Meander

East to West along a Turkish River

Jeremy Seal

W F HOWES LTD

This large print edition published in 2013 by
W F Howes Ltd
Unit 4, Rearsby Business Park, Gaddesby Lane,
Rearsby, Leicester LE7 4YH

1 3 5 7 9 10 8 6 4 2

First published in the United Kingdom in 2012
by Chatto & Windus

A CIP catalogue record for this book is available
from the British Library

ISBN 978 1 47122 891 9

Typeset by Palimpsest Book Production Limited,
Falkirk, Stirlingshire
Printed and bound in Great Britain
by MPG Books Ltd, Bodmin, Cornwall

MIX
Paper from
responsible sources
FSC
www.fsc.org   FSC® C018575

CONTENTS

MAPS

AUTHOR'S NOTE

The Turkish script, introduced by Mustafa Kemal Atatürk, is based on the Latin model but uses a range of diacritics, including the cedilla and umlaut, to establish phonetic rules for the pronunciation of characters. It also assigns unfamiliar pronunciations to some characters; those that native English speakers tend to find most confusing are given below.

- The Turkish c is pronounced j as in **j**ournalism
- ç as ch as in **ch**urch
- ş as sh as in **sh**ower
- ğ is silent but denotes a lengthening of the preceding vowel
- ı is the flat 'schwa' sound, as in show**er,** whereas the dotted i is pronounced as in **i**nk
- ö and ü are both hard to render but indicate characteristically Turkish modifications of the vowel sound; they are more commonly used in Turkish than the plain forms of these vowels

The Meander River is often given in Turkish as the Büyük Menderes, or the Great Meander, to distinguish it from at least two lesser Turkish rivers of the same name.

BULGARIA

Istanbul/
Constantinople/
Byzantium

Kuçkar Kavala

Salonika

GREECE

SEA OF MARMARA

Gallipoli   Iznik

Bursa

AEGEAN SEA

BITHYNIA

Pergamum   Eskişeh
                  Dorylae

ITALY

Mitylene   *Cyme*   Uşa

Athens   Izmir/*Smyrna*

Chios

Salamis   Ç

IONIAN SEA   Der

Sparta

Bodrum
Marmaris
Kos   Fethiye

Crete   Rhodes

Antalya/
Adalia

M E D I T E R R A N E A N   S E A

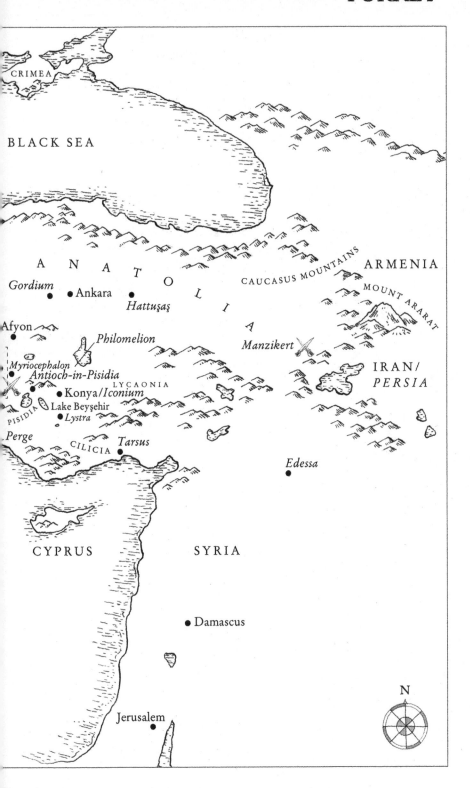

TURKEY

CRIMEA

BLACK SEA

A N A T O L I A

CAUCASUS MOUNTAINS

ARMENIA

MOUNT ARARAT

Gordium

● *Ankara*

Hattuşaş

Afyon

Philomelion

Manzikert

IRAN/
PERSIA

Myriocephalon

Antioch-in-Pisidia

LYCAONIA

● *Konya/Iconium*

PISIDIA

● *Lake Beyşehir*

● *Lystra*

Perge

CILICIA *Tarsus*

Edessa

CYPRUS

SYRIA

● *Damascus*

N

Jerusalem

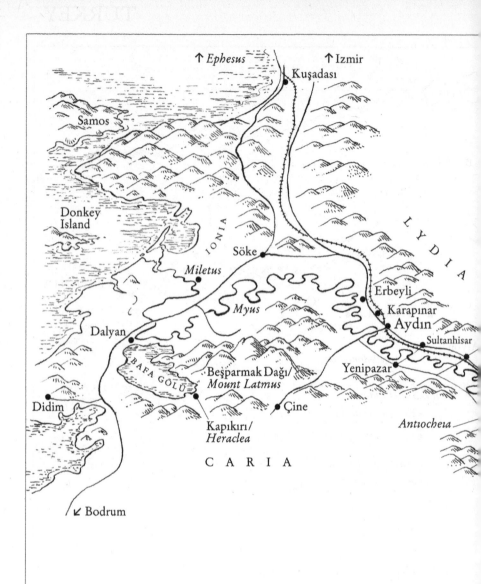

↑ *Ephesus*   ↑ İzmir

Kuşadası

Samos

Donkey
Island

L Y D I A

I O N I A

Söke

Miletus

Erbeyli

Karapınar
Aydın

Myus

Dalyan

Sultanhisar

B A F A   G Ö L Ü

Beşparmak Dağı/
Mount Latmus

Yenipazar

Didim

Çine

Antıocheıa

Kapıkırı/
Heraclea

C A R I A

↙ Bodrum

N

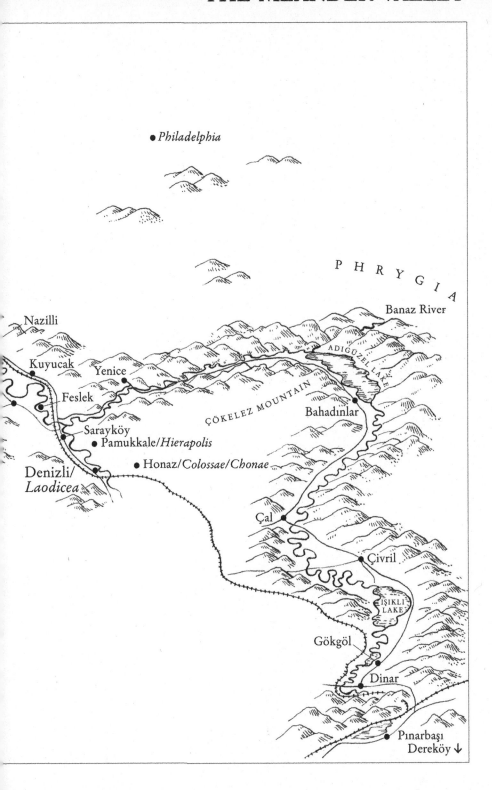

THE MEANDER VALLEY

Philadelphia

PHRYGIA

Banaz River

Nazilli

Kuyucak

Yenice

Feslek

ADIGÜZEL LAKE

ÇÖKELEZ MOUNTAIN

Bahadınlar

Sarayköy

Pamukkale/*Hierapolis*

Honaz/*Colossae/Chonae*

Denizli/
Laodicea

Çal

Çivril

IŞIKLI
LAKE

Gökgöl

Dinar

Pınarbaşı
Dereköy ↓

PROLOGUE

I would have gone down the Meander years ago if I'd known it existed.

All through my travels in the country I described for a living, however, I had never dared to imagine that this alluring proposition might lie within conventional reach; the original winding river appeared so entwined in the remote past of Anatolia, or Asiatic Turkey, as to have forfeited

any geographical place in the present. The Meander was no more accessible than the mythical Styx or the mislaid Rubicon, or so I supposed until the day I came across it.

A few years ago I was travelling in a *dolmuş*, one of the public minibuses that serve Turkey's thousands of villages, when a series of slowing jolts roused me from my back-seat reverie. Glancing beyond the window to the iron parapet of a reed-fringed bridge, I happened to spy a blue sign bearing the name of the river – *Menderes* – that we were crossing. In that instant, and no doubt thanks to some random connection triggered by my wandering thoughts, I saw at last through the Turkish rendering, and wondered that a disguise so thin could have held for so long; the Meander still ran, as it had always done, and now ran directly beneath me. It was then I realised how much more there was to know about Turkey, and what I would do about it; by the time the *dolmuş* cleared the bridge I had resolved to follow this singular river's every last winding to the sea.

Windings being, of course, what I was to expect from the Meander. The river's course from Anatolia's plateau interior to the Aegean – it showed on the map as a longitudinal squiggle, which roughly bisected the westernmost reaches of this vast and roughly rectangular land – was so sinuous that the Meander had established its byword reputation even before the first historians went to work; the earliest of them all, Herodotus, chose as his default simile the river that reached the sea just forty miles north of his home city, now Turkey's foremost tourist mecca of Bodrum, to describe a particularly mazy stretch of the Nile.

The river compelled me, of course, not only because it ran through the land whose holiday attractions had long been my subject, but because its very name embodied such resonant associations. Those associations had been actively evolving since the time of Christ when the great geographer Strabo, another Anatolian writer, was to describe the Meander as 'running in a direction excessively tortuous, so that from the course of this river all windings are called meanders'. The river's name had already embarked, in other words, on its etymological odyssey towards all manner of often conflicting meanings and resonances. It was even then acquiring a figurative currency in both Greek and Latin, one which would duly flourish among their offspring European tongues. By the seventeenth century English writers had come to use the word in a prodigious range of contexts, variously deploying that distant river's name to describe everything from the intricacies of legal process to those of the serpentine gut, from delirium or the mental effects of strong drink to the devious nature of 'oily eloquence'. By the nineteenth century its innate lack of direction especially commended the word to writers of, for example, reports on shiftless Victorian schoolboys.

It occurred to me that, in all the word's current

associations, it was this pejorative sense that predominated. To judge by *meanderthal,* a modern colloquialism that busy individuals favoured to describe dozy types given to wandering around, getting in the way in shops, or to dithering behind the wheel in streams of traffic, there was something contemptible about meandering. The dismissive coinage spoke of a sensibility, of nineteenth-century schoolmasters and metropolitan yuppies alike, which despised deviation, believing that progress was properly measured in straight lines.

Others had sensed something far more appealing, however, in the river's name. It was evidence of the word's innate elasticity that Ovid, a near contemporary of Strabo, should instead have been so patently in thrall to what he described as the loose straying of 'soft Meander's wanton current'. On this one I was firmly with the Roman lyric poet; to me, the word encapsulated the free-wheeling, romantic spirit that was the essence of true travelling.

The fitting thing, then, would have been to go to the river and go aimless when I got there – aimlessness being a productive virtue I had mislaid and thought to rediscover on the Meander. Except that I knew enough about rivers, and Turkey, to know that simply turning up, directionless as the river I meant to follow, was not wise; I had a family, after all, and was not about to cast myself adrift and unaccompanied upon a river before learning all I could about the hazards and challenges

I might be letting myself in for. At the computer and in the library I therefore set about familiarising myself with the Meander.

The basic geography was relatively simple. The regional maps, though they were poor, at least revealed that the river rose somewhere near a hinterland town called Dinar and drained into the Aegean between the resort towns of Kuşadası and Didim. Along the way it looped and strayed for some 500 kilometres, in the process losing 1,000 metres, or a single kilometre, of elevation, which is to say that the river's average gradient at least appeared reassuringly gentle.

Not that my researches threw up much else, however, in the way of bringing me to expeditionary readiness. They instead confirmed such colourful details as that the Meander Valley was famously fertile from the substantial silts carried down by the river, and quite as rich in historical figures as it was in fruit and vegetables; an epic cast of gods and mythical heroes, conquerors, kings, traders and travellers had trodden the ancient road that ran along much of its broad valley to connect the Aegean with the vast Asian hinterland. This was all of interest, of course, though at this stage I was more concerned by failures to progress along the more practical avenues of my research – like not turning up anybody, ever, who had attempted an actual descent of the Meander.

For what I urgently needed was the advice of

boatmen with hands-on experience of the river: its up-close character, that is, from the height of the banks to the caprice of its currents. It soon became apparent, however, that such men had never thought to steer cargoes down the Meander, no doubt because those in the freight trade, counting themselves with the schoolmasters and the thrusting yuppies, were deterred by the river's famously errant course. The only certainty about the one possible exception, the marble consignments rumoured to have been shipped from the Roman-era quarries at the river's midway point around Hierapolis, was that no marble man's rafting memoir had survived to throw light on the ways of the river.

My other hope was to track down modern accounts of experiences on the Meander. I soon learned, however, that expeditionary adventurers had shown no more interest in the river than the cargo men of the centuries long before them, and for reasons I readily guessed; they thought they knew enough about names to assume that the adrenaline they craved was unlikely to course through their veins on a river called the Meander.

So the Meander Valley, though it might have served as historic thoroughfare between worlds, bore a river that nobody for various reasons had ever thought to travel; a river known, then, almost entirely by the associations conjured by its name. I could therefore suppose no more than that my descent, apparently a first, was sure to be indirect, and likely to entail a feeble seaward incline; sufficiently feeble, at any rate, to have passed beneath the notice of other expeditionary parties. I hoped, being a party of one, that these intrepid types were right about the river; I was banking on the fact that the Meander might live down to its name. What I wanted was not white-water thrills but the freedom to drift gently downstream, freely attentive to the rich past of this valley on the historic borders of Asia and Europe, East and West, as well as to its present at a time when Turks especially questioned their place between these two worlds.

Against all this uncertainty I could at least claim to know my way around Turkey and speak the language reasonably well. I had also come to have a deep regard for the locals, if not for their formidable dogs, and was sufficiently confident in the sincerity of Turkish hospitality to reckon I had a good chance of finding lodgings in the many valley villages along the way; all I could otherwise do was pack as properly as possible. Before leaving home, I had therefore drawn up a priority list of every last item of gear that I might struggle to find in the Turkish hinterland. This list included maps, iodine tablets, a first aid kit and a lightweight sleeping bag. It also featured walking boots, various creams and tablets, and dry bags. It ran to a reducible walking pole sufficiently stout to fend off the dogs, and even a collapsible boat.

What it did not include was a trowel.

CHAPTER 1

Trowel was a Turkish word I didn't know, so I improvised. Hardly had I requested a pocket-sized spade, however, before the ironmonger's eyes were narrowing to wary slits.

It had not crossed my mind that laying my hands on a trowel might present a problem in a place like Dinar. How but with trowels had the chillies, peppers and aubergines that ran amok in the scruffy little town's kitchen gardens been planted? What of the geraniums that bloomed in rusty cooking oil tins at the foot of whitewashed walls? The potted pine saplings that stood in long rows at the state railway's nursery opposite the station? And the apple and cherry orchards that blossomed across the springtime plains west of the town? Dinar was where Turkey's fertile western lowlands, liberally watered by the Meander's springs, ran up against the plateau interior to breed a last-ditch growing fervour among the locals – but one that their ironmonger did not appear to share.

That said, he stocked every other item that the practical man might need; his shop was a monument to all the manual work that even now was done in rural Anatolia. Every corner, half-lit and dusty, brimmed with those brunt-bearing objects – axe handles, mattock heads, scythe blades – that interminable usage was apt to blunt or break. There were also whetstones, washers, lengths of plastic piping, buckets of nails, screws and bolts, reels of rope and chain, jubilee clips, bridles and heavy-duty sheepdog collars, their blades ferociously skewed to keep the wolves off. Wolves being something, it now struck me, that I hadn't planned for.

The closest things to trowels, however, were the spade heads. They were royal green, with tapered blades, and so like the shape of medieval shields as to put me in mind of heraldic devices. For a moment I expected to spot adjacent piles of escutcheons, chevrons and bends sinister, as if some alternative history had turned out an altogether more prosperous land; one in which Dinar's ironmonger instead ran a profitable sideline in knocking up kitsch coats of arms to order, no doubt to adorn the entrance gates that fronted the extensive spreads of the town's proliferating nouveau class, along with the same fake-grained plastic plaques bearing the carved swirls of manorial addresses standard in the affluent West. It was a fragile fancy, however, which lasted no longer than the time it took to glance through the shop door to the make-do concrete structures that in fact lined Dinar's gridded streets, the bare block walls with their hanging tongues of hardened cement, and the plots strewn with spoil. I thought of the wider town, with its shattered pavements and the tile-strewn roofscapes of rusting air-conditioning units beneath skeins of sooty cables and wires, and the scruffy villages that lay beyond Dinar, all crumbling walls of baked mud, and I had no more thoughts of entrance gates, heraldry or of prosperity in the Anatolian backcountry.

'Like them.' I pointed at the spade heads. 'Only smaller. With a handle.' The ironmonger folded his arms. He threw his head back and batted languid eyelids, which eventually reopened to reveal an elsewhere gaze, all interest drained, almost to the point of insult. It was the graphic Turkish negative, but sufficiently aggravated to express something more spirited than a shortage of stock; that the ironmonger was not minded, in fact, to sell me a trowel. On principle. He took me for a treasure hunter.

I had not anticipated such an obstruction quite so early in my journey. I nevertheless supposed it could do the lone traveller no harm to be reminded that Turks resent some things about foreigners. Not least when it comes to digging. I might have pleaded my case (that it was not, after all, a bull-dozer, or even a spade, that I was attempting to buy) but for the fact that foreigners in Turkey have the sort of digging form as to discredit even the most plausible excuse. Anatolia has haemorrhaged treasures throughout its history, to conquering occupiers from both East and West. By the nineteenth century, however, such artefacts were not the spoils of victory but articles of purchase, albeit of questionable process, as the European powers set about filling the Grecian-style halls of their newly endowed museums.

From the 1700s collectors descended upon Turkey to haggle with ruin-weary Ottoman beys and provincial governors for all manner of dirt-caked antiquities. Crated marbles were carted to the decks of waiting brigs all along the ruin-strewn littorals of south-west Anatolia; the spades, crowbars and squealing pulley blocks sounded especially loud, however, across the ancient city sites thickly clustered around the delta of the Meander River. At Miletus, the great port that had once commanded the river's mouth, the excavators found beneath the accumulated depth of silt such treasures as the monumental entrance gate that had once served the city's south agora; the gate was removed to Berlin, along with columns, capitals, pedestals and inscriptions from the Temple to Athena at nearby Priene. The temple friezes from Magnesia on the Meander, a city a few miles inland, were dispatched to Paris; and the statues that lined the Sacred Way between Miletus and the oracular temple at Didyma, the seated figures worn to an oddly modern amorphousness, went to London.

It is a national grievance that the museums of the West, to say nothing of its clandestine art collections, are often rich in finds purchased, purloined or plundered from Turkey. The soil of Anatolia even today conceals perhaps as many carved sarcophaguses, statues and inscriptions, coins, pottery and jewellery as anywhere else on earth. The Turkish state assumes that among the Western arrivals are those intent on persisting, only more covertly, in the ways of their filching forebears. The airports provide stern reminders that the unlicensed removal of antiquities from the country is punishable by a lengthy stay in prison. It's a message that clearly bears repetition, though it can often manifest more gently, as an appeal to the visitor's moral and aesthetic conscience by reminding him, typically, how 'Every flower is beautiful in its own garden. Every antique is beautiful in its own country.'

Which was not the approach they favoured at Dinar. The locals' view was that their inland region had in turn become victim to the same process of plunder that had befallen the Meander Delta in earlier centuries; that grasping foreigners, having exhausted all such coastal opportunities, had now worked their way upstream to eye the unexcavated and unguarded archaeological sites located at the top of the same river. The locals judged that the only legitimate business these same foreigners could have with the Meander was back at the river's mouth, at the beach resorts that had sprung up at nearby Kuşadası and Didim; those who found their way as far inland as Dinar must have come not as tourists but as clandestine trowellers.

That same morning a man in a brimless woollen cap, the favoured headgear among senior males in the Turkish interior, had expressed precisely these common suspicions by meeting my request for directions to the Roman theatre with a vigorous query of his own; was I, he asked, an 'accredited archaeologist'? It was only once I had strenuously argued my innocence that he pointed me up a hillside track, but with the parting discouragement that a dog – 'large, often unchained' – lived there. I had barely checked in, besides, before Turgay, the Dinar hotelier, was mentioning the old coins I might wish to view, as if my apparent interest in the local river masked my real intent, which was the illicit acquisition of local antiquities.

The locals were right in one respect: Dinar had certainly enjoyed a past worth guarding. Celaenae, as the city was first known, not only stood by the source of the storied river but also occupied what was once the most strategically significant site in all Anatolia; it commanded the pass through the Samsun Dağı range, a modest set of mountains by regional standards, but one that finally saw off the Aegean littoral as the contours stepped up to the plateau. The climb from the coastlands to the high interior, a prime communications consideration, was more easily managed at Celaenae, in the ancient region of Phrygia, than anywhere else in Anatolia.

All through its early history, from perhaps two

millennia before the birth of Christ until some four hundred years after his crucifixion, Celaenae remained a place of exceptional geographical consequence; the great longitudinal land routes across the ancient world's Mediterranean heart-lands – anywhere, that is, between the sandy shores of North Africa and the black steppe of Ukraine – necessarily funnelled through Anatolia before converging on the pass at Celaenae. The route had first connected the foremost Aegean port of Miletus, the silt-sunk city that awaited me at the end of my journey, with the early Mesopotamian civilisations of the Assyrians and Hittites. This great highway to the East – 'the public frequented road by which all travellers pass' – set out from the shores of the Aegean along the lower Meander Valley before returning to the river's headwaters at Celaenae and continuing via the pass, 'on, in a straight line, as far as India'. Vast caravans of wool, wheat and spices, marble and ivory, trundled through the pass, establishing Celaenae as the commercial and administrative hub of the western Anatolian hinterland. It was no surprise that the keepers of Celaenae's pass made immense fortunes. In the year 481 BC, for example, a resident of the city called Pythius had occasion to calculate his personal worth. His two thousand talents of silver, 3,393,000 gold pieces, plus unspecified slaves and estates, made him the world's second richest man.

For all this, however, inland Celaenae could be dismissed as a glorified toll house in comparison with Miletus, the city at the seaward end of the Meander. For in the course of the sixth and fifth centuries BC Miletus had spawned a unique crop of what Strabo called 'illustrious persons'. The great port city, which Greeks from their homelands across the Aegean had settled some centuries earlier, was home to musicians, poets and sculptors. Miletus also boasted planners, engineers and the earliest map makers, and philosophers such as Anaximander and Anaximenes, to say nothing of the great Thales, who would duly be credited with nothing less than the founding of the Western rational tradition. The neighbouring cities of Ionia, as the settler Greeks called the coastal region that encompassed the Meander Delta, were barely less impressive; Priene was a haunt of artists and home to Bias, one of the Seven Sages of Antiquity, while Magnesia on the Meander a short distance upstream swarmed with orators and singers.

This atmosphere of inquisitive and civilised enlightenment appeared coastal by instinct; in the fifth century BC it certainly did not appear to extend to Celaenae. The hinterland city, populated by its Persian ruling class and by Anatolian locals such as Phrygians, Lydians and Pisidians, failed to measure up to Miletus when it came to the production of famous sons. Easy affluence bred little, it seemed, by way of local accomplishment. The residents of Celaenae apparently felt no need to distinguish themselves beyond the breadth of their wallets. The city appeared mired in a

16

provincialism from which even its extraordinary wealth could not drag it. If the coastal Ionians knew anything of 'the pasture lands of Celaenae', it was merely that these uncultured wastes were home to the long-haired and uncouth Anatolian barbarians who were to serve as fodder at the Roman-era gladiatorial shows.

Yet Celaenae was to rise above this dearth of home-grown talent by achieving a reputation of its own, even if it was a borrowed one. The city found it in the one resource it could count upon: passing traffic. Celaenae was to make its name largely by association with the epic deeds – however far-flung their actual execution – of those who passed through the place. In this respect Celaenae recalled a small-town restaurant, the walls pinned with promotional photos, complete with scribbled wishes, of the generously disposed stars that happened to halt there. Back in an age, that is, when the stand-out stars were marchers. If Miletus was renowned for its revered philosophers, then Celaenae came to be known for the marching columns, or at least for the men in command of those columns, who took their rest there; as it was for the achievements of the head that the city at the river's foot was known, so it was for the exertions of the foot that the one at its head was to be remembered.

For in the course of the fifth and fourth centuries BC it happened that the three most celebrated ancient marches of all passed through Celaenae.

17

These had much in common, not least in terms of the infinite ambition of their leaders, but given how quickly the dust obscures the facts of ancient history it may not be facile to suggest that the most glaring similarity, however superficial, was the incidence of the letter X in their names. The first one to enter the city, exceptionally enough, had two; the arrival in 481 BC of Xerxes, King of Persia, was the very event that prompted the same Pythius to reckon his fortune, the local tycoon thinking to commend himself by offering up his wealth to serve the war chest of the new arrival, the only man in existence richer than himself. Xerxes was scion of the Persian imperial line that had ruled Anatolia – even unto its Hellenised western littoral – since 546 BC. After leading his army hordes out of Persia and along the great Anatolian road, Xerxes had arrived at the eastern gates of Celaenae. At this centre of provincial Persian rule, the King ordered his armies to rest while he took himself off to the palace that he kept by the banks of the Meander. In the company of advisers he fine-tuned his plans for the invasion of Europe. Greece, for too long defiant of Persian dominion, was now to be brought to heel.

Or so Xerxes thought. To this end the so-called Great King had assembled a force that matched the scale of his ambition; his armies, stuffed with the levies of countless subject people, were so vast that it was feared their combined thirst must drain Anatolia's rivers, if the dust the columns put up did not first turn the waters to slurry. In time, of course, the rested armies were to continue out of Celaenae, and on towards the epic events for which posterity was to remember them: the gigantic pontoon bridge, an engineering marvel, which bore the invaders across the Hellespont into Europe; the Persians' frustration before the heroic stand of Leonidas' 300 Spartans at Thermopylae; and the subsequent destruction by Greek forces of Xerxes' huge trireme fleet in the shallows around the island of Salamis.

Back to the comparative backwaters of Celaenae, however, to await the arrival eighty years later of another oft-remembered army at the city gates. Among this lot of mercenary marchers the man that history was destined to single out was one Xenophon, who would not only gain an entry adjacent to Xerxes in encyclopaedias but was also, it happened, in the pay of the same Great King's great-grandson, a Persian prince called Cyrus the Younger. Cyrus, who had been appointed the ruling satrap or governor of Phrygia, installed himself in his palatial hunting lodge by the headwaters of the Meander, just as Xerxes had done before him, where he too considered the audacious scale of his plans. The vital difference was that Cyrus and his armies arrived in 401 BC not at the eastern but the western gates of the city. Cyrus, having largely gathered his forces from among the Greek cities of the Aegean shore, was resting his armies at Celaenae for a month before leading them east to make Persia his own; the Persians were now fighting among themselves.

Like the hordes of Xerxes before them, Xenophon and the rest of the 'Ten Thousand' Greeks under Cyrus's command would advance out of Celaenae to a momentous future. The temptation might once more be to follow, accompanying these adventurers on their legendary up-country expedition, or anabasis, if the focus of this narrative did not require us to remain at Celaenae, through the levying of the tolls, the counting of fortunes and the finding of new ways to dent them, perhaps commissioning personal insignia to adorn the gates of villas, in anticipation of the arrival of the next lot of marchers at the city sixty-five years later: the armies of Alexander the Great, a Macedonian Greek intent on subduing all the world, who in 334 BC halted his men at Celaenae where they were to stay for ten days before he led them east to conquer Persia.

It is now that our loyalty to Celaenae pays off, the perspective of the city's gate men revealing the historical significance of the 150 years spanning the arrivals there of Xerxes and of Alexander in the simplest terms; where Persians had once headed west, that is, Greeks were now marching east. So the pattern of the marchers' passing through the city first told of the Easterners who meant to incorporate the West, still-born, into the vast territories of the Persian Empire, and of those who resisted, then reversed, a process of global significance.

We only know of these marches, of course, because of the writers who saw fit to describe them: Herodotus, who immortalised Xerxes' invasion march by placing it centre-stage in his magisterial *Histories*; Xenophon, whose own account of the great expedition in which he himself took part, the *Anabasis*, would soon be recognised as worthy of the great achievement it celebrated; and the Roman historian Arrian whose own *Anabasis* was just one of many accounts to commemorate Alexander's great campaign. By these literary works, mainstays of the classical canon, the place in history of the marches was assured. They have since been sanctified as key moments in the West's founding myth, and repeatedly treated by artists, poets, writers and film-makers, raised on separate pedestals to develop distinct, if overlapping, mythologies. The effect might have been to cast these epic trudges adrift, united only by a vaguely comprehended notion of a shared Near Eastern setting, if it were not that they had had Celaenae in common.

For the fact that all three marches made lengthy stops in the city and over a comparatively brief period – roughly a lifetime in each case dividing their arrivals – invited me rather to think of the marches collectively; as different stages, even, in one unfolding, archetypal event. The composition of the three expeditions – the men and the direction in which they were headed – demonstrated a classic reversal. For the process that began when

Xerxes' Persians headed in one direction to conquer Greeks – and reached a turning point when Cyrus, a Persian, marched against his own land – was to end 150 years later with Macedonian Greeks heading east to conquer Persians. History's tide had turned.

All Anatolia, and the valley of the Meander especially, has been perpetually subject to this pattern. The fall of the East and the rise of the West was to be repeated, of course, but the process was also to be reversed. The Eastern invaders who took their lead from Xerxes included the Selçuk Turks in the eleventh century, with the Mongols, Tamburlaine's Tartars and the Ottoman Turks advancing in their wake, while those who opposed their progress, in turn invoking the glorious example of Alexander, included the armies of the Byzantine emperors and of the Western crusaders. It was a process repeated even in the twentieth century when Greece's invading divisions pushed up the Meander Valley in 1919 before running into the resistance offered by the Turks – the ensuing war leading to the birth of modern Turkey. The one lesson East and West learned, though they might take turns to encroach, the East now claiming the Balkans, the West now the steppes of Asia, was where they ended and began: in Anatolia, and most especially in the plains and defiles of the Meander Valley. The river might have come to signify digression, but I was not about to forget that my subject, and my route through

22

westernmost Turkey, also wound through the historic marches, the marching lands, between two worlds.

And now I was in Dinar, where the men with the Xs in their names and their marching columns had left no impression. Along dusty streets lined with soup shops, the flat roofs topped with corrugated iron, nothing of Celaenae's glorious heritage remained. There were no reminders that the world's two richest men had once met here. In fact, at the original keystone of the Anatolian land bridge – the birthplace, that is, of the metaphor that even today defines Turkey – they were now having trouble finding me a trowel.

The city's decline had not been immediate. In fact, it was lavishly rebuilt in the third century BC with funds plundered from Persia's sacked treasures; the city was renamed in honour of Apama, mother of one of Alexander's successor kings. Apamea admittedly suffered a series of earthquakes so acute that even the Romans, those inveterate tax collectors, temporarily exempted the city from their levies. Even so, it continued to flourish down to the time of Christ when Strabo called it 'the common staple for merchandise brought from Italy and from Greece'.

It was not until the fourth century, when the rise of Constantinople to the north reconfigured Anatolia's roads, that Apamea's decline gathered irreversible momentum. Increasing volumes of traffic ignored the pass for more northerly routes and so the wealth of Apamea began to erode. Of the great palace that Xerxes had had built by the banks of the Meander, perhaps by way of consolation for the irreversible loss of his fleet and his aura of invincibility at Salamis, nothing was known; the same was true of his great-grandson Cyrus the Younger's hunting lodge. These Persian vanity projects perhaps fell victim to earthquake or plain neglect, unless their stones and marbles had been pointedly earmarked for deliberate dismantling to serve in the triumphant redevelopment of Hellenistic Apamea. Time, meanwhile, eroded the citadel which Alexander had considered so strongly positioned that he preferred to negotiate with its garrison; nothing but the foundations of the walls remained. The city dwindled and died, and the names that recalled its imperial past went with it. By the nineteenth century some locals knew the place as Geyikler, or Deer, for the wild animals that roamed the ruined parklands of Celaenae-Apamea.

Dinar, the name finally settled upon the modern town, continued to suffer from earthquakes into modern times. The most recent one struck in October 1995 when half of the town's buildings, about 5,000 in number, collapsed. Much of Dinar was not even teenage, with almost nothing of those many pasts that we have barely begun to explore – Phrygian and Persian, Greek and Roman, Byzantine and Ottoman among them – poking above the foundations when I arrived in the spring of 2008. No wonder, then, that locals like the ironmonger should have wondered what had brought me to the place.

The truth is I wanted nothing from Dinar. Not its coins nor the prospect of discreet excavations in the remains of the Roman theatre. I had no wish to dig for the potsherds liberally scattered across the hilltop site of Celaenae's once-impregnable citadel. I only hoped that Dinar would provide me with a beginning. That and a trowel.

The trowel; this was nothing more, if its purpose must be known, than a routine expeditionary necessity. With only the vaguest idea of the progress I might make along the river, and of where I would end up sleeping, I was hardly in any position to guess at the toilet facilities I might find there. The trowel was not for the secretive unearthing of treasures, then, but for the disposal of my bodily waste; all proper and responsible, of course, though I was not about to clear my name if it meant spelling out the plain facts to a Turkish iron-monger. I left the shop empty-handed, newly mindful of the unforeseen challenges that might arise before I was to experience the carefree progress I had so readily anticipated.

CHAPTER 2

I had arrived in Dinar the previous evening.

The bus did not bother to call at the town's little *otogar*, or bus station, but dropped me by the roadside before it continued east towards the city of Konya. I watched the rear lights shrink through a stain of brown exhaust as it made for the high steppe. Beneath a wide sky stuck with stars and a black minaret I dragged my luggage into the town. The streets smelt of coal and I heard their footfalls before I saw them – the solitary men in brimless caps and the women in headscarves who stooped beneath half-lowered shutters, their worn faces flaring in the spills of buttery light, to make late purchases of bread, vegetables and cigarettes.

The little hotel stood within a scruffy garden. It had been built after the 1995 earthquake, its concrete walls swagged in telephone wires, electricity and TV cables, which had been customised as washing lines where they festooned the balconies. The open-plan ground floor was sparsely furnished; a calendar and a portrait of Mustafa Kemal Atatürk, the man currently on the coins, a lifetime dead, decorated the walls. A reception desk, with a diary and hooks for room keys, over-looked the lounge area, where chairs and a sofa corralled a flickering television. At the other end of the room two metal-topped tables indicated the eating area where I found the hotelier the following morning. I was just back from a walk to the town's Roman theatre, where the views over the westerly plain had allowed me my first glimpse of the Meander's downstream seam.

Turgay Darkeye, as the hotelier's surname trans-lated, was working his way through a bunch of parsley. 'Diabetes,' he muttered. 'Only just diag-nosed.' Turgay's pronounced features confirmed the Turkic, even Mongol, origins that his surname appeared to acknowledge. He had motioned for me to join him when the shawled Mrs Darkeye, a newspaper folded under her arm, arrived to take charge. Anxious to spare her husband the least dietary temptation, Mrs Darkeye redirected me to the unoccupied table, which she set about covering with pages from her newspaper. I noticed that the paper was recent; I had not been in Turkey for long and was keen for the latest news. To a table-cloth largely composed of small ads, I therefore got the obliging Mrs Darkeye to add the front pages. By the time she returned with my breakfast – a tight-waisted glass of black tea, bread, crumbly white cheese, ship-lapped slices of tomato and cucumber, honey and a boiled egg – and with more parsley for her husband, I was deep in the lead stories.

Turkey had lately run into a political swell considerable even by its own turbulent standards. The country's secular establishment, backed by the military, was confronting the ruling administration of moderate Islamists. Dates had been set, the newspaper reported, for the case that was to be heard against the governing party. *Ak*, as the party was called, had for some weeks been facing closure for what the chief prosecutor described as promoting an Islamic, and therefore unconstitutional, programme; the government had recently sought to overturn a time-honoured ban on the wearing of headscarves in universities, ministries and public offices. The secularists, prominent in the army and the state bureaucracy, did not like Islamic headgear. Invoking the example of Atatürk, the arch-secularist Father of the Nation, who had taken a tough line of his own against the superstitious fezes and turbans of the Ottomans, they meant to close down the government for supposing that its female citizens should be free to decide what they wore on their heads in the workplace.

For almost five hundred years Turkey had been run as an Islamic theocracy. With the end of Ottoman rule in 1923, however, Atatürk's secularists gained firm control; religion's place in the public sphere was radically reduced, and many of the mosques and religious schools were closed. At the end of the twentieth century, however, the balance of power had begun to shift. *Ak*, having gained an impressive popular mandate in the

28

previous year's elections, now found itself in a position to demonstrate rather more muscle than was usual from the traditionally cowed Islamic lobby. In fact, *Ak* and its supporters had got their shot in first; months before the secularists had brought their closure case the Islamists had charged these opponents with unconstitutional activities of their own. The secularists, they claimed, counted among their number members of a clandestine organisation responsible for numerous kidnappings, executions, bombings, extortions, protection rackets, fixing of contracts and narcotics trafficking. This illicit organisation took its supposed name, *Ergenekon*, from the legendary valley in central Asia's Altai Mountains where the Turkish national story had popularly begun; from this valley the Turks, guided by a talismanic wolf, were said to have emerged to make their destined migration westwards from the sixth century.

Ak had it that *Ergenekon*'s dyed-in-the-wool secularists were behind a terror campaign whose sole design was to bring down the elected government. The objective, they claimed, was to spread such disorder that the army must intervene, as it had done in the past, and so wrest control of the country from the Islamists and return it to Atatürk's secularists. The discovery the previous summer of incriminating documents and a half-empty crate of grenades in an Istanbul flat had spurred the authorities to pick up scores of disgruntled secularists – military men, journalists, academics, nationalists and assorted mavericks – in a series of dawn raids. Some Islamic sections of the media subsequently presented these supposed *Ergenekon* operatives as members of a vast organisation, which had been responsible for almost every instance of Turkish political violence over the past decade. These unlikely claims they substantiated by linking the grenades' serial numbers with those of grenades apparently known to have been used in other incidents, as if *Ergenekon*'s entire terror campaign could be traced to the one crate of meticulously documented munitions.

The secularists contended, in turn, that *Ergenekon* did not exist; *Ak* Party schemers, they claimed, had fabricated the organisation to exaggerate the extent of the secular establishment's secret hand. These Islamists presented the rounded-up secularists as agents of the so-called 'deep state', as tools of the military-backed bureaucratic elite whose undying fealty was to Atatürk's secular vision, whatever the expressed wishes of the electorate. The actual truth, according to the secularists, was that *Ak* and its supporters nursed a secret agenda of their own, and one quite as destabilising as the secularists' was alleged to be; the *Ergenekon* investigations, designed to discredit and disarm the secularist opposition, were by way of preparation for an increasingly Islamicised, even Islamic, state.

Turgay had finished his parsley.

'So, what are you doing in Dinar?' he asked. I

was here, I replied, to spend some time on the Meander. In that word I heard the romantic character of a venture the locals would surely recognise; but what Turgay understood from my interest in the river was that I must be in irrigation.

'No, no, not irrigation,' I hastily replied.

'Fish farming, then? Hydroelectricity?' I did not much care for our parlour-game exchange. Turgay's alarming assumptions, a local's view of the Meander, conjured a different river from the one I had imagined. Anxious to head off his next best guess, in case it was that I must work in sewage treatment, which might fatally undermine my own enthusiasm for the project, I told Turgay what had brought me to Dinar. The hotelier appeared puzzled.

'History?' he echoed. 'So you'd be interested in old coins?' he asked, brightening visibly. It was then that three policemen entered the hotel.

They were from the *Zabıta*, the paperwork police, and they wore pressed blue uniforms, with holsters. At their gesture the hotelier wiped the parsley from his mouth and followed them into the front garden. I watched through the open door as they gathered by a tree. They had slipped beyond my hearing. Deliberately, I supposed. I guessed I was witnessing one of those whispered visits that small businesses were commonly presumed to suffer east of the Balkans; an irregularity detected in the hotelier's tax affairs that the *Zabıta*, as servants of the state, were duty bound to refer unless a discreet cash consideration, one the officers were happy to disburse, could be found to resolve matters.

'Trouble?' I asked knowingly once the police had left.

'The chief's after a new tree for his garden,' Turgay explained. 'He wondered if he could take a cutting from my linden. Now, for the *Menderes*. The man you want is Truehero.'

Mehmet Truehero, author of a local history, made his living as a defence lawyer. I was directed to his office opposite Dinar's judiciary building. It did not resemble any legal practice that I knew; the lawyer ran his business from a single room, workshop-style, which gave directly onto a bustling lane along with the clouds of cigarette smoke that billowed through the open door. There were no ecurity buzzers, lobbies, reception desks, appointment books or obstructive assistants. One apparently sought Truehero's services much as one might pop in to the key cutters, or drop off a frayed shirt at the tailor's. This refreshingly open approach had attracted a crowd of chatting smokers and tea drinkers, which was already larger than Truehero's premises had been designed to accommodate. The office, though it aspired to legal gravitas, with shelves of Turkish law digests and a prominent desk topped by a brass-effect name plaque, more convincingly functioned as a favoured tea salon. I had barely peered through the window when the man at the desk was beckoning me to join the gathering.

The men assembled at Truehero's turned out to be farmers and small-time business types; their interests included cherry orchards, machine workshops and kebab houses. They discussed the drought, the price of diesel, tractor parts, impending marriages and irrigation systems. The noise they generated was impressive, even overpowering, though it did not appear to disturb the meeting even then taking place between the man at the desk, whom the plaque identified as Truehero himself, and the large client in a suit with a shimmering grey weave who sat opposite him. It might be said that the congenial and good-humoured hubbub in fact sustained the two men in their toil across the arid wastes of legal discourse; even that their friends and acquaintances had assembled precisely to supply the wayside wells of conversational distraction that might refresh the pair and so provide them with the necessary strength to continue. Truehero, I sensed, had bigger interests than the law. As for the client, he especially appeared to welcome those interruptions that acknowledged his authority on subjects such as diesel, then as expensive as anywhere in the world, or the price of cherries, or big business. Big business, the client declared, breaking off from the meeting, was all this government cared about. The farmers, as far as the politicians were concerned, could all go hang.

'Yes,' came a voice from the crowd. 'But you've got to credit what they're doing for the poor.'

'Poor or rich, yes,' the client conceded, warming to his theme. 'It's the ones in the middle they're squeezing.' The cigarette smoke parted to reveal a boy bearing a shiny tin tray of glasses of fresh tea.

'Poor or rich but definitely religious,' someone added. 'That's what you need to be in this country.' As the client raised a forefinger to signal his further intervention, Mehmet Truehero took the opportunity to lean across and shake my hand. The lawyer had an angular frame, with thinning hair and sallow skin, and his eyes brimmed with curiosity.

'And how can I help you?' he asked. Not, admittedly, with anything for which he could readily charge me; but then I had already reached the welcome conclusion that Mehmet Truehero was not the sort solely interested in those he was paid to represent. It was instead his historical knowledge I sought, hoping it might lead me to what must be my beginning, the Meander's true source, which neither my researches nor the maps in my possession had quite confirmed. The topography of the Meander's headwaters had always been contentious; some of the doubts that Richard Pococke, a pioneer traveller, had expressed in the 1740s – the 'many difficulties in relation to the account, which different authors give to the rise of these rivers' – even now remained unresolved. So I told Mehmet Truehero that I meant to trace the Meander's route all the way to the sea, and must therefore begin at the very top, if I could only find my way there.

Mehmet rose promptly from his desk, grabbing a set of keys. 'Something's come up,' he informed his client. 'We'll pick up again later on.' As the relieved client threw himself into the general conversation, Mehmet led me outside to a little brown car.

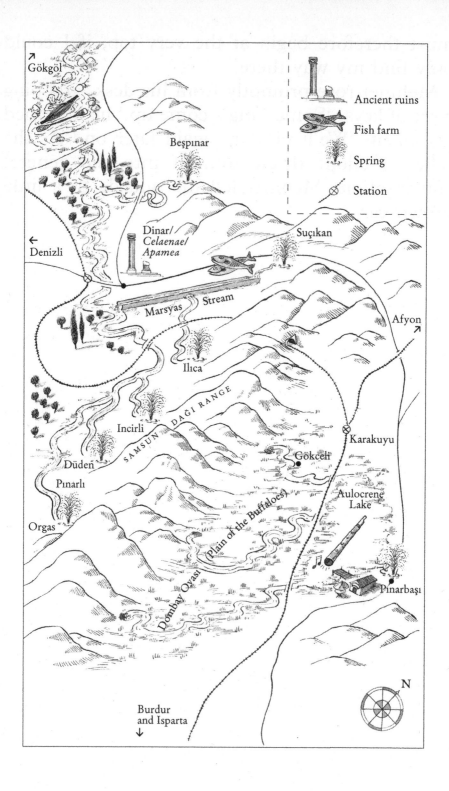

Gökgöl

Beşpınar

Ancient ruins

Fish farm

Spring

Station

Dinar/
Celaenae/
Apamea

Suçıkan

Denizli

Marsyas   Stream

Afyon

Ilıca

SAMSUN DAĞI RANGE

Incirli

Karakuyu

Gökceli

Düden

Aulocrene
Lake

Pınarlı

Plain of the Buffaloes

Orgas

Dombay Ovası

Pınarbaşı

Burdur
and Isparta

N

CHAPTER 3

It was almost as if I had done Mehmet the favour. For having turned up, out of the blue, to rescue him from another day of legal tedium, he actually made me feel generous – if not, from the moment he shoved the car into gear, safe. Mehmet drove with one hand. With the other he sifted the back seat for papers, articles and books, and flung flapping law tomes aside, smoking the while. We made unsteady progress out of Dinar.

'We'll start with the Orgas,' Mehmet declared, tossing me a copy of the local history book he had written. We turned south, following the foot of the Samsun Dağı range where it edged the unfurling plain. The fields were fringed with a pink blur of distant cherry blossom.

I was busy with Truehero's account of the Orgas, one of the Meander's celebrated tributary streams, which had featured on the coins of Roman Apamea, when with a lunge a set of spittle-strewn teeth briefly loomed at the passenger window. It was a roadside *kangal*, or Anatolian sheepdog, a creature I so little cared for that I was convinced something

37

must give; the collar, the straining leash, the ring bolt or even the scruffy farmstead to which the creature was secured, the entire edifice ripping free of modest footings to strew a cascade of roof tiles in the road, the fearsome hound surging from the whitewashed wreckage of worm-eaten timbers to chase us down. I focused on the road ahead. A sign indicated Pınarlı village.

'Pınarlı, pah!' exclaimed Mehmet, suddenly cantankerous. The name translates, prosaically, as 'With a Spring', and some decades earlier had replaced the ancient name, Norgas, as Mehmet had known the village in his childhood.

The twentieth century, its early decades especially, had witnessed the remaking of Turkey and Turks alike. Atatürk's social revolution turned people and place towards a modern, Western future. A Latin-style alphabet was drafted. The people were urged to dress in modern clothes and a new law code came into use. Surnames lifted, it could sometimes seem, from comic books were introduced.

The new Turkey, though Western in its adopted modes, was also to be Turkish in its avowed origins. A programme was therefore devised to rid the nation's villages of foreign-sounding names. Norgas, in which the local stream's ancient name was clearly preserved, had the taint of Greek; a replacement was found for it, as for many village names where other foreign influences, chiefly Armenian, Kurdish, Arabic or Persian, had been detected.

The other target was religion. Names that made reference to superstitions or to religious figures – local shrines, one-time resident dervishes – also fell foul of the authorities. One such Dinar village, the supposed site of King Xerxes' pleasure palace, had in more recent centuries been named after a Muslim holy man called Sheikh Arab Sultan. The village was duly renamed Bülüçalanı; Mehmet had no idea why 'Place of Small Chickens', as the replacement translated, should have been chosen. Less imaginative alternatives, often topographical, were more commonly employed to rename villages; the likes not only of Pınarlı but also Çamlıyayla (Pine Pasture) were repeatedly deployed to remake some 25,000 villages across Turkey.

'It means we lose our history,' Mehmet growled. The echo of the brook's classical name, undistorted beyond a snagged 'N', could no longer be heard. Its erasure by bureaucratic intervention had done for a tenacious fragment, one that time alone had failed to erode, from Anatolia's distant past.

That same brook, Turkish now, closed on the road as we drove into low hills. A dwindling dirt track halted at a scruffy picnic site where concrete tables stood among pine trees and rising red rocks. The stream twisted among the rocks, the banks climbing to form a modest defile. Mehmet and I set out on foot, tracing its course upstream. We had not gone far when the stream pooled beneath an overhanging rock, briefly bubbled, and disappeared into the hillside.

'The Orgas spring,' said Mehmet. He flipped a fresh cigarette between his lips. If one thing was clear, it was that Mehmet had not led me to the head of the Meander; nor was the source-seeker's standard prescription – continue upstream, keeping to the main fork, to the end – about to bring me there. The Orgas went where I could not follow; the pioneering Richard Pococke had a point. A consequence of the especially permeable local limestone was that the water courses tended to plunge beneath obstructions rather than circumvent them by the usual surface route. It was a trait that the epic poet Nonnos confirmed when he described the Meander 'lurking in the secret places with his water in the lap of the earth – who rolls deep through the earth and drags his crooked stream towards the light, crawling unseen and travelling slantwise underground, until he leaps up quickly and lifts his neck above the underground'.

The Meander's tributaries, Mehmet explained, did reappear above ground along their upper reaches beyond the mountain; there they crossed a high plain before running into the eastern flanks of Samsun Dağı. It was at those rising slopes that they went underground, and in the dark, like ropes pushed and twisted, the gathered channels unbraided before emerging as the Orgas and as the other springs, which rose all along the western base of Samsun Dağı. But the water courses above the mountain were for another day; Mehmet clearly meant me to visit these secondary or lower springs before introducing me to the one where my journey was truly to begin. I felt a twinge of impatience before admonishing myself; it was not in the spirit of things to fight indirection on the Meander.

So we returned to Dinar to draw up below the theatre hill – the heights of Roman Apamea – which I had visited earlier that morning. Before an arcade of crumbling arches, where a raised road had once run, was a pool roughly finished in a combination of crazy paving and off-white, institutional tiles. The water was clear. A few bubbles rose. Small fish shoaled in the pool. There were also floating patches of scum. Plastic bags and tins were strewn across the weedy bottom. The spring the pool housed pushed a bead of water over the tiled ledge to disappear down a culvert. 'I swam here as a child,' offered Mehmet, suddenly subdued, and I could not tell whether it was his childhood or the pool, long since neglected, or even the ancient glories of his home town that he mourned. The spring, Mehmet explained, was known as Ilıca, or Hot Spring. In fact, the water was barely tepid to the touch. Any thermal activity had dwindled broadly in keeping with the fortunes of the town. A muezzin announced the midday prayers but a stray dog, a safely small one, was all that stirred, and only to crap beneath one of the arches. At that moment it was harder than ever to credit that Celaenae had ever been home to pleasure parks and palaces, or had played host to armies whose leaders meant to conquer the world.

The truth was that the city, call it Celaenae or Apamea, had been captivating readers in the cloisters of European academe from the seventeenth century. In their Anatolian studies the early accounts of Celaenae's illustrious past, and the magnificent ambitions of those who had led their forces there, had lent the city a particular prominence. Not so much among the treasure hunters, who tended to favour the coastal sites precisely because they were accessible and their antiquities readily extracted, but among the less nakedly acquisitive antiquaries who made their way to Turkey. For though these scholarly travellers were quite as zealous in their pursuit of ancient objects, coins and inscriptions especially, they tended to see their finds not as lucrative collectables they might flog to museums so much as clues in an exploratory process, one that paralleled the momentous geographical discoveries taking place elsewhere. Just as James Cook and Alexander von Humboldt, Henry Morton Stanley and John Franklin sought glory in the New World, in Africa and in the polar regions, so these erudite men, often ex-soldiers and one-time diplomats, serving clerics or leisured nobles, were quietly bent on retrieving Anatolia's classical past; a past that the Turks even in our own times, to judge by the village brook now known as Pınarlı, sought to wipe clean.

From their reading these scholarly men knew Asia Minor – they favoured the Latin designation over the Greek-derived Anatolia – as the cradle of Western civilisation; it was the birthplace of history and philosophy, of Homer, Heraclitus and Herodotus, of coinage and town planning, and defining advances in medicine, mathematics and architecture, and was latterly the seedbed of a Christianity newly alive to its missionary reach. The more adventurous, beginning with the likes of Richard Pococke, now began travelling to this unimaginably rich historical repository to see for themselves. What they found was abandonment beyond all their expectations. The last millennium had done for the place.

For Anatolia, weakened by centuries of relentless raiding, had from roughly the time of the Crusades suffered a protracted decline. By 1300 the Byzantines were in headlong retreat towards Constantinople, abandoning the Anatolian provinces to the Selçuk Turks, and then to the devastating ravages of the Tartars and Mongols. The Turkish clan that finally eclipsed the Byzantines, the Ottomans, put expansion, primarily westwards into the Balkans, above any social or economic consolidation of the imperial backyard. The land that the travelling scholars subsequently discovered was not only unmapped but subject to the sometime law of local chieftains, where brigands and raiding Turkish nomads ruled the roost well into the nineteenth century. One such scholar,

Richard Chandler, evoked a Wild West atmosphere, where bodyguards and tooled-up desperadoes came as standard, when he described his travels through western Anatolia in the 1760s. 'We now perceived four men riding briskly toward us, abreast, well mounted and armed,' he wrote. 'Our janizary and Armenians halted, as they passed, and faced about until they were gone beyond our baggage.' Such security concerns only increased as the party ventured inland. They eventually forced Chandler to abandon his cherished plan, which was to explore the lands around the headwaters of the Meander.

Many problems – a shortage of supplies and lodgings, the dreadful roads, constant ill health, ferocious *kangals* – confronted these travelling classicists. Perhaps the greatest challenge, however, was the one they had set themselves; relocating ancient history in the contemporary landscape. Nowhere had the constituents of the classical and early Christian canon – places, events, individuals, myths – lost touch with the original settings more comprehensively than in Anatolia. The route described, for example, in Xenophon's *Anabasis*, among the most widely read of the classical texts, remained largely unlocated. Equally elusive were the Anatolian cities of St Paul's evangelising mission and what might be found there; so profoundly mislaid was Colossae, the city Paul had addressed in one of his epistles, that its citizens were mistakenly associated with Memnon's

Colossus of Rhodes, a monumental wonder of the ancient world, and therefore assumed to hail from that island. Other Anatolian places visited by Paul – Antioch in Pisidia, Lystra, Derbe – might have been prominent in Christian history; geography, however, had not touched them. It was no surprise, then, that the classical map of the Anatolian hinterland should have largely struck the Reverend Francis Arundell, scholarly-minded chaplain to the English factory at Smyrna in the 1820s, as a sorry blank. 'What spaces yet remain unappropriated, and to how many cities of importance is the modest and hesitating mark of interrogation affixed!' he wrote despairingly.

Classical topography taught those who presumed to master it all manner of tough lessons, chiefly that time never stopped; the problem in the case of Anatolia – the name derived from the Greek for 'east' or the 'sunrise land' – was the degree to which place had also moved on. Earthquakes had not so much reduced the sites as reconfigured them, at once turning them into quarries of conveniently dressed stone. The stones were often carted away to be reused, and the telling inscriptions they bore were concealed, often lost for ever, in the rude constructions of later ages. Even the language, in a rare example of the conqueror's tongue prevailing, had changed. Original Anatolian or Greek place names had progressively lost out to Turkish replacements. 'The reader can now form a very good idea of the extreme difficulty,'

Reverend Arundell concluded, 'of fixing with positive certainty the sites of ancient cities.'

Such sites as had been positively identified, Ephesus, Miletus and Xanthos among them, mostly lay close to the coast and served only to peg the ancient past at the region's geographical edges; Anatolia's classical topography therefore resembled a loosely secured tent, but one that these redoubtable scholars were bent on making fast. As they set about extending the identification of Anatolia's lost classical sites, so the available sources of information, often slight or unreliable, soon taught them the comparative value of classical literature in their search. The ancients, for all the inconsistencies in their texts, had had much to say about Celaenae, a place Colonel William Leake, another explorer-antiquary, considered 'a point of great importance to the ancient geography of the western part of Asia Minor'.

We have previously glimpsed something of Celaenae's abundant ancient detailing: in his chronicle of Xerxes' great march Herodotus had occasion to emphasise the city's conspicuous rivers and springs; Xenophon described how the Meander ran through the grounds of Cyrus's hunting lodge, near the palace of Xerxes, before winding past the city; and Arrian detailed a citadel so impressive that even the all-conquering Alexander was minded to negotiate a settlement with its defenders. Strabo's *Geography* also noted the city's springs;

46

they were fed, he added, by a lake that lay beyond a mountain. The likes of Pliny and Livy weighed in with further contributions.

These sources evoked a place rich with association, then, but their chief value to the antiquaries was in the abundant topographical clues they provided. No lost city of the Anatolian interior occupied such a setting; one so distinctive, besides, that no amount of earthquakes could have re-contoured it beyond all recognition. It was surely possible to locate the city, and so provide a crucial fixed point for the identification of further sites deep in Phrygia and across neighbouring regions. Celaenae-Apamea, as some scholars termed the site, consequently acquired a particular significance for the region's early topographers, Leake among them, who expressed frustration that the place remained undiscovered as late as 1824. 'There cannot be a stronger proof of the little progress yet made in geographical discovery in Asia Minor,' he wrote, 'than the fact, that the site of Apameia still remains unexplored.'

The truth was that Richard Pococke had come tantalisingly close to finding this Anatolian El Dorado as early as 1740. Not that the pioneer traveller had known it. He reached modern Işıklı some forty miles north-west of Dinar, only to lack there the 'opportunity of an onward caravan'. He did subsequently include, however, in his published journal a second-hand description of 'a high hill . . . and a village called "Dinglar", where the

Meander rises, and, as they say, falls down a hill from a lake at the top of it'.

That very sentence, if attentively read in the context of the classical sources, should have sufficed to reveal the modern location of the lost city. Pococke had been proved so awry in his identification of other ancient sites, however, hopelessly confusing many of their locations, that those travellers who followed in his footsteps paid little notice to his notoriously unreliable journal. The clues contained therein were to remain overlooked for more than eighty years. Only then did Leake recognise Pococke's account as containing nothing less than an X-marked map; in his own book he was to concede that the 'Dinglar' details chiefly provided by Pococke accorded 'precisely with that of Celaenae as given by several ancient authors'.

It was Francis Arundell, conveniently based at Smyrna, who was first to act on Leake's observations. Reaching Dinar in 1826, the chaplain soon convinced himself that 'the ruins could be no other than those of Apameia'. Classical topography had its Anatolian breakthrough; here was the fabled city. Credit for the discovery went to Arundell, even if it was Pococke's observations and Leake's deductions that had largely led him there. The discovery's significance was accounted such that other travelling scholars were soon to weigh in with competing claims; they buoyed their nineteenth-century Anatolian travelogues, a remarkably crowded literary sub-genre, with their own reiterations of the Apamea find, as if it were only the subsequent support they lent the discovery that finally confirmed it. One pronounced that he had 'little doubt that Apamea and Celaenae stood at the present town of Deenare'. 'After examining the whole of the country in the vicinity of Deenair, the course of the various rivers, and its distance from those places, the situations of which are ascertained,' another loftily declared after a visit in 1835, 'I have no doubt that it stands upon the site of Apamea . . .'

These wandering scholars therefore found the past they sought, though the price they paid was the extent to which they seemed unaware of the present. Perhaps it was their intense focus that blinded them to so much of their surroundings, not least to the inhabitants. William Leake typified the European attitude, writing off contemporary Anatolia as 'modern barbarism and desolation'. Another antiquary, travelling in Anatolia in the 1830s, concurred. 'As the most interesting period of the history of this country was the time of its accommodation by the Greeks,' he wrote, 'so the remains of their cities form now the chief attraction to the traveller.' The locals, in terms of what foreigners tended to make of them, were left to choose between the treasure hunters, who stole from under their noses, or the antiquaries, so caught up in the remote past as to see clean through them. Which was the greater offence, I wondered; being fleeced on one's own patch, or being ignored there? I rather suspected, whatever the answer, that vestiges of these attitudes must cling to modern travellers. I therefore made a point of reminding myself that Mehmet Truehero, though he appeared grateful for my company, had put himself at a stranger's disposal, despite the fact that I had given no notice whatsoever, in a way unimaginable in the West.

Our time among the lower springs, that said, was beginning to drag. Once Mehmet's tour had taken in Beşpınar (Five Springs) and the lake-like Düden, I was done with these hydrographic curiosities. So much so that the stand-out feature of the fifth spring, Incirli, or Place of Figs, was that it stood in the grounds of an outdoor restaurant.

We passed beyond flaking concrete and exposed chicken-wire walls into a pseudo-grotto, the Incirli Family Park, where an obelisk of rough concrete stones surrounded by a low slab wall marked the spring. The waters spilled into a network of concrete channels, some spanned by miniature willow-pattern bridges, to low tanks where farmed trout swirled. Our table was topped by a white paper cloth and surrounded by a sort of moat. The waiter, in shiny shoes and pressed white shirt, arrived to indulge our pretence, expressed with vague pointing gestures, of selecting particular fish from the tanks. Mehmet lit a cigarette. A plume of smoke rose through the still air into the fig trees. He was sixty, he told me, and a native of

Dinar. His people, Bosnian Muslims, had settled in Turkey during the upheavals of the 1920s. Mehmet had lived an eventful life, having been arrested as a political activist at the time of the 1980 coup, so it was in keeping with the tenor of his story that he should have lost his home, and narrowly escaped with his life, in the 1995 earthquake; that he should have spent much of the following year in an aid agency tent writing his book; and that *rakı* drinking – Mehmet had since forsworn the aniseed-based national spirit – had done for his first marriage.

He had since remarried, to a woman called Pınar; that word again. Springs are revered in most cultures but in Turkey, where the word is a common girl's name, the veneration seems particularly heartfelt. The Trueheroes had gone a stage further, calling their daughter, now nine, Nehir; a River issuing, then, from a Spring, in the local fashion, but with an obstetric literalism that bordered on the graphic. I asked Mehmet about his feeling for the Meander.

'It's our history,' he replied. 'It used to be a beautiful river. But with all the irrigation schemes, the factory effluent and the fish farms, they are destroying it. The flow is nothing like it used to be. I have still to show you Suçıkan, the best-known of the lower springs, but I remember the many watermills it drove when I was a child.' It had initially struck me as wondrous that a classical river should have endured into the modern age,

51

but by their words both Turgay and now Mehmet warned me that a price had been exacted.

The trout arrived, slack-jawed and strewn with sprigs of rocket. Mehmet lifted a laden fork to his mouth, laying his cigarette aside at the last moment. 'And it's not only the river they are destroying,' he added. 'They are closing schools. All they're building are mosques.'

Mehmet venerated Atatürk; the lawyer was a staunch secularist. I asked him about the court case against the *Ak* Party – the fortuitous acronym, which stood for Justice and Development, formed a word meaning white or pure.

'They are talking about closing it down for unconstitutional activities, and banning the party leaders from politics for five years.' Mehmet spoke approvingly. I suggested that Europe would regard such actions as undemocratic.

'Europe?' he replied. 'I can't see Europe admitting us under any circumstances.' We were continuing in this gloomy vein when Mehmet's phone rang. It was the client wondering when his meeting was to be resumed.

'I should get back to the office,' said Mehmet, beating me to the bill. At my objections Mehmet's throat rose through a series of tuts as if it were that of a seabird opening its gullet to an intake of sprats.

'You are my guest,' he said, peeling off some banknotes. On the way back to his car he offered to lead me to the true source of the Meander the following day.

'Can I drop you at the hotel?' he asked. I asked if he could instead point me to an ironmonger's.

That evening a crowd of men gathered around Turgay's television to watch the weekly episode of *Wolves' Valley*. This Turkish drama featured black-suited mobsters who carried black mobile phones. They travelled in black cars, chasing each other along empty roads before simultaneously slewing to halts, without apparent reason, but separated by such distances that they were required to take careful aim at each other over the rolled-down windows of their opened car doors. There were summonses to the homes of gangland bosses where shaven-headed security men ushered the visitors into interiors, spare except for elegant women and white but for the yellow frames of abstract art pieces, there to receive whispered instructions, which they acknowledged by patting their bulging holsters.

Wolves' Valley told the story of a Turkish agent who had gone undercover to infiltrate the country's shadowy underworld. The series had been transfixing Turkey's TV and cinema audiences for five years. In the very name, of course, it was hard not to hear a reference to that valley, *Ergenekon*, whence a wolf had once led the Turkish people on their national journey.

It was a connection I might have further pondered if it had not been for the distraction caused by the advertising banner, which repeatedly flashed across the bottom of the screen; the message touted, with a startling lack of euphemism, 'genital hygiene wipes'. *Wolves' Valley* must have what marketing people knew as a female demographic, though there was no sign of one at Turgay's hotel that evening. The guns were still going off, the tyres squealing, as I made for bed.

CHAPTER 4

Mehmet turned up at the hotel, as promised, the following morning. He skidded to a halt, *Wolves' Valley* style, and fixed a suspicious eye on my walking pole as I climbed into his car. 'The stick?'

'The dogs.' I aimed an explanatory stab at the glove compartment before feigning the whine of a chastened *kangal*.

'No dogs in my car,' announced Mehmet. It did not impress him, apparently, that I should have felt the need to arrange my own security. He spun the wheel and we made our way through Dinar.

The road had barely cleared the town before we entered the historic pass to the east. An observation post topped the heights to our left where the national flag – red, with a white star poised in the jaws of a crescent – hung within a thicket of barbed wire. To the right a giant figure in boots and khaki plus-fours, a *kalpak* or high astrakhan hat on his head, rose from rusted supports; it was a stooped, defiant Atatürk in the garb of the Independence War, which had raged through much of western Turkey, the Meander Valley especially, before the

Turks finally drove back the invading Greek armies in September 1922.

Far below those elevated symbols of nationhood, however, the nation itself appeared in a more ruinous state; the series of watermills that Mehmet had mentioned stood derelict, their neoclassical façades and rust-stained balcony balustrades visibly crumbling. Of the spring that had once turned the mill wheels – Suçıkan, or Rising Water – there was no sign.

'It rises among the trees directly below Atatürk,' explained Mehmet. 'These days, it runs down that roadside ditch. But when I was a boy the water that used to flow through here! I remember it flooding our house.' What with those floods and the earthquake, Mehmet's various homes had clearly suffered their share of natural setbacks. It struck me as odd, even so, that he should have mentioned the house without thinking to indicate its whereabouts.

'We're driving over it just about now. They flattened it to widen the highway about twenty years ago.' Mehmet spoke without sentiment, and with a pothole jolt we had left the site of Mehmet's sometime-submerged childhood behind us.

The road climbed out of the town into clouds of exhaust. The car closed on the labouring trucks, their green tailgates overpainted with the red petals of tulips and lines of yellow Arabic script, and it raced erratically towards an eroded grey skyline. Cresting the pass, Dombay Ovası, the Plain of the

Buffaloes, stretched ahead. The transition was immediate and impressive. The lush orchards were gone; a treeless expanse of spring pastures patterned by the odd rectangular plot of turned earth now ran to snow-lit uplands. William Ramsay, prominent among Anatolia's scholarly wanderers, might have been describing this very plain when he wrote how the 'bright and varied' scenery of the Aegean land gave way to this 'continuation of central Asia, vast, immobile, monotonous'; for the first time the Asiatic steppe stretched before us.

The road made south-east across the plain towards hills where an indistinct azure spill gradually resolved into a lake. In the shallows dazzling egrets appeared freshly laundered, and there were yellow buntings among the reed beds. At a sign to Pınarbaşı, Springhead, Mehmet turned down a rough track to draw up by a water-side restaurant.

'The true source of the Meander,' he announced theatrically. Mehmet had delivered me to my proper point of departure, the bonus being that I could now expect to have travelled in his car for the last time. It was an unworthy thought, of course, given the debt I owed the lawyer. The only thing for it was lunch, and on me this time. Mehmet accepted, but with a resigned dip of the shoulders as if my gesture had devalued his hospitality, and him in the process.

He led the way into a crumbling concrete foyer, empty except for a fridge. The fridge shuddered alarmingly, having somehow succumbed, it seemed, to the cold it itself had generated. The appliance had now begun to work its agued way across the floor, shuffling towards the sunlight – it and David Beckham who gazed from the poster taped to the fridge's door. An awning covered a terrace of immaculately laid tables, which protruded into the lake. We were the only guests. Brown nets hung from floating platforms: fisheries, which spared us requesting the menu.

'Trout,' proposed Mehmet, lighting up a cigarette. I looked out, like Beckham, past the reed beds and the buntings to the lake, and remembered the myth that had once taken root along its shores.

This lake the Ancients knew as Aulocrene, or Flute Spring. The reeds harvested there had historically served as mouthpieces of flutes or pipes, a usage supposedly preserved from that uncertain time when men, gods and lesser immortals were forever consorting and colliding with each other across these lands. It was said that the vain Athena, playing by the lake, caught her own reflection there and at the sight of her puffed-up cheeks threw down the pipe in self-disgust. The discarded pipe was found, inevitably, and by one who could not begin to appreciate the instrument's fatal significance: Marsyas. This satyr, whom some dismissed as a hirsute, cloven rustic but others revered as a close consort of Cybele, the Anatolian mother goddess, soon demonstrated a particular talent for the pipe. In time Marsyas came to reckon himself a musical match for anybody, even for the god of music himself. It was a challenge that Apollo, whose writ ran strong through the Meander Valley, was eager to accept; and an affront, besides, that the lyre-playing Olympian was not prepared to tolerate.

So the two went head to head, but not before the stakes had been signally raised; rather than the celebrity that passes as reward in our age, the winner in this case was to enjoy the ultimate freedom, which was to do with the loser as he wished. To the assembled panel of Muses, mythology's on-call sages, the contest's special significance was all too apparent. Each participant played not merely to prove his own musical supremacy, nor even to establish the inherent pre-eminence of the tradition – strings or wind – at which he excelled. The judges' decision would ultimately find between the cultures that laid claim to this land: the indigenous Anatolian civilisation represented by Marsyas or the encroaching Hellenism of the Olympian Apollo.

It was an age-old, even defining, opposition, one that preceded any Persian interest in the land by centuries. In key elements it constituted a ritual-ised retelling of another scrap that had once taken place on Anatolian soil, albeit on an altogether grander scale: the Trojan War, with historical foot-ings that were to serve as the setting for Homer's epic *Iliad*, had first pitched Anatolians against invading Greeks, an Eastern people against a Western one, around the twelfth century BC.

From roughly that same time the victorious Greeks had been extending their influence into Anatolia, securing preferential advisory appointments in the courts of Eastern potentates, working as physicians or establishing trading interests in ports all along the peninsula's coasts. From the tenth century BC migrants from southern Greece began to colonise the coastlands around the mouth of the Meander – the region they called Ionia. Hellenic colonies were duly established around the coasts – the Black Sea, the Aegean and the Mediterranean – of Anatolia. By the sixth century BC the cities of the Meander Delta, Miletus chief among them, had emerged as the undisputed cradle of Western art and philosophy; the pressing question was how far the West might extend its influence inland into Asia before running into the torpid oriental headwind that traditionally blew there. At the source of the same river a face-off, the original talent contest, was staged to settle the matter.

So beautiful god and bibulous satyr bent to their respective instruments. Their performances proved so impressive that the Muses were unable to reach a verdict; the siege of Troy, it will be remembered, had similarly been heading towards stalemate. The deadlock was broken in this instance when Apollo proposed a deciding round in which each should play his instrument reversed. Marsyas, despite an exceptional ear for music, clearly had no kind of nose for guile; just as the Trojans fell for the Greeks' gift, the wooden horse and its bellyful of concealed warriors, so Marsyas rashly accepted his rival's challenge. He proved unable, of course, to coax notes from the wrong end of his flute; Apollo, all back-handed dexterity, was left to sweep the field. And so to a settling of accounts; the god, not content with bringing his vanquished opponent down a proportionate peg or two, perhaps by condemning the despised piper to a season working the mythical equivalent of the pub circuit, instead had the satyr flayed.

Talent show rejection no doubt hurt; the world had had a considered look at what was on offer, after all, before it passed. But it was not like flaying; even crucifixion was a written warning by comparison. A preliminary flogging was administered not so much punitively, though it can have been no less painful, but by way of preparatory process, for it was in a tenderised state that the skin was most easily worked. With a forensic clarity Ovid detailed Marsyas's torment:

'As he screams, his skin is stripped off the surface of his body, and he is all one wound: blood flows down on every side, the sinews lie bare, his veins throb and quiver with no skin to cover them; you could count the entrails as they palpitate, and the vitals showing clearly in his breast.'

Flaying was commonly practised across the ancient world. One Persian king had a judge flayed for accepting a bribe from a party in a lawsuit; the king then ordered that his victim's chair should be reupholstered with the skin of the very man who had lately sat in judgement there. The Scythians, a feared race of warlike barbarians, were said to flay the bodies of their defeated enemies. The deities were equally partial to flaying; Athena herself had sanctioned its use on her own father, for attempting to ravish her, and on the monstrous Medusa, for being a gorgon. Corruption, defeat, incestuous violation, hydra-headedness: while the case might be made that all these crimes justified such punishment, the ultimate sanction may seem excessive in such a case of mere musical presumption.

Except that Apollo saw his Dionysian rival's transgression in less forgivable terms; any challenge to the supremacy of the Apollonian lyre, whose seven strings were said to represent the planets over which Apollo ruled, was a threat to the very harmony of the spheres. The ancient writers broadly sympathised with the occupying Olympian's view; to them, Marsyas's grisly fate appeared as a deserving instance of hubris. Certainly, the god meant to make an example of the uppity satyr, suspending his tanned hide from a plane tree by the shores of the lake where the native nymphs, spirits and deities of the land gathered to mourn him. The hide remained on display as late as the fifth century BC, according to Herodotus, though it had by then been rehung more prominently in the centre of Celaenae. Herodotus, of a time in which men and gods, events actual and mythical, were forever slipping between the permeable membrane that divided them, felt no compulsion to question the true provenance of Marsyas's skin. Our rational age, relic-wary, would assume it must in fact have been some conspicuous animal pelt, opportunistically press-ganged into serving a myth that had achieved a durable resonance: the triumph of the West.

For Apollo displayed his gory trophy as a raised finger; it was like a hawk hung from a fence post, a deterrent used even today by sheep farmers in rural Turkey, or a highwayman's tarred corpse strung from a roadside gibbet in eighteenth-century France. Marsyas had transgressed, not by thinking too much of his musical abilities but by rating himself with his superiors. His fate warned against Anatolian presumption; it served to remind the people that they should accept subjugation as their natural state; as they had once been subjects of the Persians, they must now bow to their Western overlords. The place of Marsyas's punishment marked the edge of a cultural claim, a hammered stake asserting that Anatolia, at least as far as the Aulocrene Lake, had historically belonged to the West; and even had been Westernised, some would claim, to a degree that no subsequent occupation could quite erase.

So my journey was to begin precisely where the seam between worlds had once run. According to the ancients the West and the East met not along the shoreline of the Aegean and the Bosphorus, as modern geopolitics had it, but where the coastal lands visibly gave way to the steppe. The Meander's source had once marked the end of the West, as our surroundings indicated. For while the floating fisheries to our left told us only what we could expect for lunch, the foundation stones clearly visible in the lake shallows to the right confirmed an ancient frontier.

These footings marked the floor plan of a Roman garrison fort. The fort, known by the lake's corrupted name Aulutrene, guarded the eastern border of the Roman province of Asia; the so-called region, that is, within Asia Minor, as the Romans knew Anatolia, which in turn was contained, like etymological wooden dolls, by the vague but vast continent of Asia. This border the Roman authorities, making good their point, had further confirmed in the first century by raising a monumental column dedicated to the frontier gods in the hills just above the lake. Time was that Roman territories had extended far beyond the column, of course, to Persia, Syria and to Bactria, just as Greek possessions had done under Alexander. Passing the column into wild Pisidia, however, a region renowned for its brigand resistance to outside rule, was to leave the sphere that the Greco-Romans had truly made their own. It was to venture beyond the homelands.

William Ramsay was among the last of those to

have witnessed the frontier marker intact, and among those whose conspicuous interest had condemned the 'large inscribed column thrown from its base' by convincing the locals that it must contain concealed treasures, which a few well-aimed blows were sure to expose. The shattered column, with not a hidden cache to show for it, was long gone, like the fort before it, and by what had become a thoroughly Turkish lake the Marsyas myth had also faded.

What continued was the perpetual argument over the identity of Anatolia; a struggle that seemed to derive, even now, from oppositions as fundamental as those that had once consumed Greece and Troy, Greece and Persia, Apollo and Marsyas. European antiquaries once combed the landscape for a classical past; local bureaucrats duly pasted Turkish names across the least such evidence of a classical heritage. The rusting image of Atatürk, the great moderniser, loomed over Dinar, but across that *Ak* stronghold mosques were being newly built and most women wore the headscarves that the leader's supporters desired them to remove. Across the country Islamists and secularists indicted each other. Some Turks dreamed of being enfolded within Europe; others instead cherished hopes for a greater Turkey that might extend its influence across the Muslim world.

We finished our meal, thanked the waiter, who was busy levering the errant fridge back into position, and strolled down to the shore. The water, strewn with lily pads, was still except where it rose a few yards from the fort footings to a restless, braided camber no larger than a manhole. From this underwater spring the Meander slipped into being. Meaning to honour the moment of departure, however makeshift my arrangements, I took from my rucksack the small jar I had emptied only that morning; it still smelled of the evicted garlic tablets. I thrust the jar among the blooming bubbles. The water was cold and pure. I screwed down the lid and returned the jar to a rucksack pocket, theatrically patting down the flap to seal the ritual of departure.

With an expressive twist of his open palm, however, Mehmet indicated in the Turkish way that he had not understood.

'I'm carrying the water to the sea,' I explained, ready to leave, and offered Mehmet a grateful hand, which his own, twisting to signal his continued confusion, was not ready to receive. 'Where are you going?' he asked.

'To Dinar.' Mehmet gestured patiently at his car. It had not occurred to him that I meant to walk; I now understood the remark with which he had greeted me that morning, that I was to encounter no dogs in his car, had been literally meant.

'I'm going to follow the river,' I explained.

'To the sea?'

'To the sea. Today, though, just to Dinar.' Mehmet stared at me.

'You're going to Dinar on foot?' he eventually

asked. The man had survived flood and arrest, divorce, alcoholism and earthquake, but the prospect of a four-hour walk apparently floored him. Many Turks proudly claim descent from Anatolia's nomads, the Yörüks, a tribal designation said to derive from the Turkish word for walking; the odd thing was how little they thought of the activity for which their descendants were named. They could argue, I supposed, that their calloused forebears had done quite enough walking to count for all their descendants, for ever. Or that Allah had clearly signalled the walking should cease by providing people with cars. Or that the ambivalence was the damaging consequence of an extreme overexposure to walking, much as miners' descendants might not feel the homely warmth of a coal fire without bitterly recalling the racking coughs of their emphysemic grandfathers.

I was heir to no such feelings; rather, the discomfiting obligation to sit – through a long education, then the daily regime of the writer – had left me fidgeting to leave precisely the same seat that Mehmet cared only to occupy. I could wait no longer. So when my companion again offered a lift, casting a palm in the car's direction, I raised the walking pole to signal that my intention was fixed, though I did fish out my phone and promised to use it in case of the least trouble. Then I set off along the shore of the lake.

Alone, I looked out across the lake where the infant Meander's diluted drift lay lost among

the reeds. Kingfishers flitted among the seed heads; the little blue flashes they trailed lingered against the retina, and I felt my spirits lift. The sun was high, and from the lake's marshy fringe a gravel embankment rose into the sky. It carried a railway line, a single track, which made off in the direction I meant to go. At the outset of my journey, yet to gain my bearings, I wished only that my progress be certain; as certain, for instance, as where the Dinar Railway must lead me. So I climbed the slope and set out along the tracks, my stride hobbled by the sleepers, as I covered a first few kilometres to the north-west.

After some time a raised farm track cut across the line, heading across the high plain for the boulder-strewn slopes of Samsun Dağı. I followed it, thinking to pick up the river's progress beyond the lake. The shoreline proved indistinct; beyond the open water was a thick ruff of reeds, which gave way, like a broken hairline, to a few scattered stalks at the fringe of the grazing land. All along the lake's western edge furrowed streams seeped from its punctured rim and nudged curling routes across the little that remained of the plain. Where they reached the foot of the hills these streams had formed dark pools. I stood beside one, ten feet across, and I watched the catkins turning in its lazy gyre grow sodden before they followed the flow into the sinkhole, burrowing downwards by unknown channels to emerge at Orgas, Ilıca or one of the other lower springs. The river had gone where I could not follow. So I retraced my steps to the railway line and walked north, past a series of raised concrete irrigation canalettes, past the empty dirt lanes and rough-tiled roofs of Gökceli village, until I came to the station at Karakuyu.

The junction halt stood isolated and incongruously neat. Baskets of flowers hung from the pitched platform roof, and the Victorian-style lanterns were freshly coated in black paint. A moped, aged but cared-for, was parked outside the stationmaster's office. A harmless dog lay across the doormat. A little way along the line a work gang had broken for tea. They had gathered by a track-side tent, a cone of faded white canvas, where a kettle wheezed on a coal brazier. The men beckoned me to join them. They were dressed in flat caps and stout boots, and wore their sleeves rolled up. They seemed, with their native courtesy and sweat-stained evidence of honest industry, like people from another age. Their foreman, the spit of James Mason, spoke for them, fielding their whispered questions to quiz me on exchange rates, on the retirement age in my country, and on the availability there of procedures to fit prosthetic knees. I was still pondering the knees when Mason spoke again.

'A practical people, the British,' he ventured approvingly. 'They built this railway.' The line, the very first in Turkey, had from the 1850s linked the Aegean port of Smyrna with the city of Aydın along the lower Meander Valley. By shadowing the once-great road to the east, the Meander Valley Railway had wrested from the Turkish camel drivers the lucrative carriage of grapes, figs, opium and all manner of other agricultural goods. The railway's success encouraged its owners to extend the line eastwards, by stages, until in 1889 it followed the lead of the ancient road through the pass at Dinar, to Karakuyu, and on past the source of the Meander. I guessed I would be seeing more of this neat, compact railway, then, in the course of my journey. I commended the workers on their repairs.

'They needed doing,' Mason replied. Not that

they reflected, he was quick to assure me, the least discredit on the original British contractors. 'After all,' he conceded, 'the work they did was a long time ago.'

We drank our tea in companionable silence. When I rose to leave, Mason rose with me. He took me by the wrist and raised my hand in the direction of the railway line, touchingly oblivious to the possibility that he might achieve the same effect by pointing there himself. I was to follow the line onwards to Dinar. I thanked Mason and his men, gently freed my hand and set off. The men were returning to work when I looked back, and I noticed now that one walked with a pronounced limp, and I understood the enquiry about artificial knees had not been baseless.

The railway line began a gradual climb towards the smoke-grey limestone heights. Then it suddenly veered straight for the hills, destined to collide, until a tunnel swung into view. At the entrance I knelt and put a precautionary ear to the rail before I passed beneath the mountain. The light faded with every step. The entrance at my back, suspended like a diminishing lamp, was eclipsed and finally extinguished by the tunnel's curvature. The dark was total; what light this place had ever known – from the lanterns of the tunnel's one-time diggers or from the windows of passing trains – was either old or occasional. It was a darkness to set the mind adrift. I thought of the river's own progress, spilling blind down the passages it had itself made, immeasurably gradual digger of its own tunnels. I surfaced, dislocated, from the darkness. I blinked in the sunlight and scanned the landscape to establish my path, finally recognising a distinctive shape on the skyline; it was the rusted reverse of the Atatürk outline. I descended through orchards to the one lower spring I had not yet visited, which Mehmet had pointed out that same morning: Suçıkan, which the Ancients had known as Marsyas.

For it was from the tears of the flayed satyr's mourners that the same waters that had overrun the boyhood home of my lunch partner were said to have sprung. The spring was set in a wooded park where ancient inscribed marbles had been displayed; here I came across a young couple dissolving their relationship in a hail of insults. I backed away, taking refuge in the pleasant tea garden where a sign above the entrance quoted Arif Nihat Asya. 'Friends,' the Turkish poet declaimed, 'it would be remiss not to tell that I saw at Dinar the very birthplace of the Meander.'

I knew otherwise, of course, but Asya's twentieth-century rhetoric echoed an assumption local people had long shared; it was from this watered grotto at the foot of a romantic crag, according to popular belief, that the Meander issued into being. The setting of Suçıkan was more persuasively attractive than that of upstream Pınarbaşı; another certainty was that it had always been more accessible, given that here had stood 'the very market-place of Celaenae'. The lower spring's

72

urban location, all things considered, constituted a more suitable setting for the display of that talismanic hide – and its relocation appeared to have caused the entire myth to up sticks and move to Suçıkan, even to the point of the Meander's primary source being repositioned there.

In reality, of course, rivers rarely rose in such suggestively attractive spots; they rather more typically seeped from nondescript bogs high in the watershed. Rivers were born plain, without fanfare, which did nothing for the claims, however widely held, of pointedly good-looking locations like Suçıkan – and for that matter Pınarbaşı. For if the tale of a local peasant was to be believed, a third source for the Meander merited consideration.

The tale in question was told in 1929. It supposedly related to events that had taken place some twenty years earlier (but had no doubt related to twenty-year-old events, that safely remote time lapse, all through the history of its telling). Once, let's say, a shepherd was digging at Dereköy village some fifteen kilometres east of Pınarbaşı when he came upon an underground spring. The shepherd was curious to learn where the freshly revealed spring emerged. Into the water he dropped the object that happened to be at hand, which was his music pipe. An encampment of Yörüks duly chanced upon the pipe in the lake shallows at Pınarbaşı. If the tale's narrative purpose was to confirm the lake's ancient association with flutes, then it was not without interesting incidental implications: that modern Anatolians seemed as ready to discard their flutes as Marsyas had been eager to pick his up, certainly, but also that the Meander might have its true beginnings on some drear upland known only to a local shepherd.

Not that Dinar's townfolk were about to acknowledge these prosaic geographical realities; what was there, besides, in the way of tea rooms that could possibly merit the slog out to rustic Dereköy? And how could the views there compare with those at Suçıkan, especially given the topographical improvements the locals had carried out? For barely had the waters bubbled out of the grotto when a rusted pump diverted them to the top of the crag to create a cascade. The effect was picturesque even if the artificially assisted flow did happen to fall directly beneath Atatürk so that the great leader appeared to be doing nothing so much as taking a torrential leak. The waters, having apparently passed through the Father of Turkey, then collected in an ornamental pond where tethered rowing boats bobbed. Fishermen dangled home-made rods from a wooden footbridge. This harmonious scene was disturbed by the appearance of the girl who had evidently failed to resolve her argument with the young man; tearfully wresting the ring off her finger, she flung it into the water and ran out of the park. Two men in freshly pressed shirts, arms linked, lowered their heads at her passing. I recognised the men from the hotel; we had watched *Wolves' Valley* together the previous evening. We traded distressed winces and the handful of freshly picked green almonds that they placed on my table seemed like a gesture of universal conciliation. I drank the tea and ate the almonds, soft furry shells and all, then I began my descent down the Marsyas.

It was a stream which had enjoyed a long reputation, quite unlike the river it was soon to join, for energy and spirit. Herodotus knew the Marsyas as the 'Cataract'; it was, according to Ovid, 'the clearest river in all Phrygia'. An antiquary on a visit in 1887 described the stream emerging 'at the foot of a precipitous cliff, from a dark hole . . . and flowing through a narrow wooded glen, to presently dash down a steep slope through the modern town of Dineir'. By the spring of 2008, however, it resembled no such thing.

Beyond the boating pond, where a portrait of Donald Duck adorned a sun-bleached slide in an abandoned playground, the stream disappeared without ceremony down a metal sluice. On the far side of an empty municipal swimming pool it resurfaced but briefly, like a gasping gangland victim invited to talk, before a gully dragged it through a hole in the block-built shed wall of an adjacent fish farm. The Marsyas emerged, fouled with fish shit, to drain into a steep-sided concrete ditch, which ran beside the road. At a shop selling canned drinks, cigarettes and disposable razor blades, approximately where Mehmet's childhood home must once have stood, it ducked beneath the road. On the far side it resurfaced to run beneath the concrete span of a miniature Italianate bridge in the gardens of the Pines Pavilion Café. An open culvert frogmarched the stream along the rear of some empty shops before forcing it underground opposite the petrol station. It reappeared as an open ditch, which ran across a patch of waste ground until another ditch, concrete-lined, arrived from the left. There the combined waters of four other springs, the Orgas, Incirli, Düden and Ilıca, joined with the Marsyas. So these united tributaries were lost in the river, which here bore the name it would carry to the sea; I found myself by the banks of the true Meander. So I might have expected more of the moment than the green beer bottles, tins and discarded CDs that were strewn across the shallow river bed. Nothing remained of the Persian palaces and the hunting parks. Modern times meant a tough infancy for the Meander.

Mehmet appeared relieved to learn that I had survived the walk to Dinar. He insisted on buying me dinner. Over another plate of fish the conversation ranged across the long history of Mehmet's home town before settling upon a single event that had occurred here in the second century BC. About 160 years, that is, after Alexander the Great had passed through on his way to subduing all Asia, another arrival had taken place at the city gates, though this time it was not a passing army but a column of carts and footsore civilians, some 2,000

Jews, who had been relocated to Apamea from their homes in distant Babylon. The reigning Seleucids, dynastic successors to Alexander the Great, rated the Jews for their civic reliability; at this time of particular instability their presence in Apamea was intended to have a moderating effect on the regional tendency, especially among the neighbouring Pisidians, to rebellion.

This ancient displacement interested me. It instanced, for one thing, a theme of Anatolian history that recurred with an institutionalised regularity: all through their history the inhabitants had been subjected to forcible resettlement. Those who controlled and administered the contested peninsula – the kings and satraps, emperors and governors, sultans and emirs – habitually shifted and shuffled the population packs under their control. With no regard for the regional attachments of their subjects, but with a close eye on their own security and prosperity, they regularly transplanted communities so as to dilute insurrectionist instincts, to bolster depopulated frontier regions, or to improve thin soils by reassigning industrious agricultural communities there.

In the Meander Valley especially, where new arrivals originated from elsewhere in Anatolia but also from further afield, ragged communities had been raising walls among new ways, among unfamiliar languages, dialects and soils since Herodotus recorded how the Paeonians, a people of Macedonia, had some 2,500 years ago been forcibly settled 'in a Phrygian territory and village by themselves'. Some settlers received attractive inducements; the veteran soldiers of successful campaigns were encouraged to make comfortable lives in the lands they had helped to subdue. The authorities in Apamea sweetened the exile of the 2,000 Babylonian Jews by offering them prime housing plots and productive land for their crops and vines.

Others came, however, as prisoners of war; in the fourth century gangs of captive Goths were dispatched to Phrygia and compelled to toil until their Byzantine masters required them for military service. There were mass transportations of captured Slavs to the region during the seventh century. In the twelfth century, as the Byzantine authorities settled Serbians, Hungarians and Petchenegs in imperial lands, newly established Turkish emirs busily abducted Christian families from the protection of rival warlords and dispatched them to areas under their own command. It was a practice that continued in recent centuries; eighteenth-century travellers to Anatolia regularly stumbled across picturesque communities of Cossacks and 'Old Believers', ultra-orthodox religious sects, whom the Ottomans had taken prisoner in the course of successive wars with neighbouring Russia. Mehmet, himself the grandson of refugees from Bosnia, was living evidence that the same process that had brought all manner of formerly scattered peoples to the headwaters of the Meander continued to shape the population across this land.

As for the 2,000 Jews, the new community settled well in Apamea. It helped that they were able to furnish their new home with the old myths they had transported there; a chief claim emerged that the Ark of Noah had come to rest not on distant Mount Ararat but in the very hills that rose above the Jews' adopted city. Perhaps the frequency of the floods, the same floods Mehmet was to experience during his childhood, helped to establish the story. It certainly flourished; Apamea came to be known by the common epithet Cibotus – Apamea of the Ark – and several coins issued during the third century commemorated the association.

It must be admitted, however, that my particular interest in this ancient story was hardly historical. The truth was that an ark, even a mythical one, constituted a big improvement on the dinghies I had seen on the Suçıkan pond; as a grander precedent, that is, for my own boating ambitions.

'Your own what?' asked Mehmet, twisting his palm. He did not speak until I had finished.

'You've a boat in a bag?' Mehmet eventually asked. 'Which you're going to paddle down the river?'

CHAPTER 5

The bag was at the hotel. It was heavy, but not for what it contained. From the moment I had first stumbled upon the Meander I knew that the only way to tackle the river was by being *on* it; there a man might surrender to the windings, pit himself against the currents and so get closer to the truth of things, all the while putting himself beyond the reach of the local *kangals*.

The boat, which I had bought in England, suggested a convenience as high-tech and portable as a folding bike. The collapsible craft, to give it another name, actually had established expeditionary antecedents; canvas kayaks had served in the Second World War, and the *Lady Alice*, the transport that had carried Henry Morton Stanley down the Congo a century earlier still, had likewise broken down into transportable sections. The Victorian explorer was on a considerably bigger river, of course, and where he had hundreds of native porters at his command, I currently relied on the bemused goodwill of a Turkish lawyer. The sections of Stanley's boat, so much bigger than the component parts in my bag, built up into a forty-foot steamboat; mine was a one-man canoe weighing just eleven kilos. It was hard to believe that there could be sufficient room for my luggage, little that there was of it, though the more immediate worry was not so much fitting into the canoe as fitting the canoe into the Meander.

For Dinar's ditches had been troubling me from the moment I first encountered them. It was not possible to believe that anything could ever come of their sorry litter-strewn flows and brutal lines. Industrialisation appeared to have done for the historic river that I had discovered in my researches and even now imagined it to be: the river that Cyrus's forces on their way to Celaenae had once crossed by a prototype pontoon bridge almost 200 feet wide; that a nineteenth-century visitor, alive to his readers' reference points, had compared to the Moselle, or to the Forth at Stirling; and that numerous ferry crossings were still serving in the mid-twentieth century. While it might be argued that the Meander must be given time to grow, the complaint stood that it might by now have provided for a canoe at home on the most modest trout stream. So much, then, for the departure that might have been, Trueheroes, Darkeyes and *Wolves'
Valley* watchers all wishing me well as I paddled out of town. The only thing for it was to walk on until the river grew big enough to accommodate the canoe.

Turgay Darkeye was sorry to see me leave. 'We love you,' he declared. I appreciated the sentiment, supposing that Turgay spoke for the wider hotel crowd, but it was the parting gift, a box of baklava tied with a pink ribbon, which touched me. I liked baklava, and I liked Turgay Darkeye, the more so for having made me his pastries proxy. Those that ill health barred from such sweet pleasures often tended to begrudge them to others. Diabetes, though it had put him on a parsley diet, had in no way embittered Turgay. It would be a privilege to honour his generosity by eating the baklava, but later, when I might also be able to congratulate myself on successfully negotiating a first stretch of water. I embraced Turgay and set off into the bright morning.

I rejoined the Meander at the confluence of its feeder streams, where I had left it the previous evening, and followed the ditch through Dinar's nondescript outskirts. I passed close to the train station, traversed an empty market area and reached the edge of the town. Here a prison stood by the banks of the Meander.

Turkey has an unenviable reputation when it comes to prisons. The encounter might then have been suggestive, substantiating my fears by confirming the Meander's poor start in life; the tough infancy having apparently led to an inevitable first spell inside. It might, less fancifully, have added up to a tableau so depressing – nick, ditch, concrete, rubbish – as to have stopped me in my tracks.

Except that this prison bordered on the picturesque,

its features apparently lifted from black-and-white breakout movies: a single guard in a tin helmet surveying a square compound from a whitewashed watchtower with pointy overhanging roof; a washing line hung with what I took to be inmates' smalls; high wire-topped walls, in the way of a proper jail, but with a gate so oversized it might have been the entrance to a giant's castle; a dinky visitors' waiting room for doting mothers; and, against the outside perimeter wall, an outdoor basin with a mirror hung above it.

The basin felt like the telling detail, indicative, whatever sorry episodes might have taken place inside, of what Turkish society demanded above all else of those released from prison; a certain level of personal hygiene. Turks traditionally put a high value on cleanliness, as their ritual ablutions prior to prayer, their extensive patronage of *hamams* (steam baths), and their prime-time adverts for genital wipes amply confirmed. The thought reminded me that I was a comparative scruff, with every chance of becoming a superlative one during the off-road weeks ahead. I had washed that morning. What I did not know was where I would wash that night. From now, since I could only guess at the next tap, I would do well to use facilities whenever they appeared, starting with the prison basin. I made a point of washing my face there before making my way, free and freshly presentable, out of Dinar.

The river had barely passed the prison when it

too went free, slipping from the concrete ditch to run between root-veined banks of earth. For a moment, conditioned by captivity to its linear lot, it held course; then it remembered its name and the freedoms it had known above Suçıkan, and at last it began to deviate, throwing loops, which grew full and fat. Beyond the river, lines of spring wheat shoots unfurled in the sunshine. Shawled women, rears to the sky, bent with their mattocks to weed around spinach seedlings. Willow trees rose along the banks. Coots scuttled across the clear stream, and the wing strokes of rising herons sounded like beaten carpets beyond the trees. Turtles basked on the banks, ditching inelegantly at my approach. Fish showed distinct in the sunlit shallows. It was beautiful but for the last rafts of town rubbish – plastic bottles, aerosol cans, margarine containers and discoloured polystyrene chunks – which had gathered behind the scummy booms of fallen branches.

The river began to fill out, but even as my canoe worries were dispelled, fresh concerns took their place. The arable lands had given way to pasture where fresh droppings signalled sheep – and warned of the dogs that commonly attended them. I gripped my walking pole and hurried on until I reached the relative security of a low bridge where a lane ran. Beyond the bridge the river formed a basin with gently shelving banks, which I immediately knew to be the place. I took out my mobile phone. 'I've found the launch site,' I told Mehmet.

The previous evening had proved a challenging one for Mehmet; he had barely come to terms with my walking before he learned that I was to take to a boat, and while walking was merely unnecessary, cars having made it so, boating was positively outlandish. The people of Turkey have never been notable sailors; the Ottoman Navy, though it might have had its moments, was mostly manned by subject peoples of traditional seafaring lands, Greeks especially. Nor did the Meander, as we have seen, boast much in the way of boats: one legendary ark and some rowing boats, unsubstantiated rumours of marble-bearing rafts, a few cable ferries and the odd fish farmer's dinghy did not constitute a rich, river-going history. Mehmet might have tried to dissuade me but for the discovery that my luggage contained a boat; he was enough of a realist to accept that people who packed boats in their luggage probably meant to use them. It was to his credit that we were yet to finish our fish dinner before he had worked out how he might be useful. 'You find your launch site and I'll deliver the boat,' he had proposed, thereby offering the use of his car without me having to go in it.

When he drew up at the bridge some time later, he was with a friend. Adnan was from the *Dinar News*.

'Your ark,' said Mehmet cheerfully. He hauled the boat off the back seat. I unzipped the bag and tipped its contents onto the grass. The canoe comprised a skin, or hull, of red rubberised fabric. Lightweight metal rods, in elastically connected sections, constituted the craft's basic frame. The bag also contained cross ribs, inflatable tubes and seat, air pump, spray deck and paddle.

'What are you doing?' demanded the portly Adnan. I had expected journalistic inquiry; but the tone from the *Dinar News* sounded more like censure. Mehmet might have left his own reservations behind but had apparently brought backup in this regard. I got the strong impression that a literal answer was not what the newsman wanted; rather than describe the assembly process, detailing how the rods fitted together to provide the canoe with its keel and gunwales, I was instead to justify a project Adnan clearly considered ill-advised. I took the romantic line, explaining that I had not thought beyond following the river to the sea. Adnan looked along my gesturing arm but saw nothing at the end of it to satisfy him.

'Why are you travelling without a friend?' he specified. I clipped the inner cross ribs to the frame, which served to stress the canoe, and considered my answer. I had myself wondered whether it was recklessly dangerous to make the journey alone; but Adnan's objection, I suspected, was rather that it was unnatural to forsake the companionship essential to any enterprise. I liked travelling alone, I replied, though the truth was I suspected my expeditionary tastes were sufficiently obscure to have deterred all potential companions.

A craft of sorts was now taking shape. I fitted the support struts. Then I inflated the air tubes, which lay between the frame and the skin, further stressing the structure and providing buoyancy. The thing had begun to resemble a canoe.

'Do you know how to use it?' queried Adnan. I had done some canoeing, I replied, which was true, but my diffidence only encouraged Adnan to prod the other gaping holes he had detected in my plan.

'Where will you sleep?' I explained that I was depending on the Turkish reputation for hospitality to find lodging in the villages.

'They will not be expecting you. They have not seen canoes on this river. They have never seen tourists on this river.'

'Then I can sleep by the bank,' I replied, patting my sleeping bag; I could think of worse predicaments than spending the odd spring night under the Anatolian stars. I inflated the canoe's seat before beginning to stow my luggage. Bags, rucksack and air pump went into the limited space astern, while the walking pole and the dry bag, in which the mobile and other valuables were stored, went forward. I squashed my boots into the bow, lashed the laces to the frame and snapped together the tubular sections of my paddle.

'And what will you do,' Adnan asked, 'about lunch?' There was nothing like lunch uncertainty, it seemed, to endanger a man on the Meander, and this from one who had clearly missed very few of them in recent years.

'Which reminds me,' said Mehmet. He scurried back to the car to return with Turgay Darkeye's baklava. I wedged the elegant box, tied in a pink bow, as best I could against the rucksack. The effect was less than expeditionary. I embraced Mehmet.

'You must call tonight,' he said, containing his own concerns within a single instruction. I promised to do so, clambered into the canoe and pushed off. I was on the Meander.

I had not owned the canoe for long. Its maiden launch had taken place near my home a few weeks earlier. On that English river I had learned that the craft's lightness, a vital asset when it came to the portages I expected to make, had been traded at a price; the canoe was unstable. The manufacturers assured me that I would get used to the thing with practice; I now regretted that lack of familiarity as I moved with the exaggerated wobble of a tightrope clown out onto the narrow stream. It reassured me that I had seen enough of the river, with its shallow gradient, to feel confident of a forgiving introduction. The Meander was sure, now of all times, to stay true to its name.

It did no such thing. Around the very next bend there appeared a different river. A sudden fall in the land's lie, though it was imperceptible, caused the river's languid curves to tighten into bends. The surface of the water was embroidered with sudden ruffles and swirls. Fallen branches littered the channel. I cursed myself for not having made a precautionary foray. If I had checked the river

88

for another hundred metres beyond the bridge, I would have known. But I'd been watching the river since Dinar. And beyond every such hundred-metre stretch another one awaited, and another, onwards until the current slackened and the water turned to salt. Much was to be learned, no doubt, from quizzing the locals and from checking the available maps, but the time always came when there was nothing but to go with the river. To trust the river at one's back for the one that lay ahead.

This, though, was not that time. On this occasion I should have walked for another hundred metres.

I was still settling into the canoe, finding my balance, when I felt the narrowing river gather pace beneath me. I sensed a momentum not my own. I was being led. I looked ahead as a sharp left turn swung into view. Water broke white over a fallen branch. I was on the bend in no time. I dug in my paddle astern, looking to swing the bow round, but the canoe's right flank soon rose where the water heaped up on the branch. The canoe tipped onto its side and threw me into the waist-deep stream. The water was cold. I clambered to my feet. I dragged the canoe to the bank. I emptied it of water. I climbed back in and went at the next corner, which I cleared, and the one beyond it too, only for the next one, in the way of next ones, to arrive. A fallen tree lay across the river, forcing the flow through a narrow chute where a protruding branch prevented passage. I reverse paddled to avoid the chute and went broadside against the submerged tree. The canoe flipped. I came up spluttering, grabbed my paddle and the canoe's painter rope, and staggered towards the bank. Something pink caught my eye; Turgay Darkeye's box of baklava disappeared down the chute.

I dragged the waterlogged canoe up the bank and overturned it in a field of young wheat. Adnan had been right. I had thought too much of my own abilities and not enough of my opponent. What had I thought by taking a river's ancient name as surety? I had barely started before getting soaked and shocked. And I had lost my baklava.

It was then that I became aware of the snake, a benign creature that spilled its liquid green coils through the wheat shoots at my feet. The snake sensed my presence and froze, not so much to immobility as inanimacy, its raised head an iridescent circlet. I watched the snake; it was some time before it continued towards the river, as it had intended. The creature had disappeared by the time I followed its lead back to the bank.

I walked downstream, searching for somewhere to attempt another launch. Beyond a pair of fields I came upon a clear stretch of low-lying bank. I returned to the canoe, unpacked my sodden luggage and transferred it to the launch site. I went back for the canoe. I repacked the canoe. I put myself back on the river. I pushed off, adrenalised, and clattered down a long ramp of little corrugated waves. The banks of earth and roots rose high, the sunlight strobing through the long grass. I slalomed down a gully to a bend that turned more sharply than I could. My bow slammed into the bank and I stretched to take hold of a passing tree root so that the current did not catch me and spin me round, blind to the river at my back.

There were other such bends. And fallen willows. What riverside willows did, I learned that day, was fall. On occasion, where the banks were high, I was able to find a way beneath the trunk, forcing a route through the foliage to emerge caked in web and leaf, and the dusty, fluff-tufted bracts of catkins. Elsewhere, when the blockage was total, there was nothing for it but to clamber up the bank before working my way back to the water, all the time dragging the laden canoe behind me. The hauling proved exhausting. Once, looking over my shoulder, the boot soles that protruded from the canoe's bow caused me to imagine that they contained the feet of some stretchered person, and as they were my boots it was natural I should have begun to think that the stretcher was for me and that I would not get down the river.

I fought the exhausting river for a long time. Then the current began to slacken as suddenly as it had run, and over the quietening water I again heard the chatter of sparrows and the splash of turtles. The relief was complete. I loosened my grip on the paddle, flexed sore palms, and looked about me. The woven spheres of weaver birds' nests hung from overhanging branches. In the late light seeds had patterned the water's still surface. A lone boy, his face stippled in shadow, watched me from the bank. I had passed before he offered the gnomic encouragement that I was heading in the right direction. The banks had begun to lose their height. The river yawed gently left before spilling into a still lake, which the low sun had slicked with gold. Geese flew black against the mountains. I paddled across Gökgöl, or Sky Lake, past a few scattered fishery platforms towards the village on the north shore.

Fairy lights twinkled in the trees close to the water's edge, and beyond the insects that played in their vague penumbra could be seen a few tethered dinghies stuck with roughly stowed oars.

Among them was a yellow pedalo. It had twin bows, each bearing a wave-cresting dolphin, and flicked tails for sterns.

Outside a concrete building a man with a bull neck, hands on hips, watched me put ashore. The man told me that I had arrived at a *pansiyon*, with a *restoran*. He led me upstairs, and along a corridor lit by unshaded bulbs, to a room that the man made mine by plugging his fingers into the necks of some empty beer bottles and tipping a butt-filled ashtray out of the window. I did not think much of the place, nor of the effort that had gone into readying it for me. It was only when I found a mirror that I thought even less of myself. I was caked with drying mud. There were weed smears, and bits of twig all over my T-shirt. One ear was draped with a spider's web and many catkins had snagged in my hair in the manner of miniature rollers.

I showered, washed my clothes and hung them out to dry. I went downstairs to eat. In the vast dining hall tables stretched to infinity. An extravagant plastic flower feature, which might have adorned the shrine of an Iranian martyr, rose from the middle of the hall. A pall of cigarette smoke engulfed the only other guests, six men in suits arranged around a bottle of *rakı*. Maddened insects flung themselves at the harsh bare lights. The owner brought me a plate of fried fish. He laid it before me, helping himself to a chip as he did so. I sensed not boorishness but deliberate insult.

This was behaviour that the antiquary David Hogarth, who travelled extensively through this region in the late nineteenth century, would have recognised. Hogarth stressed the importance of travelling 'with a certain train of pack-animals and attendants; the Englishman who, proud of his power of endurance, discards all superfluities and travels with what he can carry on his own horse excites no admiration but much contempt in the minds of the villagers. "This is a poor man," say they, and he is shown only just as much of what he wishes to see as will silence his importunity.' The *pansiyon*'s owner had taken exception to an approach he considered not original but aberrant. Gökgöl did not do canoes and river filth. If it was respect I wanted, I should have turned up tidy, in a hire car or, better still, a tour party.

I ate the fish and remaining chips, and stepped into the night. The lake was skeined in moonlight; from the far shore there came the distant honk of geese. The canoe lay in a deflated muddy puddle. I dragged it under cover. Then I kept my promise to call Mehmet.

'You made it?' he said. 'We saw you get wet at the first bend. But we thought it was best to let you get on with it.' I told him I had arrived in one piece.

'Good,' he said. 'We'll be with you in the morning. With a television crew.'

CHAPTER 6

I was sore the next morning, shaken even, and made myself the waking promise that I would find out what lay ahead before having anything more to do with the Meander. People were commonly lost, after all, in Anatolian rivers; the German emperor Frederick Barbarossa had drowned leading his Crusader armies across the Calycadnus River, the modern Göksu, in 1190. While I could take comfort from the relative risks we seemed to represent – the emperor's horse, its rider weighed down in armour, had none of the buoyancy benefits of a canoe – it nevertheless paid to take care.

So I turned to the maps; I had packed several, largely because no single map among all those I tracked down had struck me as in the least reliable. The theory was that the maps might prove unreliable in their own ways, but with a corresponding range of virtues, so that the whole sheaf, consulted in combination, might just help me find my way. Once they had dried out from the soakings, that is, they had received in yesterday's capsizings. I had the previous evening hung them out along the aerial cable that ran from the back of the TV to the window

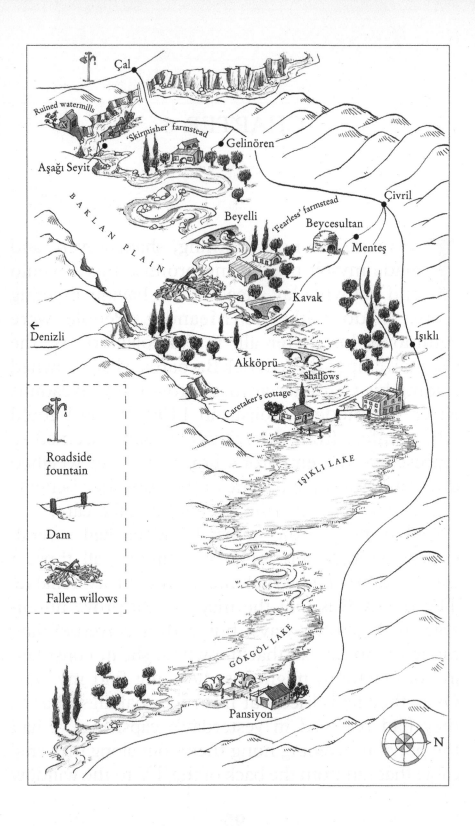

of my room. From that makeshift laundry line I collected them, crinkly now, and unfolded the one the Turkish military had published.

The map should not have been in my possession. Its unauthorised use was illegal. The more pressing drawback was that it dated from 1944. For all its archival interest – confirming, for example, that the village of Pınarlı had indeed once been known as Norgas – the map was patently unable to help with any obstructions or dangers that might have appeared on the landscape since the Second World War. The map's great asset, that said, was a scale far larger than anything offered by the competition; at two kilometres to the centimetre, it was sure to provide useful detail, even if much of it might be historical.

According to the military map – once, that is to say, and possibly still – the waters along this stretch of the Meander resembled a pair of lifters' weights, cartoon-like in their unequal sizes, and attached by the stretch of river that ran between them; beyond little Gökgöl the river briefly re-formed before draining into another, larger lake, Işıklı Gölü, whose extent was represented by a wide ruff of marshy tussocks. My practical objective that day was to find my way across the two lakes and in each case pick up the river where it continued beyond their indistinct fringes. To cross-reference the military map with something more recent I returned to the sheaf and selected the pages I had photocopied from a

Turkish road atlas, wondering, as I did so, if any motorist had ever unfurled a sea chart across his steering wheel.

Turkish maps were not up to much. They never had been, to judge by one nineteenth-century antiquary, who had found them 'incorrect in the highest degree; in fact, absolutely useless'. My own hunch was that a correlation might exist between the quality of available maps and the historical incidence of invasion across the region they purported to cover. Such a correspondence was liable to throw up all manner of insights into the local insecurities, particularly in the case of much-trampled Anatolia. William Leake, reflecting upon his travels of 1800, recognised that experience had taught the Turks to view foreigners as thieves, not only, as we have seen, of the land's ancient artefacts but even of the land itself, maintaining that the inhabitants were unable to 'imagine any other motive for our visits to that country, than a preparation for hostile invasion, or a search after treasures among the ruins of antiquity'. Anatolia had been subjected, after all, to invasions by Persians and Macedonians, Romans and Avars, Gauls and Goths, Arabs and Slavs, Mongols and Tartars, Franks and Mamelukes, Russians and Bulgars, the British and the Anzacs, French and Italians, not forgetting the Turks themselves and, most recently, the Greeks whose invading forces had advanced from Smyrna up the Meander Valley in 1919. It was therefore no surprise that the authorities should have come to view those who sought to know Anatolia's topography with particular suspicion, and to assume that it was the land itself that the paymasters of these inquiring individuals – spies, in short – were after. Maps were weapons, then, no less than armaments. The army had always made the best maps in Turkey. And it meant to keep them for itself.

Enter the road atlas, a large-scale, mass-market and informative innovation, which threatened to lay bare every last secret of Turkey's topography. Except that very little, as I was quickly discovering, could actually be learned from the Turkish product; at least in terms of relating the roads, which it covered tolerably well, to the surrounding landscape. I was quick to notice conspicuous errors in the road atlas's coverage; the railway where James Mason's gang at Karakuyu had served me tea, and quizzed me on prosthetic knees, was represented as running round the wrong side of the Aulocrene Lake, while the Meander was placed on the wrong side of the road that ran between Dinar and the village at Gökgöl.

All of which I might have put down to cartographical inexperience or under-resourcing if it had not been for the military map, and its assertion, even now, that the landscape was not mine to know. Blame *Wolves' Valley* perhaps, but I found myself imagining some clandestine agency of the deep state charged with ensuring that road atlas publishers incorporated in their product a degree of deliberate inaccuracy. Not in their coverage of the actual roads – which was too much to expect, even in the interests of national security – but at least in the bits of cartography that might be accounted of minimal interest to road users; hills and pastures, say, since nobody but shepherds went there, rivers and railways too, and perhaps such strategic installations as power stations, if only because people who bought road atlases for their proper purpose had no business being interested in such things. So it was that a topographical blackout, partial but permanent, awaited the next wave of invaders, wherever they might come from, even if in the meantime it inconvenienced those, canoeists included, whose only design on Turkey's sovereign territory was to pass through it more safely than Frederick Barbarossa.

Beyond the roads, then, I was not to trust the road atlas, even if in this instance it broadly agreed with the military map; two lakes, linked by a short stretch of river, lay ahead. The second lake appeared as much as ten kilometres across, with an unbroken expanse of open water beyond a marshy rim. I had little confidence, however, that this lake might not prove to be an unnavigable swamp. Or a drained expanse of farmland or orchard, the river traversing it by a concrete culvert. Or off-limits in some way that I could not even imagine. I decided to ask the fishermen.

I found a pair of them by the waterfront, scooping up farmed fish with hand nets and tossing them with practised ease back into various pens. It soon became clear, however, that they had put such effort into the acquisition of their fish-sizing skills that they had learned nothing of the river beyond Gökgöl. I tried my luck with another fisherman who was wandering the *pansiyon* grounds in waders, touting a brace of freshly caught, fearsome-looking fish. When I showed interest in the creatures, thinking it might assist my search for directions, the fisherman told me that they were known in the village as *turna*, more generally as the literal *dişli balık*, or teeth fish, and were excellent eating, even at breakfast, and hardly expensive, at least not for me. It turned out, however, that he knew no more than his colleagues of the river's onward route. Beyond Gökgöl the Meander might spill off the edge of the world for all these fishermen cared. The lake was merely their workplace; their travelling they did by the local roads – to Dinar and Burdur, Afyon and Denizli, Işıklı and Çivril – which they could describe with complete reliability. What I heard from the fishermen was the same advice, in short, on offer from the road map, and from Adnan and Mehmet before it; mine was not the way to go.

I retired to the restaurant to consider my position. I breakfasted there not on the local piranha but on bread and olives, and a pan of fried eggs whose yolks had formed a triangle of spheres, perfectly symmetrical, in their unified whites. It was still early, when the hotel man's disdain for

his maverick guest seemed half-stoked, even concil-
iatory, and I felt bold enough to ask him about
the way ahead. The man took a biro from his top
pocket and began to draw on the greaseproof paper
that covered the table, helping himself to an olive
as he did so. It was a predictably bad map, but
the same cartoon weights could be made out in
it; little Gökgöl was connected by a short stretch
of the Meander to Işıklı Lake. This appeared to
be no more informative than the two printed maps
until I noticed that the larger weight, Işıklı, had a
decidedly flat end, which the man, lifting another
olive, emphasised in bold.

'*Baraj*,' he said emphatically; dam. The post-war
landscape had indeed acquired an addition of
strategic value – as I might have surmised by the
road map's failure to include it – and of relevance
to my journey. Beyond this dam, which the man
said was easy to spot, the Meander continued
westwards – at least when its flow was permitted
to do so. The very fact of this first dam, and its
intimations of industrial interference, might have
registered more alarmingly if I had not simply
been content to have found a visible landmark to
aim for. I had now got a plan for the day. So I
thanked the man, who had just put the printed
maps to shame, by offering him the last of my
olives.

I was running an eye over the canoe, relieved
that it appeared no worse for the battering it had
suffered the previous day, when Mehmet and

Adnan rolled up at the head of the promised press convoy.

Mehmet emerged from his car unshaven, in sunglasses and an open-necked shirt; it was a dramatic makeover suggestive of a multi-media impresario. As he approached, he threw a thumb over his shoulder at the television van. 'From Afyon,' he declared with the easy poise of one whose influence now extended north across the highlands of Phrygia to Opium, as the provincial capital's name translated, whence he could summon not merely free-sheet hacks like Adnan but fully equipped film crews.

The crew consisted of a middle-aged director, who did his own filming, and a female assistant. This young woman sported an uneven fringe of brown hair and a slight, oddly affecting stoop. But the director, rolling his eyes in frustration, was quick to advertise his immunity to her allure.

'The stills camera,' he snapped. 'You were supposed to bring the stills camera.' With a theatrical flourish he folded his arms and watched his wayward charge make for the van, as if only his close scrutiny would prevent her from falling into the lake, forgetting where she had been sent or returning with the wrong camera. It was a long walk back to the van; long enough that the director might have punctuated his vigil by making a public acknowledgement of the girl's shortcomings with an indulgent shrug, a knowing wink, or even some derisive utterance, confirming a meaner streak in his character. He did no such thing but continued to watch the girl intently until the rest of us transferred our attentions, one by one, from the girl to the watching director. As the impatience drained from his posture and the lines of his face lost themselves to reverie, it was clear to all of us that the man was in the grip of something more disabling than a professional dissatisfaction. By the time the girl drew near, the correct camera slung across that canted shoulder, he had slipped involuntarily into some whispered song. Only as the girl arrived among us did he break the trance and remember who he was supposed to be.

'I shouldn't have to remind you,' he told her. So we set about making our item for a regional news programme. The director filmed as I prepared the canoe for the water. I was inflating the tubes when the girl's shadow briefly fell across the director's shot. 'Stay right beside me,' he scolded her, but not one of us heard his words as a cinematographic instruction. The man was in thrall to emotions that no show of professional irritation could conceal. They came off him in crackling waves, coursing through the air with an energy so palpable as to rouse the dogs who shook the strange sensation from their dozy heads, and the fishermen flexed their fingers, casting glances skywards to check for thunderheads among the clouds. The feeling was so all-consuming it was impossible to believe the film would not convey it; the TV audiences in distant Opium must know that the foreign canoeist who thought it something to paddle down the Meander had merely been the sideshow that morning at Gökgöl.

The director declared that he was done except for the footage he wanted of my departure. He sent the girl back for a fresh battery and watched her go. In the silence Adnan turned to tell me that he had fished on Işıklı Gölu as a young man. 'There's nowhere for lunch,' he advised. 'The lake's deep in the middle and the wind can get up,' he said, shaking my hand. 'Keep to the left bank. And that will bring you to the dam.' Adnan's campaign to stop the canoeist, every objection exhausted, had run its course. The assistant returned with the battery, and with some bananas, which she kindly handed me.

'No need to ring tonight,' said Mehmet, who was to follow no further. He embraced me at length. 'Just when you get to the sea.'

I stowed the bananas, made a mental note of Adnan's advice and pushed off. The water was like a screen, and where the blade shed its droplets a faint kink rippled through the reflected willow trees. I had pointed my bow at the channel, enjoying the moment of pure solitude before loneliness began to sour it, when shouts reached me from the shore. It was the film crew. They had commandeered the pedalo. Its twin dolphins were moving out across the lake. Pivoting the canoe to face them, I was reminded how the dolphins of myth traditionally saved men imperilled by shipwreck or storm; and it almost seemed as if that yellow pair, one with a stove-in beak, were bearing the television crew to a higher realm, beyond the social constraints of conservative Anatolia, and onto a stage worthy of the director's passion. He trained the camera on me for a moment before signing off with a raised thumb. Then he briefly rested a hand on the girl's shoulder before joining her at the pedals. They trundled away in a wide arc.

Alone again, I passed outlying fish pens where rope lines, running shallow to stakes on the far shore, chafed beneath the canoe. A man at the furthermost pen had noticed that the tethers were hampering my progress. Holding to the platform with one hand, he worked his way out along the rope to clear my passage, weighting the line until the water drew round his heels. He bowed theatrically as I passed, occasioning a wobble from which he barely recovered.

'Shit!' he exclaimed, putting up a local heron. 'Tea?' I paused, for I was not one to turn down tea, from fishermen on tightropes especially, but it was already past noon.

'I've a way to go,' I declined apologetically.

'All the more reason for tea,' he riposted.

'And I'm not even sure,' I persisted, 'where I'm going.'

The fisherman took rejection with good grace. 'Onwards is where!' he exclaimed. 'The way is clear.'

And with that reassurance I slipped into the channel, settling into my stroke. Reeds closed in on either side, rising green from their fronded bases to a bleached palisade of crackle-dry seed heads. Above their fluffy tops, to the east, I saw sunlit limestone uplands. The rounded summit of an earthen *höyük*, or Neolithic mound, rose from the western plain. Fish broke surface in iridescent arcs. Where ponds breached the reed beds, the yellow bursting globes of water lilies rose on snub stems from foundering pads. Prey birds, alive to the massed clamour of frogs, ranged above the reeds. Egrets trailed their legs, blowsy and vaporous, across the sky. It was a beautiful morning, though the unease I felt at depending upon a poorly drawn map to get through this reedy maze, the scribbled directions of a man who held me in low regard, rather dented my appreciation of the fact.

Beyond Gökgöl, I found myself back on the river where it passed beneath a country bridge, then swung to the north and broadened, its banks ravelling away like stage curtains to reveal Işıklı Lake. The greaseproof sketch had not failed me. The lake's stippled expanse stretched to the foot of the mountains that rose along the shore. Remembering Adnan's advice, I kept left where the shore was banked by a high concrete levee. Işıklı Lake, a one-time marsh where the writ of the season had run without interference, had since become a reservoir. Not that I, having fretted over the apparent lack of water only the previous morning, had cause to complain. The lake teemed, besides, with life; frogs and fish, and tiny water snakes, black and yellow, which fled as the waves from my paddle overran the lily pads where they basked. White storks stood in the shallows, fastidiously immobile. Whiskered terns dipped overhead, their angular wings diaphanous in the sunlight, and above, against the snow glare on the heights of Akdağ, White Mountain, a procession of pelicans passed, their wings in lazy unison, like a half-remembered vision of hands waving from the windows of a passing train. I put ashore where a faded blue boat lay abandoned, the reed-punched hull rotted to wafer, though the gunwale supported my weight, and glad of the birds I ate the bananas in the sunshine.

The west wind got up after lunch. A procession of waves bore down on me as I paddled through the long afternoon. Alert for my landfall, I kept an eye on the horizon where a faint grey rectangle rose from the tree-lined haze. I powered through shallows stuck by drowned trees, past a drift of pochard ducks, the wind ruffling their henna plumages, and at last closed on the building to put ashore in the long shadow it now cast. The man's map had done its job, delivering me to the pumping station beside the dam. Beyond the levee, where I dragged the canoe, smoke drifted from an orchard. Families sat beneath the trees, barbecuing lamb kebabs.

At the sight of me a woman rose from her table and strode across. 'This is State Water Works land,' she announced briskly.

'I hoped I might leave the canoe here,' I replied, thinking to find a room in the nearest town. She threw back her head in the expressive negative.

'I'm following the Meander,' I told her, playing the romantic card.

'You can't leave it here,' she confirmed, walking away. It was then that I brandished the letter I had secured from the state tourism ministry. The effect was instant, halting the woman mid-stride, before she turned to take the letter. At its contents she nodded approvingly. I followed her lead through the long grass in search of the caretaker, dragging the canoe behind me.

I had arranged my own laissez-passer, having

been repeatedly struck in preparing for my journey by the prominent role that written permission had played in these parts. Francis Arundell was forever flashing his *firman* – the word originally denoted an Ottoman imperial decree – before he was given leave to proceed. In the Dinar area, where foreigners were regarded with particular suspicion, it proved of special value. 'Returning through the market place, for it was market day,' Arundell wrote, 'we were followed by a Turk, who asked for our firman; and having sent it to the aga, he obligingly gave us permission to go where we pleased.' Arundell was once making out inscriptions when he was interrupted by Dinar locals, 'some with evident marks of displeasure, but "they have a firman" was at once a conclusive and satisfactory answer'.

We found the caretaker outside his cottage where he was scything a knee-high meadow. He had worked his way round two small dozing dogs to leave them undisturbed on their grass islets.

'The man's got authorisation, Mehmet,' the woman said. 'He came across the lake.'

'And where would he be going?' he asked.

'He wants to store the boat for the weekend,' she explained. This Mehmet was much younger than his Dinar namesake. He wore, however, a brimless woollen cap of the kind that the dapper Truehero would not think of wearing, I guessed, until his own Nehir had made him a grandfather, for it was a hat traditionally associated with dotage. The caretaker came from a village further downstream. He had circumscribed horizons, and admitted to knowing nothing even of Gökgöl when I told him where I had paddled from.

'You can put the canoe under cover,' he said, lifting one end and leading the way to a nearby shed. 'Wouldn't want the dogs to eat it.' I thanked him, explained that I would be back in a day or two, grabbed my rucksack and walked out to the road.

The last light was draining from the blossoms in the dusky cherry orchards. Silhouetted hawks perched on telegraph poles. By the road a donkey tugged at its staked tether. A car pulled up and I made space for myself among the rods and nets on the back seat. The driver and his friend, both bank staff, had had a disappointing day by the lake.

'Not a bite,' said the driver. He sniffed the air discreetly.

'Nothing but birds,' his friend confirmed, winding down his window.

'And a red canoe.' I owned up to the canoe.

'So did you have more luck?' the driver asked. I admitted I wasn't a fisherman.

'You were in a boat,' his friend observed.

'I'm travelling down the Meander,' I explained. A lengthy silence followed.

'Let's hope you don't go aground,' said the driver.

The small town of Çivril's main street had high crumbling kerbs, and unlit windows with displays of bubble-wrapped fridges and saucepans printed with vegetable designs. There were several banks.

'His branch,' said the driver, pointing at one of them.

'And his,' said the friend. We drew up by a side street where the driver indicated a building outlined in orange fairy lights.

'Hotel,' he said. 'With a shower.'

CHAPTER 7

A palace once stood a few miles south of Çivril, by a tributary of the Meander, at a site now known as Beycesultan. The palace had long since disappeared beneath a grass-topped *höyük*, along with all trace of the settlement's original name; the tributary now served as an irrigation ditch. I was making my way there the next morning, walking a road that passed through poppy fields, when a kitchen fitter drew up in a van.

Ali was taking his wife and son to visit relatives in the nearby city of Denizli. I squatted in the back of the van where loose screws skittered among the chipboard offcuts, spanners, U-bends, washers and tile samples. There were glossy German brochures but so neatly stacked, with careful folds at the page corners, that I suspected Ali only ordered their designer taps and baths in his dreams, the one place his clients could afford them. Even so I was quick to point out, with the fluent insincerity of the hitch-hiker, that Ali's kit clearly marked him out as a quality fitter. Ali nodded, though he seemed less keen on discussing

113

kitchens than in learning how his lift might spend Sundays back home.

'Well, like you,' I offered. 'Visiting friends or relatives.' A family meal, I continued. A walk.

Unsatisfied, Ali eyed me in the rear-view mirror. 'And church?' he asked. 'I understood Christians went to church on Sundays.' I owned that there were better Christians.

Ali frowned. 'You are a Christian, then?' he asked. 'But not a good one?' Beycesultan was insufficiently distant for getting into, never mind out of, exactly what I was; so I merely nodded.

'You do know that there are other religions?' Ali asked. 'Ones that might suit you better?' I told Ali that I was aware of the fact.

'Awareness is one thing,' he replied, slapping the steering wheel. 'But are you actively looking into the matter?' I admitted that I was doing no such thing.

'You should,' said Ali. 'Everybody needs a religion.' He handed me a business card in case my kitchen could also do with an overhaul before dropping me, mildly admonished, where Beycesultan rose visibly from the plain. The carcass of a kingfisher lay in the road, one extended turquoise wing tipped with cobalt and edged, like a condolence, in black.

Mounds like Beycesultan were once dismissed as topographical curiosities, or taken to be the tumuli of ancient nobles. Advances in archaeology have since dignified these sudden hills by

114

recognising them as reminders that agricultural civilisation substantially began in Anatolia. What caused these mounds to rise from the plains was neither veneration of the deceased nor geological quirk but patterns of settlement that favoured established sites, as long as some at least of the virtues that had commended them to their founders – viable communication routes, water provision, good farming land and security – still held. There were, besides, obvious advantages in adapting ruins rather than starting from scratch. So it was, as successive settlements stacked up on the spoil of former ones, that these mounds gradually acquired distinctive contours and archaeologists latterly came to recognise them as repositories of the little-known pre-classical past; the beginning, in short, of Anatolian history.

Excavations on central Turkey's Konya plain at one such mound, Çatalhöyük, duly uncovered evidence of Neolithic settlement dating back some 9,500 years. The earliest remains at Beycesultan, where excavations were conducted through the mid-1950s, were found to be 6,000 years old while the palace there was dated to around 2000 BC. The building, perhaps eighty metres in length, indicated a culture of remarkable sophistication. With seventy rooms, extensive sacrificial areas and corridors, staircases leading to upper-storey reception halls, and floors carpeted in reeds and corded bundles of hay, it proved unlike anything else discovered in Anatolia. Of this remarkable structure, and of the civilisation that built it, history knew nothing; at least not until the contents of the 10,000 clay tablets uncovered in 1906 at Hattuşaş, 500 kilometres north-east of Beycesultan, began to be understood.

It is with written record, of course, that the archaeological evidence of earlier human existence gives way to history; the history, with the discoveries at Hattuşaş, of the Hatti people, latterly the Hittites, who had their capital there. These cuneiform writings, the earliest in Anatolia, turned out to be the annals and letters of the Hittite kings. The deciphered hieroglyphs told of an empire that spanned central Anatolia and Syria from early in the second millennium BC. One consequence of their deciphering was that a number of the mysterious hieroglyphs inscribed on prominent Anatolian rocks could now be identified as Hittite. If the clay pages gave a first sense of these shadowy inland traders and warriors, then the landscape turned out to have been inscribed with their literal marks of passage and settlement. Hittite routes were revealed, most notably the major one that ran west from Hattuşaş to the Aegean; this route passed right by the city settlement at Beycesultan, which had once belonged, the tablets suggested, to the rival state of Arzawa.

A palatial city, its ancient name unknown, on the great road through the land of Arzawa: history struggles for purchase beneath such weight of speculation. A tablet hoard may eventually be uncovered to do for the Arzawan civilisation what the one at Hattuşaş did for the Hittites by providing it with a spectacular dust-down of its own. Until then, though, we cannot claim to know the Arzawans except as a footnote in the history of the neighbouring Hittites, the same people who pushed west to absorb Arzawa around the fourteenth century BC. The judicious advice might be to leave the Arzawans well alone if it were not for the fact that the palace they seem to have built at Beycesultan some six centuries before their conquest by the Hittites suggested extraordinary possibilities to the site's archaeologists.

In the view of these archaeologists the Beycesultan structure, though unique to Anatolia, bore a striking resemblance to the contemporary palace complexes belonging to the pre-eminent civilisation of the period, Minoan Crete, an island located barely a hundred miles from the Anatolian coast. The archaeologists noted similarities in the sacrificial quarters, the central rectangular courtyard, the use of light wells, the corridor layouts, the hearth designs and the upper-floor locations of the state rooms. Specific parallels were observed in roofing technique, with the same distinctive clay layer filling the same sandwich of packed earth and brushwood, and even in the way the walls were painted with broad red horizontal bands.

The core question, then, was how these similarities came about; did the Minoans learn their building techniques from the Arzawans, or were they in fact the teachers? Which culture informed the other? Was it the western Minoans, known by pottery findings to have had settlements at Miletus around 2000 BC, whose builders first pushed up the Meander Valley to offer Cretan construction know-how to the inland Arzawans? Or was it rather the case that the same Minoans, learning of the fabled palaces of the interior, dispatched craftsmen up the broad valley to master these latest techniques and replicate them for clients on nearby Crete? Or was it in fact the Arzawans who took the initiative, exporting their expertise to the cities of the Aegean coast and the islands beyond?

Archaeology was far from providing anything approaching a definitive answer, though the probability was that these neighbouring civilisations had in fact been bartering ideas and techniques for centuries, and that these palaces were effectively the result of a cultural partnership. Certainly, the Western assumption that the backward Anatolian hinterland had long been impervious to the transmission of new ways and ideas was scotched by the discoveries at Beycesultan. The interior had been in active correspondence, communion even, with the Aegean almost from the beginning, and via the Meander Valley. Beycesultan instanced the inherent momentum with which traded or otherwise transmitted ideas, techniques, advances and inventions, even ways of seeing, flowed along the Anatolian conduit; the same process, in fact, by which German tap brochures came that Sunday morning some four millennia later to be in the back of a Turkish kitchen fitter's van.

If the excavations at Beycesultan established any one fact, however, it was the great fire that had engulfed the palace around 1750 BC. The seams of ash uncovered in the digs strongly suggested that the city was sacked, perhaps in the course of a Hittite border raid; they were a timely reminder that conflict was as much an Anatolian common-place as contact.

I left the road and took a track to the north. A *kangal* was chained to a farm building. The creature had worked itself into a foam-flecked lather by the time I drew level. In the dust it had made concentric semicircles, its ring of paw scuffs fronted by a broken line of crusted spittle to mark the extent of its reach. I hurried on across undulating grasslands to the mound's twin summits. An Ottoman *türbe*, a tent-shaped shrine, had made a final stand against the site's abandonment. Its octagonal walls of stone, brick and inscribed marble rose to a beehive roof fuzzy with wild grasses. The *türbe* had recently been topped with a faux-Victorian lantern, whose base was repeatedly wrapped with a long length of wiring, as if the absence of a power source on this lonely hillside had occurred to the lantern's installer, cuffing his forehead in frustration, only after he had measured out the cable. I entered through an arch of Byzantine marble. A spare, square tomb, rendered in whitewashed plaster, was backed into the wall. It might, but for the carved stone turban at its head, have been the sleeping platform of some hardy anchorite. Haphazard gestures of reverence – crumpled braided cloths and patchworks, thumbed copies of the Koran – topped the tomb alongside such incongruous items as a wooden mallet and a metal file, which I took to belong to the toolkit of a stymied electrician.

A young man appeared in the doorway. He was not the type I had expected to meet at Beycesultan; a passing shepherd, perhaps, or a reverential rustic, but not a man in a well-cut grey coat and modish glasses, a digital camera slung over his shoulder. Ahmet was an agricultural consultant employed on a nearby irrigation project. He indicated the works site, stepping outside the *türbe* to point out a distant scrum of brightly coloured earth diggers clawing at the plain. He had wandered up here in a break from his duties, he explained, to check out what he described as 'the shrine of some dead old sheikh'. Religion, I figured, meant rather less to Ahmet than it had to Ali the kitchen fitter.

'You know,' he asked, 'that our state is bringing a closure case against the governing party?' I nodded; I had read about the case at the breakfast table of Mrs Darkeye in Dinar a few days before. The case was scheduled for later in the year.

'It must be done,' Ahmet continued. '*Ak* is threatening the nation's secular constitution.' Local mayors were repealing alcohol licences. Mosques were being built across the country. Women proclaimed their right to wear religious headdress in the course of their work or study. Despite his support for the proposed closure, Ahmet acknowledged that such an action could only profit the Islamic movement. He wondered whether a coup was in the offing.

Coups had been a prominent feature of Turkish life over the last half-century. They were the political equivalent of earthquakes and happened about as frequently. As earthquakes were preceded by seismic tremors, so coups tended to be presaged by political ones; Ahmet saw the closure case as such a presentiment. Turks commonly feared coups for the disorder they threatened, for the damage they did to the nation's reputation abroad, but mostly because they emphasised the country's cultural fault lines. It was as if Turkey had so long been warred over as to have ended up, inevitably, at war with itself; Western secularists squaring up to Eastern Islamists along the old fault line between the two worlds.

The coup, that Turkish institution, had conspicuously evolved over the years. The first one occurred in 1960 when a scheming cadre of ambitious army officers, tanks on the streets, arrests and executions, effectively represented Turkey as a banana republic. In a country with democratic and European ambitions, of course, such old-school interventions were an acute embarrassment. The powerful military achieved the same objective rather more subtly in 1971 merely by issuing a memorandum that demanded the formation of a national government. The prime minister resigned accordingly. The military consequently learned to develop subtler arts of interference, in part by working in concert with more malleably pragmatic institutions such as the judiciary and some sectors of the press. In fact, since widespread disorder regularly threatened Turkish society, many Turks tacitly supported army interference as a means of restoring stability. In recent years, however, such support had become increasingly eroded.

The main threat to society had shifted, or so some believed. While the issues in 1960 had largely been economic mismanagement and social repression, had been revolutionary political unrest a decade later and economic collapse in 1980, the so-called 'post-modern' coup of 1997 was in response to something else entirely: the rise of political Islam.

When an Islamic party, Welfare, was able in 1996 for the first time to form a government, albeit in coalition, the military should not have been surprised. It had, after all, actively encouraged political Islam as a counterweight to leftist and separatist ideologies during the 1980s. Now, however, rather than protect the country from economic or social chaos, it was the nation's secular character and constitution that the military vowed to guarantee. Further evidence of Islam's advance into the public sphere – the government's decision to close state agencies early during Ramadan, allowing observant employees to be at home in time to break their fast – finally spurred the military into clandestine action in 1997. The government fell.

Welfare and its leaders were subsequently banned from politics. Political Islam proved hydra-headed, however, duly reappearing under other names – Felicity, then Virtue. When these parties were also banned by the courts, Justice and Development replaced them; this same party, *Ak*, the judiciary was now threatening to close. It seemed less likely, then, that Turkey's Islamic constituency would lose all ideological steam than that its political parties would run out of words by which to name themselves.

A measure of the military's waning influence was that its latest interference, which took place the year before my journey, should have ended in humiliation. In April 2007 a memorandum appeared on the website of the Turkish general staff. The memorandum threatened action if the *Ak* Party pushed ahead with plans to install a pro-Islamic candidate as the next president, a post secularists held sacred on account of the fact that it had been originally occupied by Atatürk himself. *Ak* responded by calling general elections; the landslide majority they won not only endorsed their presidential candidate, but delivered a public rebuke to the generals and to those who would prioritise secularism over democracy. The current closure case represented yet another battle for the *Ak* Party as the military-backed establishment accused it of subverting the secular constitution.

'The Islamists are definitely getting stronger,' Ahmet insisted. 'Ramadan is more strictly observed every year. They have used democracy to get into power. But don't expect them to respect it if it looks like preventing them from staying in power. Which is why I hope the courts stop them. Whatever trouble that may mean.'

I left Ahmet behind me. He was still there when I looked back, sitting in the grass, staring into space. A hawk, light spilling through its splayed tail feathers, hovered above him and the mound of those who had been there before; the early people who had settled by the tributary banks 6,000 years ago, the Arzawans and the Hittites, the Phrygians, the Persians and the Greeks, the Romans and the Byzantines, the Mongols and the Tartars, the Ottomans, their dead sheikh entombed where the past broke surface, and, finally, an agricultural consultant in a raptor's shadow pondering Anatolia's present troubles.

Beyond the muddy bed of the irrigation canal, the fields were stippled with the ragged purple blooms of the opium poppy; the produce of these same fields, now harvested under strict government controls for the pharmaceutical industry, had once fed the widespread addictions of eighteenth- and nineteenth-century Europe, famously inspiring Samuel Taylor Coleridge's *Kubla Khan* and soothing the toothache and travails of Percy Bysshe Shelley. The use of this 'poisonous drug', largely grown in the watershed of the upper Meander and north to Opium, the regional processing centre, was banned in Turkey during the 1820s. But it continued to be harvested for an export market enthusiastic for Turkish opium's high morphine content and for the quality of its preparation. Turkish opium accounted for as much as 90 per cent of British imports of the drug for much of the nineteenth century. The harvested crop was processed into black, paste-like cakes wrapped in leaves, which went down to Smyrna by mule or camel train to be packed in zinc-lined cases and sent abroad.

At the nearby village of Menteş shawled women sat by roadside piles of reddish cherry prunings, which they hacked unceasingly into kindling. A mother in baggy *şalvar* trousers, belted with twine, punched at wet and soapy laundry in a blackened tin; her young daughter, wrapped in a knitted green coat, fed fragments of a tinderised tomato carton into the fire at its base. The men of the village motioned me, meanwhile, to join them in the shaded garden of the tea house. The older men took my visit as an excuse to recall their *Gastarbeiter* years in Europe; a tailor had found piecework in Paris, stitching jacket linings, and a mechanic had worked shifts in Austrian factories. Their memories had grown indistinct, however, for the villagers no longer went abroad to work.

'Europe doesn't want us,' the tailor said. He was

settling back into the sun-splashed afternoon when a van drew up.

'Fish!' yelled the driver as he clambered from the van. The man stood a wooden box by the roadside and topped it with a rough tray into which he emptied the slithering contents of a plastic bag. These tench were greenish-yellow except where livid discolouring around the organs showed beneath translucent underbellies. The man spread his catch across the tray. He then busied himself by arranging the shoal as if it were still alive, turning errant fish among them so that they all presented their sightless stares to those who might buy. The tea house fell silent in the shared suspicion that no amount of presentation could commend these fish.

'More tea?' somebody murmured, waving a discreet hand before his nose. I was reminded of an ancient Phrygian taboo against the eating of fresh-water fish; William Ramsay, travelling the region before trout farms were established here, claimed not to have found 'a single stream which furnished palatable fish, and even where the fish seemed of good quality they were most unwholesome and could only be eaten with the greatest of caution'.

'We call them *kadifer*,' the tailor told me with a grimace. 'From Işıklı Gölu.'

'Ah,' I said. 'The lake I crossed only yesterday.' The men at the tea house showed no more interest in my travels, however, than in the tench. The men of Menteş, though the older ones had been to Europe, knew not what to make of a passing canoeist.

The tailor eventually broke the silence. 'It was all of thirty years ago that the river last had proper water,' he declared. 'I doubt you'll get a boat through there now.'

I had all but given up on Menteş when an old man stirred in a corner of the tea garden. He struggled to his feet, steadied himself against a chair arm, and like the Ancient Mariner, a vision the product of these very fields might even have helped inspire, he fixed a cautionary finger upon me. 'Watch out!' he bellowed. 'Watch out for the old watermills at Aşağı Seyit.'

★　　★　　★

I dined that evening in Çivril's only restaurant. I was alone among my surroundings; caryatid Cleopatras, spangly chairs backed with enormous satin bows, plastic yukkas and palm trees swagged with year-round tinsel and Christmas bells. A half-size shepherd girl, carved from meerschaum, cradled a basket of plastic blooms and frosted pine cones. Plastic ivy was entwined around the television cables. The walls were embossed with gilt bells, which housed orange art-nouveau light fittings. There were football club pennants, portraits of family patriarchs, Atatürk memorabilia, clocks and paintings of tumbling rivers. The kebab I ate against such a background seemed hopelessly prosaic. So I followed it with the plate of baklava I had been promising myself since losing Turgay Darkeye's gift to the river.

I wandered into the evening. A spring warmth was in the air. Çivril's park, partially lamplit, was deserted except for a youth preening himself in the wing mirror of his moped. A bronze Atatürk in educational mode clasped the hands of two studious children, books beneath their arms. A sparrow clamped the tip of a discarded ice-cream cone in its extended beak. Beyond rusted tables were brightly painted swings.

The park's main feature was an elevated and oversized amphora, tipped to send an ornamental stream winding through the park. The stream's course ran beneath low hump-backed bridges lined with ornate iron railings. The setting consciously recalled, in degraded form, the paradise gardens of the Persians; the shaded pavilions, the blooms, flowerbeds and fragrant trees, all alive with the murmur of streams and the song of birds, like the parklands by the Meander's banks at Celaenae.

Herodotus acknowledged the particular Persian regard for rivers. 'Rivers they chiefly reverence,' he wrote; 'they will neither make water nor spit nor wash their hands therein, nor suffer anyone to do so.' The same was true some 1,500 years later of the Mongols and Tartars who, though they might have scourged the land and piled up the heads of the inhabitants, refrained on principle from urinating or washing in rivers. It was a reverence today's Turks, with their affection for such names as Pınar and Nehir, and for kitsch paintings of tumbling streams and waterfalls in sylvan settings, consciously observed. Except that Çivril's ornamental stream was bone-dry. And rubbish was strewn all along its concrete bed.

CHAPTER 8

In the morning I searched Çivril for a belt of sorts. Along the streets of the country town sprays of budding cherries spilled over crumbling garden walls; cardboard signs marked *zehirli* – poisonous – claimed that the trees from which they hung had been treated with chemicals, as if to caution the cowherds against risks to the health of their wandering cattle, though I suspected that these warnings had in fact been fabricated to preserve the cherries for their exasperated owners.

In the shade of an alley stacked with cement sacks I found an ironmonger.

'For belts,' he explained, 'we go to the *butik*.' This patient man might have been reciting from a Turkish primer. The man's exaggerated clarity, though it cast me as a halfwit, was not so mortifying as his ready surmise that I must be after some fashion accessory. I hastily emphasised my expeditionary credentials, explaining that I actually needed something to cinch tight a rucksack, which I'd been having trouble fitting within the stern frame of my canoe.

'Your canoe no less,' the ironmonger replied with

exaggerated courtesy; and standing corrected as to how this customer preferred to think of himself he wandered off into the dusty recesses of his shop. When he returned it was with a functional leather strap, about a yard long, with a heavy-duty buckle.

'For a rifle,' he said, laying it along the counter between us. 'But I dare say it will also do for your sack.'

Back at the dam, I surprised the caretaker in a private examination, which finally explained the brimless cap I had noticed at our first meeting. A stooped Mehmet was peering with visible concern into the wing mirror of his ancient motorbike. He had removed the cap to reveal an irregularly threadbare pate, tufted in the way of the terminally ill, which he smoothed with a tentative palm. Mehmet moved to replace the cap the instant he saw me, though the knowledge that he had been observed soon caused him to abandon any attempt at pretence.

'It was the shampoo,' he confessed sheepishly, straightening to shake my hand. 'The advertisement promised to thicken my hair. Instead, it's made it all fall out. All over the country there have been people complaining about the stuff. I heard on the television.' In the coverage dominating Turkey's broadcasting – items about the etiquette of headscarf-wearing, updates on the threatened closure of the ruling party, the *Ergenekon* arrests – I had heard of no such national outbreak of hair loss. Nor was I in any position to advise, though the caretaker appeared to think otherwise, fixing me with a searching look that anticipated I might have the solution. I was reminded how country Turks had habitually regarded travelling Westerners as repositories of medical knowledge. William Leake regarded 'an assumption of the medical character' as nothing less than a chief necessity for successful travel in Anatolia; such consultations were so commonly sought that the sardonic Reverend Arundell came to regard visits from Turks as 'affording me an opportunity of displaying medical talent'. Certainly, Mehmet seemed disappointed that I could do nothing for him. It was only when I told him I had feared he must be properly sick that he acknowledged the implied inconsequence, even the comic value, of his predicament with a thin smile; one which broadened when I promised not to say a word. We shook on it.

'Then I'll help you carry the canoe,' said Mehmet. He led the way to the shed, which he had gone so far as to padlock over the weekend. I thanked him for the care, true to his calling, that he had taken of my canoe.

'Not at all,' he replied, lifting the bow and leading off in the direction of the dam. 'It's just I can't see you getting much further in it.'

What Mehmet meant did not become clear until we had set down the canoe and made our way across the dam by the railed walkway. It was a modest installation, a series of gates and sluices set low in the concrete levee, but noisy for its size; a considerable crush of water was being drawn from the lake though it was not being released, it happened, into the river. The torrent foamed through a sluice and tumbled hectically into an elevated concrete canalette, which smuggled it off to irrigate the nearby cherry orchards.

William Hamilton, geologist and topographer, had in June 1837 witnessed a pre-industrial version of the same process not far north of Çivril, where villagers were 'busy preparing channels and water-courses for the summer irrigation'. The description, though spare, conjured a practice that had obtained in its generalities beyond Anatolia, even unto the high-summer vegetable gardens of Hamilton's native England; the retrenching by mattock or spade of the old channels that had previously carried water from river, spring or tank, or the digging of fresh courses in newly tilled ground, with soil dykes at the junctions to regulate each watering.

Hamilton witnessed the skilled application of a water husbandry that had continued unchanged for thousands of years, and with no discernible effect upon the source. It was a view I envied, given the sickening sight that now greeted me below the dam. The river was almost empty. Glazed patches of its bed, humped slicks of mud, had broken surface. No birds, for all their abundance on the adjacent lake, frequented the half-lit mire. The only living things were the midges, dancing in a frenzy over the stretches of standing water.

I stood horrified and recalled the dry, litter-strewn bed of the ornamental stream in the park at Çivril. It now appeared as a presentiment of trouble on the river, and by no means the first: the pumps that had diverted the water at Suçıkan; the concrete ditches of Dinar; the regrets Mehmet Truehero had voiced about his beloved river; Turgay Darkeye's repeated assumption that I could only have an industrial interest in the Meander; and the recurrent doubts, expressed most recently by the caretaker himself, as to how much further I was likely to get. My journeying appeared done, here and now, for the employees of the State Water Works, by the buttons they pressed and the levers they pulled, had diverted every last drop of river water to the surrounding orchards. They had severed the river from its headwaters, terminally decapitating the Meander.

Mehmet was wringing his hands; this empathy was to his credit, as was his insistence that I should not now abandon the river. Mehmet, seeing that my canoe required hardly any water and judging that the river might yet recover, urged me to attempt a launch. With his encouragement I stowed my newly strapped rucksack, shoved the canoe into the shallows and thanked Mehmet for his help.

'Good luck,' said the caretaker, embracing me. 'And remember,' he whispered, pointing towards his head. 'Not a word.'

I drifted out across the stagnant water, my paddle stirring the cesspool contents; particle clouds mushroomed to the surface, painting my wake with grey, cauliflower growths. I followed a weaving course between flats of mud and rock; their exposure appeared quite as ominous as the weed-wrapped ruins of spires and gables that were said to rise from the cracked beds of drought-struck reservoirs. The going was arduous and only with regular shoves of the paddle was I able to punt myself clear of the groundings; high above me, meanwhile, there passed the banks where the springtime flow must once have jostled, tugging at the trailing willow branches, back before the irrigators and their farming clients stole it all for cherry juice.

The river, as Mehmet predicted, had managed a partial recovery by the time I reached the first bridge of the day. Three arches of pale ashlar carried the handsome Akköprü, the White Bridge, across the river. The bridge was Ottoman, though the crumbling footings on which it rested were far older; some of the stones might even have known the weight of the vast column of chariots and carts, horsemen and foot soldiers, greaves and helmets catching the spring sunshine, which had crossed the river here in 401 BC.

Some fourteen centuries had passed since the sack of the palatial city at nearby Beycesultan. The Hittites, having absorbed the Arzawans, had themselves given way; in the ruins of their abandoned cities another people, the Phrygians, had long since settled. The Phrygian kings, the legendary Midas among them, had established themselves over much of western and central Anatolia.

By 401 BC, however, Midas had himself passed into fable, and not in a manner that would have been to his liking. The soldiers at the bridge knew him, if they knew him at all, not as the venerated former monarch of the lands they were crossing but as storied fall guy of the Olympian gods; another victim of Apollo who, having dealt with Marsyas's

136

musical impertinence, now turned on the Phrygian king for having sided with the cocksure Anatolian flautist and gave Midas the ears of an ass, as if his patently defective hearing deserved them. The Olympians further reduced Midas by granting his ill-judged wish that everything he touched might turn to gold; his every touch, it turned out, of his lips as well as his fingers so that the king had no sooner enjoyed infinite wealth before he was subjected to intolerable hunger and thirst.

The Phrygian people themselves had not done much better than their ridiculed ruler. They had not quite disappeared but had become subject to the rule of others, occupiers from the east. Phrygia had since 546 BC been a satrapy, or province of Persia. In 401 BC it was under the regional command of one whom we have already encountered among his marching forces at Celaenae; Cyrus, who had spent a month at his Celaenae hunting lodge, reviewing his forces and awaiting the arrival of reinforcements from the Greek lands of Thrace, Sparta and Arcadia, before he led his forces out of the city and onwards to the bridge at Akköprü.

To the distant sound of an engine refusing to fire I put ashore, hauling the canoe up a shelving bank pitted with the mud-cast hooves of watering cattle. I strolled up a farm track to the bridge and looked out across the plain to a truncated furrow where a farmer in rubber boots was climbing from his stalled tractor.

The forces under Cyrus's command, following

a three-day route that ran roughly parallel to my own, duly reached the river crossing where I now stood. Not that Xenophon chose to mention the crossing in his account of the great march. Its omission from the pages of the *Anabasis* was understandable in that barely a blister had been suffered by this stage of the march. The crossing must have been routine, certainly compared to the many hazardous ones that lay ahead. Many hundreds of parasangs, the Persian measure of distance, and a good many months were yet to pass before the men of the expedition would be called upon to demonstrate the exemplary endurance, fighting spirit and solidarity that posterity was to celebrate.

Those events, destined to play out in the distant uplands of eastern Anatolia, were to be remembered as a classical Dunkerque; in this regard Xenophon would have been technically correct to have called his account the *Katabasis*, or Retreat to the Sea, since the primary events it detailed constituted an evacuation, albeit one of unquestionably heroic endurance, rather than an advance. The doughty forces, finding themselves outnumbered and leaderless following Cyrus's death in battle near Baghdad, were compelled to reorganise and beat a winter retreat over snowy passes and swirling rivers, fending off hunger and hostile tribesmen. The triumphant cry they put up at their first glimpse of the Black Sea's Hellenised littoral – The Sea! The Sea! – has reverberated through Western history.

Back at the bridge and barely embarked on their

march, however, the same men could have had no idea that the Black Sea might lie ahead; not the least intimation, in fact, that they were destined to be remembered for anything. Xenophon and his mercenary fellows had not even been informed as to where they were actually headed or whom they were to fight when they got there. They thought to have signed up for a routine mission; the word put about by Cyrus himself was that he meant to subjugate the rebellious Pisidians whose lands lay just east of the source of the Meander. Persia, in short, was merely dealing with one of the minor insurrections to which any vast empire was occasionally subject.

History never ended, of course, though at that time the Persians might have believed that theirs was the one empire that would endure, whatever the successive eclipses of their predecessors in the region – the Arzawans, Hittites and Phrygians – might have taught them. By the fifth century BC the Persians had established their rule over all Anatolia, west beyond Phrygia to the Greek port cities of Ionia, and had even filled the city states of Greece itself with the spectre of invasion.

By this time, however, Greek pride and civic culture were allied with an increasingly sophisticated fighting know-how. There were even those, both in Greece and along the Hellenised shores of Ionia, who sensed beyond Persia's extraordinary power and might something of the Easterners' fallibility. Some dreamed not only of driving the

Persians from their own cities but even of uniting one day to push east and invade the lands of the Great King himself. Aristagoras, a Greek whom the Persian authorities had unwisely entrusted with the satrapy of Miletus, in 499 BC rallied the city to rebel by mocking the ruling Persians for the trousers they wore and by claiming that they 'were wont to carry neither shield nor spear and could be easily overcome'. With the abject failure of the subsequent Ionian Revolt, an independence bid bolstered by the support of some mainland Greek states, Aristagoras was proved wrong, though not many years were to pass before it appeared that the man may have had a point about the Persians; at Marathon not far from Athens just nine years later the invading Persians, despite every numerical advantage, suffered a crushing defeat at the hands of the heavily armed Greeks.

For that stinging reverse the Persian kings swore eternal vengeance. In honour of that pledge Xerxes led his armies west through Celaenae in 481 BC. Xerxes' invasion of the West failed comprehensively, however, when the Greeks crushed the Persian trireme fleet the following year at Salamis, consolidating that success with further victories in 479 BC on both shores of the Aegean. Defeat in 460 BC at Eurymedon in southern Anatolia dealt another blow to the Persians, a people who not only wore trousers in battle but were quite willing to drop them, it was gleefully assumed, when otherwise required; vases painted in Athens after the Battle of

Eurymedon, probably not intended for family use, depicted a Greek, erection in hand, advancing on the presented rear of a prostrate Persian.

Not that this posture resembled the one adopted by the noble Persian leading his forces out of Celaenae in the spring of 401 BC, though Cyrus's intentions were certainly unorthodox; the satrap had reversed the Persians' traditional direction of travel. Cyrus, though his own forces did not yet know it, was after his own brother, the Great King himself, whom he meant to overthrow and so claim the Persian throne. To secure what he saw as his birthright he hardly relied, moreover, on any significant degree of support from fellow Persians. Instead, he had signed up some 10,000 Greek mercenaries hardened during the Peloponnesian Wars that Sparta and Athens had concluded just four years earlier. On this point Cyrus had been specific, instructing his commanders that they should 'enlist as many Peloponnesian soldiers of the best sort as they severally could'. Addressing his Greek mercenaries, whom he held to be better and stronger than many barbarians, the broad-brush slur by which the Ionian Greeks denoted the uncultured Asiatics, Cyrus appeared to believe in his words beyond their morale-boosting capacity. In Western military prowess, technique and armament, he reckoned, the East's huge numerical supremacy might now have met its match.

Cyrus's hired hands, for all their paymaster's confidence, would no doubt have baulked at the sheer ambition of his actual plans, not least on account of the footslog the project entailed. It was for precisely this reason that the satrap had fobbed them off with his talk of a routine regional mission. Cyrus's stated plan – driving the Pisidians 'out of his land entirely' – was one that his mercenaries initially had no reason to question. Until the day, that is, when he led them out of Celaenae in quite the wrong direction. Geography had it that the mercenaries must advance by the great pass at Celaenae and continue beyond the site of the mythical musical scrap at the source of the Meander if they were to sort out the Pisidians. Instead, Cyrus led them north-west, and back to the banks of a river they thought to have left behind.

Over the plain which these ancient mercenaries had once crossed there now came a series of increasingly frustrated clangs. The farmer lay flat beneath his stricken tractor, only his boots protruding. With every ringing blow of the farmer's spanner, the storks that had gathered to pick along the fresh furrows unfurled their white wings in readiness to fly.

Although Xenophon passes over the bridge in silence, it was here, it is to be assumed, that some among his fellow marchers must have felt their doubts deepen. It was only logical, given that river crossings were a primary measure of progress, that some should have wondered why they had doubled back to one whose famed sources they had already reached at Celaenae. If this was not the way to

Pisidia, then the satrap must be leading them, and by a patently roundabout route, against some other foe whom he clearly did not mean them to recognise. Was it here, then, that some might have had the first intimations of what truly lay ahead? That they would be the first Greeks to take the fight, literally, to Persia?

The anabasis commemorated a pointed moment in the process of Persian eclipse; when Greek military power, albeit under Persian authority, set out to conquer Persia just as Xerxes' Persians had advanced on Greece eighty years earlier. Indeed, Cyrus largely followed the very route of his great-grandfather but in reverse, rolling up the Persian advance and with it the last great gesture of Eastern imperial might before the West was to take its turn. The anabasis might initially have been about rivalry between royal Persian siblings; its actual effect, it turned out, was to inspire an era of Hellenic expansionism. The Roman historian Polybius regarded 'the retreat of the Greeks under Xenophon from the upper satrapies, in which, though they traversed the whole of Asia, a hostile country, none of the barbarians ventured to face them' as the chief inspiration for Alexander the Great's Asia campaign seventy years later. The West had learned not only how to defeat the East, but also that it must tramp across Anatolia to get at it.

Of all this there was now no sign. Out on the plain the farmer wiggled out from beneath his tractor and clambered to his feet, brushing the soil from his worn jacket. Then he threw down the spanner and set off in search of help, and along the half-ploughed furrow storks hopped out of the irate farmer's way.

Below Akköprü the Meander was severely choked. From the angled trunks of fallen willows branches rose like banister spindles. I sought out the gaps and pushed through the half-submerged crowns to emerge in a slick of cobwebs, catkins, bits of branch and river weed. Floating branches had boomed rotting reeds into stinking rafts, which I inched through by hauling on overhanging branches. The going was hard, and I began to wonder when I would reach the next bridge.

It was about this time it struck me that the Meander was not proving the carefree experience I had imagined. It seemed I was always in a hurry on this river; today because I could not afford to reach the next bridge after nightfall if I hoped to find lodgings there. Villagers could not be expected to take in strangers if they could not first view them in the full light of day. I felt less like a free-spirited wanderer than a Transylvanian coachman, whip raised against the setting sun, as I dug in my paddle to drive through the willow brakes. The relentless bends added to my frustration, the low sun shearing away from the bow; only when the sun's glare was back in my eyes did I know that I was heading west, towards the next bridge, which was where I was meant to be going. What I really wanted that evening, for all my earlier protestations, was the odd straight stretch of water. But this was hardly the river to want that from.

The sun had set by the time the drone of thinly spaced cars advised me that I was finally getting close. The crossing that swung into view was an arched Ottoman bridge, partially collapsed, and beyond it a concrete replacement carrying the tarmac road. I ran the canoe ashore and made my way across a rough pasture where a tethered horse was staked. The village at the crossing took its name, Kavak, from the poplar trees that rose, along with the spike of a minaret, out of a mean cluster of block-built dwellings and dusty vegetable plots. I met the headman in the lane and asked if the village could put me up. He looked at me.

'We don't have the space,' he said. 'The nearest hotels are in Çivril. But you can leave your canoe in the schoolyard.' He dispatched a young man to help me. Together we walked down to the river.

'Your boat's full of bits of tree,' said Gökhan, bending to pick up an end. We carried the canoe back to the school and lifted it over the low wall.

'And there's a nest in your hair,' he remarked. I thanked Gökhan, shouldered my rucksack and walked out to the road; there was nothing for it but to overnight again in Çivril. The moon was rising above a cooling earth, silvering the willows along the course of the river. I watched a pair of lights bore out of the darkness. As the *dolmuş* drew to a halt I brushed myself down and prepared to board.

CHAPTER 9

I was back in Kavak early the next morning. A ragged chicken watched me retrieve my canoe from the deserted schoolyard. It flexed its stubby wings to follow me across the empty road and down to the river, apparently caught, in the village way, between seeing me off its patch and shipping out itself.

I launched below the collapsed Ottoman bridge and passed beneath the stained concrete slab that carried the modern road, only to run into the partially submerged remains of yet another crossing. These rotted stumps, all that remained of a wooden footbridge, might have conjured a picturesque past for Kavak if they had not more immediately served as a jagged reef, which threatened to hole the canoe's fabric hull. My main concern, though Kavak might once have been more appealing, was not being stranded in the unlovely place, with concrete crossing and territorial chicken, that it had since become.

I had cleared the village and was making steady progress, relieved that the stumps had caused no lasting damage, when the first fallen willow of the day appeared. I was getting used to these obstructions. I liked to think I was learning to read them; canoe-height clearance, in this case, hard by the right bank beneath a foliage overhang that my seated torso could push through, I reckoned, without too much scrape or scratch. Until something stirred beyond the bank. And then began to growl.

I could barely see the dog through the willows, but was at least relieved to hear a clinking sound. The chain told me that the creature's reach was limited, though what shadowed that conclusion was the realisation that any such restraint was likely to be of a length that the dog might drink from the river, if only to save on water bowls. That necessarily put the dog in reach of the only place where I might pass. When it began to bark I abandoned these considerations and took up a holding position in the middle of the river, there to contemplate the fearsome reputation of Anatolian dogs.

Turkey's dogs had always been a fear of mine, and in this I was not alone. The *Anabasis*, that monument to Hellenic valour, tended to focus on such hazards as conflict and snow drifts, hunger and exhaustion; it made little mention of the ferocious mutts Xenophon and his comrades may have encountered along the way. Large packs, however, of what Herodotus described as Indian hounds were known to have accompanied Xerxes' invasion force across Anatolia on its way to Greece in 481 BC. These creatures were impressive but essentially recreational, there to accompany the Great King when he was minded to hunt – unlike the dogs of Magnesia, a city on the lower reaches of the Meander. When Magnesia's horsemen made war on the people of neighbouring Ephesus, they first threw their enemy's lines into confusion by setting their dogs upon them. Pliny wrote how the people of another city of the Aegean littoral, Colophon, raised entire detachments of dogs to fight alongside their soldiers.

These warring canines had long been demobilised by the time Reverend Arundell set out in search of nineteenth-century Apamea. It seemed, even so, that they went about their civilian functions, as guardians of the sheep flocks, with all their old belligerence. They behaved like outlaw irregulars, taking to the hills where they paired up or formed bands before descending upon any strangers who dared to trespass upon the dogs' self-proclaimed, shifting territories. Nor did they seem much interested in the role they had been assigned except, like nightclub bouncers, for the action it might bring, even to the point of abandoning their woolly charges to take on passing vehicles.

The heavy-set, short-haired *kangal*, which seemed to have taken its colourings, chameleon-like, from the straw and dun tones of the surrounding steppe, resembled the mastiff-type hunting dogs depicted on ancient Persian reliefs; it might have descended from Xerxes' Indian hounds. Modern Turks had found, however, another lineage rather more persuasive for their national dog, much as Turkish names were preferred over Persian ones for their villages, and instead traced the *kangal*'s descent from the dogs of the Turkish nomads who had first migrated to Anatolia in the eleventh century.

The Reverend Arundell, though he did acknowledge that *kangals* were 'rather worrying', preferred to make light of them by emphasising the beasts' 'noble appearance' and 'the brave fidelity with which they guard the flocks and herds of their masters'. More revealing was Arundell's observation, referring to his travels near Işıklı in 1833, that his companion's whip was regularly 'in full exercise against the dogs'. This detail, which conjured the local dogs in all their pack-like ferocity, appeared to concede that Arundell's expressions of *kangal* admiration were worked up retrospectively, and on the safe side of his nightly billets' secured doors.

I had rather more in common with another traveller, William Childs, who proved himself refreshingly craven when it came to the dogs. In 1912 Childs crossed central Anatolia, not far from the very district which gave the *kangal* its name. 'Nothing in Turkish travelling, indeed – neither the filthy khans nor universal dirt, nor risk of disease, nor chance of robbery – equals in unpleasantness this plague of savage dogs,' he wrote. Childs, who was subjected to *kangal* attacks daily, defended himself not with a whip but with a 'heavy, steel-pointed stick'. He eventually took refuge in his *araba* – Childs' 'walk' was supported, somewhat questionably, by an attendant vehicle – whenever a warning 'flock of goats or sheep appeared ahead'.

Born into a time that had rather marginalised the use of whips, I had instead taken my cue from Childs; the reducible walking pole I carried was stout, with a spiked end. How I thought to have truly stolen a march on the man, however, with his dubious cart and driver arrangement, was by taking to the river. That a dog should have blocked my way even here came as a rude surprise. I attempted to drive it back by slapping the water with the flat of my paddle and nosing the canoe forward until I could see something of the creature beyond the foliage; my truncated view was of braced paws, which briefly left the ground with every bark but showed no sign of retreating. I conceded defeat and put ashore on the opposite bank.

I lashed the canoe to a root, grabbed my walking pole and scrambled up the bank. A smiling youth stood beside a field of maize.

'Hello,' said Hasan Fearless. He offered a hand, extending it like a toy soldier. 'You are welcome. We were expecting you.' I had guessed, knowing Turks, that I might be welcome. But I had not expected, as I told Hasan, to be expected.

'We read about you in the newspaper,' he explained. 'In the *New Century*. You will drink tea.' It transpired, then, that Adnan's article had enjoyed a life beyond the *Dinar News*, graduating from that small-town free sheet to feature in the regional newspaper that served the Turkish Aegean and its hinterland. The syndicated article, having outgrown its home town, had burst out of Dinar and raced down the valley, all the time finding new readers, to alert the Fearless family that a foreigner in a canoe was closing on their isolated farmstead. Where there was to be no continuing, it seemed, until he had stopped for tea.

Hasan led the way past the fallen willow, along the bank to a footbridge of poplar trunks clinkered with knot-edged planks. We crossed to a low-built house with a tiled roof above walls of cracked bare plaster. A Turkish flag and a framed photograph of Atatürk hung above a doorway draped with a faded floral muslin. The sepia photograph happened to show the great leader himself emerging from a door, a grander portal admittedly, and flanked by saluting officers. The conjunction was such, however, that it might have been the Fearless family home that Atatürk was leaving, and the Fearless family itself, drinking tea at an outside table shaded by a hanging vine, to whom the leader was doffing his determinedly Western bowler; to Mr and Mrs Celal Fearless, to their teenage daughter

Adile, and to Ayşe, whom their son Hasan was to marry the following month. Certainly, it was precisely the sort of family to have found favour with the great social revolutionary, the champion of modern values and the European dress styles that were supposed to complement them, not least because the Fearless family men were free of reactionary brimless hats and because their women went unshawled. It was harder to know, though, what Atatürk would have made of Ayşe's *No More Heroes* T-shirt; a sentiment that seemed not only at odds with the particular surname Ayşe was so soon to adopt but also in defiance of the generally valiant tenor of Turkish surnames.

'Welcome,' said Celal Bey. 'So you're going to the sea, God willing. I was there once. But here is where we have been for sixteen years.' He gestured at his riverside plot, and the blessed sky above, laying a contented palm across his chest.

'Tea, tea,' said Mrs Fearless, pressing a glass upon me. 'The man must be thirsty.' I admitted that I had come no further than Kavak that morning.

'Kavak,' Celal Bey mused. 'My birthplace.' I wondered if the village's last smile had left with him.

'We knew something must be on the river from all the barking,' said Adile. 'Bosti doesn't much bark yet. She's only a few months old.' So I learned to my shame that a puppy called Bosti was what had halted my progress.

'You'll stay for lunch,' said Celal Bey. I declined the offer. I had a lot of river to cover.

'Then we'll make you a picnic for your journey,' said Mrs Fearless. 'Adile! Boiled eggs for our guest. Three. And some salt. Ayşe! Almonds.'

'You really don't need to worry,' I protested. I had bought bananas and biscuits that morning in Çivril.

'Nonsense,' said Mrs Fearless. She bustled off to pick me some plums. Ayşe, meanwhile, had settled herself beside a chopping block. She set about a pile of almonds, shattering their shells with a mattock. A flying shard landed in my tea. I wondered just what might remain of the almonds once the redoubtable Ayşe was done with them;

Hasan would soon know, I rather guessed, what it was to be married.

'Come,' said Celal Bey. 'Let me show you round.' Rows of rocket, lettuce and parsley, arced with soil-stuck willow branches that had supported winter polythene cloches, furled now, grew in early profusion. There were peppers, chillies, tomatoes, aubergines and cucumbers. Beyond were orchards of almond, plum and cherry, and I stood in the shade of walnut trees that the Fearless family had planted just six years before. The farmlands of the Meander valley, accounted the richest in all Turkey, had always been 'the orchard of Asia Minor'.

It was a measure of this abundance that the Roman deity of this river, the eponymous Meander, was commonly represented in a pose of voluptuous plenty, with flowers in his hair and 'a cornucopia in his arms, overflowing with pineapples, pomegranates, grapes and other fruits of the valley'. The bearded god's bounty was acknowledged on Roman coins minted along the river from Apamea to downstream Antiocheia. All through its history the valley has produced a remarkable diversity of highly prized and abundant produce. The upper valley has long been known for its grapes and cherries, apples, capers, wheat, and the poppies whose seed-head secretions once fed the pipes and tinctures of Europe's restless addicts. Along the lower reaches figs, citrus fruit and strawberries, tobacco and cotton, sesame and silk, liquorice and olives have traditionally predominated. The

Meander Valley's abundance has commonly proved a source of astonishment; 'such crops of wheat', as one visitor declared, 'as to astound one who contemplates the fact that since the days of antiquity these fields have, without fertilization, fed hordes of Romans, Greeks, Turkish and other nations as empires successively rose and fell. In fields about the river Meander . . . I stood in wheat which, thick as grass, rose above my head.'

Until the twentieth century, when the building of dams began to interfere with the process, this historical productivity was the natural consequence of the rich topsoil silts that the regular winter floods deposited evenly across the plain. This plain had grown, particularly along the lower reaches, to become disproportionately broad and exceptionally flat; magnificent farming country through the summer months but seasonally subject to extensive winter flooding. These floods, though they had once fertilised the valley every winter, also caused their share of disruption. It was said that the god Meander so regularly washed away riverine tracts of land that he was subject to beggaring fines; landowners affected by the flooding, that is, were compensated by payments taken from the local ferry tolls. One historical consequence was that valley settlements, especially downstream ones, had learned to keep back from the flood plain. I wondered if Celal Bey had given any consideration to floods before settling his family right beside the river.

'Floods?' Celal Bey laughed. 'This river's flooding days are done. It hasn't flooded since they built the dam on Işıklı Lake. Believe me, too much rain is the least of our problems. Yours too, though there should be enough water to get your boat through. Though I can't say beyond Çal. And you wouldn't want to be out at night.'

'On account of the wolves,' explained Mrs Fearless, carrying a handful of the sour spring plums Turks are so fond of.

'Wolves?' scoffed Celal Bey. 'Only on Çökelez Mountain, woman.' Mrs Fearless was briefly silent.

'Scorpions, then,' she said. 'Now, let me make the man a sandwich. Adile! I need some baby green almonds for our guest's sandwich. And spring onions!'

'Spring onions! Coming!'

'The wife's right, though, that you'll need somewhere to stay,' said Celal Bey.

'And a cucumber, Adile!'

'Cucumber!'

'See if you can make Gelinören. They're sure to put you up there. Just ask for the headman.'

'Ayşe, tomatoes, once you've done the eggs!'

I jammed the bulging picnic bag in the bow of my canoe.

'You can come through this way,' said Hasan, hauling the branches clear at the bank. I drove the canoe into the gap.

'Thanks,' I said. 'And best wishes for your marriage.' Bosti had followed Hasan to the water's edge. The dog pounced as I passed, but only to lick my ear and I mused that *kangals* were not the monsters I had taken them for. Celal Bey was waiting for me at the footbridge.

'You forgot this,' he said, and reaching to shake my hand he passed me down my walking pole.

I paddled through the warm day and slipped past the country bridge at the hamlet of Yahyalı where I noticed a welcome chafing on the surface of the water; the current, absent since the dam, had resumed. The wonder was where the water had come from, and I sensed secret capillaries freshening the river long after the spring rains had stopped, the skies set fair for summer, even reclaiming water stolen to irrigate the orchards. The fish, flashing bars of black, had returned to the river. Sparrow gangs were out after bedding, stripping the crackle-dry debris that crested the bank-side stands of reed. Nests of weaver birds, felted baubles, hung from the tips of willow branches, and for many reasons – the river's miraculous recovery, my growing confidence in handling the canoe, the generosity of the Fearless family, Bosti's lick – I was happy to be on the river.

A fresh concern was arising, however, by the time I had made a few more kilometres to stop for lunch at the bridge by the village of Beyelli. It related to the third and final map in my sheaf; the local tourism department's one of the province, Denizli, into which I had lately crossed. This map I had until recently ignored, doubting my ability to compute the value of yet more conflicting carto-graphical information. The previous evening, however, I had given it a cursory glance and could no longer ignore its alarming contents. I now spread the map before me on the grass, weighting its corners with the bags of Fearless almonds, plums and boiled eggs. The map was even less use than the others; its particular deficiency was to demonstrate provincial tourism department thinking at its most wishful. The map had recast the local landscape according to its own agenda. It was dotted with recreational symbols – tents, campervans, horse riders, picnic benches, para-gliders, fishermen far better equipped than the ones I had seen, even a waterskiing girl in bikini bottoms and life vest – which bore no relation to my own experience of the river valley. So I might have dispensed with that fantastic map entirely except that the photomontage abutting the prov-ince's irregular boundaries – not only of mountains and waterfalls, but of such unlikely attractions as conference facilities and glasses of wine – included a rubber dinghy manned by helmeted paddlers chuting down a white-water rapid above the legend: *Menderes – Rafting*.

I was done with rapids, especially ones as big as those in the map montage. Rafting rapids were not meant to be in the programme. Not on the Meander. Over a sandwich of chopped green almonds and spring onions I carefully considered the evidence. The tourism map's claim was both insistent and specific in that the photo in the montage was supported by a whole series of raft symbols showing repeatedly along the river below Beyelli. Since arriving in Turkey, however, nobody had made the least mention of rafting on the Meander. In fact, rafting on the river seemed even less likely than running into a curvy waterskiing blonde there. I decided a better plan, knowing what I did of Turkish maps, was to ignore this one in favour of my own instincts. I would stay on the shallow river and make, as Celal Bey had suggested, for the village of Gelinören.

It proved a long afternoon, one in which I came to believe that there might indeed have been thrill-seeking rafters on this stretch of river, but only back before the building of the dam by Işıklı Lake. This section of river would have been perfect for rafting, I reckoned, if only the water had not gone missing. The gradient visibly steepened, and the rock-ripped waters that remained ran faster down the tilted bed. The waters rushed across the shallows, grounding the canoe, which clock-handed wildly on stony pivots. Repeatedly I climbed from the canoe and walked my battered boat down the ankle-deep river, and thought how the dam had done for the river, its sloshing tide backed up there to serve the seasonal fattening of the local cherries. The banks rose higher still above my bottoming canoe where once the waters had deepened beneath bobbing rafts. The trough that I travelled was now deep in shadow, and I even feared that the banks might close above me, the river disappearing down a sinkhole just as it had done above Dinar. It was late, besides, and where a fallen willow forced me from the river, up a steep bank, the last of the daylight was raking a meadow of poppies and cornflowers. On the low rise beyond, skewered to the earth by a single minaret, there chanced to be the village. I stowed the canoe in the deep meadow grass and walked into Gelinören.

Clusters of shawled women, mattocks hanging from their rough hands, were returning from the fields. At the edge of the village they parted with abraded nods and made for home, padding down tributary paths grooved by the passing of their own feet. Rising up from the river, and along a path I by contrast could expect to walk just twice, and only so I might return to the canoe, I never felt so rootless. I felt quite as lost as those sorry wanderers of the Phrygian plain to whom one Lityerses in mythical times had commonly offered food and lodging in exchange for help, Kibbutz-style, in his fields along the Meander. Lityerses, according to some sources the bastard son of King Midas, proved a harsh host when it came to those who failed to work their stay. These he decapitated before wrapping their torsos in the same sheaves they had so signally failed to cut and dumping them in the Meander. Lityerses was to meet his match, of course, as mythical Anatolians invariably did, at the hands of some avenging Olympian; it fell to the superhero Heracles, Roman Hercules, to carve up Lityerses and consign him in his turn to the same river as his victims. Modern interpreters of myth have taken Lityerses' end to instance the emergence of a less conditional notion of hospitality towards strangers; one for which Turks in their homes were justly famed and which might, I hoped, obtain in this shabby village, with its minaret, its flat roofs and rubble walls, and the twilit agro-barn that one woman pointed out, in reply to my question, as belonging to the headman.

At the far end of the open barn, with shit-splattered cattle pens to the fore, the headman's house squatted beneath an industrial expanse of sheet-iron roof. Agricultural implements rusted in long grass around the toilet block. The headman was sitting beneath the house's awning, dressed in a threadbare suit and dandling an infant on his knee. Ali Ihsan Skirmisher was in his middle years. When he proudly repeated his name it was to indicate, with a gesture to the infant, that he shared it with his first grandchild. Among fluttering moths I settled gratefully into the rickety chair he now offered.

'And little Ali Ihsan is very beautiful,' I offered.

The child was fine but the compliment was an awkward attempt at ingratiation. I had not forgotten how my direct attempt the previous evening to secure lodgings had been unsuccessful. Time had been when beds were commonly sought in Turkey's villages, and foreign travellers thought nothing of rousing homeowners at any hour. Visitors knew the form; they were confident in the knowledge that the *oda* or village room, maintained at the expense of some prominent villager, existed expressly to accommodate them. In these honoured institutions they commonly enjoyed remarkable displays of hospitality; the archaeologist Charles Fellows was lodged in a house near Kütahya 'when in came nine people each bearing a dish . . . I was informed that it is the custom of the people, strictly enjoined by their religion, that, as soon as a stranger appears, each peasant should bring his dish; he himself remaining to partake of it after the stranger has fed . . . The hospitality extends to everything he requires; his horse is fed, and wood is brought for his fire.' Payment, moreover, was rarely demanded, though some did use money to secure exclusive access to the accommodation. Reverend Arundell, loath to share the 'magnificent fire', the spread mattresses and provisions freely provided at Dinar, bought off the two other would-be guests – 'gaunt, bony, six feet gentlemen, by occupation beggars, and literally heaps of filth and rags' – with a few piastres.

And now it was growing dark.

'What a beautiful farm,' I ventured. Ali Ihsan, inclining his head at my excessive courtesies, frowned in a dignified bemusement.

'If it is that you need to stay,' he said, 'then you are welcome.' He confirmed the offer by calling for a plate of green almonds. A daughter appeared from the house and placed the almonds, served with salt, on an upturned olive oil tin beside us.

Six-year-old Yağmur, whose name meant Rain, spun on a theatrical heel and stared fixedly into the dust.

'Why,' this inquisitive child asked me, 'do ants work so hard to collect things in the spring?' I replied that the spring must be a busy season for ants.

'For people too,' said Ali Ihsan whose own son was still out ploughing the fields. Yağmur continued to scrutinise the same patch of ground. 'And why do ants like green almonds so much?' she asked. It was dark by the time Ali Ihsan's wife called us in to eat.

The family gathered around the stove in the main room. We formed a cross-legged circle on the rugs; Yağmur placed me between herself and her inflatable Tigger. I noticed how Mrs Skirmisher and her daughter-in-law, a girl of striking green-eyed beauty, wore their headscarves; they had fashioned them in the manner of high, elaborate turbans, restraining the hair but making no attempt to conceal their faces, necks or throats. I had registered other styles of headscarf among the valley's womenfolk; some knotted them at the chin while others wore them in the way of wimples. They were artless, the traditional arrangements of working women, and were not to be confused with the avowedly Islamic veils that were behind the current political lather. Such veils, the outriders of Islamic revolution and of *sharia* law in the secularists' judgement, no doubt even of public amputations in the opinion of some, were worn pinned close to the face, often crossed at the neck, and were sometimes complemented with a shapeless full-length coat. Even so, facial concealment was rare in this part of Turkey where women and male strangers plainly could eat together, and there was little sign of the sequestering outfits favoured in Arabia and Afghanistan, and I thought it strange that female headdresses should have thrown today's Turks into such convulsions that they meant to close down their government over the issue.

We were helped to a battered pan of Black Sea *hamsi*, or anchovies, their tails turned up like the dried-out bristles of lacquered paintbrushes, and to bread and salad. The anchovies proved popular: Yağmur, hard pressed to keep Tigger from burying his snout in the pan, was admonished by her mother. We ate in a television flicker. When Ali Ihsan had finished he rose without a word, pocketed his cigarettes and mobile phone, and led me outside to his car.

Insects spiralled in the headlights as we drew up among the tractors parked outside the tea house at the neighbouring village of Dayılar.

'He came by canoe,' said Ali Ihsan by way of introduction. 'He's taking it to the sea.'

'Are you carrying your own water?' asked a farmer, stroking his stubble.

'I fill up my bottle along the way,' I explained.

'I meant to float on. After all these years of drought you won't find much of it downstream.'

'Before that, though, you should watch out for the old watermills at Aşağı Seyit,' another man advised me. It was not the first time I had heard this warning. And when I asked the man what he meant, he lifted a horizontal forearm from the table and angled it steeply downwards, his other hand driving a current before it.

A crescent moon had risen by the time we returned to the silent farm. In the pile of shoes and slippers by the doorway pink-eyed kittens stirred. I washed in a tiny bathroom where the mirror that lay among Ali Ihsan's shaving kit was from the wing of a car. My host dug out some nightclothes for me, a pair of shorts and an under-sized cerise towelling robe, which I had not the heart to turn down. Being required to dress like a bantam-weight boxer did not compare with the treatment meted out by Lityerses, certainly, but it was a reminder that there had long been a down-side to Turkish hospitality. The hosts dictated terms and had always felt free to call on their guests after dinner; even to make sizeable inroads into the supplies of medicaments and coffee, which foreign travellers tended to have about them. Nor were the mornings much better; Charles Fellows wrote how locals turned up at his door at dawn bearing 'cream and honey as an excuse for remaining to see me dress', while Reverend Arundell was woken one morning at four o'clock by 'smoking Turks, full of curiosity to witness our operation in dressing and shaving'.

We were to share the main room; Ali Ihsan, who had spread blankets for me on one of the divans there, now made himself comfortable on the other one. We both settled down to watch the television. I dozed fitfully, repeatedly surfacing to television noise – football highlights, gunshots, updates on the closure case against *Ak*, more *Ergenekon* arrests – or to Ali Ihsan's explosive snores. It was a long night. And by the time dawn came, I knew it was time to get off the river.

CHAPTER 10

I rose early and rummaged for the military map, which I carried out into the early light. Beyond the barn the village women were already returning to the same fields I had watched them leave the previous evening. In faded floral *şalvar* and headscarves they re-formed their stooped rows. A male overseer stood by, running a wheat stem between his teeth.

In the night it had occurred to me that the military map could at least be trusted when it came to the gradients; gradients being unlike dams, roads, villages and village names, that is, in that they could not have changed much since 1944, and being of such strategic importance that the Turkish Army's map men had no doubt got them right. Gradients had been uppermost in my mind since the previous afternoon, when I had sensed the valley begin to close, the river quicken, and especially since hearing the warning repeated at the tea house. A glance at the map confirmed my misgivings; brown lines positively tidemarked the river's banks just a few miles below Gelinören. What remained of the plain, patched with poppy

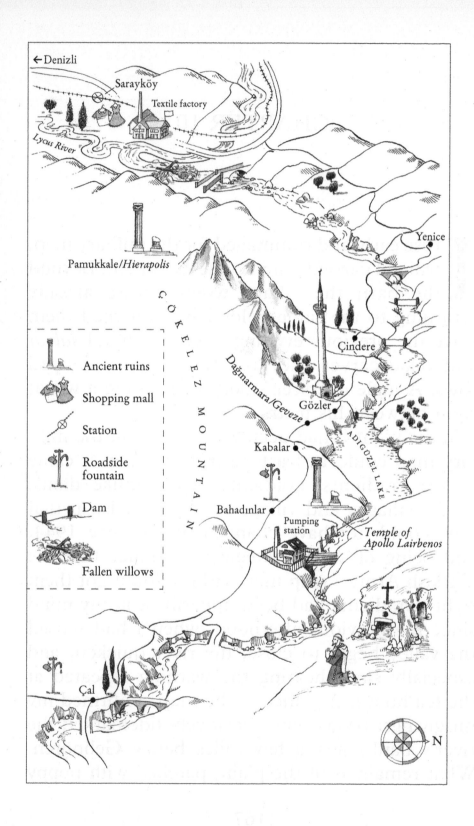

← Denizli

Sarayköy

Textile factory

Lycus River

Pamukkale/*Hierapolis*

Yenice

G
Ö
K
E
L
E
Z

M
O
U
N
T
A
I
N

Dağmarmara/*Geveze*

Çindere

Gözler

Ancient ruins

Shopping mall

Station

Roadside
fountain

Dam

Fallen willows

Kabalar

ADIGÜZEL LAKE

Bahadınlar

Pumping
station

*Temple of
Apollo Lairbenos*

Çal

N

and wheat fields, had already begun sliding south towards the town of Baklan; the river, meanwhile, continued west, and the closely contoured uplands through which it carved a course looked like no place for a lone canoeist. I had prepared myself for the possibility that I might have to leave the river, and had not the least regret about putting away my paddle, for now at least, and pulling on my boots. I walked down to the river, bagged up the canoe and shouldered it back to the farm.

Tigger had deflated during the night. Yağmur puffed away at the toy before parking it in the breakfast circle. We ate *yufka*, stove-warmed sheets of flat bread, with thick cream and tomatoes. Yağmur, who liked cream, tugged inquisitively at a ringlet of brown hair. 'How would an ant,' she asked, 'carry cream to its nest?'

It was time to leave. With a dignified air of apology Ali Ihsan accepted my offer of payment. He carefully pocketed the folded notes, promising to put them towards the street light the village was saving for. Only when I asked if I might leave the canoe in his care until I could arrange for its collection did Ali Ihsan realise that I was now without transport.

'But I'll drive you,' he protested. I explained that I meant to continue along the banks of the river on foot, thanked the Skirmisher family for their kindness and walked out of the village.

The river's mazy seam ran towards the hills. Across the valley bottom, cut sticks had been

169

planted four-square, like Zimmer frames, around gnarled vines whose budding branches were further supported with frayed ties ripped from old feed sacks. A white-haired man in a buttoned jacket of faded checks steered a horse between the scraggy rows, the plough turning the red sandy silt to level the bold yellow daisies and podded vetches. These ploughed plots, the vineyards and the stands of spring wheat initially showed as regular blocks. As the valley narrowed, however, and the rocky heights closed on the river, so the confined fields and the vine rows lost their shape, running liquid to the flat land's broken edge as if to seek out every available indent.

By the time I reached Aşağı Seyit, a sun-struck sprawl of rutted lanes and slumping tiled roofs, rising red bluffs had closed on the river. The path, forced from the riverbank, rose out of the gathering gorge and I followed the faint score of its track across pine-covered slopes. The river fell away but its roar increased. I heard its torrents clattering through the choke of trees. I had done the right thing; if I had not made the decision to leave the canoe, then there was no doubt that I would have abandoned it rather less voluntarily by now.

It was then that I heard bells; not the church peels that the Ottoman sultans had once banned as an infidel affront to the muezzin's sacred call, but the arrhythmic clank, thin as knocked pots, which alerted herdsmen to the whereabouts of their charges. The sound, generally accounted bucolic, triggered more alarming associations in my case. Just as the sight of flocks or herds had caused William Childs to make for the safety of his conveyance, so the bells had me grabbing for my walking pole. I was braced for snarling *kangals* when a pair of placid cows appeared through the pines; the herdsman who followed in their wake wished me peace, which I returned, before the two of us lapsed into bemused silence. Company came as a surprise on this lonely hillside, and it was some time before either of us could make sense of the other: a stick-wielding foreigner, without apparent purpose and on a path where foreigners were not seen, and a local herdsman, face weathered to a walnut, and wearing a ripped T-shirt with English words printed across the chest:

Inside From The West World
X-Position
Mission Available
Loading

'You're travelling alone,' the herdsman remarked; this was a familiar observation among a people who regarded solitude as unorthodox as recreational walking, and solitary walking as cause for outright suspicion.

'So are you,' I countered peevishly. I was contemplating the message on the man's T-shirt – which made no more sense to me, despite every linguistic and educational advantage, than it could have done to its wearer – when the herdsman threw an impatient arm in the direction of his cattle; one went with the cows where he came from, the gesture implied, while the apparently purposeless wanderings of strangers, without cows, might legitimately be called to account.

'I'm looking for the old watermills,' I offered.

The herdsman pointed into the gorge. 'There were several along the river,' he said. 'They were abandoned back when the electricity came. People don't go there mostly.' Nor should I have thought of doing so if it had not been for the tea house warnings. I was curious about the watermills. The locals spoke of these mills as they might have referred to old mine workings or to the quicksands of tidal flats, to ice-covered ponds or the craters of rumbling volcanoes; I sensed it might pay this visiting canoeist to understand the local view if only because watermills meant no more to me than innocuous echoes of a pre-industrial past, a stock feature of picturesque period landscapes, high wheels turning harmlessly within the barred confines of their leats. I asked the herdsman the way to the mills.

'You'll find a path down a little further on, where the slope eases. But there's not much left of them.' I had thanked the herdsman and was continuing on my way when I heard his voice above the bells.

'Is Turkey beautiful?' he called out. Reassured by my fulsome reply, he turned and with his stick rapped the rump of a lingering cow, hurrying it towards Aşağı Seyit.

Where the herdsman had advised I descended across a rock-strewn meadow of wild flowers and waist-deep grasses. A thick wall of foliage lined the river. With my pole I hacked at the tangle of briars, hollyhocks and dog roses until I had made a hole through which I could poke my head. The river, half-lit beneath the green canopy, surged past in forbidding white braids that slapped at the banks. Feeling for the bank with my feet I discovered a choked channel, perhaps a metre wide, which ran beside the river. I knelt and picked the moss from the channel's sheer sides to reveal concrete. It was a leat, and a mill had once stood where the watercourse disappeared into impenetrable thickets. Downstream I could make out the broken walls of several other mills.

It was clear what distinguished these mills: the lack of the trademark vertical wheels, and the fact that they were not regularly spaced, in the way of more temperate lands, but were conspicuously clustered, as I now remembered the ones along the banks of the Marsyas at Dinar had been. Anatolians, when they first learned to put their river gods to work, soon discovered that they must resign themselves to a fitful supply of aqueous muscle. It was in accordance with the region's unreliable rains that they designed their mills – water, its fall maximised, turned the paddles of a horizontal wheel whose rising spindle directly rotated the grinding stone up in the milling chamber – and learned to locate them where water flowed fastest. As Canadian bears grouped at waterfalls to gorge themselves on migrating salmon, these mills were traditionally gathered to catch the best of the current; in the case of the millers who served the Baklan Plain, this was along the steep stretch below Aşağı Seyit. Every rural Turk knew by instinct that watermills were found where the land fell away; the foreign canoeist had to work out for himself, however, that the cryptic warnings issuing from the tea houses were to be equated with the brown lines on the map.

These so-called 'Greek' mills appear to have originated in the region; first attested at Byzantium, they were one of the transforming technologies of the Hellenistic Age. That period of Western pre-eminence, which marked the end of the ancient Persians, is generally considered to date from the moment that Alexander the Great crossed the Hellespont into Anatolia in 334 BC. It was not until the following year, however, that the age's scope was truly confirmed when an ancient oracle identified Alexander as the man who was to subdue all Asia.

By the time of his arrival at Celaenae the young Alexander had already subdued the coastal cities of western Anatolia. On a rising reputation the brilliant Macedonian commander now marched out of Celaenae, as the Persian Cyrus had done sixty-eight years before him, to rendezvous with his forces further north. At Gordium, ancient capital of the eclipsed Phrygians, Alexander made offerings at the Temple of Zeus. There he happened upon a sacred object, which figured large in the Phrygians' founding myth.

It was a farming wagon, its wheels solid timber discs, which spoke, like the sturdy carts of the South African Boers or the early settlers of modern America, of a national pride that was at once peasant and pioneering. The Phrygians' forebears were said to have come, like Alexander, from Macedonia. These ancestors, the story went, had been advised that they were to take as their king him who first appeared to them in a wagon; and in that same totemic wagon the peasant who duly turned up, Midas, led his people out of Macedonia to their new home in Asia.

This legendary journey appeared in several key respects to presage the one that the ambitious Alexander was now in the process of making; early Macedonians, though history might have since swept them away, had once made their mark in these parts. These correspondences, in which Western dominion seemed prefigured, perhaps caused Alexander to heed an oracle that appeared to confirm the same ideas; he who could undo the famously insoluble knot of the wagon at Gordium, that is, would rule over the East. The Gordian Knot was undone, either by the power of the sword or by subtler contrivance, and within ten years Alexander had conquered Persia and extended his control beyond Afghanistan to India.

It was left to Alexander's generals, following his

death in the East, to cement Hellenic rule across the region. These generals, though they were eventually to sunder Alexander's vast inheritance by their competing claims to it, nevertheless established a Greco-Macedonian dynasty flush with the wealth of Persia's plundered treasuries. The Seleucids, as they were to be known, set about extensively redeveloping the native and Persian settlements of Anatolia's archaic age, especially the cities that guarded the great road along the Meander Valley. Kings like Antiochus and Seleucus renamed many of these lavishly restored cities after themselves or similarly honoured mothers and wives such as Apama and Laodice. They commissioned splendid gymnasia, council buildings, libraries and medical schools, on gridded plans and amidst an abundance of two-storey colonnades. Fine houses went up; the first closed drains and private piped water systems appeared. Public spaces were landscaped. Not only watermills but also aqueducts were built. Schools were founded, and the arts and sciences – geometry, astronomy, philosophy, rhetoric, oratory and drama – were rigorously studied. A uniform system of Greek law was established. Athletic training, often undertaken naked, grew rapidly in popularity. Greek began to marginalise native languages like Phrygian, Lydian and Carian. Subject peoples, the more readily assimilated at least, took Greek names that they might more easily pass among the influx of Westerners: these settlers included veteran soldiers who had been apportioned generous plots of land, administrators, magistrates and merchants, architects who refashioned the temples and artists who carved cult statues, in the Greek style, so that native gods were gradually absorbed by the Olympians. The Greeks extended a Hellenising skein of language, culture and thought into the Asiatic interior, and the meaning of those fabled Anatolian reverses was fully revealed. The defeat of Marsyas and humiliation of Midas at the hands of Apollo, and Lityerses' decapitation by Heracles, demonstrated that West had finally bested East, and could now do as it wished with it.

The sorry experiences of those mythical and legendary natives echoed, in fact, the actual plight of the Anatolian peoples. The Phrygians and their regional neighbours had plainly suffered under Eastern dominion as they were to at Western hands, at least to judge by the experience of Pythius, the world's second richest man, whom this narrative last encountered offering up his fortune in the service of the Persian war machine. The Celaenae tycoon, who came from the neighbouring Anatolian region of Lydia, rashly assumed that his generous offer somehow afforded him special pleading rights with the Great King. Since his five sons had all been drafted into the Persian ranks, the Lydian tycoon thought the oldest at least might reasonably be excused from service in the invasion of Greece. Xerxes was outraged. Pythius's eldest son did not go to Greece but only because he rapidly became in no condition to do so; the youth's carcass, cleft on Xerxes' orders from head to toe, was left by the roadside to remind the King's serving subjects of the fate that would-be draft dodgers should expect.

By his action Xerxes reminded this family of prominent Lydians that they were nothing but his absolute subjects, their purpose to serve his merest whim; and that Anatolian peoples such as the Lydians or Phrygians, Pisidians or Lycaonians, almost as obscure to Xerxes as they appear to us, represented an underclass that was born to subjugation. Xerxes quite forgot how the Phrygians under Midas, and the Arzawans and Hittites before them, had in their time all created viable Anatolian empires of their own. Anatolians were ethnic elements that were to be subsumed either into his empire or, if it came to it, that of his Greek enemies, the great Xerxes even going so far as to claim that his invasion must end in one of two ways: 'that what is ours be under the Greeks, or what is theirs under the Persians; there is no middle way in our quarrel.'

In all this any notion of an independent Anatolian identity appeared comprehensively lost. An all-or-nothing duality, East versus West, was at play, one that Xenophon reflected in the *Anabasis*; the account, after all, of a Persian leading Greeks against Persians, and latterly of retreating Greeks fending off Persians. The Anatolians, who might truly have felt the land to be their own, tended towards invisibility in the *Anabasis* where they were largely dismissed as barbarians; the term, first used by Homer to denote the babble-speaking Carian peoples whose lands lay immediately south of the Meander River, progressively broadened in scope to include all Anatolians, all Persians and peoples ruled by Persians, all Asiatics, and finally all uncivilised foreigners. If Xenophon specified Anatolian races, it was only because their moral deficiencies served to highlight Greek virtues: the pesky Pisidians whose red-herring role was to conceal the identity of an enemy more worthy of the Ten Thousand's attentions; or the Lydians, the original retailers, whose effeminacy led them to wear rings in their ears and whose only talents were profiteering from their management of the mobile markets that provisioned the expeditionary army, and making prostitutes of their female children. The Anatolians had been so long marked down as subject peoples, destined to lose their languages and identities in favour of superior ones, that it was no surprise European antiquaries of the nineteenth century should have largely considered them beneath notice.

In the afternoon I reached a bridge, where I followed a rising road out of the hot valley. At the first village, Yukarı Seyit, a fountain stood by the road. The fountain began impressively enough, with a marble base, sponsor's name and lugubrious inscription – *Some evening some time I too will fade with the sun* – but grew increasingly gimcrack

towards the latter stages of its construction; it was
finished with offcut bathroom tiles, carelessly
grouted, with the sort of push tap usually associated with public toilets, and furnished with a pink
plastic mug. Turks traditionally fulfilled the
charitable acts their faith required of them by
the provision of such fountains; those who
worked the land benefited from these fountains to
perform the holy ablutions required of Muslims
before prayer, though the proximity in this case
of the village mosque, with its own fountain,
suggested that personal prestige might rather have
influenced the siting of this one. I filled the pink
mug and drank deep and, the prospect of my own
fading temporarily deferred, I continued footsore
along the empty road.

A town of sorts eventually rose out of the land. Çal, standing at 850 metres, was a forlorn place. Beyond a few apartment blocks, dirt lanes wafered away to wilderness. Children in blue tunics silently padded across the pine needles carpeting the school-yard. A queue of farmers trailed from the town's cash machine. Tractors trundled past. The only place to stay was at the Forestry Directorate, a compound of block buildings behind a barbed-wire fence, the walls hung with long-handled fire beaters and red-painted buckets. The directorate had a guest wing where I found a bed that was not broken, and set about washing my stinking clothes in a large saucepan sneaked from the communal kitchen. I hung my laundry over a railing and looked out over the grounds. Potted saplings, pines and firs, stood in long rows where a man walked a hose. His care recalled the roadside signs – 'To Every Village a Forest' – I had seen; and I wondered why it should be that the Turks looked after their trees rather better than their rivers.

The guest wing was free of visiting foresters, so I sought out diversion on the streets of Çal. Most of the townsfolk had disappeared from view, and the only activity was in the internet café where the shadows of careening cars and jinking foot-ballers flickered across the pale faces of young men. Beyond the pavement a donkey chewed at its staked tether. I was making for an early night when music reached me from the pine trees in the

181

town's park. The music had an experimental, arbitrary quality, layered as it was with dissonant phrases that were soon submerged beneath ones that had no business keeping their company; snatches of oboes and violins, electronic keyboard riffs, a volley of drums, a falsetto voice, each confronting and consoling the others in what I took to be some intriguing musical face-off. For just an instant I thought I had stumbled across an avant-garde soirée; the descendants of Marsyas himself defying their peasant expectations by what they had made of themselves. It turned out that the noise came from a makeshift combo of mobile phones. A group of youths were slouched beneath the pines, spitting out the husks of sunflower seeds, while they passed the time comparing ringtones.

CHAPTER 11

It rained through the night, and at Çal's Forestry Directorate the rows of saplings slumped in their black polythene pouches. The clatter across the roofs ceased at dawn, and from a clearing sky the sun soon began to retrieve what water the earth was yet to absorb. Steam heads were rising off the meadows by the time I reached the river, and villagers and their tethered horses evaporated to wraith-like outlines in the vineyards, the blossoming apple orchards and vegetable plots.

It was an enchanting scene, at least until the mist lifted to reveal the concrete canalettes, and the concrete posts with their metal spreaders that ran support wires along the vine rows, and the tractors, if only of the few who could afford them and the diesel costs. Rural Turkey was industrialising, shedding its picturesque ways, and I regretted that the earth-dug irrigation channels had not the carrying capacity of the canalettes; that the makeshift vine props I had seen the previous day did not provide the support of the concrete posts; and that no horse could pull a plough like a tractor. Much had gone the way of the watermills but the main regret, I guessed, of those who still hitched plough to horse, and who gazed upon the tractors of their luckier neighbours, was that they themselves were yet to be spared the grind that passing foreigners had always thought so appealing.

The Meander had made a decisive change, meanwhile, in direction; running up against the foot of Mount Çökelez, it turned sharply to the north. The river would not trend west again, as the military map revealed, until it had cleared the hoop-shaped gorge it had in its own slow time scoured around the base of the mountain.

What the military map did not show, of course, was that much of the same gorge had since disappeared beneath the lake, which had backed up behind the hydro-electric dam they had built near the village of Adıgüzel during the 1990s. I knew of the lake, which I meant to reach that evening, from the other maps; the tourism one had it as nothing less than the haunt of the curvy blonde on waterskis. The farmer at the bridge thought not.

'You'd be lucky to find so much as a fisherman there,' he said. 'And you won't get through by following the river.' He stamped the mud from his boots. 'What you want is the asphalt.' He pointed at the marvellous innovation beneath our feet before lovingly tracing its route up the valley's western flank, detailing every bend with a calloused finger. He was wading into a stand of maize when I thanked the farmer for his advice; it was a useful reminder that tough terrain lay ahead as I approached the most remote stretch of the Meander. Unlike both the river's headwaters and its broad lower valley, astride the ancient highway and richly described since the time of Herodotus, this conspicuous midway kink had remained unexplored into the nineteenth century.

It was easy to see why, most especially to those travelling not down but *up* the Meander Valley, the European antiquaries among them, who typically ventured inland from the coast by the valley road that brought them to the lower side of Mount Çökelez. There they arrived at a defining junction; the great road continued into the interior by the Meander Valley's natural easterly extension – the valley of the classical Lycus, the Meander's main tributary – while the Meander made off into the high canyons behind the mountain.

Only in 1826 did a European, Reverend Arundell, first think to leave the well-trodden road for the route of the unexplored river above its junction with the Lycus. 'I was now entering upon the principal object of my journey,' Arundell wrote with expeditionary anticipation, 'to discover the course and sources of the River Meander.' Leaving the highway's broad valley and turning north into the shadow of Mount Çökelez, he soon found himself on 'a pathway not a foot wide, and sloping towards a precipice of great depth'; the road was 'at best extremely intricate, and scarcely distinguishable'.

The Meander's unknown course evidently attracted other scholars' exploratory instincts. In 1835 William Hamilton declared that his 'first object . . . was to examine the course of the Meander between its junction with the Lycus' and the river's headwaters; to explore, in other words, the river's wilderness wanderings around the back of Mount Çökelez. No sooner had he begun, however, than Hamilton 'became fully alive to the difficulties of getting through this part of the country, intersected as it is by so many deep fissures, as I may almost call them'.

This lost world, now threatening to close about me, had remained little known as late as the 1930s; at that time the few tracks that served the Çal region, considered too rough even for carts, were passable only by donkeys. Even now the metalled roads were sufficiently novel that the local people could not imagine that anybody might harbour a preference for the same footpaths that had so wearied their forebears. I suspected the farmer's enthusiasm for the asphalt was the reflex response of one who had not trodden the old ways for many years and knew nothing of their condition, and could conceive of no circumstances in which a foreigner could possibly have any interest in following them: remaining loyal, if the farmer must know, to the river, if not to the canoe, which was why I turned my back on him and his road, and crossed the bridge to the right bank where a rough track ran beside the tumbling river.

This track dwindled before ending at a gate; the gate was easily climbable, though it did carry a crudely painted sign which read PIG TRAPS ON THIS LAND. The sign might have sounded a sincere caution, as the cardboard ones slung from the sprayed cherry trees in Çivril had perhaps done; the fact, however, that Turks specifically disliked pigs, creatures proscribed by their religion, gave rise to the same nagging suspicion – that these particular porkers had been fabricated, along with the dire prospect of being trapped alongside them, to dissuade people from passing over the gate.

It had been my experience, that said, that the only Turks intent on keeping people out were the military, and this they did with formidable fences and signs of unmistakable intent. The rest seemed perfectly happy, proud even, that I should wander their land at will, and it was a measure of their refreshingly unfenced approach that only fallen willows and invitations to drink tea should so far have blocked my way. I therefore read the sign to indicate that I was perfectly free to proceed, but that there were pig traps on the land, which is to say that I advanced gingerly through the field, toeing aside the wild rocket, with its faded lemon petals, to check for the least glint of gaping iron jaws or even for a brush-covered pit, set with stakes, the better to do for the unholy swine.

The field proved quite empty, and beyond the ruins of a remote farmstead, where a rusted children's swing was lashed by lengths of electricity cable to the bough of a walnut tree, the valley drew decidedly to an end. The river now squirted into a high-sided ravine, and the only way onwards was by scrambling up a steep slope and grabbing at the holly oaks, thick with dusty webs, which thrust from the crannies. Here, where the sun could not reach, land crabs sidled away; from the safety of rocky recesses they swivelled yellow eyes to watch me pass.

I found myself on a narrowing rise. The deepening ravine fell away to my left while to my right rose a sheer rock face set with the regular shadows of the arched or rectangular entrances that had been cut there. Many of these cell-like caves, patently hewn by hand, were now inaccessible; they must once have been served by ropes or by timber footholds in the form of driven pegs, which had long rotted away. I managed to reach the lowest cave where I ran a hand across the rough rounded roof, expecting a sandstone sufficiently soft and powdery to have encouraged the cell's excavator to take it on. This rock was seamed, however, with quartz; it was a granitic gneiss so unyielding as to suggest an occupant committed to a life lived, whatever effort the readying of his quarters might have cost, on that especial ledge. Other than this evident determination there were no further clues to conjure the cowled reclusives who had once settled these remote rocks. Nothing but an old ash pile and the single quill of a porcupine, banded brown and white, now lay on the floor of the hermit's cell.

It was then that the slope opened up. Among the remains of stone terraces I pictured the anchorites, grateful for a break from the chiselling, taking turns at tending produce they had once raised here. Now only a sunlit sweep of dandelions stretched to the ravine's edge. Martins rose from the river and winged over the grasslands, careless of the breeze that bludgeoned the yellow-black swallowtail butterflies there. A stork soared on fixed rectangles, its pink legs trailing, and I followed the flit of its shadow far below me, crumpling and unfolding across the contours like the shadow of a descending aircraft observed from its own cabin.

Then I came to a track not tramped into being by ancient usage, but machine-made and newly graded, which coiled downwards to draw up beside the river. On the far bank stood a pumping station, which was reached by a footbridge of planks nailed across a pair of stripped poplar trunks. The path, confronted by the cliffs that reared before it, crossed the bridge to continue along the far bank, but not before it had run beneath the high gate at the far side of the bridge and wound its way across the pumping station compound. It was only when I reached the gate, finding it locked, that I was reminded what bridges were in fact for.

For during my time in the canoe, free as I was to paddle between the banks, bridges had served not as crossing points but as something else entirely; they were the exits where I might leave the river for the roads or tracks the bridges carried. I had accordingly come to see bridges as junctions – which generations of watering cattle had perfected by trampling the adjacent banks to gentle shelves, foliage-free slopes, as if their mission had always been to assist the landing and launching of river craft, and their need to drink merely the consequence of the effort it had taken them. Here was a reminder of the actual use for which bridges had been built, for crossing rivers; but only, in this case, by those who had legitimate business with the pumping station on the far bank. I was stuck.

Nor was I the first; river crossings had historic form as prominent obstacles to Anatolian journeying. There were the mountains, of course, but the challenge they represented was embodied in their sheer substance. Before many bridges had appeared – early ones, around roughly 500 BC, were constructed on pontoons – most rivers subjected travellers to delay, effort and expense even as they allowed tantalising views of the far bank. Their modern equivalent was negotiating the remote border post, the difference being that the river crossing was not merely tiresome but fraught with danger; this danger being the last thing, of course, that Barbarossa was to discover before he was pulled under by the weight of his crusading armour. As today's travellers hope to find border officials in tractable mood, so ancient ones held out for favourable fording conditions;

waters, in short, which did not rise above the chest, and a current sufficiently weak that men might stay on their feet. Thales, the great engineering philosopher of Miletus, gained renown for reducing a river that blocked the advance of an army intent on taking on the Persians; his solution was to dig a canal, splitting 'the river into two streams, which were both easily fordable'.

The Persians preferred to dispatch magi, their priestly wonder workers, to propitiate the deities of the river; on Xerxes' Greek campaign they even sacrificed white chargers to the waters of the River Strymon. When the forces of Cyrus's anabasis succeeded in crossing the Euphrates at Thapsacus, where the river was generally reckoned unfordable, the active support of the gods was presumed. On that same great march can-do types occasionally engineered ingenious solutions to the problems the rivers posed; a man from Rhodes offered to transport Xenophon and his comrades across a river in eastern Anatolia, 4,000 at a time, on a pontoon bridge made from the inflated skins of local livestock. Elsewhere on the same expedition the men filled their tent coverings with hay and made floats of them by stitching them tight.

Whereas I got to call out, prosaically enough, in the hope of attracting the attention of a key-wielding attendant; to decide, when none appeared, that safety considerations prevented me from attempting to wade the turbid river; and to retrace my steps to the bridge where the farmer had shown me the only way forward earlier that same day. I followed his finger's course through a long afternoon. I passed the hours pondering how perspectives – on everything from asphalt to watermills, on the various uses of bridges or trowels – were what distinguished us.

The rising road wound through fields, scattered villages and scrub-covered rocks, beneath a black sun, and not a vehicle passed. At length I grew weary, and my head drooped to fix stupidly at the asphalt I had thought to avoid. Only the accumulation there of cowpats signalled my approach to a final village. Beyond the crusted shit and the stir of flies I plodded unsteadily into Bahadınlar. At the road bend was a village shop, tiny and half-lit, where I found Cola and a packet of biscuits. The news of my arrival spread through the village. Murmuring men crowded the open door of the shop, the only light source, so that I paid in gathering darkness.

'Who is he?' somebody inquired.

'Give us some light!' the shopkeeper protested. 'I can't see the man's money.'

'Is it Peter?' another villager asked. I drained the Cola, wondered who this Peter could be and shouldered my way though a crush of soil-streaked farm labourers.

'Maybe he's here to see the tourism place,' somebody suggested.

'The tourism place?' I asked, instantly interested. A young man in a torn suit jacket, checking the time on his wrist, stepped forward and offered his hand.

'I'll show you,' said Mehmet Halil Blessed. In no time we were heading north down a rough track in the village *dolmuş* while Mehmet Halil asked me if I knew said Peter.

'Peter,' he insisted. 'The historian from England.' We passed between fields; then, at the plateau edge, the land ran wild and the track plunged down the steepening slopes of the Meander Valley. It flattened off at a promontory where a hill protruded from the valley slope. The driver pulled up. We climbed through the breeze-blown grasses to an eroded summit and looked out over the crumpled vastness of the empty land. The ravine lay far beneath us. I looked back to the high-sided gorge, with its mysterious hewn rock cells, where I had walked that morning. Beneath us the river widened into a silvered expanse, which zigzagged between myriad capes and headlands. I had reached the lake, my day's objective, where there was no sign of the waterskiing blonde. Instead, the remains of a classical site – marble blocks, monumental stones, chunks of carved architrave and column drums – lay scattered along the hilltop.

'The tourism place,' said Mehmet Halil. 'Peter came here some five years ago.'

And others before the mysterious Peter; an archaeological research team led by William Ramsay and David Hogarth had discovered the site in May 1887. They travelled up the Meander

Valley by train, Turkey's first railway having been extended a few years earlier as far as Sarayköy, the town at the south-west corner of Çökelez Mountain. At Sarayköy, however, the modern world's advance was abruptly halted, and the team continued their progress to Çal on horseback. There they learned 'of the existence of ruins in or near Badinlar, three hours away to the north', and were duly guided to what Hogarth described as 'the site of a small temple situate on a conical eminence' above the Meander gorge. 'Only the platform on which the temple had stood remained in situ,' Hogarth wrote, 'and very few fragments could we find of columns or cornice: such as remained of the frieze showed by their formal ornament the Ionic of Roman period.' Beyond the memorable setting there was not much, in short, to be seen; it was remarkable, given the more extensive classical sites in which the region abounded, that the remote site should have detained the scholars. Yet something caught their eye; the discoveries made at the temple were to provide an extraordinary insight into the workings of religion at the end of the first century, when the temple's extant remains were dated to.

Almost half a millennium had passed since the conquests of Alexander. Through the intervening centuries the Emperor's Seleucid successors established an avowedly Hellenic culture across the region. They warred as much among themselves as with others, however, and thus did much

194

to hasten the dynasty's decline. The rising power of Rome, in harness with its regional client, the adjacent Anatolian kingdom of Pergamum, inflicted a series of defeats upon the Seleucids, who agreed humiliating terms at Apamea in 188 BC; the payment of massive war indemnities and the cession of western Anatolia, the Meander region included, to Pergamum. When Pergamum's last king died heirless in 133 BC all his territories passed to Rome. Under imperial rule, the region was formally established as the province of Asia. In the Meander's lavishly refurbished cities, at Apamea, Laodicea and Tralles, Hellenic culture was soon partnered by Roman writ. Out in the sticks, however, the old ways largely endured; what Ramsay and Hogarth discovered at the lonely temple site below Bahadınlar, a large number of inscribed stone slabs or steles, revealed an impressive cult to the local god Apollo Lairbenos.

The pagan gods of Anatolia had long been conspicuously diverse. Native deities, often Hittite or Lydian, jostled for influence with popular incomers from Zoroastrian Persia, like Mithras, Isis and Osiris from Egypt, and established Olympians such as Apollo. What decidedly crowded the devotional landscape, however, was a strong variant tendency among the established archetypes; the likes of the moon god, Men, and the great mother goddess, popularly known as Cybele or Leto, came in local versions, growing epithets, or prototype surnames, to indicate their particular constituency communities and distinctive powers. Apollo cults in particular flourished across western Anatolia where the god not only practised his established talents – the guardianship of a pure musical tradition, as we have seen, along with prophecy, harvest, sun worship and medicine – but had also sprouted specific, often pointedly singular functions; one, Apollo Smintheus, slew mice and was represented accordingly, a triumphant heel poised above some cringing rodent, while Apollo Culicarius made it his business, like a divine spray, to repel mosquitoes. The meaning of Lairbenos has not been established; it probably referred to the people of these uplands, the Lairbenes perhaps, whom the god held in his tyrannical sway. For the inscribed stones uncovered in the vicinity of the temple site compellingly cast these Lairbenes, for want of a better name, as victims of Apollonian harshness, as the land's mythical figures had been before them.

These inscriptions were to prove hard, hard as the herdsman's T-shirt that had so baffled me the day before, to decipher. They were in Greek, which all through the Roman period continued to denote refinement and education in these Eastern lands, but rendered by a people whose linguistic carry evidently did not reach far beyond their native Phrygian. Ramsay, expert in Anatolian epigraphy, described the inscriptions as 'mis-spelt, corrupted, distorted so much as to be sometimes

196

unrecognisable', while Hogarth remarked on 'the extraordinary barbarism of their orthography and etymology'.

What the decrypted steles eventually revealed, nevertheless, was a people in thrall not only to a fancy foreign language but also to an excessively ritualised theocracy. By their inscriptions the Lairbenes sought absolution for their sins, which were apparently many, and at once confirmed themselves as obedient subjects of the god. Their steles resembled the legion testimonies heard in charismatic churches, at once confession statements and oaths of loyalty. The Lairbenes admitted to all manner of transgressions: the theft of sheep, of clothes from a bathhouse, and of firewood from a sacred grove. One individual had consumed improperly sacrificed goat meat; another had had sex while in the service of the temple. A lie had been uttered that somehow related to the sacred pigeons housed in the temple precinct; there had been a failure to attend divine service. The author of one stele owned up to having masturbated – if his coy euphemisms were correctly interpreted – while the hapless Apelles even felt compelled to admit that he had once contemplated sex with his wife at a time when such thoughts were evidently proscribed.

Many of the inscriptions bore witness not only to the actuality of divine power but also to the fact of a deity willing to deploy it; the contrite Lairbenes commonly acknowledged having suffered some kind of retribution for their transgressions. These chastisements the rationally minded Hogarth mostly identified with ailments such as the 'disease, perhaps malarial fever, which always hangs about the valley'. According to the subject mind it was Apollo who brought the sickness, as Ramsay well understood. 'When illness struck an individual, especially fever, the unseen fire in the body,' Ramsay wrote, 'he searched his conscience to find where he had sinned, confessed, made atonement, and recorded the circumstances as an example.' So it was that one Sosandros, having 'sworn falsely, and being impure on that account', and having been chastised, warned 'that no one should despise the god Lairmenos, since he will have my stele as an example'. Another, Kleonymos, 'punished by the god set up this tablet even as he punished me, for my oath, for consciousness of guilt, and for pollution. I warn all that none should slight the god.' An institutionalised guilt, general and visible, appeared to hang over this Anatolian tribe.

We made our way across the hilltop, passing the information board the tourism department had lately erected, and looked out across the view, which the dam had transformed over recent decades; what qualified this beautiful prospect was the fact that these wild waters, now tamed, had been herded into a body of water where they were condemned to mill until their time came to turn turbines.

What was left of the shrine, however, the extensive platform, the stubs of columns and plinths of statues, the fallen pediment festooned with fruit and foliage and the odd in situ stele, remained much as they had been when Ramsay and Hogarth first found them. In this respect the hilltop site had lost nothing of its resonant atmosphere. In my mind I was able to retrieve the scattered stones, and raise a colonnaded portico, with coffered ceilings, above the platform. By the sacred groves, thick with roosting pigeons, I laid out the courtyards and furnished them with the deity statues, long since removed to museums, and with the steles, numerous as gravestones, where local consciences were laid bare. At the temple I caught my first unmediated glimpse of the native Phrygians who had hitherto been excluded from the history of their land. Among the incomers – Persians, Greeks, Jews, Romans – Anatolia's own now appeared. It felt, however, like a sorry entrance.

History could only know these people for what they admitted to having done wrong. It was from their criminals that most societies wrung formal confession statements, and from their marginalised that they demanded oaths of loyalty; the steles showed that the average Lairbene habitually endured both. The fate of these people was to read divine displeasure in their every misfortune. The assumption that they had brought their trouble upon themselves duly led them to the deluded belief that they could do something about it; if only, that is, they could work out what they were supposed to have done wrong.

For by the imaginative range of their confessions the Lairbenes appeared as much to propose possible misdemeanours as to acknowledge them. These people willingly owned up, in a language not their own, to any conceivable transgression; anything to lift the fever, to prevent more deaths in the family or losses of livestock, to protect the crops from hailstorms, or otherwise to guard against loss of livelihood. The confessions had the look of statements given under duress; the work of sorry souls racking their brains not for the truth but for the words their torturers might wish to hear. I sensed, and not for the first time, a people stalked by victimisation.

Mehmet Halil was tapping at his watch to signal some unknown commitment. We made our way back to the *dolmuş*.

'Does he know Peter?' the driver asked over the straining engine. Peter was the last foreigner, it now transpired, to have visited the temple site. He had been here fully five years ago, and had not stayed long. It seemed, even so, that the villagers had invested this Peter's visit with particular significance. His name was invoked to substantiate the outside world's interest in the temple, bring tourists to the tourism place and thereby transform local livelihoods, as it had done at the great archaeological site at nearby Hierapolis, which I meant to visit over the next few days. I was no coach load, of course, but could perhaps be said to constitute a start in the process. It may be I was thought worthy of cultivation. The *dolmuş* had not reached the village, where a shawled woman slapped a stick against the threadbare rear of a donkey bundled with vine prunings, before Mehmet Halil was inviting me to stay.

He lived at the end of a cobbled alleyway, among scruffy chickens and vegetable plots, on the first floor of a small stone house. Steps rose to a raised patio; an ancient marble column, fitted out as a heavy roller, served for flattening the mud floor. Mehmet Halil welcomed me with a sweep of the arm but this familiar gesture of village hospitality had a contemporary twist, concluding with a motion that indicated the particular socket, the one that worked, where I might charge my mobile phone. He lit a brushwood fire in the open hearth and dispatched a cousin to get vegetables. The young boy returned with lettuce, green peppers, spring onions and tomatoes gathered from a nearby plot. When Mehmet Halil went off in search of a chicken, I therefore thought to hear the frantic wingbeats of a cornered bird followed by the rude termination of its protesting squawk. He reappeared, however, not with plucked feathers trailing in his wake but with a family pack of frozen drumsticks he had picked up at the corner shop.

Mehmet Halil arranged the drumsticks across the hearth, poured cups of home-made wine and told me about his life. He was born in Bahadınlar and had attended the village school until he was thirteen. He did not have a proper job and had no prospect of one. With only occasional farming work, Mehmet Halil was in no position to attract a wife. The unspoken probability was that he would grow old in the village, without a family of his own.

'Eat up,' he urged, tapping his watch as he laid a plate in front of me. 'And then we'll go to the tea house.'

Night had fallen by the time we left Mehmet Halil's house. We made our hurried way through the village beneath a crescent moon, passing beneath the enormous spread of an ancient plane tree, its trunk sundered by lightning strikes. The region was renowned for its great planes; on his invasion march Xerxes had halted not far from here to admire such a tree before bedecking it with golden ornaments raided from the imperial war chest and furnishing it with a troop of guards. It was all of 900 years old and sacred, according to Mehmet Halil, who might have told me more if he had not been so keen to reach the tea house.

In no time he was steering me into a large room, the walls bare but for the commercial calendars of tractor parts distributors, suppliers of fertilisers and animal feed, their tear-off stubs some two months out of date, where a few flat-capped men and youths were warming their hands around a central stove. Most of the village's men had already parked themselves, however, before the television, with only the strewn husks of sunflower seeds to show where their chairs had once formed conversational clusters. These chairs were now arranged in neat rows, five deep, before the screen; we were among the late arrivals, pushing through the door with a sort of premiere excitement, who dragged chairs across the bare boards to join the audience. With a last look at his watch Mehmet Halil motioned me to sit beside him. The talking stopped and the clink of tea glasses fell still, and through the window the sound of cattle briefly carried.

'*Wolves' Valley*,' whispered Mehmet Halil.

★   ★   ★

The steles discovered around Bahadınlar, dated to the end of the first century, do not appear to have featured in earlier ages. Around that time, then, something caused the Lairbenes – some signal shift in their relationship with their god – to make these public displays of their legion transgressions. It was as if, in fact, Apollo Lairbenos and the god's pagan sponsors sought overt confirmation of civic devotion; the old guard reassuring itself by this insistence that the Lairbenes affirm their subject status. The cult of the gods, complete with imperial imprimatur, was reconfirmed; but in the face, of course, of the new creed that was sweeping Anatolia.

That creed, in William Ramsay's judgement, had already left its mark among the Lairbenes. For one stele inscription appeared to admit to an offence not of ritual but of actual religion, as if its author had in fact been flirting with a dangerous hetero-doxy. The inscription, Ramsay reckoned, amounted to a forced recantation of Christianity.

CHAPTER 12

Mehmet Halil had neither a spare room nor much spare space in his own one. I bedded down where a wife should have been, as Mehmet Halil would certainly have preferred it. In the proximity of strange male company it was I, however, who had trouble sleeping. My thoughts drifted back to the squealing tyres, the poly-wrapped bricks of banknotes, the reflector sunglasses, the shiny black gloves and the practised fitting of pistol silencers that had featured in that evening's episode of *Wolves' Valley*. An agent of the state had morphed into a gang boss, and viewers in the Bahadınlar tea room and across Turkey watched transfixed.

Wolves' Valley reflected a profound national cynicism; it was as if James Bond had agreed to allow some evil genius's bid for world domination – so long as they cut him in on the proceeds. The Turks had long trusted the 'Father State', as they once referred to it, to protect the national interest at any cost, even if it meant deploying agents in a range of clandestine operations. Such activities were typically legitimised as confirming a heroic tradition in the service of national salvation: the training of guerrilla units and caching of weapons, for example, whereby the Turks under Atatürk had prepared for successful resistance after the Ottomans' defeat in the Great War, and the secret provisions made during the 1950s to prepare for possible occupation by Warsaw Pact forces. Many Turks also acknowledged, albeit with rather more ambivalence, that such shadowy forces had been responsible for many of the killings committed in south-east Turkey during the Kurdish insurgency of the 1990s.

This trust was shaken, however, when the extent to which the state was mired in common criminality became explosively apparent on a wet night in 1996. A black Mercedes – *Wolves' Valley* to a tee – left a hotel in the resort of Kuşadası to collide with a lorry hours later near the town of Susurluk. The car was found to contain: a high-ranking police commander; an MP who had made a fortune hiring out his private armies in actions against Kurdish separatists; a heroin-smuggling gangster wanted by Interpol; and the gangster's girlfriend, predictably enough a former beauty queen. Three died in the crash – the only survivor, the MP, lost all memory of how he came to be in the car.

Which was prudent, given that it excused him from explaining either the company he had been keeping or the contents of the Mercedes' boot: pistols and silencers, quantities of cash, a diplomatic passport in the gangster's name and a host of other incriminating documents. Ensuing investigations revealed that the gangster held a whole array of diplomatic passports, identity cards and gun licences; he had been operating as the state's assassin, and in return had been permitted to continue his heroin-smuggling and money-laundering activities unopposed. The state not only sanctioned the extra-judicial executions of its enemies – those businessmen suspected, for example, of funding the Kurdish insurgency – but did so in a partnership richly rewarding to its criminals. Many Turks were not so naïve as to assume that their politicians and policemen were all above suspicion. What shocked them was the complicity revealed in the wreckage of the Mercedes. It was no longer possible to distinguish – in Turkey as in *Wolves' Valley* – between criminals and agents of the state.

The more immediately relevant question, come the morning, was what lay beyond the lake I'd seen from the temple ruins. More river rafting, according to the tourism map, as well as biking along the riverbanks, horse riding, and the chance to sample local wines in long-stemmed glasses, perhaps at one of the picnic tables handily sited along the trail. Mehmet Halil thought not.

'Beyond the dam?' he gruffly echoed my question. 'Another lake. Leading to another dam.' He forked some tomato slices onto his breakfast plate. 'And below that they're building yet another dam.'

The entire gorge at the head of the loop had apparently been given over to a series of reservoirs; vast quantities of river water, stored heads of hydroelectric energy, which stepped down the sheer-sided canyons to power the flickering light bulbs of the neighbouring towns of Buldan and Sarayköy. The tourism map did not include bull-dozers and heavy machinery, it seemed, in its coverage.

I was being progressively distanced, I felt, from the river. Since there was no way through the gorge, not even on foot, I had no choice but to continue by the lane which, all three maps for once agreed, shadowed the gorge for its entire length. This road would return me to the Meander once it had reverted to a river, below the dam they were currently building, and not far from the town of Yenice. At Yenice, then, I could think about retrieving my canoe.

'There's a hotel at Yenice,' added Mehmet Halil. After a run of largely sleepless nights I could do with a room of my own, I reckoned, and deter-mined to reach Yenice the same day, though it was at least forty kilometres away. I packed at speed. Mehmet Halil, aghast at my offer of money, embraced me as I strode out into the morning.

The narrow lane ran through fields flecked with green shoots. Hunched villagers dug fertilising hearth ash into the red earth around the roots of their vines. The day had already turned hot, and the clouds were floury wisps above the distant gorge. There were few buildings and I spotted the roadside hut long before I reached it. It stood beside a mulberry tree and in the shaded interior there was an armchair, shabby but serviceable, with a clay washing bowl set in the earth floor beside it. Two old amphorae were propped against the rough stone walls, with wooden lids hand-fashioned in the shape of table tennis bats. I lifted one; the amphora brimmed with water freely offered as Mehmet Halil's hospitality had been, and I drank deep, wondering about the plainly good person who must come, if I waited long enough, to replenish the water, pat the dust from the chair where I now sat and rinse the plastic cup I now drained. It was a kindness, apparently anonymous, and one that required repeated atten-tion; the tap fountains, which entailed no such maintenance, appeared by comparison like monu-ments to the beneficence of local worthies. The regular readying for others of this place was all the more affecting because most of those who might once have stopped here no longer even noticed it, passing as they did in their *dolmuş* seats or on the trailers of tractors. The world sped by and ever-dwindling numbers, the odd indigent or itinerant, came to the hut for its shade and water. It could not be long before the place fell into disuse and yet another ruin would mark the land-scape, and plastic bottles thrown from passing windows would instead indicate where travellers got their water from.

For now, however, a stranger's care had sanctified the contents of the roadside amphorae. The State Water Works might be busily turning the last of the canyons into hydroelectric stores, but the water that came chilled from that earthen darkness felt like the gift of life. It lightened me on my way and in that marvellous morning I glimpsed the lemon flash of a golden oriole among the trees outside a place called Kabalar. It was a plain village, a bare cluster of block-built houses, but in the little square a woman stopped to learn who I was and where I was headed. Women in rural Turkey did not generally accost male strangers. Perhaps it was because she was decidedly matronly, beyond all that, or that she had learned to see things differently during her years in Switzerland where her two children now worked as an architect and in the computer industry; prosperous and married, with children of their own, ambitions fulfilled in a way, I feared, that Mehmet Halil was not to know.

All morning I followed my shortening shadow across the silent uplands. I passed through hillside pine forests. In the chill braids of a milky stream I bathed my feet, the current sweeping the sweat towards the gorge as I laboured onwards to reach the village on the high slopes. It was a cluster of flat-roofed hovels and whitewashed cottages where poplars in their spring brilliance rose like Day-Glo fireworks. The village was now called Dağmarmara, or High Quarry, though the military map knew it as Geveze, or Windbag, a plain silly name proving quite as unacceptable, apparently, to the modern bureaucrats as a foreign or religious one might.

The village was empty. The flank of a sleeping dog heaved in the shade of a blue water bowser. Beyond it, where a wide plain ran to the horizon, I left the road. A path led through scattered plots of corrugated soil. Among those irregular strips, their straight edges giving way to violin curves where boulders and scrub oaks intruded, I found the villagers of Dağmarmara. An elderly couple weeded a field of thyme; a gang of women, their hoes abandoned, hitched up their baggy *şalvar* to squat around a blackened teapot in the shade of a pine tree. In the wake of a slow tractor a disc plough trailed neat lines of tobacco seedlings. Seated workers, the women in floral shawls and the men in brown rubber boots, topped the plough. They slipped the seedlings into notches on blades that revolved to release them upright in the newly turned soil. I asked where the crop would end up.

'Izmir!' exclaimed the moustachioed patriarch who sat at the wheel of the tractor. 'And where might you be going?'

My answer caused him to smile. 'Ah, Yenice,' he enthused and at my good fortune threw up his arms. It was a gesture that did wonders for the hotel there, instantly furnishing it with foyer and ornamental fountain, and I lengthened my stride against the sun.

I was making for the minaret I had spied in the

west. It appeared from a rift in the plain, where I thought to rest and drink tea in the village of Gözler. Clearing a final limestone bluff, however, I saw that there was to be no tea. The minaret, patterned with blue-glazed bricks and rising to a round balcony, stood amidst a ruined village. Fields enclosed by low broken walls, waist-deep in thistles, edged the abandoned settlement. The minaret rose from the tumbled walls of a mosque whose roofs had been scavenged for building materials; I reckoned it might just be climbable.

I had never been up a minaret, which felt like an omission; the question was whether it was wise that I should begin with a derelict one. The mosque had been reduced to a pile of bramble-choked rubble and a fig tree thrust from the arched doorway at the minaret's base. Beyond the fig tree, however, the minaret's staircase looked reasonably sturdy. I had often been struck how minarets commonly defied their slender fragility to outlast buildings they had once served – like the legendary one at Jam, Afghanistan – no doubt because the modesty of their roofs, in this case a steep cone of stainless steel topped by the traditional star and crescent, preserved them from the ingress of rain. Even so, it was only the consolation of a memorable epitaph – *Died in a Minaret He Himself Had Caused to Collapse* – which finally persuaded me to push past the fig tree, hung with spiders' webs, and start up the cramped spiral.

The stairs of rough concrete proved solid. I had soon ceased to worry about the structure of the minaret. By the time I had climbed all of its eighty-eight steps I was instead thinking of the muezzin who had made the same ascent, five times daily, to pronounce that Allah was great, and that there was no God but He; whatever others, long since banished, had once claimed for numerous other deities from Apollo Lairbenos to the god of the Christians.

A sunlit archway gave onto the balcony where the parapet had partially fallen away. So I halted there and looked out over the land's deep folds and the limestone outcrops. From my high outlook I now saw that one other building had survived amid the wreckage; it was a stone house of some distinction, which must once have been home to the village landlord or *ağa*. The house, squarely built, with thick walls, Gothic window arches and a sagging roof, stood within a walled garden where a *kangal* had been chained to assert an absent owner's claim. The creature was less anxious to defend the property, however, than itself – and from the falling tiles which the roof regularly shed. Smashed tiles lay across the garden, leaving not a single patch of clear ground; not one so big, that is, that a *kangal* might safely shelter in it. It appeared that the dog had been suffering in this way for months. In the process the traumatised creature had come to survey the sky whence it had learned to expect strikes. It now caught sight of me there and, taking my high tower for the haunt of a tormenting deity, it gave a long whine of submission, and I figured I might finally be done with worrying about *kangals*.

I passed the village of Çindere, which clung to the plateau rim high above the half-built dam, in the late afternoon. Wicker baskets heaped with fresh-cut meadow fodder stood in the dusty lanes, and the road beyond the village began a sweeping descent. The watered western flank of Çökelez Mountain was thick with pinewoods and with the lilac blossoms of the Judas trees. Bleached jade poppies stood slashed with ragged purple petals.

Box beehives the colour of old denim patterned the hillside meadows. The only traffic I encountered was a pair of donkeys bearing an elderly couple to Çindere. He sported a coal-black flat cap, a fob watch hanging from his tattered purple waistcoat, while his wife wore a high turban, extravagantly tied, and patterned in ivory and gold. They were mounted on embroidered saddles, with high wooden pommels, and the firewood sticks they had gathered protruded from their saddle-bags, feed sacks reinforced with stitching, like desperado musketry. They were magnificent.

'You're out late,' the man observed, glancing over his shoulder. His meaning might have been mundane, that he doubted I would get a lift, but I had the thrilling sense he might once have used the same utterance to warn against ruffians and brigands; that a lonely road, the light fading, even now remained no place for strangers. I told him that I was making for Yenice.

'Ask for the hotel,' he said, kicking at the flanks of his donkey. I now saw a low-lit bar, heard a piano and even fancied a line of flagpoles at the front.

It was an evening among the heavens. The last sunlight was so low among the plane trees that it caught the undersides of the leaves. The long shadows grew indistinct and a lowland warmth rose up the road to meet me. I plunged through woods and fields, and had almost reached the valley floor by the time the lift came. The tractor came barrelling out of the gloaming, a wide-eyed driver staring down the beam of the one functioning headlight. I clambered gratefully onto the trailer and had barely sunk to the wooden boards when we were clattering over a bridge. The Meander slid beneath us. I glimpsed lines of current, stronger than I had expected, which were scored in silver across the chipped surface of the river. The headlight illuminated a rusted sign bearing a message I had not yet seen on the Meander: *Entering the Water*, it said, *Is Dangerous and Forbidden*.

The tractor drew up in what I took to be a poor part of Yenice (alt. 263 metres). There was a scruffy park and a broken sequence of street lights, and the little shops, open to the street, sold bags of crisps and disposable razors. A youth emerged from a barber's shop. He introduced himself as Menderes, which I took as a good sign. I told Meander that I was very pleased to meet him and wondered if he could direct me to the hotel which I understood to be in the town. Meander thought not.

'Hotel?' he queried, and went to check with his friends in the barber's shop. He then returned, shouldered my rucksack and led me down the street. When he stopped and wished me goodnight, it was not before an illuminated building, with flagpoles and landscaped flowerbeds, but at an unlit concrete block. On the wall, in red paint, was scrawled the word *OTEL*.

CHAPTER 13

I rose early, delaying only to arrange the retrieval of my canoe, before I walked down to the river. It was a first opportunity to return to what was, after all, my theme. The river, besides, was my way out of Yenice. The little town and I had not got on.

It did not help that the travelling had done me in. Three long days of walking had left me sore and blistered. My rucksack reeked of river rot. The broken nights in villagers' bedrooms had left their mark. I was weary to the point of seeing things, though not the standard mirages; regular drinks from the roadside fountains and clay jars had at least spared me the shimmering lakes that parched travellers thought to drain in single draughts. That I was able to stay well watered had only made space, however, for more banal visions; of the neat and prosperous outlines, in fact, of quality accommodation. The shame of it was that I wanted nothing so much as somewhere nice to stay. The same softness at my centre that had caused me to hold out, however remotely, for the likes of waterskiing blondes now deluded

me that an oasis of country comfort awaited at
Yenice.

It was therefore a disappointment to discover
that the hotel there did not even run to a name.
The Turks might have borrowed their word for
hotel from the French, as the absent 'H' in their
phonetic rendering signified, but they had learned
little else from those hoteliers par excellence. Turks,
who preferred to bestow hospitality rather than to
sell it, had always been better at opening their
homes to visitors than at running hotels for them;
this was to their credit, of course, though the
consequence was hotels like the one at Yenice.

Hotels needed names, I reckoned, no less than
people did. The lousiest establishments had
them. When the water supply failed, or scurrying
cockroaches gleamed in the harsh flicker of naked
bulbs, or the midnight mutterings along the corridors betrayed the tawdry travails of fellow guests,
the one consolation was the magnificent presumption of a place that called itself, say, the Silk Palace.
A hotel without a name, on the other hand, trampled the least illusion that it might have foyer or
bar – or, for that matter, carpets, breakfast or bed
sheets. Or even resident staff.

I had found the hotel locked the previous evening.
So I pushed the bell. A man eventually answered
the door, which was made of industrial metal, but
not from the other side; a dictum, I vaguely
recalled, had once impressed me with its solid
advice that the only door worth stepping through

must be opened from within. It was out of the night, and to the clack of his walking stick, that Hüseyin instead appeared, summoned by some improvised relay of messages. I followed the elderly man through the door and up the half-lit stairs, which he took one at a time, levering himself on his stick and pausing to draw my attention to a notice in his own hand that he had posted there.

'No drinking, no smoking, no making noise on the order of the Council's manager,' it decreed. Into one corner Hüseyin had squeezed a subsequent commandment. 'No eating seeds' it read, and I pictured Hüseyin ankle-deep in sunflower shells, stick and broom to hand, resolving to rain down ordnance on those who would litter his floors.

I ate in a nearby kebab house. An aged mute, all gestures, came to sit with me. My journey seemed to awaken old, scurrilous memories in the man, who, throughout my meal, scrawled picaresque bullet points – '1976', 'Baghdad', 'Rotterdam', 'Lorry', 'Dutch girls!' – across scraps of newspaper torn from my tablecloth. He laid them neatly beyond the chipped rim of my plate, even reordering them there, like the parts of a jigsaw puzzle, in the conviction that a minor adjustment was all that could be keeping me from taking a proper interest in his own wanderings. Out on the street a youth sidled up, collar raised, to advise me in a lascivious whisper that there were girls working in the nearby beer hall. Travel allowed all manner of liberties, of course; the one that then mattered, however, was the freedom to leave Yenice without looking back.

So to the river; the road that led to it sported a tattered pink bunting of oleanders, the first such flowers I had seen on my journey. The surreal, even discomfiting colour that they brought to sun-bleached landscapes had never endeared these botanical flamingos to me but the fact that they favoured Turkey's lower elevations meant that these plants for once functioned usefully, as an altimeter, to remind me of the contours I had shed since Çal; almost six hundred metres, more than half the Meander's overall fall, in just sixty or so kilometres, which meant a descent some ten times steeper than the river's overall gradient. In time, of course, the river would achieve a more uniformly steady rate of descent; through geological time, in fact, steadiness had been its guiding ambition. It was a physical law that running water, which had shaped these lands from the first raindrop's fall, sought only such constancy. By the brush of its gathered current the Meander had been gradually eroding the irregularities, boulders and pebbles alike, along its bed. It was in thrall to a process that must always continue. The river was destined in some unimaginably distant future to run down a uniform incline, and in its progress to that smooth ramp erase all evidence of the dams men had once built when they thought themselves masters for ever of the river's power.

We were now reunited, the river and I, at a sunlit bridge beyond the oleanders. The surprise was the weight the Meander had put on. I was aware that various tributaries had since thrown in their lot – most notably the Banaz River, which drained the lands north of the gorge – but I had feared the dams were sure to have absorbed them, even reduced the river once more to a sorry trickle. As it was, the Meander certainly looked to carry me out of Yenice, which was fine, but at a considerably greater speed than I might welcome; it was clear that the river's steep descent continued. A racing current tore down it, bearing trails of spume ripped from the riffling crests of the waves lining the stream's V-shaped sides; waves that jostled but never advanced, the water sliding beneath the frozen form of the rucked surface. I followed the rip current downstream, and passing through the vineyards that lined the banks, I scanned the river for the reassurance to relaunch there. I walked a long way before I found it.

It was midday by the time I got back to Yenice. On the main street, where tractors hauled pesticide sprayers, the man I had phoned earlier that morning was standing by a taxi. He pointed at the bag he had left by the door of the hotel. It was my canoe.

Around AD 47, roughly half a century before the Lairbenes had set about erecting their steles high above the Meander, a ship had docked at the port

221

of Perge on the southern shore of Anatolia. Among the passengers were two men, Paul and Barnabas, who headed north into the interior. The road was long and the men were vulnerable to all manner of dangers, with nothing to propel them but an absolute conviction, which they meant above all to share; that gods were not multiply incarnated, in fact, in Roman emperors, Macedonian generals and Persian kings, in the deities of the Olympian pantheon, in the sun and moon, in rocks and trees, but singly, and in a carpenter from Nazareth in Galilee. A new faith had set out to seek its fortunes in the uplands of Anatolia.

The young religion would duly have to contend with that dense crowd of pagan deities, Apollo Lairbenos included, which it so utterly denied. First, however, it must survive its own mother religion, Judaism, whose orthodox elements had from the very beginning sought to smother the unwanted offspring. The Pharisees, Judaism's self-appointed guardians, dismissed as a charlatan the Jew who had been crucified some fifteen years earlier in Jerusalem, and those who proclaimed him the Messiah they condemned as blasphemers against the Law of Moses. Paul, himself a Jew, had once been a prominent persecutor of the Jesus sect; it was as Saul, name of the first king of Israel, that he had set out some years after the crucifixion to inveigh against Jesus's followers in Damascus.

The scourge of Christianity never got there; on the road to that Syrian city, and in a demonstration of the new faith's potency, he was recast as its foremost advocate. This transformation appeared miraculous, though the man's biography, however poorly documented, suggests that divine intervention merely hastened a conversion its subject might in time have managed independently. He who stumbled out of the light had not so much been transformed, that is, as restored from aberrancy; he was the natural product of a cultural background that militated against orthodoxy. For Paul, though an avowed Jew, was not of Judaea. He was instead from Tarsus in south-east Anatolia. A diaspora Jew, possibly the product of the same imperial policy that had in previous centuries settled Jews and their Ark legends at Apamea and elsewhere across Anatolia, Paul was necessarily shaped as much by contact with the codes and cultures of the Hellenist Roman Empire; his newly adopted name may even have been the form he had always preferred in his dealings with non-Jews. Through his upbringing in Tarsus the world of the Gentiles had touched Paul, and through his calling he now set about reshaping that world fundamentally. This process – the early advance of Christianity – was to begin along the same great road that rose in the Meander Valley, ran through the pass at Apamea and some eighty kilometres east reached Antioch in Pisidia before continuing to Iconium (modern Konya) and the provincial towns of Lystra and Derbe.

There had been increasing contact between

Gentiles and Jews since the conquests of Alexander in the fourth century BC. Just as the ruling Seleucids and their Roman successors had settled Jewish colonies across Anatolia, so Greeks were increasingly stationed across Judaea. It was predictable, of course, that each people should have found fault with the customs and codes of the other. A chief issue was male circumcision; what Jews regarded as the very mark of their covenant with God, the Gentiles abhorred as vile mutilation. A ban in the second century BC on their rituals had caused the Jews to rise against Seleucid rule. Rebels had forcibly circumcised captured Gentiles; the authorities had responded by slaughtering Jewish mothers along with their circumcised infant sons.

Other Jews and Gentiles rubbed along rather better, however, and in learning Greek Paul was by no means alone. Many such Jews were schooled in rhetoric and philosophy. They frequented the gymnasium and the theatre. Their culture, abraded and adapted, arrived at an accommodation with that of the ruling Greco-Romans.

The striking thing was the extent, given the Jews' subject status, to which this syncretic process operated in reverse. Many Gentiles admired the Jews for their prosperity and the influence it bought in, for instance, securing top seats at the theatre or prime plots for the raising of synagogues. Others seem to have been attracted by the moral vigour and clarity of the Jews' faith; one God, unquestioned and for ever, which perhaps left Hellenist paganism's overlapping collage of oddly consti-tuted deities looking like the wonkiest kind of bet hedging. Certainly, sufficient numbers of Gentiles had come to revere the One God of the Jews as to acquire a particular designation – God-fearers – at the very time of Christianity's emergence.

These lapsing pagans, as we may call them, are known to have frequented the synagogues, discoursed with Jews and even partaken of some rituals in a tentative experimentation with Judaism; this unestablished monotheist minority was in the market, then, for a faith it could call its own – though it was not, finally, to be that of the Jews. Judaism had no missionary interest in receiving outsiders. It insisted upon absolute adherence to the Law of Moses, circumcision included, which deterred many God-fearers from converting. The fact of these spurned monotheists may explain the apparent facility with which Christianity took its earliest steps, in Anatolia especially, where Gentiles and Jews freely mingled from Miletus to Apamea, from Ephesus to Iconium.

For the Christian message – that the Messiah had indeed come, and that all *this* faith essentially required of its adherents was that they believe in Him – was appealing in its simplicity. Where Judaism barred its doors, in short, Christianity's stood open. This same line Paul and Barnabas preached on their arrival at Antioch in Pisidia. If the message played well with the God-fearers who had gathered to hear him at the synagogue, however, it outraged many Jews by defying their assumption that the new faith was no more than a minor offshoot of Judaism, and its followers unconditionally subject to Jewish law. Paul's riposte was to accuse the Jews of rejecting the word of God and declaring his missionary intent in one of the New Testament's most resonant phrases: 'lo, we turn to the Gentiles'. So Christianity first broke with Judaism at Antioch in Pisidia. The new faith spoke, of course, to a constituency, the God-fearers, which was predisposed to hear it; Christianity was yet to set its sights on the multitudes who worshipped the pagan gods of imperial Rome, and therein lay the greater prize.

Paul, recalling the dangers he had faced on his missionary journeys through Anatolia, wrote of beatings and stonings, and of being robbed. First, though, he mentioned the rivers.

At Yenice, I saw why. The river ran fast, and even if it had broadened, allowing me at least some space to manoeuvre, I was unconvinced that my decision to return to the water was a sensible one. Just below the bridge, where an open stretch of gently shelving shingle edged the Meander, I therefore reassembled my canoe with particular care. I checked that every last rib was clipped securely into place. I adjusted the inflatable tubes to achieve the perfect balance of rigidity and pliancy. For stability, I ballasted the bottom of the hull with the heaviest kit items and fitted the inflatable seat as low as possible. I made sure to lash down every last object. Then I retired to the shade of a nearby scrub oak. I was practising with the paddle there, summoning strokes I had not used for days, if only because I might now need them in a hurry, when a tractor appeared from the direction of Yenice. The driver had barely glimpsed me before he braked so abruptly as to spring moulded ingots of sun-baked mud from his tyre treads. He was not accustomed, it seemed, to seeing foreign boatmen on the river. When he lit a cigarette and sat back to watch, however, even thinking to cut his engine, I had the uncomfortable sense that something more than mere curiosity had brought him to a halt; the feeling, as I slid the canoe into the shallows, that the driver guessed he might just be in for a treat.

The shallows were slack, though there was not much of them; they barely contained the canoe. I was still settling into my seat when the current's braided rim snagged the canoe's wavering bow and began coaxing it onto the water. I back-paddled, grounding the stern on a mudbank while I took stock. Beyond the stretch of open shingle thick foliage soon crowded the banks. Willows tumbled out over the water. To clear that wet thicket, and the trailing branches that tore white strips in the stream, I must take the current on. I settled my hips, seeking balance, and suddenly, as if to catch the current unawares, I drove the canoe hard across the stream. I held a fighting line until the last moment; as the current threatened to overwhelm my faltering forward momentum I dug in at the stern, spinning the bow to face downstream. I caught the outermost willows, busted through, and slipped out onto the river. At my back the tractor moved slowly off.

I had safely launched. I had denied the tractor driver his entertainment. The way ahead looked wide enough, moreover, to take a fallen willow and leave space for a passing canoe, which had been my particular hope. It was this formula – one willow's height plus one canoe's width – that it came down to; that much river and I reckoned my progress was assured. On a growing sense of confidence I surrendered to the current, paddling only to correct my line through gouts of rising turbulence, which spread bubble-strewn slicks across the stream, and I raced through the spinning vortices. The banks slid by in a blur of trees, reeds and stands of purple-topped thistles. Up came a bridge, a thing of two roughly equal halves comprising a handsome Ottoman span, all pointed piers supporting keystoned arches, and the crumbling concrete slab it met midstream. It was a typically Turkish repair, inelegant but serviceable, which I took at the time to have been caused by a typically Turkish instance of long-term neglect. I was later to discover, however, that the damage to the bridge was deliberately done by locals intent on halting the advance of Greek forces in the war of 1919–22; a preview, in short, of what modern history had in store for the river and an early intimation of the devastation that was to descend upon the Meander Valley from almost a thousand years before that final war.

As it was, I had barely seen the botched bridge before the current had slung me through one of the arches and swept me downstream. I was not far beyond the bridge when the banks began to steepen. The reeds that lined them thickened with every moment. A familiar gloom settled upon the river. A drowned cow, a yellow plastic tag stapled to its ear, floated upright among the willow brakes; it had swollen like a drum and lost one eye to the birds. In my seat I hunkered down and raced downstream where a heron, half-lit, rose gracelessly from a dead tree, taking the last of life with it. For a moment I thought I might be swept down a riverine plughole. In this darkening netherworld I tore round a bend where the channel came to an abrupt end. At two fallen willows.

These trees had once faced each other across the river; and just as they had chanced to grow in each other's shadow, so they had merged in their falling, the splintered branches of their half-submerged crowns meshing mid-stream. The blockage they formed was total. From one bank to the other the trunks ran a uniform boom where a grey scum rose in agitated wavelets, and the few plastic bottles that had collected there, fretting against the sodden, peeling bark, bobbed furiously against the pull of the ducking current. I braked hard, back-paddling and at once turned the canoe tight. But I was too late. The canoe broadsided the willows with a thump. I felt the craft flex alarmingly. Then the current kicked in, the hull rode up the trunk and the canoe began to tip, and it occurred to me that I had miscalculated the river's vital measure; a canoe's width plus the height of *two* willows, then, being the requirement if one was sure to pass.

The canoe did not quite capsize. Its rising edge caught against a branch, wedging it at an angle while the current boiled around it. But the boat was taking a battering. It had begun to ship water over its lower gunwale. I instinctively pushed against the trunk, thinking to swing the bow upstream, even as I knew I had no hope against the current. I leaned along the canoe, grabbed at a willow branch and heaved hard. For a moment nothing happened. Then something gave and the canoe, its fabric skin squealing in protest against the willow, began to bump along the trunk. I pulled again and again, and the current began to lessen as I closed on the far bank. The canoe finally slipped back onto an even keel.

I was breathing heavily as I ran under the bank, a high palisade of plainly impenetrable reeds. There was no way I could get myself off the river here, nor begin to extricate the canoe. The only possible exit out of this trap was upstream. What now signified was not the river's width but the rate of its flow. To escape the river I must paddle the canoe at a speed to outrun the current. Otherwise, I could only wait for the current to weaken, which might take days, while my own weakening proceeded apace.

I faced the canoe upstream, the stern resting against the willow boom, and pondered my escape. The current ran weakest by the banks; but by running among the foliage I would be likely to snag the paddle and lose vital headway. I sighted my bow accordingly, taking a line to clear the willows and reeds, drew down a deep breath and drove in the paddle. For a moment, there was nothing but the frantic churn of water. Then, slowly, I felt the stern ease free of the willow and the same backdrop that had fled past minutes earlier – trailing branches and dead trunks, desiccated reed tops and weed tresses – now inched into reverse. I began to make gradual ground, but I was sprinting. It was no time before I needed to rest. I grabbed at an anchoring branch so as to bank the few yards the flurry of strokes had earned me. In this manner I made my way upriver. The paddling spurts soon began to shorten, the rests to lengthen, and all the while the reed stands stretched along either bank. Something bumped against the canoe; it was the cow's bloated corpse, idly spinning in the current, as it slipped downstream.

I must have covered some 200 metres, and was drenched in sweat, when I saw the plastic irrigation pipe. Broad and blue, it ran down the left bank.

To install it, the farmer had cleared a passage through the reeds before trampling the bank to a moderate gradient. I had noticed such pipes on the river's upper stretches and cursed them for the ecological damage they did in depleting the water levels; I now blessed them, and irrigators all, and with a final dig of the paddle drove the canoe into the reeds beside the pipe. I clambered unsteadily up the bank, dragging the canoe behind me. At the top my legs gave way beneath me and I found myself lying in a damp field of green barley.

For some time I did not move. I looked up at a blue sky scored white by gliding storks. A rim of mountains was cloaked in a grey haze. When I finally got to my feet I found the barley stood to my midriff. The crop fringed the river into the distance. One thing at a time, I told myself, starting by traversing the field and clearing the fallen willows. Then I could try to find a way back onto the river. I offloaded the rucksack and stowed the paddle. The rucksack was heavy on my shoulders; it was sodden on account of the water the canoe had shipped. I flipped the canoe until the water had drained out. Then I wrapped the painter round my fist and ran it over my shoulder before setting off across the field. The canoe, its fabric skin sliding over the smooth green stems of the flattened barley, moved with ease; more easily than I did, sinking to my ankles with every step. Into the field the irrigation pipe had delivered not only me and my canoe but also considerable quantities of water – which was, after all, its purpose.

The sun was spiralling out of the sky by the time I trudged past the fallen willows that had blocked my way. Beyond them, however, a fringe of impenetrable reeds ran unbroken to the horizon. The river remained quite out of reach. I continued on my way, insects about my ears. When I looked back, the canoe's wake through the parted barley resembled the runner marks of an Arctic sled, stretching out of sight. The barley finally ended at an earth rampart, which ran at right angles to the river. Thistles grew all over it. With my paddle I hacked a way over the top to discover the earth was spoil freshly dug from an adjacent irrigation canal. The way to the canal's banks was clear, and the canal ran unchecked back to the river. I wept, but not for long, because the sun was low. Then I repacked the canoe and launched on the canal.

I noticed it the moment I rejoined the river; the current had spent itself. In the course of my progress through the barley the river's bed had finally levelled out. The plummet that had begun at Çal, and had caused the river to lose more than half its overall fall, had ceased. The Meander no longer tumbled down its crevice; it had cleared Mount Çökelez to turn sluggish in a broadening valley.

Through the thinning willows I now spied an expanse of low-lying meadow and copse; the emerald and jade tones of another valley, wider, and out of the east, lying roughly at right angles to the Meander. This was the valley of the Lycus, the historic road's continued route into the interior; the effect of the Lycus's approach was to head the Meander, at first gradually, from its southerly course. Beyond a final bend the tributary closed on the river and was lost in it without ceremony, but not before nudging the Meander further towards its original bearing. I felt the river turn until I was paddling into a setting sun. I was back where I was meant to be; heading west.

I had completed the great hoop; the Meander,

its wilderness wanderings behind it, now rejoined the same arterial route it had last touched at Dinar. That the river was once more in the company of the railway and the main road prepared me for the roar that rose from the bridge; refrigerated pantechnicons, speeding Mercedes, police vehicles and gleaming overnight coaches streamed beneath the road lights towards Sarayköy and Denizli. The carts, thyme fields and plough-bent villagers of the uplands already felt like a fond dream.

The surprise was that somebody should have marked the Meander's return to the modern world with something so fitting as a riverside factory. A chimney-topped edifice sat behind its security fence, belching smoke into a darkening sky. A sign, which announced the Meander Textile Factory, bore a stylised wave, which appeared to claim a harmonious association with the river. From where I sat, however, the view was of a one-sided, even abusive relationship. What I initially mistook for the chimney's reflection in the water in fact turned out to be its submarine counterpart; a broad pipe from which a heavy brown effluent, gold along its edges, spread out into the water. The river now changed colour, and it began to smell.

I passed under the bridge and beached on a shabby shore in the half-light. I rolled the canoe into a stand of wheat, shouldered my rucksack and crossed the bridge where another discovery struck me by its aptness. Beside the road, at the point where the Meander turned west, an outlet store had lately been built. The store, now closed for the night, was plastered with Euro-style brand names: Puma, La Notte, Tivolyo, Colin's, Loft and Sevenhill. The lights from the main road revealed shelves of trainers, racks of T-shirts, jackets and belts, and bins of footballs. The window also bore the reflection of an itinerant of the sort – mud-caked shoes and trousers, dripping rucksack hung with bits of barley and willow – that factory outlet stores tended to discourage. Hearing somebody call out, I turned to the sight of an approaching pair of security guards in pressed blue uniforms and feared the worst.

'Tea?' one asked. The men led me into their office and made me their honoured guest, sitting me in a chair before a bank of screens that displayed the several views provided by the CCTV cameras; my trail of mud was clearly visible in a number of the images. The guards were too intent on enthusing about the outlet store to notice my filthy state; they described how the store, which had opened six months earlier, had attracted gawping crowds of wide-eyed shepherds, housewives and imams alike, and from as far as Nazilli and Burdur. They brought me more tea and regaled me with the news that Galatasaray, an Istanbul football team, had been crowned Turkey's champions the previous day. I in turn asked them about the river.

'No problem,' said one. 'At least as far as Feslek.' One of the guards, who was going off-duty, offered to drop me in nearby Sarayköy (alt. 153 metres) where there was a hotel.

From Antioch in Pisidia Paul and Barnabas journeyed east to Iconium where their teachings once more stoked hostility among the local Jews. The two men fled to Lystra, a modest country town, where Paul miraculously caused a cripple to stand. The locals, who spoke the regional Lycaonian, took the two strangers for gods and prepared to sacrifice an ox in their honour. Paul and Barnabas rent their clothes to express disapproval of these heathen ways. 'We are also men of like passions with you,' they exclaimed, 'and preach unto you that you should turn from these vanities unto the living God, which made heaven, and earth, and the sea, and all things that are therein.'

Christianity thereby set its sights on the pagan world.

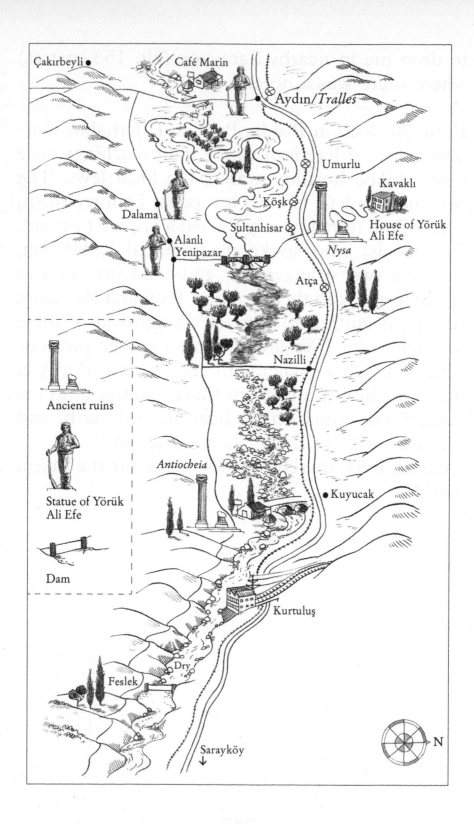

Çakırbeyli •

Café Marin

Aydın/*Tralles*

Umurlu

Kavaklı

Dalama

Köşk ⊗

Sultanhisar ⊗

House of Yörük
Ali Efe

Alanlı
Yenipazar

Nysa

Atça ⊗

Nazilli

Ancient ruins

Antiocheia

Kuyucak

Statue of Yörük
Ali Efe

Dam

Kurtuluş

Dry

Feslek

Sarayköy
↓

N

CHAPTER 14

In the year 110 the Roman governor of the Anatolian province of Bithynia wrote to Trajan, alerting the Emperor to a growing Christian presence in the region. The cult, having at first found few takers beyond the urban God-fearers, had since flourished across Anatolia's pagan hinterlands. The likes of the Lystrans, the Lairbenes too, had evidently been listening.

Not only were these increasingly numerous Christians of all ages, as the governor's dispatch reported, but they appeared immune to such deterrents as denunciation or trial. As well as prohibition and sometimes brutal persecution the authorities had also tried promotion, staging lavish spectacles in honour of the pagan and emperor gods, but their efforts seemed only to spur Christianity's advance across western Anatolia.

In the Lycus Valley – at the three cities of Colossae, Laodicea and Hierapolis – some of the first Christian missionaries had been operating for fully half a century; from around the time, in fact, of the letter that Paul, then under house arrest in Rome, had addressed to the people of Colossae.

Paul's 'Letter to the Colossians' served to steer the new religion's initiates with an impassioned blend of instruction, succour and correction. It also included some specific requests: that its contents were to be circulated among the Laodiceans, and that the people of Colossae should be sure to read the separate letter, since lost, that Paul had sent to Laodicea. These orders might have been passed over as nothing more than routine reminders of the need to foster common understanding among neighbouring Christian communities; particularly, that is, if Paul had addressed such a letter to the third city, Hierapolis, or specified that the other letters were also to be circulated there. That Paul contented himself, however, with merely passing on the respects of a fellow evangelist to the Christians of Hierapolis suggested that such differences as existed between the cities might merit investigation.

Of the three it was certainly Colossae and Laodicea that had the most in common, even if Laodicea – sumptuously endowed by the Seleucid kings, the residence of the Roman proconsul of Asia, home to a distinguished crowd of rhetoricians and the like – had outgrown its declining neighbour by the middle of the first century. For from their comparable locations on the valley floor the two cities had both prospered from the trade that flowed along the great highway, from the richness of the soil and from manufacture, particularly of garments woven from local wools prized for their softness and for 'their dark or raven colour'. The two cities were extensively Hellenised, moreover, and their cosmopolitan settler populations, Jews and Greeks especially, made for a devotional diversity.

Hierapolis, just six miles from Laodicea and as far again from Colossae, was distinctively different, with a conspicuously elevated, even sanctified setting on the southern slopes of Çökelez Mountain; a fitting location for the 'holy city', which even under Roman authority remained, in the words of Ramsay, 'the centre of native feeling and Phrygian nationality in the valley'. At Hierapolis paganism's roots ran deep.

The devotional piety that characterised Hierapolis was heavily cut, moreover, with a cultic, even orgiastic sensuality. For though the city's patron deity was Apollo, the same Lairbenos who had tyrannised his subjects from the nearby temple above the Meander on Çökelez's northern slopes, the primary influence largely resided with fecund Cybele: the Anatolian Earth Mother, She of the all-over dugs, whom by conflation the Ephesians knew as Artemis. For Hierapolis had long been a focus of an inherently Phrygian devotion to the primal life force. Women once honoured Cybele by serving as prostitutes, a sacred calling, in the courtyards of her temples. An ancient cult of the phallus had widely prevailed, one that a modern tourist trade in graphic clay figurines acknowledged. These satyrs, with their impressive erections, made tacit reference to a dark, chthonic deity known as the Echidna, which had risen from the earth's bowels at Hierapolis to impregnate the Mother Goddess and so spawn all life; to this swollen-cheeked dragon serpent the local population was once in thrall. Conception's special association with Hierapolis was reinforced, though the protagonist this time was female, when the third-century AD epic poet, Quintus of Smyrna, located there the ravishing by the moon goddess of mythical Endymion; the beautiful shepherd caught the eye of the goddess, Selene or Luna, who dosed him with some divine Rohypnol before subjecting the stupefied youth to a prolonged bout of procreation.

These unbridled associations and their attendant rites the mannered Greeks and Romans sought to moderate. They set about civilising Hierapolis with a veneer of seemliness, in part by promoting the healing properties of the city's famed thermal springs. This reminder, that the gods could restore people to health as surely as they made the transgressors among them ill, played a significant role in the recasting of Hierapolis. Under the aegis of medical deities like Aesculapius and Hygeia, who shared image rights on the city's coins with Apollo, the sacred massage parlour and place of conception progressively morphed into a halfway respectable health spa.

What did not change was Hierapolis's essential opposition to Christianity, to the point that the circulating there of letters that championed the subversive faith may well have been as foolhardy as the hawking of bibles in modern Mecca. The particular instructions Paul included in 'Colossians' may evidence, then, the care with which the new religion's proselytes trod in that bastion of paganism.

Not that Christianity's hagiographers, strangers to stealth or strategy, would have it so. According to the apocryphal 'Acts of Philip', excised by the New Testament's fourth-century editors, no doubt for exceeding plausibility's outer limits with mechanisms such as talking leopards, pagan Hierapolis spectacularly surrendered to Christ in the course of a productive visit by two of his apostles. John, fresh from a successful crusade against the Artemis cult at Ephesus, came with Philip to the city where 'the men of the place worshipped the snake and had images of it'. The natives proved predictably hostile; they bound Philip, piercing his wrists and thighs, and also vowed to drain every last drop of John's blood, to mix it with wine and serve it to the Echidna. When they came to take John, however, they found their hands had been paralysed. Philip turned up the heat by calling upon God to open up the earth and swallow the entire place, 'about 7,000 men, save where the apostles were'. Things had turned apocalyptic, even by apocryphal standards, by the time the risen Jesus appeared over the city. He rebuked Philip for his wrath and condemned the apostle not only to die but to endure a chastening delay of the statutory forty days before being admitted to Paradise. Jesus then released the 7,000 citizens of Hierapolis from the abyss, excepting from his mercy only the city's wicked authoritarian, the Roman proconsul, and the dreaded serpent itself.

So it was that Christianity took the city; the impressionable minds of the time could best account for the coming of a new age, and for the passing of the old one, by resort to the reductive certainties of fantasy epic. I had a hunch, however, that the 'Acts of Philip' might yield a more rational explanation for the same historical process, one Anatolia had repeatedly experienced, when I set out for Hierapolis the following morning.

Along the busy road out of Sarayköy sunlight streamed through the windows of the crowded *dolmuş*. It flashed on the cheap watches of the grizzled farmers, and with every pothole it jolted up the ginger twine binding the cardboard boxes with which the shawled women had immured themselves. Beyond the orange groves snow scraps glinted on the heights of Babadağ, Father Mountain, which faced Mount Çökelez from the south side of the valley. The *dolmuş* drew up at Denizli, the modern city that occupied the slopes above Laodicea's column-strewn ruins, and I transferred to a vehicle where I suddenly found myself among foreign tourists. The sight of all these elderly Germans and young Italians, the first Westerners that I had seen on my journey, caused me to bridle, and some time passed before I had worked out the stimulus to this powerful adverse reaction: it was the money belts and the padlocked rucksacks, and the guidebooks the tourists now consulted, apparently to guard against being overcharged for the cost of the bus ticket, which was about £1. After all the kindnesses I had received – from Mehmet Halil Blessed and Ali Ihsan Skirmisher, from the Fearless family and Mehmet Truehero, the proffered handfuls of green almonds, the tractor lifts, the fountains and clay jars, the gift of baklava and the glasses of tea – this default defensiveness added up to an affront; the assumption that they must expect trouble in Turkey had caused these visitors to don their travelling riot gear.

Not that such concerns would keep them from Hierapolis, a site firmly established on Turkey's tourism trail. For the place the Turks called Pamukkale (Cotton Castle), and eighteenth-century travellers Pococke and Chandler knew as the abbreviated 'Pambouk', now came with that top-drawer tag: World Heritage Site. Richard Chandler was certainly impressed. From his campsite at the foot of the cliff below Hierapolis he witnessed a view 'so marvellous, that the description of it, to bear even a faint resemblance, ought to appear *romantic*'. 'The warm waters here,' concurred Richard Pococke in his comparatively sober register, 'are the greatest natural curiosities in Asia.'

The bus passed restaurants and souvenir kiosks, to draw up somewhere near Chandler's one-time campsite. We removed our shoes and in the manner of pilgrims proceeded up the flank of a dazzling white hillside. Over the millennia, Çökelez's thermal springs had covered the hill in a thick calcareous deposit, which one early visitor compared to the shell of cuttlefish; this observation, visually accurate but no more appealing for that, Chandler improved upon by evoking the wider scene as 'an immense frozen cascade, the surface wavy, as of water in its headlong course suddenly petrified'.

To Quintus of Smyrna, however, the remarkable landscape at Hierapolis evidenced nothing less than the spillage that attended unbridled fecundity. 'There,' the poet related, 'Luna had once descended from the sky to Endymion, while he was sleeping by his herds; that marks of their bed were then extant under the oaks; and that in the thickets around it the milk of cows had been spilt, which men beheld still with admiration; for, such was the appearance, if you saw it very far off.' This description, though it ascribed the milky puddles to the leaking udders of Endymion's neglected charges, was sufficiently suggestive as to have left Quintus's readers in no doubt that they were in fact the surplus secretions, in keeping with the myth's insistent theme, of the loved-up swain himself.

The chemical reality, as Quintus conceded, was

that the landscape was in fact formed by 'clear or warm water, which in a little while concreted round about the channels, and formed a stone pavement'. That pavement, braided with rivulets of water, now lay beneath our feet. The steaming water spilled turquoise from the rims of scallop-shaped pools, which projected from the slope, rounded like art-nouveau balconies or nightclub stacks of cascading champagne glasses. The tourists, their trousers rolled, composed themselves into photographic poses among the so-called travertines. As ivories may denote piano keys, coppers coins, so the Turks did not distinguish between these signature formations and their substance, a marble-like stone formed from water-borne deposits of carbonated lime, which even today was quarried across the region.

Some five years earlier, in a factory east of Denizli, such a block of travertine was being sliced into floor tiles when a fossil was fortuitously exposed. The surviving section was from the skull of an early human. It was estimated to be several hundred thousand years old and was rich in identifying clues; a prominent brow ridge suggested that the subject was probably male, the degree of cranial closure indicating him to be aged between fifteen and forty years. Lesions consistent with tuberculosis were discovered, furthermore, in the skull. Susceptibility to tuberculosis in prehistoric times is generally associated with the inability of dark-skinned people to create sufficient vitamin

D. The palaeontologists therefore suspected that their man must have come from Africa.

Among such warm pools, where the tourists now took photographs, a distant wanderer had once lain down to die. I had not thought that our distant forebears might be embedded among such rocks, in the manner of ammonites, and even inhabit our banal surroundings – the tiles of shower walls, the floors of kitchens and car showrooms – with such haunting proximity.

These travertines, rich in association, had on an earlier visit impressed me as a one-off natural wonder; they were the most remarkable manifestation of a process that also turned earthen irrigation channels into lime-faced runnels, coated the paddles of the nineteenth-century watermills along the Lycus River so that they needed daily descaling, and left even today a crusty glaze across the paintwork of washed-down vehicles.

In the course of my journey down the Meander I had, however, come to see these calcite formations in a different light; as yet another, albeit extreme, manifestation of the surreal and suggestive featuring that characterised the wider landscape. Across these topographical borderlands steaming streams turned to milky stone as rivers ducked underground by shadowy swallow holes to emerge reborn from grottoes and caves. Springs bubbled into sudden lakes. Against the constant rumble of seismic activity – which lightning storms, like natural *son et lumière* shows, were said to attend

– age-old *höyük* mounds, sheer-sided gorges and gigantesque plane trees proliferated. These bizarre features extended beyond the river valley. To the north and east, in the Phrygian high country and across Cappadocia, rose rock formations the Turks knew as fairy chimneys but which convincingly resembled giant toadstools, over-sized hay stooks and, most compellingly, phalluses on a scale worthy of the Echidna itself. To the south, in Lycia, the perpetual fire that vented from a singular hill-side betrayed the lurking presence there of the fire-breathing monstrous Chimera. Back at Hierapolis, meanwhile, a gaping hellhole known as the Plutonium allowed the egress not only of the rampant Echidna but of gases so pestilential that asphyxiated birds had once plummeted from the sky.

The region's volatile geology was noted by Strabo who wrote how 'nearly the whole of the country about the Meander, as far as the inland parts, is subject to earthquakes, and is undermined by fire and water'. It was a land where nature had apparently tired of its more quiescent conventional role, as seasonal master of ceremonies, to emerge as an act in its own right; a wilful and spirited bill-topper, which accounted for the ubiquitous sacred groves, holy springs, river gods, sacrificial rites, underworld presences and other manifestations of an entrenched nature cult. The paradox was that Christianity had by the third century made more headway here, in Phrygia, than anywhere else. By some counter-intuitive process, though the landscape bristled with pagan installations, Phrygia of all places had proved the new religion's beachhead.

All manner of reasons have been suggested to explain this striking advance: chiefly, that the sheer profusion of the pagan gods, and the availability of a manufactured deity for every eventuality, might have seemed unduly pragmatic, cynical even, compared to Christianity's devotional constancy; that paganism's view of sin, an outward contamination one might salve by sacrifice, by sprinklings of water or blood, was plainly otiose, even intellectually simple-minded, compared to Christianity's intriguing proposition that sin might lie within, and it might even be within one to combat it there; that paganism generally promised to deliver in this life, which it but arbitrarily succeeded in doing, while Christianity could never be known to fail, at least not demonstrably, in its pledge to deliver in the next; and, finally, that the imperial persecutions, which one second-century theologian called the seed of the church, had by claiming high-profile Anatolian victims, among them saints as familiar as George and Valentine, dotted the landscape of the third century with the chapels of local martyrs, which were to serve as rallying points for the Faith.

In the case of the Lycus Valley, however, the timely occurrence of a momentous natural event may have been quite as influential in Christianity's advance as all these factors combined; the massive earthquake that was known to have levelled the region in AD 60. There may be no rational way of accounting for much in the 'Acts of Philip', not least talking leopards, but the gaping abyss into which Philip cast the population of Hierapolis may preserve a memory of the catastrophic rupturing of the seismic fault which attended the great earthquake, a fault which even today visibly runs through the site.

The same earthquake's dramatic effects may also inform some of the Christian legends associated with nearby Colossae. There the local pagans, pantomime villains to a tee, had attempted to destroy the church by diverting the course of the River Lycus. They had not reckoned on the Archangel Michael who, invoked by the local priest, struck with his staff a rock, which duly gaped open to accommodate the rushing waters. The city was subsequently known as Chonae, or funnel, in honour of the sudden appearance of the subterranean sluice that saved the church and thereby caused the Church to flourish.

The earthquake appeared as a sacred endorsement, then, of triumphant Christianity; by the same logic the local pagans could hardly fail to read anything but divine displeasure in the spectacular disappearance of their settlements and rivers alike. Nature, the very pulse of Phrygian paganism, had itself overthrown the lands, even the sacrificial temples, of its own devotees. Here, then, was one cause of the chill foreboding that passed among the pagan gods and their agents, and which we have already sensed on the northernmost slopes of Çökelez Mountain, where the devotees at the sanctuary shrine of Apollo Lairbenos were made to feel the additional weight of their increasingly insecure god's tyrannical hand.

Apollo, it happened, was represented at the Hierapolis Museum, though no such end-of-days uncertainty dogged his image. On the panels of a frieze recovered from the city's theatre the god appeared at the height of his authority; he was at the headwaters of the Meander, overseeing the flaying he had ordered. As a beast hung by trussed hocks from a meathook the bound Marsyas was being stripped of his skin.

It was an image that had proved resonant through ancient times, serving a purpose primarily political rather than purely artistic. Representations of Marsyas in his agony, images and statues alike, were tacit reminders of the natives' subject status. Like CCTV cameras, patrolling police squads or Big Brother posters, they were an integral part of the age's security apparatus. They were a blunt expression of imperial, and Apollonian, power.

That power derived from the god's broad portfolio of interests – music and justice, the sun and the harvest – but it was on account of his prophetic expertise that Apollo especially prospered. Devotees endowed lavish oracular temples to the god who knew the future, most famously at Delphi in Greece, but most numerously along the littorals of western Anatolia, where they spent fortunes securing access to his advice.

Given this prophetic knack, it is tempting to assume, of course, that Apollo of all the deities must have foreseen that it could not last; that he and his power must die as the gods of Arzawans and Hittites, Persians and Phrygians had died before him. The devotional momentum, for one thing, was evidently with Jesus Christ – though the first signs of Apollo's decline were instead implicit in the voices that began to be raised on behalf of a rival from an older tradition: Marsyas. In a process that started around the first century BC the satyr who was once regarded as deserving victim began to be represented as freedom's symbol, especially in Rome where he came to symbolise plebeian rights. His statue was raised in the forum, the centre of Roman political activity, where it became a focus for demonstrations and served as a poster board for anti-authoritarian verses. The power struggle between the common people and the elite, which came to dominate Roman political debate, was mirrored by the contest between Marsyas and Apollo; coins carried satyr and god, one on each side. One coin, minted in 80 BC, represented Marsyas as wearing the *pilleus*, or Phrygian cap; this item of headgear, originally denoting little more than the Eastern otherness – barbarianism, in short – with which the Anatolian lands were closely associated, came to be recast as the badge of freedom, an association it was to retain even until the French Revolution. Ovid was repeatedly drawn to side with Marsyas, and in later evocations of the story it was increasingly easy to tell where the sympathies of Dante, Titian, Caravaggio and the like substantially lay. The appalling fate of the tree-bound Marsyas even came to stand as a non-cruciform version of Christ's passion. It was inevitable, of course, that the satyr's reinvention as redeemed martyr should have exposed the divine disciplinarian as amoral torturer.

Despite this onslaught by an increasingly politicised urban underclass, Apollo and his agents clearly recognised Christ as the main threat to their authority. Apollo, whose local proxy had defended his patch by wringing public loyalty oaths from the Lairbenes, now deployed his extensive oracular influence to shore up his embattled position. Apollo's oracles began actively to champion the piety of ancestral belief. They then went on the offensive, advising supplicants as to how they might deter family members who had shown an interest in Christianity and increasingly cutting their prophecies with sideswipes against 'those who have forsaken the ways of their ancestors'. They condemned those who worshipped the mortal remains, torn and broken, of Jesus Christ. With the passing of the centuries, however, these utterances looked like desperate attempts at self-justification.

It was in the year 303 that Apollo made one of

his last recorded utterances. The Emperor Diocletian asked Apollo's great oracle at Didyma, near the mouth of the Meander, what he was to do about the increasing disobedience of the empire's Christians. The oracle's response was that the impious hindered Apollo's ability to provide advice. On the court's insistence that the oracular reference to the impious could refer only to the Christians, Diocletian acceded to demands that the minority faith be exposed to state-sanctioned persecution. Apollo thereby put his name to the razing, slaughter, burning and boiling that followed. The trademark cruelty that had begun with the flaying of Marsyas was not to save him; ten years later, as Christianity was first legalised across the empire, it was apparent that Apollo's final utterances had merely foretold the end of Apollo.

The city's healing gods had fared better, if only because their sacred pool retained its former function. A large sign confirmed the various conditions that the pool's thermal waters were known to benefit; these included diseases relating to 'head function', blood pressure, obesity, chronic gastritis, constipation, catarrhal diseases of the upper respiratory tract, bronchitis and inflammatory rheumatic disorders. In a case, in short, of blisters and weary muscles, a dip could do no harm.

The one-time home of nymphs and dryads was occupied by coachloads of the tourists who daily descended upon Hierapolis; swim-suited Russians swam briskly past, exhaling in chesty Slavic satisfaction, as I settled upon the weed-festooned flutings of a half-submerged column. Plumes of tobacco smoke rose from tables across the poolside patio where waiters brought tea and beer. In the warm water I lazed for the first time in weeks and let my thoughts drift.

I reflected how the sacred pool had continued in use all through the centuries of Hierapolis's ruination. A local *ağa* arrived to bathe, it so happened, at the time of Richard Chandler's visit in the 1760s. It proved a fraught encounter; the *ağa*, backed by 'a considerable retinue', proved implacably hostile, alleging that Chandler 'had knowledge of hidden treasure, and had already filled with it the provision chests, which he had seen by our tent'. Of this imaginary hoard the *ağa* demanded a substantial share. Chandler's party, 'apprehensive of immediate violence', fled without delay.

I wondered what had prompted me to recall this episode, which appeared historically remote, until it struck me that the same misunderstandings and suspicions persisted even today; they were evident, indeed, in the money belts and padlocked ruck-sacks I had noticed that very morning. Westerners persisted in the traditional view that Turks were roguish thieves – as Turks maintained their equivalent assumption that Westerners were diabolically clever ones whose educated noses always led them to treasures hidden on lands not their own. Just as Westerners had learned to keep their possessions close in Turkey, so Turks knew not to sell trowels to their guests.

The Westerners were way off in their preconceptions, as my own experiences had so comprehensively taught, but the Turks were no more correct in theirs; it was the locals who had caused the greater destruction, though largely out of ignorance rather than malice, of the land's ancient treasures. Visiting antiquaries and scholars were commonly horrified by the extent to which inscribed stones, even statuary, were blithely recycled as building material. Charles Fellows once noted a statue – the 'beautiful body of a child, about a foot or eighteen inches long, with one arm over its breast' which had been 'built into the wall of a house; the head and legs had been broken off'. Carved pieces were commonly mutilated to adorn gravestones; stone cutters traditionally set up shop at 'quarries of white marble wherever the remains of a temple are to be found'. Fellows also noted a headstone hacked from 'a robed female statue of white marble, stuck head and shoulders downwards into ground; the projecting feet had been broken off, but the folds of the drapery showed that the statue must have been of good Greek workmanship'. At Denizli Reverend Arundell watched a 'stonemason, who was chipping most unmercifully a beautiful frieze, to accommodate it to a Turkish tombstone'. Troughs and cisterns were recycled from 'pedestals, capitals of columns or tombs'; roadside wells with 'Attic bases of columns perforated, and placed over the mouths' as copings were commonly encountered. Inscribed blocks served as hearths and doorsteps.

This wholesale destruction of artefacts continued into the twentieth century, and with the connivance of the Turkish state. William Guthrie, commissioned to seek out and copy ancient epigraphs across Anatolia during the 1930s, ruefully conceded how 'in the advancement of civilisation the making of roads comes before the preservation of ancient monuments . . . Many an inscription is ground up for road metal, and more go into the walls of the Government's schools which are springing up.' Inscribed stones poked from newly built railway platforms. In one village Guthrie was called over 'to where building was actually in progress to see, before it took its place in the wall, a little tomb-relief, a quaint representation of a native art which must have been almost untouched by Greek or Roman influences'.

After my soak I dressed and continued my tour of Hierapolis. The staff of the Italian Archaeological Mission, guardians of the city's Roman heritage, were busy erecting interpretive notice boards. Red poppies bloomed between the quake-shaken ashlar seats of the theatre. Mottled lizards, motionless but for their pulsing throats, clung to the carved mouldings of fallen architraves. I walked north until I had cleared the main settlement where I followed the course of an ancient processional way through the ruin-strewn grasslands. It led to a Byzantine building: an impressive octagonal hall, its dome long since collapsed, with arched doorways leading to a ring of outer chambers. It was the martyrium, or sacred burial place of St Philip, which appeared to acknowledge that a further fact – the apostle's death at Hierapolis – was preserved among the fantastic details packed into the apocryphal 'Acts'. The martyrium, which dated from the fifth century, was designed to lodge the pilgrims who increasingly visited the holy place through Christianity's early period.

These pilgrims, weathered from the long road, had no doubt followed the path up through the remarkable travertines. They continued beyond the great baths and the sacred pool to pass a colonnaded building, which they no longer had cause to notice. For the few who now entered the Temple of Apollo did so with the same furtive discretion that the first Christians must once have shown in Hierapolis – if, that is, the pagan temple had not already been closed or requisitioned by the adjacent theatre for the storage, say, of props and other such stage devices.

CHAPTER 15

I breakfasted at the outlet store where the security guards had entertained me some nights before. Amid the chrome and glass of the café, stacks of plastic serving trays shook to the celebratory beat of Galatasaray's footballing triumph. The boy at the till, whose T-shirt declared *Dance Hall – Fervent*, rang up my double portion of *börek*, a steppe lasagne of sorts that was filled with crumbly white cheese and parsley, and my glass of black tea; the very first tea, in fact, that I had paid for on the entire journey. The purchase appeared to signal the end of the exemptions I had enjoyed in the uplands, as the thyme fields had given way to factories, the fob watches to T-shirts and the horse-drawn carts to refrigerated lorries, at least until my bottle of mineral water brought the boy up short. He set the water aside.

'You don't want to buy that,' he advised, pointing out the fountain on the patio at the front of the mall. With its futurist taps and stainless-steel case, this minimalist dispenser was of a part with the café. It might have furnished the open-plan offices of some metropolitan design agency. Even so, the fountain did a job no different from the clay jars of the back roads. At this mission post of Westernised retailing they could not bring themselves to charge for the drinking water they themselves stocked. Heartened, I filled the steel beaker I found at the fountain and crossed the patio of polished travertine, where the ghosts of wandering hominids lay compressed, to eat at a sunlit table.

In the upturned canoe, which I had left in the wheat field below the bridge, spiders had set up home. I shook them free, wicking away their cobweb skeins, and dragged the dewy craft down to the water. It was only now I noticed that the river had broadened considerably since absorbing the flow of the Lycus. Remembering how Cyrus's Greek mercenaries had required a bridge supported by seven pontoons to get them across this stretch of the Meander, it seemed safe to assume that fallen willows, however diabolically they might combine, would no longer block my progress.

The river had also recovered the trademark character it had comprehensively lost all through the gorge; the largely undeviating arc of its steep descent now gave way to windings more expansive yet than the ones that had waylaid me back in the first days of my journey. The loops that now carried my canoe north and south, even back towards the east, were more capacious than ever. This was to be expected; it was along the broad lower valley that the Meander most famously strayed, expressing its freedom by following a course so convoluted that 'the letters of the Grecian alphabet', as one seventeenth-century traveller observed, appeared inscribed in it. What struck me was that rivers and humans covered the ground in oddly antithetical ways – the same steepening gradients that put the twists and turns into men's mountain roads and paths being precisely what led rivers to straighten. The converse was also true; where the ground levelled off, and the kinks disappeared from those footpaths and roads, was where rivers began to wander.

Rivers were not subject, of course, to turned ankles or brake failure, theirs being a life free from all fear of falling; but while this immunity might account for the headlong descents that rivers favoured, it did not explain why the broad plain should cause them to lose all sense of direction, this river most dramatically, as it did that morning.

Men had speculated as to the reasons for the Meander's windings. Strabo thought it might have something to do with the soil, which he described as 'dry and easily reduced to powder, full of salts, and very inflammable'. The underlying principle was, in fact, one of differential; what caused the outer wheels of a cornering vehicle to revolve more quickly, covering a greater distance in order to keep up with the nearside ones, similarly encouraged a river's flow to run fastest at the outer bank – thereby causing the greater scouring to occur there. This erosion necessarily deepened the curve at the far bank even as the silt scoured upstream was deposited on account of the comparatively slack current along the near one; these two forces working in concert, in short, were what deepened the river's bends. The slightest kink in a river's course was subject to this cumulative process; a silt transfer, working like strong liquor, which caused the river to weave across the plain.

Not that the Meander's mazy twists disturbed me that morning. In fact, I hadn't felt so happy for a long time. I was quite content, mindful of the trouble I had had on the Yenice stretch, to follow wherever that wide and sedate stream took me. It particularly pleased me that the river had come to resemble the one I had initially imagined. As the canoe bow swung through the compass bearings, so my mind wandered free, for once without the least practical consideration to dictate its direction, and the river I travelled at last proved true to its name.

I had often wondered, knowing all that it had come to mean in modern contexts, what the river's name had originally signified. Its etymological journey had begun in one of the original and no doubt interrelated languages, now all but lost, of the ancient regions where it flowed; from its sources the Meander passed through Phrygia before leaving that land to form the historic boundary between Lydia and Caria – at about the point where I now found myself. Since none of the recovered Phrygian, Lydian or Carian inscriptions makes mention of the river, the earliest surviving form is the Greek Maiandros, which carries no hint of the name's original meaning. All it gives us is a distorted echo of how the word might have sounded – but an echo that may not be beyond restoration. One verifiable fact about these ancient languages is that their place names commonly concluded with 'anda', as this cluster of vowels and consonants is best transcribed, which raises the intriguing likelihood that the modern English version of the river's name may happen to be a pleasingly phonetic match with the original.

I had had reason to think about the river's name and the evolution of its etymology the previous evening. I found myself at an empty kebab restaurant in Sarayköy where the waiter, making an exception for the foreigner, sent out for beer, which arrived in a brown paper bag, prohibition-style, along with the whispered request that I keep it beneath the table.

The forbidden brew went down well. In fact, those surreptitious sips on top of the afternoon's long soak at Hierapolis soon reduced me to a kind of meditative stupor in which the restaurant's décor had my glazed attention. For a long time I scrutinised the kitsch wall painting of a silvered tumbling river spanned by a timber bridge before transferring my attention to the patterned paper border, discoloured and peeling, which ran round the restaurant walls. I had noticed the same pattern at Hierapolis, where it was engraved across the old masonry, and around the border of the doormat at my Sarayköy lodgings; a repeat sequence of rectilinear spirals, like a succession of cresting waves, and widely known as the Greek key. Since at least the first century BC, when Virgil used the word to describe a cloak hem's decoration, the pattern has also been known as the meander.

This ubiquitous band or border motif and its related variants are known to have occurred from China and the South Sea Islands to Mexico. It is with the ancient Greeks and their Roman successors, however, no doubt for the prominence of their decorative legacy – their stonework, pottery and coinage, of course, as well as their clothing – that the pattern is most closely associated. It was a common motif on glazed pottery as early as the eighth century BC, and had acquired identifiable associations by the fifth century BC; on vases featuring the Minoan myth of the Minotaur the pattern signified the Cretan labyrinth where Theseus had tracked the monstrous bull. A more recent, anthropological assertion is that the pattern simply reflected the age-old design naturally created by woven reeds along the edge of a hand-worked basket. Others saw stylised serpents, adjudged the pattern a symbol of infinite cyclical recurrence, or even detected in it an ideogram of the human face.

The most oft-invoked association, however, was with water. The pattern commonly decorated the walls and mosaic floors of Greco-Roman bath-houses. The columns and walls of ancient temples, traditionally sited on holy springs, also featured it. Most compellingly persuasive, however, was that the pattern, however stylised, patently represented water not only as the cross-sectioned wave but from another, equally archetypal perspective: as a rectilinear rendering of a meandering river's aerial view. These associations confirmed an ancient reverence, which somehow appeared to have survived in modern Turkey, to judge by the girls' names – River, Spring, Rain – and the roadside taps and clay jars, even the textile factory's logo and, finally, the instinctive reluctance of the boy in the *Dance Hall – Fervent* T-shirt to sully the stuff, and his common humanity, by selling it to me.

It was an exquisite morning. Across a blue sky storks beat upstream until their white plumages were lost against the high snows of Babadağ. The river coiled broad and clear across the plain, gradually trending towards the valley's southern edges. Wild olives, hazed in the swaggering lowland heat, grew from the reddish rock slopes. A fig tree, choked in vines, murmured with bees and cicadas. I passed beneath a bridge where a red-ruled marker post showed 2.5 metres of water, and with a jolt of joy I figured that nothing could now stop the brimful river from delivering me to the Aegean.

It was then that I came to a place signposted as Feslek, a name that was vaguely familiar, where the black gates of a regulator reared lock-like between the banks. At the base of this metal barrier churned a bolus of rotted weed, plastic bottles and discoloured chunks of polystyrene. From the walkway running along the top a man was waving me in the direction I had come. I paddled upstream to put ashore at a shingle shelf. I dragged the laden canoe through the knee-length grass of an untended olive grove, thinking to return to the river below the gates until I saw what lay there. The river had disappeared.

The locals had repeatedly warned me, of course, that I would find no water on the Meander; but as this had usually turned out to mean insufficient water to allow passage of whatever craft it was that they imagined me to possess, invariably something larger and more deep of draught than my canoe, such statements had soon ceased to alarm me. The security guard at the outlet store had clearly meant it, however, when he told me that there was no water at Feslek. Beyond the regulator there was not so much as a puddle. The damp seam that ran dark down the middle of the riverbed was flanked with a peeling crust of dry mud. I remembered how Mehmet, the tufted caretaker at the Işıklı Lake dam, had at least been on hand to offer encouragement the last time anything like this had happened. There was nothing positive, however, that this watchman could possibly say to a canoeist. The only utterance was my own.

'Gone,' I intoned, slack-jawed.

'Gone,' the watchman confirmed. 'For hydro-electricity and irrigation,' he added, motioning that I follow him across the walkway. Here the water disappeared in a high-pressure tumble, just as it had done at Işıklı, but this time in sufficient quantities to fill two broad concrete canals. Beside the brimming canals stood a sign. *Let's Keep Our Water Clean*, it urged. I asked the watchman if he knew of any plans to open the gates.

'Oh, only if they need to meet irrigation demand downstream,' he said. 'Or' – he wrinkled his nose – 'when the rubbish needs flushing through.'

'How far do you reckon before there's water in the river again?' The watchman cast an open palm up the empty river bed, as if I must find out for myself, though the gesture appeared to concede that it might be a while. He offered tea to see me on my way.

It increasingly occurred to me that the story of the region had for some time been following my own progress down the Meander, and in good chronological order. The river and its history unspooled as one. It was therefore fitting, consolingly so, that I should have run out of water just as I came up against a major historical blockage. The Byzantine Age, a millennium, roughly calculated, appeared as much a challenge to the continuance of my Anatolian journey as any drained river bed.

For from their first appearance in the fourth century the Byzantines had always appeared an exclusively metropolitan lot, with no easily imagined place out in the Anatolian provinces: the very name by which they are known to the modern world exclusively associates the people of the Eastern Roman Empire – ever the *Romaioi*, or Romans, as they styled themselves – with the great city of Byzantium. The empire takes its very dates from their occupation of the city on the Bosphorus which their founding emperor was soon to rename in his honour; what began with Constantine's adoption of the city as his capital in the year 324 ended with Constantinople's loss to the Turks in 1453. It is no surprise, then, that urban backdrops should materialise unbidden in any evocation of the Byzantines: the gilded chambers of Constantinople's Great Palace, for example, or the offices of the holy Patriarchate, or the domed interior of the Haghia Sophia basilica where these chamberlains and tributes, presbyters and patriarchs performed their arcane rituals, intrigued and pointed ring-laden fingers grown long with the endless scoring of obscure philosophical points.

All of which inevitably consigned the Byzantine legacy across the Anatolian provinces – the land they knew as *Romania* – to a corresponding faintness. In the Meander Valley, in fact, it appeared to the modern traveller that the Byzantine centuries had been subjected to a campaign of concerted erasure. No trace remained of the evocative objects – icons fashioned from heated wax, painted books of purple parchment and silver ink, gilded iconostases and gold altar cloths – which were the stuff of their culture. Then there were their structures, which Turkish archaeologists had not always respected in their haste to uncover the classical ones beneath them. In the process of the Byzantine decline and extinction many churches like that of the revered St Michael the Archangel at Colossae had been sacked; others had been turned into mosques. Going back over my journey, the only expressly Byzantine remains I had seen were the monastic cells hewn into the cliffs of the Meander gorge, and the martyrium of St Philip at Hierapolis.

These ruins were not much to go on. They did serve, however, to confirm that the sacrifices of Paul, Philip and the rest had borne fruit in Byzantine Anatolia; Christianity had triumphed there. They might even have been cues as to the particular character of that society – the pilgrims who made devotions to martyred apostles, and the penitents who found fulfilment in the ascetic example of Egypt's Desert Fathers, the devout and the marginalised retiring to remote monasteries and hermitages to lead lives by turn communal and solitary. So I now perceived those abandoned rock caves as home to communities committed to poverty, spiritual wealth and the service of the sick and the indigent. I pictured the monks who lived out their lives after the examples of the blessed saints, in prayer, study and contemplation, in the tending of their plots and the pounding of grain, in treating the sick and in giving alms to the poor. The land prospered under the tenure of Christianity's guiding principles.

Except that this is to ignore the faith's zealous aspect, which had been increasingly to the fore from the moment Christianity was legalised in the year 312; the time had come to turn on the pagans who had once persecuted the early Christians. From the end of the fourth century, when Christianity was declared the Roman world's only legitimate religion, religious dissent was no longer tolerated. In the sixth century the Emperor Justinian, builder of the great basilica of Haghia Sophia in Constantinople, ordered: 'If any unholy or defiled pagan does not make himself manifest, whether living here or in the countryside, and run to the churches with his household, that is to say wives and children, let him submit to the aforesaid penalties, let the revenue confiscate their property, and let them be given over to exile.'

The work that occupied some Byzantine monks, then, was the razing of pagan temples. John, Bishop of Ephesus, set about converting the pagans of the lower Meander in the year 542. 'When God opened the minds of [the pagans] and made them know the truth,' he wrote, 'he aided us in destroying their temples, in overturning their idols, in eradicating the sacrifices which were offered elsewhere, in smashing their altars defiled by the blood of sacrifices offered to pagan gods, and in cutting down the numerous trees which they worshipped, and so they became estranged from all the errors of their forefathers. The saving sign of the cross was implanted everywhere amongst them, and churches of God were founded in every place.' Over a period of thirty years the bishop reckoned that he and his shock troops had forcibly converted some 80,000 pagans.

Even so, the old beliefs endured. When a city north of the Meander Valley, Pergamum, came under siege in 717, a sorcerer persuaded some desperate residents that they might spur themselves to a last-ditch defence by sacrificing to the pagan gods. A pregnant woman was found and killed, her foetus boiled in a cauldron in which the citizens sought divine protection by dipping their right hands prior to taking up arms. These diabolical rituals prevented neither the city's fall nor the slaughter of its citizens; a chronicler of the Pergamum siege judged that the god of the Christians, appalled as ever at such pagan atrocities, had allowed the city to be overrun.

It did not occur to this Christian chronicler that the besiegers must have seen it differently; the men who fought their way into Pergamum were not Byzantines reducing the last outposts of paganism, but raiders from the Arab lands who inevitably credited their success not to the retributive Christian god but to the active support of their own, newly revealed one. In Byzantine Constantinople Christianity might have continued to reign supreme for over a thousand years. Across much of Anatolia, however, the Christian centuries appeared abbreviated by the persistent paganism at their back and the advance of Islam before them. Christ's enforcers, as events at Pergamum in 717 revealed, were yet to eradicate the last of the pagans before the first of the Muslims swept in from the south.

I drank tea with the watchman and left the bagged-up boat in his care. With a supportive slap across the shoulders, the watchman saw me on my way. There was nothing for it but to continue along the river on foot.

The going was not good. With every step the crusted mud yielded to a fetid green smear. I slid and stumbled down the silent course. The leaves of the bank-side willows were brown and brittle; their roots poked from the collapsed banks like rusted cables. Desiccated tresses of river weed, brittle and grey, lay as they had once streamed upon the water, seawards, a sun-cast memory of current. The birds had fled but for a single heron, which stabbed at the putrefied remains of a turtle. The State Water Works had turned the Meander into a stinking gully, a rubbish flush, and then they had erected a sign that lectured the local people on the need to keep the water clean.

I stumbled on, tired and outraged, until a square grey building rose above the banks. It was a hydro-electric station. Above the protruding metal pipes and sluices the words *Abundance Energy* were painted large across the walls.

CHAPTER 16

I had barely returned to the path the following morning when the river got some of its water back. The diverted flow, having passed through *Abundance Energy*'s turbines, rejoined the Meander immediately beyond the power station; just not enough of it to float a canoe nor even, apparently, to stop a man from crossing on a moped.

I watched the man squeeze his aged machine through a gap in the cobweb-starred trees and brambles lining the far bank. Then he sped down the slope into the Meander's bed, barely slowing for the water. The same river that Cyrus's expeditionary Greeks had crossed only with the aid of seven pontoons – and which an impressive Roman bridge, all six stone arches of it, had once spanned at nearby Antiocheia – this man now forded without wetting his shoes.

From those shoes, and from the man's flat cap, tattered suit and even his moped, all colour had long since leached. Only his face and hands, a deep varnished walnut, relieved the monochrome effect. With a sharp twist of the throttle the man gunned his moped up the bank, trailing blue exhaust, only to brake at the sight of me. He wished me good morning, offering a calloused hand.

'You must be the foreigner I read about in the *New Century*,' he said. 'Except they said you were travelling by boat.'

'For that I'd need water,' I replied tartly. I was curious for my part how long it was since the farmer had first been able to cross the Meander on two wheels.

'On and off, all through the drought years,' he reflected. 'Just twenty years ago these fields regularly flooded in the winter. Back in my childhood, in the 1950s, the current even in summer was so strong that our parents only let us swim if we promised to stay close to the banks. The only way across in those days was to wait for the ferry.' The farmer described a flat-bottomed timber raft with a knee-height gunwale, a stout fixing post and a wide stern, of the sort that had operated at various points along the Meander's lower reaches. This transport, which

the local ferrymen winched across by a cable secured between the banks, was typically capable of carrying perhaps twenty passengers, along with a cart, some livestock, or even the occasional motor vehicle.

By effectively the same arrangement earlier travellers had crossed the Meander. What Richard Chandler called 'a triangular float, with a rope', Richard Pococke detailed as 'a sort of boat like a sledge in shape of a half lozenge, the sides of it not being about a foot high. They tie vine boughs together, which are about an inch and a half diameter, and from ten to fifteen feet long, which are fixed across the river; a post in the boat rests against it, and keeps the vessell from being carried down by the stream and by the help of this three men pull the boat from one side to the other.' Such river crossings had not changed in their essentials between the mid-1700s and the mid-1900s; from the 1950s, however, industrialisation had begun transforming the valley.

As for the drought, this was not the first I had heard of it. Since Dinar the lack of water had been the talk of the tea houses. Farmers and smallholders glanced skywards and with a shrug gave themselves up to Allah's plan; they submitted to the caprices of divine will, at once absolving their fellow men of responsibility. The statistics might confirm that Turkey had indeed received less rainfall than its customary portion in recent years, but it was also the case that just ten kilometres upstream the Meander brimmed with two and a half metres of water. The real problem was the concrete culverts, which smuggled away every last drop, and the vast volumes of river water retained behind the dams at Adıgüzel and Çindere, not forgetting the additional waters that would be withheld to fill the dam now being built there. I had barely begun to fulminate against the dams, culverts and regulators, however, when the farmer began to lose interest. He who had been pleased to reminisce now appeared awkward, apparently finding his time to be short. I was in mid-flow when he wished me good travels, kicked his moped into life and drove off into the morning, casting a beseeching look at the cloudless sky.

Back, now, to the Byzantines and the faintness of the impression they had left beyond the city; a more substantial bar to sensing their presence in provincial Anatolia may in fact be that they were often short of Anatolian provinces, at least ones they could unconditionally call their own. The Byzantine emperors who went east did so not to tour peaceable provinces but to contest ones they had recently lost.

For the peace secured under Roman rule had begun to fray by the sixth century. Anatolia once more found itself overrun by invaders, and not for the first time from the Asian East. A thousand years after Xerxes had crossed into Europe the campfire plumes of the latest Persian dynasty, the Sassanids, rose from the eastern shores of the

Bosphorus. Then the Saracen Arabs, newly aflame with the revelations of the Divine Prophet, poured through the Taurus Mountains, the formidable rampart at Anatolia's southern rim, during the seventh and eighth centuries. They swept north beyond the Meander Valley where they sacked cities such as Pergamum, and on three occasions even besieged Constantinople itself.

These regular *razzia*, or raids, might have marked the very seasons in Anatolia; every spring the Saracens came from the south and every autumn, as the mornings turned chill, they led their spoil-laden camels back to homes in the Levant and Arabia. In their wake they left smoking ruins, tumbled apses and trampled fields, the communities reduced by slaughter and abduction, and stripped of provisions and what few valuables they possessed.

The Arab raids certainly brought depopulation, dread and hunger, but the country Byzantines learned to endure; the Saracens would pass as surely as tax collectors, locust swarms, earthquakes and conscription officers. Insecurity had always appeared in the weave of the contested land. The raids, though they continued for centuries, only confirmed the fundamentally conditional nature of Anatolian existence. A consequence of the Byzantines' forbearance, stiffened by their faith, was that the Arabs failed to maintain a permanent presence in Anatolia. William Ramsay went so far as to claim that they 'never held a foot of land beyond Taurus outside the range of their weapons at the moment'.

Those Byzantines who by chance or by their age survived the *razzia* were left to pray for a few years' grace. They wished only that they might be granted time to rebuild their churches and restock their herds, plant their fields and replenish their granaries, repair their threshing floors and raise their walls, and all the while watch their boys put on fighting sinew. They knew they must expect to fight again. If anything gave historic purpose to the provincial Byzantines, it was their achievement in denying the Saracens, at their own great cost, the Anatolian platform whereby they might finally have reduced Constantinople. The city was the very key, of course, to the continent beyond, and the Saracens' failure to take Constantinople stemmed the Arab advance into Europe, diverting its flow to the south, along the coast of North Africa, so that Islam would first penetrate Christendom not by the eastern marches but by its Iberian underbelly. The forgotten heroics of these provincial Byzantines, their memory all but erased across their Anatolian lands, were to have the most profound effect upon European history. Without them, the Arabs might have made the West their own as Alexander had made the East his a thousand years before. As it was, the Arabs were to leave only the faintest mark upon Anatolian culture.

Which could not be said of the next lot of invaders – whom Byzantine fortitude could do nothing to deflect. They came this time from the vast Eurasian steppe, which lay north-east beyond the Caucasus Mountains and the Caspian Sea. These grasslands, irregularly watered, turned from green to tawny with the seasons. Any settlements that sprouted there withered under the alternating effects of summer sun and winter freeze; a shortage of natural defences left the rest vulnerable to sack. The only thing for it was to travel light and chase down the sudden sweet greening beneath the rain clouds where the herds might grow sleek and rich in milk. To this end alone the steppe people roamed, no doubt in the familiar orbit of their forebears, but unburdened by sentimental attachment and only for so long as the ancestral lands continued to serve. In times of drought, or if a succession of good years had so swelled the herds that the traditional pastures could not sustain them, the nomads were suddenly gone, the steppe coughing up whole tribes and hawking them in the direction of whatever settled peoples happened to lie in their path. Some centuries before, just such a migratory paroxysm had carried the Mongolian Huns and the central Asian Avars westwards, shunting into the tribes they encountered there through the fifth century; the people they displaced, the Goths and Vandals among them, duly overran the Western Roman Empire. Something similar was now about to befall the Byzantines in the Roman East.

In the Anatolian lands that were destined to bear

their name the Turks had first registered only as a conscripted element among the Sassanid and Saracen raiding parties; a hardy steppe people who made excellent soldiers. These Turks originally hailed from the mountain fringes of the distant Gobi Desert – from that secret valley of legend Turkey's more fervent nationalists now knew as *Ergenekon*. The temptation was therefore to assume that the Turks had taken a very long run-up in breaking down the Byzantine door. In fact, they had meant no such thing; with only a modest name for metal working to distinguish them, and the watering whims of their sky god by way of propulsion, these animist nomads had seemed more interested in escaping their Chinese persecutors than in entertaining the least ambitions towards territories in the distant West.

By the eighth century, however, a complex combination of motives, unspecified but no doubt rooted in the exigencies of grass and ground, had energised certain tribes of Turks and caused these pigtailed nomads to muscle their way across the eroded ranges of central Asia and close on the Persian borderlands. Here, they honed the skills for which they were renowned, as horsemen and archers, and meantime discovered the foil for their martial zeal in the militant creed now pulsing out of its Arabian hub. The Turks took readily to Islam; the males, from sultans to soldiers, were thenceforth to favour the name of the Prophet, which their language rendered as Mehmet.

So the Turks' wanderings, no longer in thrall merely to the seasonal cycle, acquired a missionary sense of direction. With Persians and Arabs they came to contest not only the pastures on which they once had solely depended but the settled lands too. These steppe skirmishers now acquired the weapons and wherewithal to take cities. To the sound of the kettle drum, to the swish of the scimitar they took on all comers. By the eleventh century a federation of Turkish tribes known as the Selçuks, named for their founder, held sway over much of Persia. In 1045, with their first incursions into Anatolia, the Selçuks set their sights on the grasslands of Byzantium. Twenty-five years later, they had raided beyond the headwaters of the Meander to reach the Lycus Valley. In the nave of the great basilica at Chonae, built on the site of the fabled church St Michael the Archangel had once saved from the diverted waters of the pagans, these Muslim raiders now shook off their steppe dust, stabled their war horses and made plans to stay.

Ploughed fields ran from the banks of the straying river. The turned earth, which storks wandered on their jointed red legs, abutted expanses of wheat stubble, orchards of orange and pomegranate trees, ordered lines of walnut trees and olive groves. The view recalled the same alluring patchwork – 'the whole plain in highest state of cultivation, abounding with rich pasturage, cornfields, vineyards, olives and fig trees' – that Reverend Arundell had admired in earlier times. The valley had produced, after all, the famed 'Smyrna' figs and 'Sultana' raisins that the British, the Edwardians particularly, had consumed by the shipload 'to titivate fog-dulled appetites'. One visitor early in the twentieth century marvelled at bottomlands that 'have been cultivated from the beginning of history, and yet are so fertile as to make one question the possibility of their exhaustion'; the cornucopia that the bearded god Meander held aloft on the statues and coins appeared set to overflow through all time.

Except that the enriching silt had for the best part of twenty years not been nourishing the valley but accumulating uselessly at the foot of upstream dams. The water the Turks otherwise appeared to revere was, besides, largely missing. And the Meander smelt. At one bend, where there rose a rubbish heap, it smelt particularly bad. A shawled woman with holed gloves was picking through a smouldering strew of plastic bottles and cartons, tyres, shoes, tins, stained cardboard and bloated bin bags that spilt rot, viscera-like, from their split flanks. The smiling image of a nappy-swathed baby beamed from a scrap of polythene packaging; like the tourism map, whose legend did not include riverside rubbish heaps or the impoverished people who picked over them, the infant seemed oblivious to its surroundings.

★   ★   ★

Opposite where I knew the ruins of Antiocheia to stand, set back as they were some distance from the south bank, I kept a close eye on the Meander's shallows. I was hoping the low water might at least have exposed a river-bed remnant of some sort, perhaps an old pier footing or some other protrusion, to mark the site of the six-arched bridge that had featured on the coins of Roman Antiocheia. I found nothing; which, as the bridge had been down for a very long time – certainly since 1147 – should not have surprised me.

The bridge at Antiocheia, as its place on the coins acknowledged, had been a significant crossing for centuries; it was where the ancient valley road had switched riverbanks. Unlike the modern highway, which now kept north of the river as far as Sarayköy, crossing beside the newly built outlet store, the old road had taken to the south bank here, at Antiocheia, before continuing east to Laodicea.

It was by this same road that the diverted forces of the Second Crusade under the King of France were in 1147 obliged to travel if they were then to make south for the Mediterranean port of Adalia (modern Antalya) en route to the Holy Land. But the Meander bridge at Antiocheia had been destroyed, perhaps precisely to frustrate the Crusaders' advance, or it may have been reduced in the devastation to which the Meander Valley was generally subject, and which positively engulfed the region during the twelfth century.

Half a century had passed since an appeal for assistance by the Byzantine emperor had first brought the 'base and bastard Turks' to Western notice. By the 1090s the Turks were threatening Byzantine territory to a greater degree than the Arabs had ever done; their capture of Jerusalem from the Arabs had further galvanised the Christian West. The result, the First Crusade, had in the last years of the eleventh century achieved such glorious successes as to confirm the Christians' assumption that they could depend upon divine favour should they ever again need to take up the cross against the Eastern infidels. By roundly defeating the Turks at the bastion city of Dorylaeum and elsewhere, pushing them back into the Anatolian hinterland, the armies of the First Crusade had not only secured the land route to Jerusalem but also fulfilled the sanctified mission of restoring the holy city to Christian rule. They had even established a whole series of Latin state-lets – Outremer, or Beyond the Sea – across the wider region.

The fall in 1144 of one such possession on Anatolia's Syrian border, Edessa, had alerted the West that Islam was once more on the rise. It was time to reconfirm Christianity's pre-eminence in the East by serving God's wrath on the Turks, an altogether more formidable and alien race of Muslims than the Arabs. The summer of 1147 saw Western forces, boosted not only by the papal imprimatur but by the personal leadership of two

European sovereigns, gather under the banners of Louis VII of France and Conrad III of Germany.

The German Army was the first to leave the European mustering grounds. It led the advance to Constantinople where Byzantine observers – contemptuous of these knights' wayward religious ways but fearful of their impressive fighting abilities – put the army's size beyond computation. And this without reckoning on the French columns, which were to reach Constantinople by the same trampled road a month later. It was a formidable force, one whose strategists were unlikely to have heard of a Byzantine backcountry town called Antiocheia; certainly, they had no reason to suppose in even their most pessimistic calculations that the place was ever to figure in their advance across Anatolia.

For the once-great road up the Meander Valley, which led past little Antiocheia, had long since lost out to more northerly routes. These passed through Constantinople, the world's greatest city, so that the great highway to the Holy Land, choice of traders, pilgrims and soldiers alike, only touched the Meander at its source deep in the interior. This 'straight and level' road, which ran through Nicaea, Dorylaeum, Apamea and Iconion, was crucially the route the knights of the First Crusade had taken. Many of those who now took the cross under Louis and Conrad divined in the direct nature of their itinerary, a broadly straight line to the south-east, something of the unswerving purpose of that first crusading generation. They saw that exemplary venture as nothing less than a sanctified template for their own enterprise, in all manner of ways but above all in terms of their designated route to the Holy Land. In such a spirit Conrad, first to lead his armies across the Bosphorus into Asia, set out down that same straight road in October 1147. It was not long after, however, that he and his men were comprehensively routed by the Turks a short distance from the site of the great Crusader victory won fifty years earlier at Dorylaeum.

So much, then, for God's wrath at the Turks or for the certain bestowal of divine favour; a presumption many Christians might also have questioned when He had allowed Edessa to fall a few years earlier. The same God who had seen to things half a century earlier had now left the Crusaders to prove their own mettle against a demonstrably strengthened enemy, and amid the first falls of snow and increasingly acute shortages of food.

So the Crusaders' south-easterly route began, like a headed sailing ship, to stray south; advisers proposed that Louis's armies and the remnant of Conrad's ravaged force should abandon the straight road and instead make for the Byzantine-held city of Philadelphia. They would thereby avoid the worst of the mountains and, though they would not publicly concede the fact, skirt what effectively amounted to Turkish territory. The diversion acknowledged the power shift that had taken place in Anatolia since the time of the First Crusade. It tacitly recognised the hinterland presence of the Turks whom the Crusaders wished to avoid, if only to save their energies for the slaughter they meant to serve upon them in dispatch of their sacred obligation to restore Christianity's increasingly shaky hold on the Holy Land.

The Crusaders, all said, were having a tougher time of it than the gilded accounts of the First Crusade had led them to expect. Hampered by the pilgrims, nobles' households, motley camp followers and other non-combatants under their supposed protection, sapped by the Germans' recent defeat and exhausted by the distance they had already travelled, they were now to turn aside and so bear the additional weight of moral compromise. The road to salvation was long and was, it now seemed, not even straight.

Indeed, they were soon to find themselves further consigned to Anatolia's 'crooked and treacherous byways'. Word now reached the Crusader camp that the proposed diversion to the south might also have its drawbacks: Conrad, chastened by the near starvation suffered by his broken forces on the retreat from Dorylaeum, advised Louis and his barons that they could expect similar provisioning difficulties on the Philadelphia road. The best option was to make for the south-west, fully at right angles to their intended course, and follow the coast road to Smyrna and Ephesus.

From there, revictualled and rested, they could then take the ancient road up the Meander Valley to Byzantine-held Laodicea before heading south for the Mediterranean and so complete their journey by sea.

The holy blitzkrieg was fast losing, in short, all sense of direction. The expedition, badly blunted, rambled through provincial Anatolia. Louis and his entourage spent several farcical days press-ganging upland rustics into directing them back to the path they had mislaid. Their progress along the coast was particularly sorry, with the king's chaplain, Odo of Deuil, chronicling how they encountered 'nearly every day steep, stony mountains and the deep channels of mountain torrents, which were difficult to cross even when dry and if filled with snow or rain possessed swift currents which neither horse nor infantry could swim through'. Conrad was ailing by the time he reached Ephesus; he did not need any encouragement when an imperial envoy arrived to inform him that palatial quarters had been readied for his convalescence at Constantinople. It was left to Louis to lead the advance up the Meander Valley.

So the Crusaders worked their way up the wintry plain. On their approach to Antiocheia the Turkish resistance, which had been shadowing them since Ephesus, materialised in force: bowmen on the heights, infantry across the valley and the rest, in Odo's words, 'massed on the other bank of the river to prevent us crossing'. For two days the

Crusader forces advanced up the north bank in protective formation. Losses were modest but progress was slow, and the continued harassment convinced Louis that they must find a way to cross the Meander: a river, it is to be remembered, which a bridge no longer spanned, which no regulators had reduced and which, as Odo reported, 'ordinarily was deep and wide, but at that time was swollen with water from other streams'.

The stage was set for the engagement that was to ensue by the banks of the Meander on the morning of New Year's Day 1148. The battle was not to merit a name, though this did not prevent the leading Byzantine historian of the age, Niketas Choniates, from making it nothing less than the central episode in his account of the Second Crusade. The historian may have given the battle such prominence because he considered himself a local – he was, as his name indicates, from nearby Chonae – or because he had as a child seen for himself gory evidence of the sheer extent of the conflict that had taken place just seven years before his birth. It may also have been that Choniates recognised the battle as the one event in the whole sorry venture worthy of Christian commemoration; the moment when God came to the belated rescue of the Crusaders and, it might be said, of Niketas Choniates' otherwise untriumphant account of it.

So the first dawn of the new year broke, Choniates wrote, to reveal the opposing armies arrayed in battle order along either bank. He told how the king had reviewed his troops and roused them by denouncing the barbarian 'enemies of the cross of Christ' in whose blood his men had promised to wash themselves, taking vengeance on a people whose brothers had defiled the Saviour's tomb with their feet.

The problem was getting at these Turks; in the way lay a river whose 'rushing waters formed whirlpools, making it completely impassable'. The king's proposal was brazen. 'Massed in full battle array and couching our lances,' he declared, 'let us zealously rush in and charge on horseback through the river's current; and I am fully confident that the waters shall be stayed, draw back, and the direction of their course reversed as happened of old when the Jordan River was crossed by Israel on foot.'

These words stirred the Crusaders to action; somehow the knights and their weighted horses successfully forded the torrent to storm the far bank. They soon did for the Turks who were 'cut to pieces in diverse ways and fell on one another like ears of corn; and then, like grapes pressed in wine vats, their lifeblood was squeezed by the lance-bearing knights . . . others arrayed nearby were wounded with dagger thrusts and were plunged into ruin as the bronze spilled out of their bowels. The bodies of the fallen Turks completely covered the plains, the ravines overflowed with their blood . . . To this day,' Choniates concluded, 'the mounds of bones are so many and so high that they stand like lofty hillocks bearing witness to the hosts who fell there.'

Odo of Deuil, privy to the same events, was of the standard view that a divine hand had been at work. 'I do know,' he wrote, 'that in such straits such an easy and brilliant victory would not have occurred except by the power of God, nor would the rain of iron from the opposing army have fallen without causing death or wounds.' It was said, he reported, that some people had seen 'at the ford a certain white-clad knight' who had supposedly 'struck the first blows in the battle'. God had sided with them, that is, as He had abandoned the pagans of Pergamum to the Muslims and as His archangel had guarded the church at Colossae against inundation.

This was a selective reading of recent events, of course, one which ignored such reverses as the defeat of the Germans at Dorylaeum and the fall of Edessa; the Christian forces might have known better than to rely upon divine favouritism. For the Deity, as they were obliged to acknowledge, soon withdrew His support for them. Barely a week after their victory by the Meander the same Crusaders suffered a terrible mauling in the mountains above Laodicea, Louis barely escaping with his life. The Turks so dogged the expedition's progress to Adalia that the Crusaders were reduced to feeding off the corpses of fallen horses. A few men, mostly officers, finally made it to the Holy

Land, but only to discover that the various Christian factions assembled there could not agree a common plan. The venture ended in humiliation. If the Second Crusade proved anything, it was that the Turks were firmly established across much of the Holy Land and Anatolia, and the differences between Western and Eastern Christians were such that they could not begin to settle them.

This particular instalment of the holy mission had in fact been compromised from the very beginning. Long before the knights' discovery that they were to be denied the favourable campaigning conditions that the men of the First Crusade had enjoyed half a century earlier – an on-side God to guarantee a steady stream of victories, and a straight road – these men had also learned that they must do without anything in the way of steadfast allies. For on their arrival at Constantinople they were informed that the Byzantines, for all their diplomatic protestations of goodwill, had recently made a treaty with the Turks to guard their flank in case of conflict with the Crusaders. The emperor might have extended hospitality to his ailing German counterpart, but most Byzantines viewed the Crusaders not as their co-religionists but as nothing less than 'a cloud of enemies, a dreadful and death-dealing pestilence'.

Nor did the Western Crusaders think any better of the Byzantines. Odo of Deuil compared them to the worst kind of tourist touts, offering rip-off exchange rates, letting down baskets from the safety of high walls to collect payments for goods they then refused to deliver, and in some cases mixing the barley they sold to the Crusaders with fatal quantities of lime. He listed their other treacherous failings: the Byzantines of Antiocheia had offered sanctuary to those Turks who had managed to flee the riverside carnage while the Byzantine commander of Laodicea had actually led a detachment of Crusaders into a Turkish ambush. Some of the Turkish forces that harassed the Crusaders were even under the leadership of Greeks. Any sense of common Christian purpose appeared to be beyond the churches of the Byzantine East and Latin West, officially sundered for a century, whose congregations had come to regard each other with outright hostility.

The truth was that Anatolia had already begun to turn Turk. The same Byzantines whose forebears had appealed for Western help against the accursed Turks just fifty years earlier now seemed more inclined to seek accommodations with their new neighbours from the east. Some Byzantines and Turks had begun to explore ways in which they might coexist. It was a social phenomenon that some chroniclers regarded as inevitable along the empire's contested margins, and which others saw as the understandable reaction of a populace who had long been regarded as a lumpen source of tax and of expendable soldiery, and had been generally maltreated by the authorities. The loyalty of these disenchanted Byzantines was negotiable, as some commentators noted. The islanders of Lake Beyşehir, just west of Iconion, 'by mingling with the Turks, not only strengthened their mutual bonds of friendship but also maintained strong commercial ties', and in time came to look upon the Byzantine authorities as their enemies. The populations of Christian settlements near Antiocheia, captured and deported by the sultan's forces at the end of the twelfth century, took a similar view; they were so generously 'apportioned fertile land for cultivation', provided with 'grain and seed for the growing of crops', and so lightly taxed following their arrival at the Turkish-held town of Philomelion that 'many who had not fallen into the Turks' hands but who had heard of what the Turk had done for their kinsmen and countrymen' followed their lead into Turkish territory.

This is not to say that an entirely amenable process of assimilation – that of Christian Byzantines into Muslim Turks – was under way by the time of the Crusades; there were plenty of instances of slaughter, abduction and the sack of cities, as we shall see, and even in the twentieth century the descendants of the same Byzantines and Turks would still be warring by the banks of the Meander River. Through the early centuries of Turkish dominion many Byzantines were forcibly converted; it was a condition, for example, among the young Christian men whom the Turkish authorities favoured for imperial service. Others converted to curry favour, to avoid persecution or to dodge premium taxes.

Perhaps, however, the chief influence on the Byzantine masses was the sense that the experience of their forebears had bred in them: that the time had come, as it did in Anatolia, to submit to the latest transformation. This plastic people whose predecessors had once been Arzawan, then Hittite, Phrygian, Persian, Greek and Roman, were no longer to be Byzantine but Turk. They were to change their language and bow before different gods, and so they were to survive by once more forgetting their former selves.

The bridge I finally reached was not far from the town of Kuyucak (alt. 133 metres). Beyond dusty orange groves a riverside *kahve*, a makeshift café, stood in a shaded garden. The place was deserted except for a grey-haired man drinking beer, a habit he had acquired during the thirty years he had spent in Holland. Europe had been good to Çetin. He had returned home a few years before to farm. The local orchards were his, but this year's harvest was sure to be disastrous.

'The water,' he exclaimed, his voice thick with disgust. 'When I was a child we drank straight from the river. The river brimmed with fish. There was water even through the driest summers. There's now so little, and so much filth from the factories, that I can't even use it on the orchards. My harvest will be wiped out this year.'

The stream that crept past the *kahve* was brown. The educated Çetin listed the factory effluents he knew it to contain: copper and lead, chromium and nitrates from the textile factories at Sarayköy and Denizli, and chlorides and sulphides from the leather and tanning factories at Uşak.

'They would never allow such a thing in Holland,' said Çetin, plainly disgusted.

The water was certainly filthy. But at least there was more of it; probably even enough, what with my sore feet, to float a canoe on.

CHAPTER 17

The man from the State Water Works – thigh-high in waders, sock-deep in water – was so absorbed in his work that he never noticed the approach of my canoe. He was measuring the Meander's flow below the bridge near the city of Nazilli (alt. 94 metres). In his hand he held a high-tech meter – matt black, scalloped grip, digital display – which evidently made for grim reading; like an infirmary nurse clearing a thermometer, the disbelieving man shook the meter before he plunged it back into the patient.

'Way too slow,' he muttered and cast a disapproving eye upon the river as if it were to blame for its own condition. This so rankled, given what his own organisation had done to the river, that I thought to surprise the man by paddling up to his patently unnecessary waders with an opinion of my own.

'Way too low as well,' I declared, promptly grounding.

At my words the man spun round. 'Where were you going?' he blurted. I clambered from the canoe, not for the first time that morning, and made a point of telling him how the plan *had* been to reach the sea. But by a river which, it now seemed, was unlikely to complete its own passage there.

The wonder was how those upstream obstacles – the endless loops, fallen willows and sudden bouts of current – could ever have tried my patience. I now recognised them as the river's vital signs. The same could not be said of these incessant groundings; any river that failed even to maintain the half-filled bath it took to float my canoe was not worthy of the name. The Meander, poached beyond enduring, was nearing an early end. As the man with the gadget was now discovering for himself.

That morning I had collected my stowed canoe from Feslek, brought it by *dolmuş* to the riverside *kahve* and reassembled it in the shade of Çetin's ailing orange groves. There was nobody about to see me push off and collide with what I took to be a rogue submerged sandbank only yards from the *kahve*. Further groundings followed in such quick succession, however, that I was soon down to my last hope: that I might learn to read the river anew, or what remained of it, and so dodge the riffled patches where the water was stretched so thin as to tear, just as I had once got good at negotiating tight gaps among the willows.

The hope was a forlorn one. If I learned anything that morning, it was the extent to which my trousers should be submerged – mid-shin – before I might successfully get back into the canoe, and I had relaunched repeatedly by the time the Nazilli bridge came into view. In the process I had transferred a lot of river water and mud into the canoe. The smeared clods, broken open between my feet, gleamed with veins that seemed to run with mercury.

Those factors – the mud, the effective lack of a river and now the first signs of chemical corruption – almost persuaded me to call it a day. I might have hauled out at the bridge, jabbed a finger at the hapless man from the State Water Works, upbraided his organisation, the river's supposed guardian, for having delivered it up to the power companies, to the irrigators and to the industrialists, and excoriated him for the dead turtles, and the brazen signs that enjoined the public to keep the water clean even as the same organisation turned a blind eye to the toxic effluent pouring out of the factories. The man was not solely to blame, however, and the river was not quite dead, so I pushed on, but inadvisably, because it was not long before the river became very filthy indeed.

With every advance, whether by stroke or step, the mud worsened, the churned water billowing clouds the colour of charcoal. The stuff that now splattered the canoe, my clothes and gear, had a foul, anoxic smell. That same morning I had passed some wading fishermen, stripped to the undershorts to net for gasping carp in the shrunken shaded pools beneath the bank-side willows. By

301

the afternoon, however, the same potbellied mudlarks had either come to their belated senses or expired in the mephitic mire, for I passed no more groups of them. Like the birds, the fish and the turtles, they were gone, and with them went the last faint vestiges of the Meander's pastoral allure. Beneath a flat sky the river now looped like a bowel, carrying its foul load, and me, towards evacuation.

It was then that I saw the culvert, and I shuddered; a treacly black substance was creeping onto the river. Initially the viscid filth formed a regular fringe along the bank. In no time, however, it had begun fingering out into the river, its malign ribbons drifting apart beneath the cut of the canoe bow. The spidery, grease-flecked branches dispersed until the entire river ran black, and a sour smell rose from the water. The smell, that said, was not the one I feared. Besides, the colour was wrong. That realisation lifted my spirits, but only until it struck me that I, who had recently walked by fields of thyme, and climbed a gorge in a confetti of yellow butterflies, and passed roadside urns of sweet shaded water and donkey-mounted villagers swathed in turbans, saddlebags holstered with collected firewood, was now consoled, apparently, to figure the filth that lapped at my canoe could not at least be shit. It was time to get off this river, at once and possibly for good, before it finally died, and I risked doing the same. At the foot of the next bridge I drove the canoe ashore and dragged it among some oleanders, stopping only to grab my splattered rucksack.

For once, however, the river offered no easy exit. It was a moment before I worked out the dread significance of the fact that the Meander's banks had not been trampled to the usual slopes: the waters Çetin once drank had turned so foul that even the local livestock knew better than to slake their summer thirsts here. Parched cows were not so foolish as to go where I had been, and it appalled me that I had spent the best part of a precious day wading through filth. I began to question the worth of the entire project and was soon seized with a swelling sense of desperation that I must at all costs get off the river. I threw myself, mumbling incoherently, at the bank of dried mud and scrambled headlong through the thick stand of reeds at the top. To the brittle clatter of snapping foliage, and with a sigh of relief, I heaved myself onto the plain.

It was a beautiful sight; the plain was bathed in a lemon light and gnats danced in spinning columns. Beyond the bridge the road ran north to a town at the foot of mauve hills, the last of the sun flaring against the distant windows. I followed the road through strawberry fields. The muezzin sounded, fading into the noise of traffic. I crossed the highway and the adjacent railway line, passed freight sheds and made my way into Sultanhisar. I climbed a sloping street lined with shabby apartment blocks, the balconies stacked high with wooden fruit cartons. A sign warned off pedlars and travelling salesmen, but the town had not pronounced in relation to filth-lacquered foreigners. I might have gone unregistered if it had not been for the muzzles of the pavement strays, which lifted to quiver at my passing. Even the taxi drivers in their pressed shirts, chatting across yellow bonnets in the town square, pointedly ignored me, as if my condition discounted the possibility that I might constitute a fare or that they would welcome me as one. The fountain in the square bore a plaque decorated with arabesques and an inscription: *All Living Things Were Created With Water.*

It was then I noticed how the road from the square wound up to something unexpected: a hotel, with flagpoles and flower beds, marking it out as precisely the apparition that had repeatedly teased me along the upland road to Yenice. This one did not dissolve, however, and so offered a real prospect of the comfort I had not enjoyed since my arrival in Turkey. The hotel had also attracted the only other foreigners I had seen since Pamukkale, even if the elderly Koreans then disembarking from their luxury tour coach appeared to take the place for granted. Their indifference was all the encouragement I needed to consider mine the priority claim, though I would have to hurry to press it. The wild and malodorous figure that shambled into view, shedding bits of reed and caked mud, so unsettled an elderly lady at the steps of the coach that she turned for the safety of her seat, pushing against those who were trying to follow her. In the cartoon confusion I nipped through the hotel entrance where the receptionist, visibly startled, promptly dispatched a porter to escort me from the foyer before the Koreans got there, though that was not how she put it. The man would show me straight to my room, she explained, thinking that I might prefer to book in once I had had the chance to freshen up.

Later that evening I was emptying out my rucksack to ready it for a much-needed turn of its own beneath the shower. Feeling deep in a side pocket I found something hard, which I did not immediately recognise. It was the glass jar, its contents pure as the river's waters were now corrupted, which I had filled back at the Meander's source at Pınarbaşı. I remembered how my journey had started, where I had hoped it would lead, and determined then to reach the sea even if the Meander would not carry me there.

In the morning I was crossing the narrow lane at Nysa, the ancient site in the hills above Sultanhisar, when a yellow taxi drew up beside me.

'May you be clean!' the driver exclaimed. He evidently recognised the foreign tramp who had paused by the fountain in the town square the previous evening. Aydın Greatspring, short of teeth but blessed by a generous smile, threw open the passenger door.

'Welcome,' he said. 'Why not come see their village?' Aydın indicated the two old men in the back seats, their chins silvered with stubble, and with an onward sweep of his arm also took in the hills where the village of Kavaklı was to be found. The prospect was enticing; Nysa, the cultured city where Strabo had once studied, could wait. The old men were exchanging grievances.

'No money in the soil any more,' moaned one.

'Except for the middlemen in the cities,' said the other.

'The ones who don't get their hands dirty,' the first added contemptuously.

'Can't get a fair price for anything,' the other one added, throwing up his hands. 'Not for apricots or strawberries.'

'Nor for cherries.'

'Walnuts.'

'Not plums.'

'Pomegranates. Bah!'

'Not for peaches.'

Neither man seemed willing to let the other have the last word. I feared they must continue to work their way through the list of locally grown products, which I knew to be famously extensive, until one of them signed off with a final grouse.

'And now' – he sighed – 'not even a *dolmuş* to town.' Aydın Greatspring, presently benefiting from the recent closure of the village's minibus service, directed a placatory shrug at the rear mirror. The road corkscrewed upwards. In the fields were chokes of bramble and pomegranate trees stippled with delicate orange flowers. Box-shaped timber beehives, blue like faded boats, lined winding pathways and higher up, below a ridge, stands of cypress trees showed black against the sky. With a brutal twist the road climbed to a final bluff, terminating in a tiny square shaded by the brindled boughs of overhanging plane trees. Aydın set about helping the old men with their shopping bags. I looked around, and at once saw why the *dolmuş* no longer ran to Kavaklı. Rusted padlocks hung from the door of the mayor's office and the village store. The tea house had also closed, though nobody had taken it upon themselves to extinguish the possibility that it might yet reopen, for the space I palmed in the window grime revealed chairs and cloth-covered tables neatly in place. There were ashtrays and pots of sugar, even spilt decks of cards, the whole feathered with a shroud of dust.

The mosque was yet to go the way of the tea house. It was a fine, eighteenth-century building, with a stucco exterior in which the timber door and windows were bordered with stencilled motifs in black, blue and rusty brown – domes, potted flowers, trails of chevrons – and sacred exhortations in both Arabic and Latin scripts. I pushed through the door to find myself beneath a timber mezzanine, with rough-cut hayloft steps but railed like a galleon stern, and painted in the same turquoise gloss as the door and windows.

Everything was in its place; the imam's gowns, ivory and black, and two fezes, turbaned in white calico to leave vermilion tonsures, hung on neat hooks from the side of the painted *mimber*, or pulpit, which rose to the wall like a set of aircraft steps. Across the carpets, worn but recently beaten, sunlight fell in fierce stripes. The remaining villagers evidently devoted their dwindling energy to the maintenance of the mosque; the village's young were long gone, I guessed, perhaps to Sultanhisar but more likely to Denizli or Aydın, even Izmir or Istanbul, leaving only the aged and their observances behind.

It was only on leaving the mosque that I noticed the sign – comparatively recent, and more slickly produced than the usual home-made contrivances – whose arrow pointed to the *Museum House of Yörük Ali Efe*. Aydın had not yet returned from delivering his elderly passengers' shopping, so I decided to take a look. A boulder-strewn track rose through the silent village, past sagging roofs and walls that had collapsed into stands of dank, snake-infested weeds. There was no indication of the plaque's arrow coming to land, but I knew I had found its target the moment the corner house came into view. In a village teetering on abandonment, Kavaklı's unlikely attraction was conspicuously restored, if not with any great sensitivity to the regional vernacular. The place had emerged from its makeover with a roofed and gated porch, hacienda-style, and with the walls of both the

308

garden and house crazy-paved in a job lot of industrial marble. The first-floor terrace was enclosed by an ornate filigree railing, with exterior red-brick hearths finished in a shiny varnish, which only added to the persuasive expat villa aesthetic. The ground-floor rooms were empty but for the house martins, which flitted by the margins of my vision. Nobody was in attendance; and on the subject of Yörük Ali or his house there was not a single written word. So I sat in the walled garden, by a fig tree coming into leaf, and considered the one-time occupant's name. Which told me that a nomad called Ali had once lived in this house.

Nomads were not supposed, of course, to live in houses; Anatolia's roving pastoralists, the Yörüks – or Turcomans, to give them their earlier designation – traditionally lived not within permanent walls, like those who settled beside tended plots of land, but in round tents 'made of interlaced rushes, and pointed roofs formed with bent withies'. Certainly, they had done so when the Selçuk Turks first forced Anatolia's eastern door, as Manuel Comnenus, the Byzantine Emperor, had one day had occasion to see for himself.

It was 1146, a year before the armies of the Second Crusade were to arrive. The possibility that the Western armies might sack the Byzantine lands rather than pursue their stated aim of consolidating the Christians' hold over the Holy Land had not yet occurred to the Emperor; it would be some months before he thought to guard his flank by arriving at terms with his traditional Turkish enemies.

In the meantime he had been pursuing a vigorous campaign against the Turks in the region around Iconion, or Konya, as the Selçuks knew the city where they had established their sultanate's capital in 1097. Taking a rest from the fighting, he broke off to fall back on lands that had been restored to Byzantine control during the divinely ordained successes of the First Crusade. On the plains around the headwaters of the Meander, the Emperor went out to hunt as Persia's kings and satraps had done 1,500 years before. There he spied from his horse 'movement far off in the undergrowth'. Scouts reported 'many tents assembled there, and the movements in the grove were the horses of those in the tents, grazing on grass with unbridled mouths'. This was a band of Turcomans – Turks of a nomadic, tribal and stubbornly independent cast – whom the indignant Byzantine forces drove from their tents and put to flight.

The Byzantines no doubt notched up the minor skirmish as a victory. The truth, however, was that the few wounds they inflicted, the tents they no doubt torched and the horses they rustled, could not begin to mitigate the slaughter visited upon their forces by the Turks at the great battles that had taken place both before and after this brief engagement by the sources of the Meander: at Manzikert, eastern Anatolia, in 1071 where the Byzantines and their substantial levies, ignominiously overrun, had left their emperor to fall captive to the sultan; and at Myriocephalon near Dinar in 1176 where the field was piled high with scalped Byzantine corpses. Myriocephalon lies about 1,000 kilometres to the west of Manzikert; the location of the two battles would appear to constitute an excellent means of metering the rate – roughly a kilometre a month – at which the Byzantines ceded Anatolia to the rampaging Turks over the twelfth century.

The calamitous defeats at Manzikert and Myriocephalon certainly weakened the Byzantine military machine, obliged the Byzantines to abandon strategic military outposts and fatally undermined imperial self-belief. They were not decisive, however, in determining the fate of Anatolia; what actually lost the emperors their land, and by a contrastingly erosive process, were the Turcoman incursions such as the one Manuel witnessed on the same plain where Apollo had once bested Marsyas. The Turcomans, whom Manuel thought to have put to flight, had merely slipped out of range to await the passing of the imperial force. In the meantime they raided settlements, trampled crops and poisoned water sources, all the time reducing the land until it was unable to sustain the settled Byzantines even as it provided all the grass that the Turcomans required of it. It was a strategy that the Byzantines, their orchards and fields levelled, their pigs slaughtered and cattle carried off, were ultimately unable to resist.

The difference between these trespassers and the Saracen Arabs, raiders of earlier centuries, was that they did not eventually go; they were not a merely temporary scourge that would be absorbed into Anatolia's bitter memory. For in their easterly wake these nomads had left little by way of attachments; only the trail of their Turkic language and the fading circles of dust where their encampments had once stood. With nowhere to return to, they had brought not only the tents that were their walls and carpets 'without nap, and in broad stripes and figures', but also their women and children, their livestock and their few other possessions. They were hardy, mobile and lived in the saddle, where the men learned to fire their bows, the women to wean their infants.

These wild Turcomans, who functioned opportunistically beyond the advance positions of the conventional forces under the sultan's command, their interests chancing to be aligned, were soon spilling into Anatolia in vast numbers. Drawn to the grasslands and the vulnerable settlements of the infidels, they camped in the ruins of abandoned settlements whose names and classical heritages meant nothing to them, like Dorylaeum, where an estimated 2,000 tents were reported in the late twelfth century. In 1190 there were reckoned to be some 100,000 Turcomans ranging between the Meander's headwaters and Konya. By the following century they had established such a presence that the region around Chonae, Turkish

Honaz, was commonly known as the Plain of the Turcomans. Before the advance of these people, 'numerous as locusts' in the phrase of an appalled Niketas Choniates, the Byzantine villagers retreated to the safety of the towns, the townsfolk to the cities. Walls were raised around the remaining settlements. Beyond the weakening fist of Byzantine resistance, and the ponderous counter-thrusts of its forces, the Turcomans roamed at will. The Byzantines, according to a thirteenth-century commentator, 'thus fear the Turkmens so that they do not dare to go out from their cities or castles if they do not take with them a horse. . . . For they assert that the Turkmens will kill him straight away . . .'

By reducing these lands to little more than pastures dotted by the occasional beleaguered bastion, these nomadic irregulars played a leading role in breaking the Byzantine hold on Anatolia, a fact the Selçuk authorities were quick to acknowledge, even admire. The same authorities, busy establishing their sultanate at Konya, also knew that a yawning gulf now existed between their transitional culture and that of the Turcomans; the traditional Turcoman contempt for sedentary peoples and systems of administration increasingly threatened the ordered society the Selçuks sought to build. For in the course of the Turks' migration the nomadic instinct so evident among the die-hard Turcomans had otherwise been abraded by civilising contact with the settled, comparatively sophisticated and increasingly appealing cultures – notably of the Persian Sassanids and the Byzantines – which they had encountered along the way. A chief consequence of the migratory process was that many Turks no longer counted themselves steppe itinerants by the time they reached Anatolia; to many of them the Turcomans were a throwback to their wild and untutored past. Some partially transformed by adapting to the semi-nomadic practices for which Anatolia was especially suited, moving between established winter bases and the high summer pastures, or *yayla*, where grazing was abundant, temperatures were cool and the debilitating malarial mosquitoes were absent. Others went yet further, adopting home, hearth and regulation to participate in a society that was in some respects modelled on the one they had overrun; for this reason the Selçuk Turks, betraying their own astonishment at the distance they had come and what they had achieved when they got there, chose to know their new sultanate as Rum, or Rome, much as the Byzantines had known the land. It was around this same time, however, that the Western chroniclers, in a striking acknowledgement of their own take on the new order, began referring to Anatolia not as Romania but Turchia or Turkomania.

With the passing of time, the settled Selçuks saw less to admire in their wild Turcoman cousins and more to fear from these unruly and lawless mobs. As early as the eleventh century, when Turcoman feats of arms remained fresh in the mind, one chronicler noted how there had 'arisen a certain amount of aversion to the Turkmens'. For the Selçuks were learning that living the settled life meant protecting themselves from the unregulated nomads they had themselves once been. They were obliged to erect defences around their homes, their towns and especially their *hans*, or caravanserais, where travellers and traders might take refuge at night.

The ill feeling was to deepen. The Turcomans now ranged across those formerly Byzantine territories that had since come under Selçuk control. They supplemented what livings they gleaned from their herds by preying on isolated homesteads or travellers of any colour or caste. They mounted raids against Christians and Muslims alike.

So Anatolian nomadism, which had once glittered with martial allure, fell headlong into brigand disrepute. Those valiant tribal auxiliaries who had spearheaded the advance into the Turks' new homeland came to be regarded as common bandits. For all their ostensible criminalisation, the Turcomans flourished; the Turkish authorities found them no easier to control than the Byzantines had. In fact, they were still flourishing in the eighteenth century when Richard Pococke and Richard Chandler ran into them in the Lycus Valley, and gave no better account of the Turcomans than the Byzantines had some six hundred years earlier. 'These Turcomen,' wrote Richard Pococke, 'when they attack people, strike from the woods, and travellers are wounded or murdered without seeing any enemy.' Richard Chandler told of a band of Turcomans beyond the Meander who 'had very lately plundered some caravans, and cut off the heads of the people who opposed them'.

By the time of Pococke's and Chandler's travels, of course, the Ottomans had long eclipsed the Selçuks. This tribal dynasty, which had come to power in Anatolia during the fourteenth century, had finally extinguished the Byzantines with the capture of Constantinople in 1453. It had then brought much of Arabia, Africa and Europe under its imperial sway, famously advancing to the gates of Vienna. The Ottomans never managed, however, to control these unruly *montagnards* in their neglected Anatolian backyard. The authorities were largely to blame; an empire addicted to expansion, and to the relentless production of fighting men, had no choice but to ingrain soldiering so deep in its populace that many conscripts discovered upon demobilisation how little remained of the pliant, productive peasants they had once been. The Ottomans had somehow reverse-engineered these young men, turning them back into fair approximations of the steppe itinerants who had characterised their race at the outset. They joined the upland gangs of Turcomans and made untaxed livings as brigands. They fell upon passing caravans and couriers, pilgrim groups and those villages that lay outside their local support base.

They intercepted and fleeced detachments of Ottoman soldiers whom they sent packing in their drawers. And from the eighteenth century, when they were increasingly known as Yörüks, they also preyed upon the medicine chests and purses of the foreign travellers who were often found hunting out hidden treasure in the same ruins where these nomad gangs traditionally made their camps.

The surprise, which Pococke and Chandler must surely have shared, was discovering that one of these notorious freebooters was to be accorded the honoured rank of *efe*, or leader, and to get a museum in his name.

Aydın dropped me back at Nysa before hurrying on to pick up a fare. I walked among column bases where the red gossamer petals of thin-stemmed poppies flapped raggedly in a soft breeze. Meadow grass lay freshly cut among the wild olives. Triangular shards of tile lay scattered on the ground. In the ravine that ran through the little city tortoises grazed on shaded weeds and purple sheaths thrust obscene from wide-mouthed arum lilies. A group of French visitors, silver-haired, elegant and shod in blue deck shoes, wandered through the site. The group followed their Turkish guide's commentary, but loosely, repeatedly interrupting him to hold exclusive dialogues, working up the guide's plain facts into gilded insights into Greco-Roman life, which they batted among themselves.

Nysa had been named, *soit que quelqu'un s'intéresse*, after a Seleucid queen. It was under the Romans, however, that the city had enjoyed its heyday. A renowned centre of scholarship, Nysa attracted an impressive roster of orators, philosophers and rhetoricians. Strabo had himself studied here under the distinguished rhetorician Aristodemus. The guide showed his charges the remains of the second-century library, with niches set in the tottering walls where scrolls were stored. Then he led them to the fine theatre so they might look out across the patchwork of the Meander plain, all geometric lines except for its wandering, colon-black seam.

The library and the theatre spoke of a secure

and flourishing culture; something with which the French group, given their age, station and nationality, felt a natural kinship. I might myself have lingered on Nysa's life of ease and intellectual enquiry, of lectures and theatrical spectacle, if the point I had reached in Anatolia's narrative had not left the city's golden age behind by roughly 1,000 years. The rhetoricians and philosophers were long gone. Nysa's library had come to serve, it may be assumed, as a store for emergency supplies or munitions; its upper floors had perhaps been dismantled by the Byzantine residents to provide extra tiers in the raising of the city walls. I had arrived, in short, at the final moments in the life of Nysa, as I had that morning witnessed a Turkish hill village deep in its own decline. I thought of Kavaklı's padlocks, and of the accumulating concerns and scribbled calculations that had eventually led the proprietors of the village's tea house and store to leave their doors closed one morning, a final neighbour's death or departure confirming that their own time to leave had come.

By the twelfth century the people of Nysa found themselves at the heart of the bloody struggle for control of Anatolia. By the 1170s the Turks' territorial ambitions stretched to the Aegean. The sultan dispatched an army of some 20,000 men with orders to lay waste the Meander Valley and not to return unless they brought with them 'seawater, sand, and an oar'. The Meander Valley came to serve as the front line in the conflict. All along the valley cities like Miletus and Priene, Nysa and Tralles repeatedly changed hands, the retreating forces destroying much of what they were forced to abandon. Homes and harvests were torched to prevent them falling into enemy hands. The advancing forces consumed or destroyed what little remained.

It is known that a Turkish clan chief called Menteşe sacked Nysa in 1282. No details survive, but an account of the sack Menteşe's forces shortly afterwards inflicted upon neighbouring Tralles may serve in the case of Nysa. Tralles, destroyed in an earlier sacking, had recently been rebuilt by order of the Emperor Andronicus. By dispatching his own son along with 36,000 colonists, the Emperor meant to create an imposing bulwark against the enemy; here the Byzantines would comprehensively block the Turks' advance.

The new city, accounted 'one of the most considerable places by the Meander', had barely been completed before Menteşe's forces closed in. It soon became apparent that the city suffered from a fatal strategic weakness: it had no water reservoirs and 'it seemed impossible to dig sufficiently deep' wells. It was not long before the Turks had cut off the supply from the river and also blocked the city's links with the surrounding fields. Within the walls the citizens soon grew thirsty; they were reduced to drinking the blood of their horses. The Turks starved Tralles into a submission its citizens repeatedly offered but which Menteşe was not minded to accept. When the Turks finally gained entry, the city was levelled and the slaughter was extensive. Some 20,000 survivors were carted off into an enslavement 'so harsh that they rejoiced for those who had been slain'. It may be supposed that Menteşe's mood had not been much better at Nysa.

That evening there was a wedding party in one of the hill villages above Kavaklı. A niece of Aydın's was to marry the following day. From the lane that led to the house of the bride's family I saw into shadowy corners where shawled matrons squatted over wood fires, stirring the steam from tureens of lamb stew and vats of milk pudding. Men in shirtsleeves handed over discreet dowry envelopes before helping themselves to the contents of the silver-painted plastic trays – cigarettes or boiled sweets – which circulated among the cloth-covered tables the family had set up outside their house. The men sat beneath the mulberry trees and drank lemonade or tea while whispering politics or speaking of plans to visit the *yayla* where their Yörük forebears had passed the summers until well into the twentieth century. The villagers took pride in the semi-nomadic ways of their grandparents long after they themselves had been transformed into taxi drivers, hotel workers or metering men of the State Water Works. Aydın told me he planned to take his family to the mountains that same weekend, by yellow taxi, and I was reminded of the Yörüks I had glimpsed in the mountains above Antalya a decade earlier. I had been hiking along a path on a spring afternoon when a flock of strong-smelling goats shouldered by. There followed a string of haltered camels laden with blankets, straw pallets, jerrycans, blackened kettles, axes and buckets, then the few sun-darkened figures who padded through the pine trees before the dust of the goats enveloped them, and I knew the sight was sliding into the past before my eyes; a journey made countless times, every spring, had barely a decade left to run.

The bride was dancing where the land lay flat, between the old village goalposts, in a circle of fairy lights. In a green dress and a white headscarf she danced to the rhythms of Turkish pop, alone except for the disc jockey who matched her every move from behind his bank of flickering equipment. The bride's married friends, wearing red scarves, sat on white plastic chairs all around the dance floor.

'When I married in the 1980s,' Aydın shouted over the music, 'we danced to the local village orchestra.' His words, a lament for lost traditions, seemed to express private astonishment that his youth had also got away.

The bride left the dance floor and was led to a plastic chair where a man in a grey suit appeared out of the darkness to join her. It was the groom. The couple glanced at each other before they turned, bashful, to watch the bride's friends who had replaced her on the dance floor. The friends danced in a curiously truncated way, their movements traditional above the midriff but strikingly modern below the waist, as if the scarves that guarded their heads against undue influences could do nothing to stop them getting in through the feet.

The music grew louder, and more young women, girls and grandmothers streamed through the dark trees beyond the goalposts to gather at the dance. The dancers moved faster, blurring into red flashes. As women at the back of the crowd passed chairs over the heads of those in front, and nudged hunched or elderly relatives through to better seats, so the advancing front row of the audience appeared visibly to age, losing its looks and its teeth until bride and groom were crowded by crones, and the shrinking circle in which the women danced was edged by futures in which child-rearing, fieldwork and the stirring of stew tureens were to dominate.

The music reached a peak. Pigeons rose as one from their nearby roost, flocked above the dance floor and crossed the moonlit sky in search of a silent tree, and Aydın's phone rang with another job.

CHAPTER 18

I t turned out that Yörük Ali Efe had a second museum in his honour, and with opening hours and ticket prices clearly displayed, although nobody was opening up or taking for tickets when I visited. Only the custodian's snores could be heard beyond the museum gates long after he was supposed to have unlocked them.

The museum was at Yenipazar. The *dolmuş* I caught in the morning speared south to the bridge where I had stowed my canoe among the bushes before continuing straight on across the wide valley. There were straight lines, in fact, all over the sun-struck flats; a bordered patchwork of angular orchards, strawberry fields, tomato plots, hay meadows, maize stands and fallows often seamed with reed-choked drainage ditches.

The Meander Valley's natural lines, that said, had always been contrastingly fluid ones; not only the winding river but the sinuous indents all along the outer edges of the flood plain whose remarkable extent, fully eight kilometres across, was evidence of the exceptional inundations the river had brought through its history. This explained why the watchman's hut by the Feslek regulator was the only bank-side building I had passed since the textile factory at Sarayköy. It accounted for the long walks leading from the river to settlements like Sultanhisar, settlements historic experience had taught to keep to the plain's edge, their trousers rolled, in a manner of speaking, against the winter floods. With the recent installation of the dams and regulators these floods appeared to have ceased, of course, though there was little sign anybody here had noticed. The people of Yenipazar had always known the bottomlands to be uninhabitable through the winter months, turning to muddy morasses that extended a full mile from the banks, and even now the only structures they had dared to raise there were occasional polythene greenhouses. So strictly did their homes, shops and minarets keep to the valley's edge that the town resembled a little port, and the sea-flat plain was scored by tyre wakes where tractors turned like ferry boats beneath the plumes of their stubby smokestacks.

Yenipazar faced Sultanhisar directly across the valley. It boasted no ancient cities, however, nor a hotel. There were no coachloads of foreign visitors, no railway station, and no steady flow of long-distance coaches and refrigerated trucks. All through its history the main road had kept to the more populous northern edge of this westerly stretch of the valley, with the consequence that a palpable torpor greeted the *dolmuş* as it pulled into

Yenipazar that morning: a narrow lane, Yörük Ali Efe Street, which broadened briefly to pass through town; the flattened stacks of sticks, grasses and shredded plastic bags atop the electricity poles where storks had raised their nests; an unexplained life-size elephant islanded on a tiled, dry water feature in the main square; and the yawning custodian who eventually appeared at the museum gates, sheepish face bleared by the tread of a cushion's unforgiving weave, to admit his unexpected visitor.

The custodian led the way through gardens to a ticket booth before directing me to a modest stucco house beneath a low-slung tiled roof. The house was full of heirlooms and exhibits. The walls were hung with sepia photographs of moustachioed men whose fixed, even exaggerated stares evidenced a childish wonder at the camera and an absolute attention to the instructions of its operator. Otherwise the men, arranged behind and beside their seated seniors in the manner of school team portraits, might have appeared fearsome in their military, if makeshift, mix of Great War serge and dress coats, broad belts, patent leather knee-high boots, fezes and turbans. Vitrine cases contained other costume items whose derring-do romance had not faded with their colours: bandoliers, and blue-whorled waistcoats, high-cut with tightly fitting sleeves, and black embroidered leggings, culottes, cummerbunds adorned in silverwork, and chainmail sashes. There were *yatağans*, or short scimitars, in decorated brass sheaths, and bolt-action Mauser rifles, family trees, identity cards, commendations, and campaign maps lacerated by the thrusts and counter-thrusts of colour-coded arrows.

The man himself stood on a plinth among the tended lawns and borders, a carbine slung across his shoulder, palm shielding his searching gaze against the sun. Boards displayed folk poems in his honour. Fresh flowers had been laid at the marble tomb of this Yörük, who had clearly made something of himself.

Despite the odds. Ali, born at Kavaklı in 1895 to semi-nomadic parents, could hardly be said to have enjoyed good prospects. A brutish existence had long been the lot of the common Anatolian. The nineteenth-century Ottoman elite had appeared more interested in eyeing the displays of the latest Parisian fashions along Constantinople's Grande Rue de Paris, and in boasting of their showcase capital's early installation of such technological novelties as lighting systems and an underground railway, than in relieving the living conditions of the rural masses. Provincial rule remained as backward, unjust and unaccountable as it had ever been. The people were poor. They remained pitifully educated, disease-prone and largely illiterate. A visit from authority could only mean it was once more time to find the tithes due to the local *ağa*, to contribute to the hard-pressed coffers of the Imperial Treasury, or to serve in the sultan's armies.

The Turks, accounting themselves a warrior

people, had traditionally tended to view military service with equanimity, even pride. *Jihad*, or Holy War, figured large in Turkish fighting tradition. Many Turks not only took their very name, Mehmet, from Islam's warrior prophet himself, but also saw their revered sultan in indisputably martial terms – the Sword of Islam. The imperial economy's traditional dependence on booty and tribute meant that the Turk learned to measure himself above all as a soldier. In the earlier Ottoman centuries, when the empire swept away all before it and the proceeds were so prodigious as to trickle down to even the humblest conscript, Turks were proud to serve.

By the time Yörük Ali reached adulthood, however, the Ottoman Empire was not so much acquiring new territories as fighting for ones it meant to retake along its increasingly contested borders. Beset by the independence aspirations of subject peoples and by the expansionist ambitions of imperial neighbours, the Ottomans faced national breakouts and territorial smash-and-grabs on all sides. Between 1911 and 1918 the Ottomans were to wage wars in defence of almost every frontier: 1911–12 in Libya against the Italians; 1912–13 against a Balkan coalition including Greece, Bulgaria and Serbia; 1915–17 in the Caucasus against the Russians; 1915 against British, Anzac and French forces on the Gallipoli Peninsula; and 1916–18 against British-backed rebels in their Arabian and Palestinian territories.

In this phase of terminal contraction, as it would prove, the loyal heartlands increasingly served as the hard-pressed empire's only reliable recruiting grounds. Across Anatolia, where the conscription officers most regularly came calling, the authorities progressively extended the age of conscription so that by 1916 boys of just fifteen, and men as old as fifty-five, were being called up.

These conscripts suffered appalling privation. They were undernourished, poorly paid and ill equipped. They fought winter campaigns in light-weight summer uniforms and in some instances were obliged to wrap their feet in rags if they were not to go barefoot. They endured not only frostbite but typhoid, cholera and dysentery. Disease and climatic extremes, not to mention battle wounds, caused the deaths of hundreds of thousands of Ottoman conscripts. The greatest loss to the Ottoman Army, however, was from another cause entirely; in the course of the Great War an estimated half a million men deserted. Among them was one young man from Kavaklı, a village near Sultanhisar on the northern slopes of the Meander Valley.

Little is known of Yörük Ali's desertion from the Russian front – only that he eventually made his way home before taking to the mountains where even now the old Turcoman gangs persisted; in fact, the outlaws' ranks had lately been swelled by exceptional numbers of wartime deserters and other truants. The young man who fell in with one such gang must have known that he was running from a government bullet. Certainly, Yörük Ali had no reason to suppose he might one day gain an elevated rank and two museums, not to mention statues and streets, in his honour.

We have seen the fearful impression that Yörük Ali's Turcoman kinsmen had made on the likes of Pococke and Chandler a century and a half earlier – though this was perhaps the lamb's view of the wolf. For while such men had every reason to regard the Turcomans as cut-throats and robbers – the Turcomans in turn counting such affluent strangers as fair game – the truth was that their indiscriminate raiding instincts had gradually been tempered, at least to the point of distinguishing between their enemies and those deserving of protection.

A code, a rough but chivalric tradition based on hunting and raiding, on skills such as horsemanship and falconry, had come to govern these mountain outlaws whom Western Anatolians now knew for their admired warrior attributes as zeybeks. The zeybeks, organised in paramilitary hierarchies under the command of their *efes*, turned the fighting talents that had repeatedly served the empire, and gone unrewarded, on those who drew flagrant profit from it; the provincial governors and the grasping *ağas*, the prosperous merchants and middlemen and their high-value caravans, the detachments sent to hunt the outlaws down, the *haj* pilgrims making for Mecca, the

330

couriers and conscription officers, as well as those affluent European antiquaries who happened to cross their paths. Among these was William Hamilton who described the zeybeks he came across in a roadside café near Sultanhisar, with their 'numerous pistols, dirks and yataghans', as 'the most ferocious-looking, daredevil, impudent set of fellows I ever saw'.

The local people saw the zeybeks, however, in a far better light. A century before the time of Yörük Ali, the zeybeks had begun to be viewed as popular champions, heroes of the proletariat resistance to the tyrannical demands of the authorities. These zeybeks came to be lionised among a rural populace who duly served as their constituency. The villagers, whom officialdom had exploited to the point of outright defiance, willingly gave the zeybeks their silence and secrecy, provisioned and provided them haven, and even answered their calls to insurrection. For their wild greenwood the zeybeks favoured the mountains, the natural preserve of their nomadic heritage, especially where they abutted lowlands rich in settlements and trade routes; nowhere than the cave-riddled heights fringing the Meander Valley better suited the hit-and-run strategies of these Anatolian Robin Hoods.

The romantic deeds in the 1820s of one such outlaw, Bald Mehmet, were immortalised in the folk songs and ballads that rang through the Meander Valley during Yörük Ali's boyhood. Bald

Mehmet, whose home town of Atça lay just six kilometres east of Sultanhisar, nursed the usual social grievances but was particularly incensed that his suit for a local *ağa*'s daughter should have been so airily dismissed. Thwarted in love, Bald Mehmet headed for the hills to return at the business end of his own zeybek band. The region answered Bald Mehmet's call to rebellion. The revolt rolled out on a wave of popular support, and the local authorities were put to flight. Bald Mehmet had barely made the *ağa*'s daughter his willing wife, however, before he was gunned down by imperial forces in 1830.

The authorities in Atça have since made post-humous peace with their legendary rebel by raising a statue in Bald Mehmet's memory; in the case of Yörük Ali, however, no such rehabilitation would be necessary. The state's bullet never felled him. A dramatic transformation of his fortunes ensured that the brigand from Kavaklı would be honoured by Atatürk himself, would be known as '*Efe* above all *efes*' and live to enjoy a happy retire-ment in his backwater home on the sleepy southern edge of the Meander Valley.

What redeemed Yörük Ali was one final war. The difference was that this one did not take place at the empire's distant edge where the land meant little to its bloodied defenders; a foreign army was advancing up the Meander Valley. The local Turks, with home and hearth to protect, were quick to take up arms; this time they were not about to desert.

★　★　★

I walked west out of Yenipazar. The potholed lane followed the alluvial land's very edge, winding like a tideline into the smallest indents the plain had forced among the rocks. The route of the tarmac, which gave the impression of having found its way there as liquid, was clearly meant to avoid submersion beneath those winter floods that the State Water Works had since consigned to history.

What the State Water Works had also stopped, of course, was the rich layer of silt, a 'coat of manure', which the flood waters had seasonally deposited across the plain. On the hard dry flats the soil now lay old and unrenewed. What natural process had once done for the fruit groves and maize fields, making the Meander Valley Turkey's produce basket, was now being achieved by artificial assistance; by the likes of *Mataro F1: Gives High Yield in All Conditions*, and *Foliacon 22; Nothing Better for Calcium*, to judge by the company signs affixed to the telegraph posts. I had stopped to sneak a few succulent strawberries when a hand-written sign – *Attention; this plot sprayed 15/5* – did for my appetite and I walked on.

A breeze blew through a roadside screen of poplars, riffling the leaves into dappled patterns of translucence and shade. In the stork nests' undersides, scruffy as sprung mattresses, sparrows were busy making homes of their own. An expanse of low rocks, roughly upright but uncut, stood in a walled enclosure. They so recalled Breton menhirs or the *chevaux-de-frise* fortifications of an

Iron Age fort that it was some time before I realised what I was actually looking at. It was a village
cemetery although the headstones bore no inscriptions, never had – those who lay there no more
knowing the form of their own names than their
mourners did. It was a glimpse into the gloomy
world that had persisted into Yörük Ali's boyhood;
villages of superstitious and beleaguered illiterates
who were never to recognise the resting places of
their loved ones by the miraculous secret of script
but must instead rely on some distinguishing mark
or by the headstone's position in relation to a
familiar olive tree. These were people denied the
basic components of identity. They were born to
labour and to be forgotten.

I had walked for some hours before I reached
Alanlı. The village's sweat-stained farmers beckoned me over to join them beneath the shaded
awning of the roadside tea house. I drank *gazoz*,
or sweet soda, and the men asked where I had
come from. I told them of my journey and of the
black river stretch I had hauled through.

'That's effluent from the olive oil factory,' a man
explained. 'The black sludge is what's left after
they've pressed the olives.'

'But it goes straight into the river.'

'That's because they don't need it; they've
removed the oil.'

'I meant: it's terrible for the state of the river.'
The men knew not what to make of my ecological
complaint.

'Your Queen was here,' said one of them, changing the subject. I nodded, having learned of Elizabeth II's recent state visit to Turkey from the headline – WE DID AWAY WITH OUR SULTAN; LONG LIVE THE QUEEN! – which I had seen in that morning's paper.

'But now she's gone home,' the man added approvingly, balancing the native courtesies with a proper degree of Republican ambivalence.

I walked on. The lane was still called Yörük Ali Street when I reached the small town of Dalama, with its dusty poplars and sack piles outside the seed merchants, and another statue of the man standing on a captioned plinth: *What Happiness,* it read, *To Drink from the Fountain of Dalama, the place chosen of all the Efes by Yörük Ali.* Out in the countryside the mulberries were turning pink. By the wheat fields the brick shells of abandoned houses stood doorless, and nailed to the white-washed walls of the empty rooms and the timber verandas were wooden coat hooks, which still showed the buffed sheen of dead men's collars. From the roadside rose the green-wash shrines of wandering dervish saints, makeshift tombs of stone and block cornered with ornamental globes that worshippers had wrapped with floral headscarves, and in such quantities that the hard stone could not be felt beneath their layered depths. The wall of a cistern bore the painted memorial to a young conscript martyred while on national service during the 1990s in the country's Kurdish south-east. By a lonely stretch of road an old man had lain down, his crutch laid out beside him, and I bent to check on him as I passed; his breathing was even, and in the hot afternoon a dreamer's smile showed among the lines on the man's face.

In the evening I reached a wide road, which severed the lane, heading north in a sudden rush of traffic. A *dolmuş* carried me across the Meander where I glimpsed silvered shallows. The far side of the plain glittered with lights. A sign told me that I had reached Aydın (alt. 67 metres); the name my taxi-driving friend in Sultanhisar shared with the city once known as Tralles.

The Ottomans, shattered by their involvement in the Great War and by the successive wars that had preceded it, surrendered to the Allies in October 1918. The following year delegations from the victorious nations met at Sèvres, Paris, to plot the defeated empire's dismemberment. The delegates thought not only to confirm the loss of remaining imperial territories in Arabia and elsewhere but also to apportion much of Anatolia among themselves. The Turks were set to lose vast swathes of their homeland – and chiefly to the same several Western races long before encountered in the Anatolian narrative.

It was the French, the conference hosts, who had enjoyed particular influence with the Turks in recent times; in the centuries since Louis VII's crusading armies had forced their bloody way up the Meander Valley en route to the Holy Land, relations had markedly improved. By 1918 theirs were the most privileged trading terms any country enjoyed with the empire. They were also the Ottomans' main creditors, which substantiated their claim for priority in the Anatolian province of Cilicia, one that was intended to secure extensive cotton interests there and also to buffer their hold on neighbouring Syria.

The Italians, busy playing colonial catch-up with their European rivals, were also prominent at Sèvres, where they made much of their ancient historical record in Anatolia. The parcel they claimed, the peninsula's entire south-west corner, was rich in the ruins of their Roman ancestors. Nor was the connection exclusively ancient, the Italians pointing to the fact that Anatolia's Orthodox Christians were even now known as Romans, or Rum in the Turkish; this was the small but tenacious minority whose forebears, resisting every pressure to turn Turk and convert to Islam, proudly traced their roots back to a Byzantine and thus Roman ancestry, even to the early Christian communities St Paul had fostered in the Lycus Valley. This cultural justification the Italians buttressed by presenting the territory they claimed as a natural extension of the immediately adjacent Dodecanese Islands, which their forces had won off the Ottomans in 1911. The region's coast was dotted with ports, moreover, whose names bore witness to Italy's continued commercial influence in the region. Among these was the bustling harbour of Scala Nuova, or Turkish Kuşadası; Italian interests in this Aegean port and its hinterland gave substance to their territorial claims, which extended north from the Mediterranean as far as the banks of the Meander River.

Here the Italians ran up against the rival claims of the Greek delegation who, asserting a yet more influential historic association, sought to establish their inalienable rights to the lands immediately north of the Meander, and even hoped to include the entire valley in their portion. The 'Roman' designation, as the Greek delegates were quick to remind their Italian counterparts, had always been imperial rather than ethnic in origin; the Rum people were quintessentially Hellenic and avowedly Greek Orthodox rather than Roman Catholic in their faith.

True, but it was also the case that these cussed Christian Rums, whose scattered communities amounted to a few million souls, had not been entirely immune to the Turkish centuries; many of them had lost their spoken Greek, though those who knew how to write had at least retained the alphabet of their ancestors. The bibles that America's nineteenth-century evangelists distributed among the Rums tended to be in Turkish but were rendered in Greek Cyrillic script. These were an acculturated people who largely rubbed along with their Muslim neighbours; they certainly had more in common with the Turks than with their Orthodox co-religionists in the Greek nation beyond the Aegean.

The Greek delegation at Sèvres could claim a more convincing kinship, however, with more recent arrivals in Anatolia; these were the Greeks who through the nineteenth century had left their impoverished Peloponnese and island homes, as their mercantile countrymen had done throughout history, to seek economic opportunity along the shores of western Anatolia. These settlers had never spoken any language but Greek and now did so with increasing fervour. Many were passionate champions of a culture, especially of its tongue and faith, which international sentiment encouraged them to cherish.

For from the eighteenth century Europe and America had been in thrall to all things Greek. Numerous books and pamphlets were published to enable the study of Greek grammar and rhetoric, philosophy, drama, literature and art. There was a spate of translations of Homer, notably by Alexander Pope, and numerous new editions of the Greek myths. Grand houses and civic buildings, gardens and cemeteries increasingly acquired pseudo-Grecian lines and motifs. Furniture, design, even hairstyling celebrated the Greek Revivalist movement.

No cause appeared more noble, therefore, than that of Greece's rebellion in 1821 against the Ottoman rule it had endured since the fifteenth century. Committees in London's influential Hellenist circles feverishly organised banquets and other fund-raising events for the valiant Greeks. Doctors and consignments of medicine were dispatched to treat Greek wounds. Poets and artists, lettered aristocrats, romantics and adventurers volunteered to fight alongside the Greeks; some, Lord Byron among them, lost their lives in a process that eventually led to the confirmation of Greek independence in 1832.

The Greeks were finally free, if only those of the newly constituted state; if a single ambition could be said to have emerged above all others in the heady upsurge of cultural rebirth and national destiny that attended Greek independence, it was the one known as the Great Idea – the re-Hellenising, even repossession, of the Anatolian lands which, from the time of Alexander the Great and through the Byzantine centuries, had been Greek in character. The time had come, many believed, for the Greeks to redeem the marchlands – as Apollo had once dealt with the barbarian Marsyas.

Many of these Greek settlers in Anatolia, inspired by the rhetoric of their priests, teachers and ideologues, took to the Great Idea with relish. The notion even began to find favour among those older Rum communities who had known nothing of Hellas, as liberated Greece was known, and had never thought of themselves as anything other than loyal Ottomans. One such Rum, distressed at being unable to communicate with a Greek visitor to his home town of Nazilli, was reported as having 'finally put his hand on his heart and said to the interpreter in Turkish; "Tell him that though my tongue is Turkish my heart is Greek."'

It was no surprise, then, that Anatolia's Greeks, a politically motivated and energetic minority, were quick to spot an opportunity when the negotiators at Sèvres in 1919 invited Turkey's residents to help them decide on the land's political fate. Summoning the renowned rhetoric of their ancient forebears, the Greeks of the Meander Valley and beyond were soon dispatching persuasive petitions, often in cultured French, to Sèvres. The Bishop of Söke, the main town of the Meander Delta, described the district – 'where our race largely predominates' – as the 'cradle of philosophy and civilisation of EPHESUS, PRIENE, MILETUS, MAGNESIA AD MEANDRUM etc.' – and its Greek population as the 'vigilant guardians of the tombs of our ancestors'. 'The Aydın district,' according to another petition, 'not only contained very ancient Greek cities, that have produced famous artists and scholars, among which Anthemius of Tralles who built Sancta Sophia in Constantinople, but also preserved up to this day its ethnological character even after the . . . Ottoman Turkish invasion.'

Some petitions came from further afield. One Mr Papadopoulos, self-styled 'Delegate Plenipotentiary of Denizli District', declared how 'The District of Denizli . . . was always fundamentally Hellenic, as historical and geographical witnesses attest, the excavated historical sites, the surviving monuments, the research of experts . . . the inhabitants of the region were always Hellenes.' Papadopoulos reminded the delegates how the region's cities, Hierapolis, Laodicea and Colossae among them, had 'superbly cultivated Greek literature and science', and how 'Xerxes, Cyrus the Younger, Alexander the Great, Frederick Barbarossa and others' had passed through these towns, where various Byzantine dynasties 'had fought for Hellenism against the Seljuks, Tartars and Turks'.

If these latter claims were true, then it was also the case that the Byzantines had lost their fight for Hellenism. Five hundred years had since passed. Over that period Turks had come to be in the majority across the contested area: some ten Turks to every Greek in Denizli, and as many as a hundred to one in outlying areas of the same district such as Çal.

These were contradictory facts, however, which no Greek rhetorician was about to concede. It was by guile, after all, that Apollo had bested Marsyas.

CHAPTER 19

Through the nineteenth century it was increasingly recognised that the Meander Valley, abundant source of classical artefacts, was exceptionally productive in other respects. In 1914, when the carve-up of the Ottoman territories was already keenly anticipated, the region was high on the wish list of every contending power. 'Everybody wants Smyrna and the Meander Valley,' as a Greek diplomat baldly put it in a private dispatch.

The British, mindful of the valley's historic role, had thought it might even prove central to the furthering of their imperial ambitions. When a British company began to lay Turkey's first railway up the valley in 1856, some saw it as providing them with the beginnings of an overland route to British India, as 'the channel of communication between Europe and Asia, the great artery through which the pulses of Asiatic trade must throb for evermore', much as it had done in the time of Strabo. In the shorter term, however, the railway's backers expected healthy profits from the traffic, which the first phase of the line alone would surely generate; this was to run between Smyrna's Aegean quayside and 'the great entrepot of the internal trade of Asia Minor', as a commentator described the city of Aydın.

This anticipated traffic was pointedly not in passengers, however, but almost exclusively in goods; it was the valley's remarkable fertility which the Smyrna–Aydın Railway intended to tap. A specially commissioned report, commending 'the alluvial nature of the soil', listed the valley's crops 'of all kinds from the rarest to the coarsest qualities. Tobacco, the fig, the vine, the olive, the poppy, the cotton plant and mulberry tree are all indigenous products, whilst wheat, maize, barley, beans, flax, hemp and a variety of pulse and oleaginous seeds are raised in large quantities. Valonia, yellow-berries, wool, goats' hair, dye-stuffs, drugs, skins, honey, wax and likewise abound.' The only hindrance was the primitive condition of the region's Ottoman infrastructure; by revolutionising the pre-industrial carriage of the valley's largely perishable produce, the railway company's backers meant to make a killing.

As for competition, the railway company need not concern itself with the roads; they were no better off in the 1850s than they had been in Strabo's time. On the better stretches, in good weather, bullock carts could bump along, but the usual journey between Aydın and Smyrna, by camel or mule, took four days. It could cost more to deliver the produce to market than it was worth. Aydın, though described as 'fertile to excess', was said to be home to 'large bazaars filled to over-flowing with produce of all kinds that can find no market. Two years harvest of grain and valonia are still stored there with no means at present of finding transport to get it away.' When a consignment of the region's famed raisins were finally dispatched, the considered opinion was that the festering fruit 'should have been in Marseilles or Liverpool six months ago'.

The deterioration in quality from such delays was slight, however, compared to that 'caused, particularly in delicate products, by the frequent lading and unlading consequent upon the nightly rest of the camels'. The produce, mostly carried in hair sacks, was particularly vulnerable to being set down on wet ground when the bottom 'six or seven inches' of the sacks' contents could be 'entirely spoilt'. With the opening of the railway in 1866, the company was able to move covered cargoes from Aydın to Smyrna's quayside warehouses in just three hours. The economic argument was unanswerable; the railway was soon transforming the prospects of the valley's producers.

These producers were largely foreign; many were the same migrant Greeks whose numbers had been rising steeply from the moment the line's first sleeper was laid along the valley. These Greeks were characteristically quick to form an active, entrepreneurial, affluent and educated regional minority. They wasted no time in reinvesting profits in the purchase of agricultural holdings.

They came to acquire many of the valley's commercial interests; the workshops, olive oil and soap factories, watermills and fisheries were often under Greek control. Some of them set up as traders and as inland agents of Smyrna's export agencies. They were prominent in the new railway, managing the company's freight interests and serving as station staff. Greek communities, complete with churches, hospitals, Greek-language schools and clubs, sprang up throughout the Meander Valley.

Of these communities the most impressive was at Aydın. By 1919, that 'great centre of transit trade, and a mart for the produce of the rich districts around' had spawned a flourishing Greek quarter. Home to some 12,000 shopkeepers, merchants and manufacturers, the quarter had 'its finely placed church, its well-equipped hospital, its school, its theatre, its cinema, its electric light, its flour mills, its factories for crushing olives and making soap'. Greeks had also become active in the city's bazaars and warehouses, in the tanneries and dyeing works, the cotton factories, 'silk-winderies', and machine-works. The Aydın Greeks had done well from the railway; they showed their appreciation by garlanding the train that carried the season's first fig consignments to Smyrna with sprigs of laurel and myrtle.

The local Turks felt differently; the commercial justification of the railway, as even its owners acknowledged, had never been to provide the locals with a passenger service. Instead, it overwhelmingly served foreigners' interests. With the line's every easterly extension – the railway was to reach Sarayköy in 1882, and Dinar in 1889, before continuing onwards past the source of the Meander around the turn of the century – the Turks had watched with increasing disquiet. In their view the railway had hastened the advance into their land of mainland Greeks, foreigners who had soon grown both prosperous and strident, while it did nothing for the Turks themselves. The line had ruined, moreover, the largely Turkish haulage industry, putting some 20,000 camels, 500 mules and their drivers out of work. The despised railway, a tool of the infidel interests that increasingly controlled the land, became a focus for Turkish resentment. The Turks feared it could only be a matter of time before Greek armies followed the Greek settlers up the line.

They did not have long to wait. Arguments soon embroiled the powers at Sèvres. The Italians pressed the Greeks to give up their claim to the Meander Valley in exchange for a job lot of Dodecanese Islands. The British favoured the Greek claim to the region; they thought of the Greeks as compliant allies in the furtherance of their imperial ambitions in Asia. The French increasingly resisted any settlement that deprived the Turks of the Meander Valley, in favour of either the Greeks or Italians, fearful that it would affect the Turks' ability to maintain interest payments to their French creditors.

The Italians, sensing an unfavourable wind,

decided on unilateral action to press their claim; in early May 1919 they landed troop detachments, which occupied the Mediterranean ports of Bodrum, Marmaris, Fethiye and Antalya – the jewels, by happenstance, of modern Turkey's tourism industry – before moving north to the Meander Valley where they further occupied the towns of Söke and Kuşadası. This high-handed move incensed the British, who persuaded their allies to authorise a Greek landing at Smyrna on 15 May 1919. Within days there were Greek soldiers stationed along the Smyrna–Aydın railway.

On a concrete bleacher at Aydın's stadium I sat beside a man in a suit whose card identified him as a school inspector called Mr Flag. If Turks had a weakness for flags, more even than for business cards, it especially showed on 19 May. All over the city the national Star and Crescent was draped from public buildings and from the balconies of crumbling apartment blocks. The red-and-white standards flew across the stadium and trailed in the wake of the drilled military bands, which paraded among the smart scout troops and the schoolchildren. Some among the crowd were cloaked in their flags like the football fans who usually occupied the bleachers. Others waved the miniature flags printed on stick-stapled sheets of celluloid or on balloons they had bought from the dark-eyed hawkers who traipsed the bleachers, trailing the smell of woodsmoke behind them.

The stadium had known better times. The main stand carried, writ large, the word *Champions!*, though nobody in the uninformed crowd, not least Mr Flag, seemed sure when the members of the city's football team had last been in a position to call themselves such a thing. The exultant utterance that day appeared to have a wider, national resonance. For on 19 May 1919, four days after Greek forces had put ashore to make these lands their own, the Turks had first signalled their intention to resist. Barely had the Great War in the West ended upon a thrice-repeated number – the eleventh hour of the eleventh day of the eleventh month – than the Turks' preparation for yet another war began with a trio of nineteens.

The schoolchildren marched across the patchy turf. The boys were in purple, their smocks utilitarian as those of surgeons or death row inmates, while the lilac-clad girls waved their white kerchiefs aloft. Some paraded banners bearing messages of state agencies like the health authority, which discouraged smoking or commended the benefits of walking. 'To gain a tourist,' another declared grandiloquently, 'is to win the future.' This impressively choreographed display might have recalled Ceauşescu-era Bucharest or even Pyongyang if it had not been leavened by a more maverick presence – the men who had been given leave, it seemed, to wander the perimeter at their own pace. These men were got up in a clannish period look. Their baggy shorts, felt caps covered in colourful floral baubles, high boots, purple neck scarves and shoulder-slung rifles recalled the costumes I had seen in the sepia photographs at Yörük Ali's museum; they were dressed as fearsome zeybeks. These honorary outlaw militiamen advanced in no kind of order, drifting past the goalmouths and even dropping back beyond the view of their *efe* to field surreptitious calls on phones plucked from the depths of their waistcoats, much to the amusement of irreverent elements in the crowd.

'Hey, Zeybek,' somebody called out. 'Bet the signal's better here than in the mountains.'

Mr Flag, meanwhile, was seeking to win the promised future by practising his English on the tourist he had discovered sitting beside him. The school inspector ventured a series of questions, one about my surname, before processing my answers through the digital dictionary he carried.

'An amphibious mammal,' he declared unsteadily, pointing at me. 'With flippers.' My surname appeared as noteworthy to the tedious Mr Flag, and to the surrounding crowd, as his did to me.

I had been reflecting upon Turkish surnames that same morning. In the ceremonial solemnity of Aydın's central square, where the city honoured its past, I came across a memorial to the local men who had died on Turkey's Gallipoli Peninsula in 1915. The inscribed monument, of polished black marble, moved me, and not merely because of the slaughter – of some 90,000 Ottoman men – occasioned by the desperate defence of that crucial spur of land, key to Constantinople; the greater poignancy was that the Turks had then had no effective mechanism for distinguishing between many of their martyrs.

The memorial listed the men by their first and only names. Further identification supplied by their fathers' names often proved inconclusive; of the many Mehmets, for example, a good number were given identically as the son of Mehmet, while several more were similarly indistinguishable sons of Hüseyins, or of Mustafas or Alis. Even the literate bereaved could not always know which inscribed entry commemorated their own fallen Mehmet.

Mehmet had always been, of course, the most popular name among Turkish males; it was to be expected that Mehmetcik, or Little Mehmet, should have come to denote the Turkish soldier. The usage drew broad comparison, in the fond and admiring affection that it conveyed, with the British 'Tommy'; where it differed was in signifying Turkish soldiers both alive and dead, so that its meaning also encompassed the more exalted notion of the Unknown Soldier. The Turkish war graves of the Meander Valley and elsewhere were set with marble headstones, an engraved Star and Crescent and the attendant tulip blooms picked out in blood-red paint, but were otherwise marked only as the resting places of the 'Martyr Mehmetcik'. Unlike Western military practice – the war dead only accounted unknown after the failure of all administrative and forensic attempts to identify their remains – the fallen of late-Ottoman Turkey seemed more readily prised from an identity they had never fully acquired beyond the bourn of friends and families. Just as widespread illiteracy had meant nameless headstones in the villages, so it was often impossible to distinguish the men that these war graves and memorials commemorated. It sufficed, it seemed, to remember the war dead as unidentified instances of the heroic archetype.

That legendary repulse of the Allied onslaught at Gallipoli was closely associated, of course, with the day's commemorations at Aydın's football stadium and across Turkey. What connected them was one Colonel Mustafa Kemal; the same man who on 19 May 1919 put ashore in Anatolia to lead the resistance against the latest invasion had been largely credited with leading the Turks' earlier defence at Gallipoli.

Gallipoli was where Mustafa Kemal had first made his military reputation; his example there inspired extraordinary loyalty and sacrifice from the men under his command. In the carnage by the Dardanelles he acquired the aura of dogged defiance which was to rouse an exhausted, cowed and broken Anatolia to a final act of resistance four years later. The Turks, who even now were quick to account themselves a warrior people and who revered their war heroes above all others, had subsequently raised countless statues to Mustafa Kemal. In Aydın's main square he stands opposite the Gallipoli memorial where I found him among a thicket of floral wreaths, which pledged the allegiance of the city's political parties and military, its chambers of commerce, bar association, city council and many other organisations to the ideals of the man who was to become known as Atatürk.

I had seen Atatürk, of course, all along the Meander. From the leader's giant rusting outline above Dinar to his photograph over the door of the Fearless family farm, from busts in villages like Bahadınlar and framed portraits in the tea houses to the impress of his head on every coin in my pocket, I was witness to a uniquely enduring personality cult. No state had ever fostered the posthumous memory of their one-time leader so absolutely and for so long.

A singular conjunction accounted for it; the unique impression, that is, that this man's exceptional wartime achievements had made upon a people especially entrenched in martial tradition. Atatürk had saved the Turks from national annihilation at Gallipoli; and from 19 May 1919 he was to do so all over again. The vast and enduring regard that his people came to have for him would grant Atatürk unparalleled political latitude between the founding of the Turkish Republic in 1923 and his death in 1938. Unlike his modernising peers in Persia and Afghanistan, shah and king respectively, modern Turkey's saviour and founder was able to impose nothing less than social revolution upon his people and to enshrine that order in the national constitution. Atatürk's standing furnished him with the political wherewithal to achieve reforms – in terms of such social fundamentals as religion, language and dress – which weight of populist conservatism would otherwise have surely blocked.

The period iconography was a powerful reminder, of course, that Atatürk had in fact died before the outbreak of the Second World War. The vast banners unfurled on the walls of an adjacent school presented him in a pinstripe suit, with pointed collars, and parted hair in the Edwardian fashion. His statue was decked out, meanwhile, in full evening dress: morning suit, bow tie and wing collars, waistcoat, knobbed stick and top hat. In these outfits Atatürk had appeared at 1930s state banquets and embassy functions. Even so, to such rigs there now clung an impression not of the statesman so much as the dandy; something of the European aristocrat, even of the abdicated monarch, a leisured itinerant dividing his time between hotels with names like the Bristol or the Splendid, and the local baccarat tables. The costumes that Atatürk had worn to signal the national destiny had long fallen out of fashion and now looked as outlandish to the citizens of Europe's political union as they must always have appeared to the bemused Turks. The passing of time had stranded Atatürk in a period fancy dress that spoke of exclusive privileges that Europe's masters, having never shared them with their own masses, were certainly not about to disburse among the supplicant Turks.

Atatürk's image, that said, had not always been the ubiquitous presence it is now. In fact, his face had been removed from the country's banknotes and stamps in routine fashion shortly after his death. His restoration there more than a decade later was as a sop by a government anxious to reassure the secular military that the few Islamic freedoms the politicians had introduced – allowing, for example, the call to prayer to be made in the traditional Arabic – were not to be feared as harbingers of a wider assault on the great leader's legacy. By this ploy of its political opponents, then, the secularist establishment recognised that Atatürk's passing need not prevent his continued service as a highly visible exemplar. Atatürk, co-opted into the national iconography and essentially deified in the process, became the steering mechanism by which his ideological bearing might be maintained.

Now, however, that rudder appeared to have gone awry. Certainly, the guardians of Atatürk's legacy seemed hard pressed to preserve the secular order against an impressive Islamic electoral majority. In that respect the expressed will of the Turkish people and of Atatürk seemed increasingly at odds. The speeches that sounded through the loudspeakers at Aydın's stadium seemed intent on avoiding any mention of Atatürk's Western-style secularism, fearful, perhaps, of the lukewarm reception it might induce, but instead invoked attributes on which all Turks were heartily agreed; they spoke of the great warrior who had saved the nation, whose forces had saved Aydın itself, from both the European aggressors and the Ottoman authorities who had so cravenly connived in the proposed dismemberment of the Turkish territories.

'There are and have always been two Atatürks,' declared the provincial governor, a short man dressed in a grey suit. 'The one who saved us, and the one in our hearts and our futures too.' We stood for the national anthem. When its last notes played and the band fell silent, a sound was heard from across the city. It was the Arabic chants of the lunchtime call to prayer.

The bleachers began to empty. Mr Flag pocketed his digital dictionary and slipped from my side. I wandered through Aydın, recalling the 'trees, lofty domes and minarees of mosques interspersed' that had once greeted Richard Chandler, a place of 'innumerable tame turtle-doves, sitting in the branches of trees, on the walls, and roofs of houses, cooing unceasingly'. The city also impressed Charles Fellows. 'I have in England been at fairs and races, and have witnessed the commemoration days in Paris, and the masquerades and carnivals in Catania and Naples,' wrote Fellows, airing impressive travel credentials,

> but all fall short, in gay variety and general beauty of costume, of this Turkish market. The foliage of the plants and trees growing in the streets formed a pleasant relief to the dazzling whiteness of the veils, and the splendid colours of the embroidered trowsers, of the multitudes of women attending the market; light blue worked with silver was very commonly seen in the dresses of the peasants, and every turban had its bunch of roses or flowers . . . The passing of camels and loaded asses through the crowd called forth continually the warning voice of the driver. The women had their children tied on their backs, and these, with the gay colour of their dresses and their heads ornamented with coins, contributed their part to the general picturesque effect.

In this modern city of numbered streets there was not the least reminder, however, of the doves and embroidered trousers, the camel trains and the zeybeks' floral turbans. The streets were lined by apartment blocks painted in institutional shades. Lines of washing, children's tricycles, dead pot plants, rusting air-conditioning units, and the placarded details of lawyers', dentists' and gynaecologists' premises, showed among the flag-draped concrete of the balconies.

Then I found my way by chance into 1629 Street. Here, where an older city survived, the apartment blocks were yet to intrude. Behind elegant railings stood gardens shaded by orange trees, and in the arched vaults of a high-walled *han* men in thick glasses braced themselves over antique sewing machines, firing off stitch bursts like squinting *mitrailleurs*. It was fitting that the street should have been home to Aydın's Antiquarian – or *Lovers of Old Things* in the touching Turkish rendition – Society.

The society's chairman was called Mehmet Trueblueeyed. Framed portraits of Mehmet's predecessors in the post, all ties, jackets and prominent moustaches, hung from the walls of the office, a single small room, where any suggestion of cultured association had long been lost in the cram of collectables. The members' diverse interests and magpie tendencies had done for such pretensions, transforming the office into something altogether more animated; a hoard store of enthusiasms, the shelves lined with old radios, their speakers fronted with lacquered weaves, and moth-eaten items of zeybek costume, piles of 1950s magazines whose monochrome covers featured farmers standing proud beside their American tractors, and stacks of yellow-brown bricks.

The old bricks of his native city, it turned out, were the particular interest of Mehmet Trueblueeyed. He had collected more than a hundred of them. Across Aydın he picked through piles of rubble for prize examples; bricks free from cracks and chipped corners, and carrying the clear imprint of the maker's initial or name. In the continued demolition, then, of the city's old buildings Mehmet caught precious glimpses of their creation. These nostalgic keepsakes commemorated not only their makers but the historic buildings to which they had recently belonged, and every day Mehmet learned of new sites where he might grow his collection.

'The owners of these old houses don't think to live in them,' he said. 'They only value the plots the houses occupy. They are interested in profitable development, and over several storeys. Their problem is that the old houses are now protected by law. The solution is to leave them unoccupied and unrepaired, and wait for them to fall down. The houses of greatest historical value are the ones that stand empty; the neglect they suffer is deliberate.'

Mehmet led me to a few such houses. Some stood beside empty lots, which had been readied to receive apartment blocks. Deprived of their neighbours' support, the houses had begun to sag; chunks of their stucco façades, lavishly painted with columns and capitals, had fallen into the cleared lots where they turned to powder. One such villa had wide eaves patterned in a woodwork lattice, high arched windows and faded ochre walls richly worked with neoclassical cornices white as icing, with festooned borders, elegant lintels and with the same meander patterns that adorned the baths and temples of ancient cities. The house, hemmed in by a modern pavement, was also covered in black scrawls. The graffiti were illegible but seemed nevertheless to curse the lovely structure for a Greek hindrance, seeking only its collapse.

Mehmet led the way to the banks of a deep stream, where the city's tanneries had once turned out 'fine yellow morocco' leather. The present bridge was no more than a slab of reinforced concrete; as functional as the earlier crossing there had been graceful. For, largely obscured beneath the rust-stained underbelly of that flyover replacement, there still stood the high, keystoned arch of an Ottoman-period bridge. Beyond the stream we wandered past a school and among the pine trees of parklands. We walked wide residential streets lined by 1950s homes and apartment blocks. There was no sign of the neoclassical detailing – the meanders and the vine festoons – I had seen elsewhere in the city. It was then that Mehmet pointed out two stone projections that flanked the concrete steps of an outdoor café. From these rounded bases, badly chipped and painted pink, the columned entrance of St George's Church had once risen. The pedestals were all that remained of Aydın's Greek quarter.

CHAPTER 20

The historian Arnold Toynbee, on assignment for the *Manchester Guardian*, had occasion to visit Aydın in February 1921. Toynbee witnessed how 'ruins flanked the railway for miles as one came into Aidin' on the train from Smyrna. He also saw what had happened to the city's Greek quarter. 'The work was deliberately done,' he concluded. 'The buildings were not destroyed in the heat of battle but burnt one by one, and there is a sudden sharp boundary between the gutted Greek houses and the intact Turkish centre of the town. Here were twisted bedsteads, there safes with holes knocked in their sides, here a shred of clothing or a boot.'

This same city the Turks had also razed in 1282; they had then subjected Tralles' 20,000 surviving Christians to a captivity so intolerable that many were said to have envied their fellow dead. Toynbee's observations might then have been taken to confirm Turkish form, in Aydın especially, when it came to laying waste to the lives and homes of the local Greeks.

Toynbee's observations appeared consonant with

the behaviour that appalled Westerners had expected of Turks ever since learning of their accursed existence around the time of the First Crusade. Pope Urban II, rallying knights to the Christian cause by fulminating against the heathen race, thereby set the papal seal on a millennium of anti-Turkish sentiment – one which, it should be admitted, centuries of all-out Ottoman expansionism only helped to inflame. With the Turks' every advance or incursion the defiant but fearful invective deepened across Europe. The people of Christendom denounced the Turks in their pamphlets and prayers as bloodthirsty ghouls no less inhuman than their Mongol and Tartar kin. Masses were held in the hope that their fiendish war machines might mire in the Hungarian mud. Plays and entertainments were peopled with turbaned bogeymen, and references to Turkish body parts were liberally scattered among their pages: the nose of the Turk, for example, which went into the cauldron in *Macbeth* – not so much, it seemed, for its potion efficacy as that the audience might savour the implied fact of its one-time severance. The Turk's Head, a popular name among many pubs and hostels, no doubt pandered to their patrons' same vengeful impulses.

Such attitudes were especially prevalent from the late eighteenth century; a loathing of Turks was the natural corollary of the widespread enthusiasm for all things Greek. The historian Thomas Smart Hughes dismissed Turks as 'cruel tyrants, bathed in the blood of their own Emperors upon every succession; a heap of vassals and slaves; a people that is without natural affection; without pity; without morality; without letters, arts, or sciences; in a word, a very reproach to human nature, and that has made the garden of the world a wilderness'. It was a view that resonated in 1919 when a British Foreign Office mandarin, firmly in stride with the avowed philhellenism of his prime minister, David Lloyd George, privately observed that 'No one but a congenital idiot could be pro-Turk.'

Except for those, perhaps, who had gone to the trouble of acquiring first-hand experience of Turks. When Charles Fellows set out for Anatolia in 1838, just fourteen years after Lord Byron died of marsh fever in the sacred Greek cause at Missolonghi, it was no surprise that he should have declared himself 'strongly biased in favour of the Greeks and equally prejudiced against the Turks'. In the course of his travels, however, as Fellows was at pains to acknowledge, 'this unfavourable idea of the Turkish character was gradually removed by a personal intimacy with the people'. 'To their manners, habits and character, equally as to their costume,' he wrote, 'I am become not only reconciled, but sincerely attached; for I have found truth, honesty and kindness, the most estimable and amiable qualities, in a people among whom I so little looked for them.'

So Turks, as I myself had since learned, could

come as an agreeable surprise; and Anatolia's Greeks, if only because they enjoyed so elevated a standing, had regularly proved a disappointment. Reverend Arundell put it more strongly. 'It is impossible,' he declared, 'not to be disgusted with many prominent features of the modern Greek character . . . gratitude is not among their virtues.' Other travellers found them grasping, disingenuous, even devious. The Greeks were not always so good, nor the Turks so bad, as people liked to think. Neither race, that said, was to emerge with any credit from the events about to unfold at Aydın, which the Greek forces occupied on 27 May 1919.

The Allied Command had justified the landing twelve days earlier of 13,000 Greek troops at Smyrna on the grounds of maintaining law and order. It was a decision that incensed the Turks and a pretext they did not believe.

Nor, patently, did most Greeks. Not the newly landed soldiers who performed jubilant jigs around their stacks of equipment on the Smyrna quayside. Neither the Greek newspapers who were to invoke the great anabases, the eastward forays of Xenophon and Alexander, at every stage of the Greeks' subsequent advances up the river valleys east of Smyrna. Nor the citizens who waved Greek flags, rang church bells, and chanted the name of Prime Minister Venizelos, architect of Greece's 'Ionian' ambitions – and whose first name actually translated as 'Liberator'.

It was as liberators, certainly, that the soldiers had entered Aydın in the view of many of the city's Greeks. In elegant neoclassical homes celebratory dinners were held and glasses raised to the city's proud Hellenic heritage: Aydın had been home, after all, to St Anthemius, architect of Constantinople's Haghia Sophia basilica, the very font of Orthodox Christianity, and also to the Tralles Stone, the marble whose inscriptions had unlocked the mysteries of ancient Greek musical notation. The city's Greeks soon gave themselves over to public celebrations; there were 'continual processions with flags', as one English eyewitness noted, and 'portraits of Venizelos in all the houses, shops and cafes, their ridiculous patriotic songs, sung all day long by the street scum and the soldiers . . .'

Such triumphalism, merely tedious, soon descended into a more spiteful subjection. Some Aydın Greeks, increasingly secure in the strength of their position, did 'their level best to make themselves obnoxious, unpopular and hated by the Turks'. Turks were jostled and warned that the Greek forces could not be held responsible for the lives of those who would not replace their Ottoman fezes with Western-style hats. Prominent Turks, professors and lawyers among them, were arrested on suspicion of holding anti-Hellenic views.

As the Greek forces continued their advance, which the Allied authorities had not authorised beyond Aydın, so the hostilities and humiliations intensified. At Nazilli the houses of Muslims were attacked, men were beaten, women violated and muezzins abused while making the call to prayer. Sarayköy's Turks were forced to carry portraits of Venizelos beneath the triumphal arch that had been erected to welcome the Greek soldiers.

Tensions especially escalated from 19 June. That night the Greek forces, under instruction from the Allies, withdrew from their unauthorised advance positions. They left Nazilli under cover of darkness, 'suddenly evacuating a town without warning either the inhabitants or the Turkish forces', as a report was to censure them, 'and then pointing with satisfaction to the murdered inhabitants as a vindication of their statement that Greek domination is essential to the safety of Anatolia'.

The immediate provocation was what befell the thirty or so Turkish men who were forced to accompany the Greeks on their retreat. One, said to be unable to keep up with the column, was executed on the way. At the railway town of Köşk, possibly in response to the fire that some towns-people were said to have directed at the Greek soldiers, several of the captive Turks were killed and their bullet-ridden bodies left lying in the road.

It was evident, barely a month after the Greek landings at Smyrna, that the situation was increasingly uncontainable. The war-weary Turks, one observer judged, had largely been prepared to accept the Greek presence as long as it 'was well defined in limits and conducted in some measure of decency. Information so far received appears to show that neither of these conditions have been fulfilled.' The result had been to rouse 'Turks of all classes from [an] attitude of passive surliness to one of active hostility'. Insurrection was abroad. Greek misrule was intolerable, to the zeybeks especially.

It might have been assumed that rapid industrialisation – the modernised farms, the proliferating factories and the steady extension of the railway – had long since made colourful anachronisms of the Meander region's legendary brigands. That was certainly the impression gained from an 1873 guidebook's description of Aydın's 'very picturesque *meidan* with coffee-houses, where the zebecks may sometimes be seen enjoying themselves'; the old irregulars had been reduced to café habitués, it seemed, who earned their coin by hamming it up for the tourists.

In fact, the Greek landings had soon galvanised the zeybeks throughout the hinterland. The provocations along the Meander Valley, as an observer noted, served to endow them with a higher purpose. 'What was at one time but a normal . . . state of brigandage and highway robbery,' he explained, 'has now developed into a national movement aimed primarily against the Greek forces, but additionally against the constituted authority in the capital.' The zeybeks formed gangs, old adversaries now joining forces in common cause against the invaders and

Constantinople's collaborationist Ottomans alike. Across the expanding area of occupation they postered the villages with calls to arms. Their men broke open the poorly guarded stores where the surrendered munitions of the Ottomans' disbanded regiments had been collected, and helped themselves to bullets and rifles. Then these patriots fell upon the invaders where they knew they would find them: along the hated railway.

The railway had played a central role in the Greek advance, carrying soldiers and supplies inland. By shadowing the nearby Meander River – the boundary between the Greek zone and the occupied area the rival Italians had lately established immediately to the south of the river – the railway soon came to serve, moreover, as the Greeks' southern front line. From the south side of the Meander, in the safety of the Italian zone, the incensed Turks watched the Greek forces make themselves at home along the railway. The Greek soldiers stored munitions in the yards, billeted troops in the train sheds and warehouses, and with the enthusiastic assistance of openly supportive Rum Greek staff turned the numerous stations into armed camps. The railway had effectively declared in support of the Greeks, which was no surprise to the zeybeks, who from the middle of June saw to it that the railway bore the brunt of their resistance.

The Turks dynamited bridges and cut telegraph wires. They ransacked station offices. They fired upon passing trains. They killed and abducted station staff. They skirmished with the Greek soldiers garrisoned along the line. They attacked Greek civilians in the station towns. Reprisal attacks ensued. Greek and Turkish villagers alike fled their homes; the Greeks at the station town of Karapınar, following the slaughter of eleven of their number, a child and an eighty-year-old woman among them, fled in their nightclothes for the comparative safety of Aydın. The fields and fig orchards stood deserted. The villages burned beneath black plumes. The old pattern was repeating; the Meander Valley was once more being wasted as West and East laid ancient claim to the region.

In this febrile atmosphere a young reservist, Lieutenant Ben Hodder, was tasked with maintaining some vestige of order. Hodder, the British control officer at Aydın, was returning from supervising repairs to a sabotaged bridge on Saturday 28 June when his special train was held up at Umurlu; the town had been back in Turkish hands since the Greeks, abandoning Nazilli, had nine days earlier withdrawn to within a few kilometres of Aydın. This railway town had since become a mustering station on the fringe of the occupation zone, and the platform there was crowded with armed and excitable fighting Turks: 250 regular soldiers, Hodder reckoned, along with about 1,000 zeybeks from a wider band whose total complement was estimated at 6,000 men. The regular forces, whose officers took their orders from the Allied authorities even if their true loyalties lay elsewhere, claimed only qualified control over the zeybeks; these belligerent and impassioned men meant to march on the Greeks. The zeybeks refused to allow Hodder's train to leave Umurlu until they had handed over an ultimatum, which the control officer was to deliver to Aydın's authorities. The Greek forces had three days' notice to quit Aydın; if they did so, the city's Christians would be protected. Otherwise, the zeybeks vowed to 'burn and pillage the whole town'. The ultimatum was signed by one Yörük Ali.

The brigand from Kavaklı, now twenty-four years old, had evidently distinguished himself since deserting from the Russian front some years earlier. He now headed a powerful alliance of zeybek bands whose stock among nationalist Turks, civilians and officials alike, had been transformed since the Greek landings at Smyrna. A photograph taken that June shows Yörük Ali in the company of considerable establishment figures. He appears seated in pride of place between an army officer in broad buckled belt, high collar and astrakhan-style *kalpak*, and a local politician in waistcoat and fez. Behind this nationalist triumvirate stands a sombre but resolute crowd of rifle-bearing zeybeks and straight-backed villagers, their collarless shirts buttoned to the neck in a makeshift gesture of disciplined formality; a broadly representative sample of the force tasked, given the substantive demobilisation of the regular army, with ousting the hated Greeks and their European sponsors. Theirs was a cause, of course, with historic echoes; as nomadic irregulars had first won the land for the Turks in the eleventh century, so these men were to regain it. Beginning with this young zeybek chief, slim, solemn, and clean-shaven beneath his high turban, whose signature confirmed that the Greeks must leave the city or expose themselves and Aydın's Christians to the consequences.

By the time Hodder's train reached Aydın that Saturday afternoon, however, events had outrun the ultimatum the control officer was to deliver on Yörük Ali's behalf; some 2,000 Greek soldiers and some rogue zeybek bands were already locked in fierce fighting to the south of the city. The gun battle continued through the night. By Sunday morning it was clear that the outnumbered Greeks were losing ground. They withdrew their field guns to the heights behind the city, where the ruins of ancient Tralles stood, before resuming their bombardment of the advancing zeybeks. Meanwhile their front-line soldiers took up holding positions in the city.

'Aidin was in a state of terror,' wrote Hodder. 'Every house was closed as bullets were flying in all directions.' The control officer made an attempt to reach the train station, where he thought to receive news, but was driven back by the crossfire. He sheltered inside his quarters while the battle raged on the city's streets. The Greek forces made a stand around the station, distributing arms among volunteer Greek civilians and setting up machine guns on the roofs of houses in the Jewish quarter. The Turks, who had moved up their field guns, now rained shells onto the city. One demolished the cupola of St Charalambos Church. Another hit a building alongside the French convent where Aydın's Christian population had begun to take refuge.

In the course of Sunday the Greek forces were steadily forced back. Acknowledging that they could not hold Aydın, some determined to destroy the areas belonging to the Muslim enemy. Retreating through the Turkish area, the Cuma quarter, they began to slosh gasoline against the walls of the houses, coffee houses, businesses and mosques. 'It was not long,' Hodder reported, 'before there was a conflagration in the Turkish quarter.' From the streets and rooftops the Greek soldiers shot down Turkish civilians as they escaped their flaming homes; they looted the houses the fire had not yet reached, assaulting or killing the occupants. The Greeks then fell back north of the railway line before retiring to the heights where their field guns were positioned. As the day drew on, word of the Greek retreat spread among the city's Christians who hurriedly followed in the footsteps of those who had already made for the French convent.

At dusk, when the first few zeybek scouts began ghosting onto Aydın's streets, Hodder received a message; the chief of the zeybeks, Yörük Ali himself, wished to meet the control officer. The two men convened in a sheltered garden near Hodder's quarters. Yörük Ali had with him six men; their picturesque costumes moved Hodder to describe the troop as 'braves'. These zeybeks stood guard while Hodder invited Yörük Ali, accompanied by a French-speaking secretary, into his offices. Refreshments and cigarettes were provided and the two men conversed, the aide-de-camp interpreting, and in that moment of civilised parleying it may perhaps have been possible to forget the slaughter and the burned houses. The other possibility was that the darkness had prevented Yörük Ali from realising the full extent of the carnage wrought throughout Aydın's Turkish quarter. At any rate, the zeybek chief even now seemed intent upon negotiating a settlement, requesting Hodder's help in delivering a further ultimatum: that if the Greek commander now evacuated the region entirely and did not return again, Yörük Ali would guarantee the safety of the local Christians. This ultimatum was witnessed by Hodder before a messenger carried it away. Hodder entreated Yörük Ali to keep his men in hand, hoping that he would not allow them to behave cruelly to the Christians.

'Hodder Efendi,' exclaimed the chief. 'I have not come here to war against innocent people, women and children, but we do not and will not have the Hellenes here, we will drive them out. They may come back and drive us out again, but we shall continue to fight for our country to the last man.'

Yörük Ali's speech was unequivocal, even dignified, but the dispatched ultimatum was to prove as redundant as his previous one. The old hatreds that had historically consumed the Meander Valley would once again have their way. Through Sunday evening a thickening stream of frightened Christians made their way to the French convent. By Monday morning some 4,000 people were crammed into the compound.

The main zeybek bands, wary of ambush, had awaited the dawn before entering the shell-strewn city. All night they had smelt the smoke and the sweet stench of the gasoline; they had heard the dogs and the keening. They now saw for themselves the empty fuel barrels, the broken possessions and the ripped clothes that were scattered throughout the blackened swathes of the Cuma quarter. Turkish women and children lay dead in the streets, arms outflung in flight, flies at their nostrils. A smouldering shell was all that remained of the mosque at Dükkanönu. The zeybeks saw what the Greek soldiers had done and they now directed their steps towards the Greek quarter. On the deserted streets nobody stood in their way. At their leisure they looted the houses whose raised stucco detailing – the neoclassical columns, garlands, rosettes, volutes and meanders – appeared like proud pronouncements of Aydın's new Hellenic age. The houses burned and the inhabitants hiding inside burned with them. The fleeing Greeks the zeybeks encountered on the streets were shot without regard for age or sex. Then the zeybeks collected at the gates of the French convent.

The French flag flew over the building; the convent might have offered effective protection, even for the ever-growing number of refugees. As it was, the uncontrolled fires that threatened to engulf the compound gave its occupants no choice but to seek refuge elsewhere. The zeybeks were waiting for them; as the first jibbering civilians spilled into the street shots rang out, killing twelve of them. Only then did a dispatch of regular Turkish soldiers, who had managed to reach the city from their base beyond the Meander in the Italian zone, succeed in putting a stop to the firing. These disciplined troops were thinly spread, however, and there was little they could do to stop the zeybeks from stripping the Christians, the living and dead alike, of their purses and jewellery. The terrified crowd, shedding coats and shoes and valuables, eventually reached the relative safety of the nearby *konak*, the local government building. There the senior Turkish regular officer, Colonel Şefik, dutifully did what he could to feed and protect them.

The sheer number of zeybeks soon ensured, however, that they had control of the city. One eyewitness, an employee of the Ottoman Imperial Bank, described Tuesday as 'the most complete anarchy'. Aydın, he wrote, was entirely in the hands of the zeybeks who released the common prisoners and took it upon themselves to judge the city's notable Greeks on the basis of 'simple accusations, ancient grudges, the complaints of Muslims'. Some thirty persons, including Mrs Jean Philippides, Nico Avyeries, Dr Yorghanjioglou, the banker Mr Georgiades and the three brothers Papaconstantinou, were executed or led away to the mountains. Lieutenant Hodder, busy negotiating to evacuate trainloads of Christian refugees from the city, saw bodies everywhere: '11 women and 8 children and 3 men who had been cruelly done to death' in a ravine north of the city; 'a further lot of 13 women, 15 children and 22 men' in the city; and 'the remains of 8 children that had been burned in one house'. Both sides accused the other of rank obscenities: the bodies of some 200 raped Muslim girls were said to have been uncovered in vaults near the French convent, while it was alleged that the disembowelled remains of Greek children, entrails wrapped round their necks, had been discovered in the burned shell of St Charalambos Church.

Two days later, just as the Turkish regulars under Colonel Şefık were beginning to re-establish a semblance of control, news spread that a reinforced Greek column totalling some 10,000 soldiers was closing on the city. Colonel Şefık wasted no time in urging all Turks, zeybeks, regulars and civilians alike, to leave Aydın. By four o'clock that Thursday afternoon there was 'a veritable stampede of Turks towards the Meander'; their safety lay south of the river where the Italians, actively antagonistic towards the Greek occupation, were busy befriending the nationalist cause by offering Turks safe haven and succour beyond their protective screen. Among the last to leave the city was Colonel Şefik who called in to say goodbye to Lieutenant Hodder.

'I have done all in my power,' the Colonel declared, 'to safeguard the Christians and I hope the Greeks will behave likewise towards the Turkish population. Today the Greeks are entering Aydın and we are leaving the town, but we shall drive the troops back and enter it again.' By eight o'clock the following morning it was reckoned that just 105 out of some 25,000 Muslims remained in the city. The Battle for Aydın was over. The city had once more changed hands, as it had always changed hands. It would do so again; though it would take more than three years, the Turks would finally recapture Aydın, as Colonel Şefik and Yörük Ali had vowed.

In the meantime, any shred of pretence that the Greeks' presence in Anatolia was to maintain law and order was dispelled; this was their attempt to confirm for once and for all, by force of arms and with the tacit support of Great Britain, the historical truth that here truly was where the West extended, not where the East began. From the banks of the Meander River north to the shores of the Sea of Marmara, the roughly rectangular area occupied by the advancing Greeks soon descended into barbarous war. Ben Hodder, witness to the hatreds that had flared in Aydın, would not have been surprised; the local Turks, he reported, had developed a 'fanatical hatred of the Greek; the war is now a religious one and it will be hard to appease and settle matters'.

So it proved; with every successive springtime advance of the Greek divisions, the old sectarian accommodations that had once prevailed between the land's Muslims and its Rum Christians were obliterated in a welter of slaughter and burning. The animosities were at their most bitter along the Meander Valley where the Turks, falling back before the well-equipped Greek forces, took their revenge upon Christian civilians. Most of Umurlu's Rum Greeks were killed and thrown down the town's wells. Other Christians, often barefoot and even naked, were driven into the interior. In the burning rubble of Nazilli Greeks and Turks were buried alive. The corpses of the slaughtered were left to be devoured by dogs. On the road between Nazilli and Kuyucak, a distance I had alternately dragged and paddled my canoe in the course of a short morning, an eyewitness counted fifty-three corpses. Bodies formed floating rafts on the Meander.

By the spring of 1921 the Greeks' eastward advance up the Meander Valley had carried them as far as Çivril; they were now within striking distance of their historic frontier by the Meander's headwaters. To the north the city of Eskişehir – classical Dorylaeum, where the armies of the First Crusade had famously defeated the Turks eight centuries earlier – also fell to Greek forces. They now closed on Gordium where Alexander had cut the knot before founding his empire in Asia. The newspapers in Athens found the weight of historical precedent irresistible; with the inevitable fall of the nationalists' capital at Ankara, it seemed nothing could stop the Greeks from achieving their Great Idea by making western Anatolia theirs once more.

Except that Turks in great numbers had deserted the towns and villages of the interior for the front. In time, moreover, these irregular hordes had been fashioned under Atatürk's leadership into a formidable fighting force. It helped, of course, that the anti-imperialists in Bolshevik Russia were now supporting the Turks' cause by delivering increasing quantities of munitions to the Black Sea ports that remained under nationalist control. Even so, the Turks' supply lines were long and threadbare, and it was often civilians who bore the shells and provisions on their own backs over the Anatolian mountains to the front. Grandmothers fashioned soldiers' tunics out of carpets or learned to hammer petrol tins into canteens; workshops that had once repaired stoves now turned out daggers and bayonets. In the course of August 1921 the Turks finally brought the exhausted and overstretched Greeks to a standstill on the hills south-east of Ankara.

The tide now turned; the French, who had themselves been fighting the Turks for control of Cilicia in southern Anatolia, sued for peace, not only freeing up the Turkish divisions they had been holding down there but also surrendering large stocks of arms and munitions in the process. Britain, quick to reappraise its own interests, declared its neutrality. The Greeks, stalemated and alone, soon found themselves as short of money as of morale. There was nothing for it but to dig in and hope to hold their positions against the inevitable offensive.

The Turks eventually attacked in August 1922. The Greek line, pulverised by artillery fire and sheer weight of enemy numbers, rapidly disintegrated. The Greeks fell back, as they had done three years earlier through the streets of Aydın, and as then they destroyed what they would not be able to keep for themselves. They seized women from the Turkish villages and killed the men who attempted to shield them. They doused villages with kerosene. They torched barns and mosques. Fields were burned, orchards hacked down, farming equipment smashed. Basic possessions like copper pots were destroyed. Korans were ripped to pieces before their owners' eyes. The villagers were left to glean 'handfuls of singed grains' from their smouldering fields.

The Turkish forces continued their rapid advance. They reached Aydın on 7 September 1922 where a Greek machine-gunner resisted from the minaret of the burned Selçuk mosque; it was said that Yörük Ali, who had now attained the rank of colonel, silenced the gunner with a single bullet. A Turkish flag soon flew from the minaret. The city had changed hands for the last time.

Later that month, the Turkish forces reached the terminus of the same hated railway that had carried the Greek forces into Anatolia. At the Smyrna quayside where the Greek forces had put ashore in 1919 they took their revenge on soldiers and civilians alike. In an orgy of slaughter the infidel city burned.

In the afternoon I made my own way back to the street that had somehow survived the sackings of Aydın – 1629 Street was peaceful. The tailors were drinking tea deep in their shadowed arches. An octagonal shrine stood in a walled enclosure amid a littering of headstones. A few of the houses that lined the street still bore the hand-shaped metal door knockers that I had also seen in the Aegean islands.

Among all this, and in the Turkish way, there stood a public toilet. The old attendant dozed beneath a handwritten sign, his wrinkled hand outstretched like a turnstile across the entrance and cupped in a striking resemblance to the door knockers. I placed a coin in his palm and pushed through.

'Wrong way,' the attendant murmured. I was making, however, not for the toilet but for the adjoining garden in order to access the impressive building that had caught my eye from the street; it was built from fine old bricks and topped by domes fuzzy with grasses grown from wind-borne seeds. The door to the building stood open.

Stepping inside, I found myself ankle-deep in fallen plaster. The air was oddly sweet. Dust billowed upwards, back-swirling through the light shafts that streamed past the rusted crossbars and down the deep vaults of the windows. A fountain pipe rose from a circular marble enclosure in the centre of the room. Recessed doorways, arch-shaped and stepped in the Selçuk style, led onwards to rounded chambers, with broad alcoves where marble partitions and the lips of floor basins showed above the depth of debris. The fallen plaster had exposed the brickwork in the dome where inset panels of glass striped the gloomy interior with angled bars of light. It was an Ottoman *hamam*, or bathhouse, of cathedral splendour. The effect was to transport me back to the city Charles Fellows had known; the steam hems hanging heavy over the marble slabs where camel drivers and fig farmers, murmuring at the soreness in their limbs, had once reclined to sweat the dust from their pores.

As my eyes adjusted to the half-light I began to notice that the building had not stood empty since its closure as a *hamam*. From the rotted hemp sacks that showed through the blanket of plaster hundreds of small cylindrical objects had spilled;

they were corks. Nearby I now spied green bottles, their coarse glass strewn with air bubbles and flaws, which had been stacked in their hundreds against one wall; the lower tiers, gradually extruding beneath the weight of the heap, threatened the entire bank with collapse. Piles of old grape baskets had been reduced to raffia skeletons, wood cartons lay scattered and the walls of one domed chamber were lined with wooden barrels. The *hamam* had done time as a winery.

The vintners' office had occupied a wooden mezzanine at the top of some rickety steps. The wall calendar showed a still life of a fruit bowl overflowing, in the way of the valley itself, with oranges, grapes and cherries; it hung open at the page for December 1976. There was a road map on the wall, and shelves that had partially collapsed so that the dusty ledgers were piled in the rhomboid troughs. Bottle labels, parcelled in neat string ties, proclaimed contents 'Made from the Aegean's Excellent Grapes'; and a further set of labels was for one Mr Bluedanube's 'Excellent and Delicious' cherry jam. I felt sentimental for the passing of the vintners and of Mr Bluedanube's jam makers; it saddened me that the *hamam* should have closed, the winery too, and that a malodorous toilet was all that now occupied the site.

I heard noises. A gang of men trooped through the door.

'You must have arrived by the toilet,' observed Osman, the man at their head. Osman was a scrap dealer; he wondered what interest I could have in the place. I liked old places, I explained; it was the atmosphere they exuded.

Osman shrugged. 'Then you should meet the man out at the new mall,' he said. 'We've been supplying him with lots of this junk. Today it's barrels we're delivering.' I wondered what a new mall could want with old wine barrels.

'Search me,' said Osman. 'But once we've loaded the pickup, you're welcome to find out for

385

yourself.' So I joined Osman on his delivery run. We drove through the city, stopping at a corner stall for water. Osman drank deep. 'The stuff of life,' he gasped. Then he pitched the drained plastic bottle out of the window.

From Aydın's southern edge we headed out along the same road I had travelled up the previous evening. In the fading light I had not then noticed the collection of new buildings where we now drew up. Out on the plain, apparently confident in the efficacy of the dams and the regulators, a kind of island mall had risen; a new world of fashion stores, a hotel with flagpoles, an agricultural dealership fronted by a line of machines called rock pickers, and the Café Marin, where Osman's barrels were destined.

The mall had established itself as Aydın's prestige social destination. Black cars, expensive marques, had shoaled along the tarmac apron. From beneath parasols in the garden of the Café Marin leisured locals in bright T-shirts, their tables littered with car keys, cigarette packets, phones and sunglasses, surveyed the empty plain beyond the line of rock pickers. From self-serve plastic trays they ate 'meal choices', which fairly resembled the photographs hanging by chains above the serving counter. The uniforms of the serving staff complemented the fast-food format, one that the management had cut with a refining gallery aesthetic. Minimalist chrome chairs were scattered around, and prices for the framed prints that hung from the walls were to be sought at the various screen-topped terminals where assistants decked out in curatorial black occasionally appeared. Not yet content with this curiously textured ambience, the management had begun littering the place with artefacts in the manner of a museum. I had barely begun to take in the various displays, of old-fashioned brooms and raffia baskets, grape presses and antique typewriters, before I realised where they had all come from.

'I guess nobody had been inside that *hamam* for the best part of thirty years,' the café's proprietor, Ali Ironhand, told me. 'We were amazed what we found there. I think these old pieces look good here.'

Osman and his men had begun to unload the wine barrels. I asked Ali what he knew of the Meander. He told me how as a young man, working in the cotton fields, he had often swum in the river. He had even taken boats downstream to shoot duck around the town of Söke. That was a long time ago and he had not been to the river for years. He guessed there could not be enough water for my boat. I thought I would see for myself.

As I walked down the road towards the river bridge I noticed the message marked out large in an arrangement of white stones across the hillside within the fenced military area to the south of the valley. *The Greatest Achievement*, it read, *is the Nation's Security*. Martial hyperbole went down well with the Turks. Behind the inflated words I heard, however, a truth the river's bitter history had only confirmed. The yearning that I felt for Aydın's vanished worlds of doves, domed *hamams* and elegant villas, the nostalgia that had prompted the Café Marin's heritage artefacts and Mehmet Trueblueeyed's collection of bricks, could not disguise the fact that Turkey's past had been an overwhelmingly pitiless one. For as little as a long lifetime ago the river I was following had been a no-man's land, a boundary between implacable hatreds. Was it of any account, then, that they had not yet learned to respect the river if the land was at peace, if the bodies of the slain no longer littered the roads and choked the river?

Beneath the bridge the water showed stagnant among the Meander's braided sandbanks. For once, though, it did not matter that it would be some time before I could relaunch the canoe.

CHAPTER 21

The Turks had won, and a glorious war had earned Atatürk not only the national leadership but also the freedom to rebuild the country much as he saw fit; along the lines, ironically, of those beaten or bested nations that so recently had meant to dismember it.

The transformation was to begin, less than two months after the Turks' recapture of Aydın's cindered ruins, with the abolition of the Ottoman monarchy, the sultanate. The state was proclaimed a Republic, Western and secular, in 1923. The Caliphate, office of the Supreme Head of all Muslims, and the sole position the deposed sultan continued to occupy, was abolished the following year; the Caliph and his family were expelled for ever from the borders of the newly constituted nation. The religious courts were closed down. Ingrained Ottoman practices such as polygamy and the husband's right to divorce his wife, or any number of them, merely by repudiation were outlawed; a Western-style civil code was introduced. The bureaucrats were commanded to abandon their Ottoman frock-coats and fezes for

Ancient ruins

Shopping mall

Station

Fish farm

Samos

Mycale

AEGEAN SEA

Atburgazı

Priene

Güllübahçe

Donkey Island

Lade

Balat/Miletus

Sarıkemer

Söke

Mavişehir

Dalyan

Myus

Didim/Yeronda

BAFA LAKE

Beşparmak Dağı/
Mount Latmus

Erbeyli

Kapıkırı/
Heraclea

Karapınar

Bodrum

N

Çakırbeyli

↙ Çine

Aydın

lounge suits and brimmed hats, and the public were increasingly shamed into following the official example; the wearing of veils and the segregation of the sexes was actively discouraged. The Arabic script was replaced by the Latin alphabet. Friday, holy day of the Muslim week, was ousted by the Western weekend; the Islamic calendar, reckoned from the Prophet's flight out of Mecca, was replaced by one that instead began with the birth of Jesus Christ. In barely a decade it was done. It must have seemed unaccountable to many Turks, of course, that they were being forced to adopt the same infidel ways of the Christians whom the new nation had so recently expelled.

Many Rum Christians had needed no such prompting; they fled Anatolia before the rout of the Greek forces, conscious of the climactic bout of bloodletting it was sure to unleash. The first to reach Anatolia's ports, otherwise the richest or luckiest, managed to buy or beg safe passage on ships or fishing boats. Even as they watched their homeland recede, however, they could see the columns of footsore civilians and creaking buffalo carts that were already engulfing the quaysides they had lately left; the exodus of over one million Rum Christians had begun. The earliest of them soon reached the safety of nearby Greek islands like Samos, or cities such as Athens or Salonika, where they were billeted in public buildings, in ruins, in warehouses, in old moored freighters, even in damp caves. Later waves of arrivals fended for themselves as best they could by throwing together tents or low hutments in the camps that sprang up at the fringes of the cities. Many of the arriving refugees had been plundered of their few remaining valuables. This destitute majority, in which children and the elderly figured large, was particularly prone to hunger and illness. In the cramped and filthy camps smallpox, typhus and dysentery ran riot; in the summer months malaria further ravaged those who had not found proper shelter.

Many of these Rum refugees sustained themselves in the belief that a political settlement would eventually allow them to return to their homes and pick up their former lives. By 1923 it was clear, however, that there would be no going back to Anatolia. At Lausanne, Switzerland, the Greek and Turkish authorities agreed on an exchange of minority populations; those Rum Christians who had fled Turkey were to be permanently settled in Greece while the estimated 180,000 who remained in Anatolian regions largely remote from the war, like Cappadocia, were also to leave.

This further exodus, which gathered pace from the end of 1923, soon overwhelmed the processing capacities of Greece's port authorities. The packed coasters and steamers had no choice but to wait their turn at the quaysides; in the meantime the onboard living conditions became indescribably squalid. One observer witnessed the arrival at Salonika of a refugee ship in the winter of 1923:

They were packed like sardines on the deck, a squirming writhing mass of human misery. They had been at sea for four days. There had not been space to permit them to lie down to sleep; there had been no food to eat; there was not access to any toilet facilities . . . They came ashore in rags, hungry, sick, covered with vermin, hollow-eyed, exuding the horrible odour of human filth – bowed with despair.

Six months after being forced from their homes many others had not even cleared the transit camps that had sprung up by the Turkish ports. The horrors continued through 1924. All around the Aegean whole communities, stinking, sick and starving, huddled around campfires. Western sentiment blamed the Turks. *The Times* described the wretched refugees as the victims of the Turks' 'fanatical Nationalism, which is merely a manifestation under new forms of their traditional intolerance'; it was said that the Turks were now doing to the Greeks what the Turks and the Kurds of eastern Anatolia had done to the Armenians in 1915. The land's Christians were treated much 'as Asiatic conquerors dealt with the conquered in the times of the Old Testament. They interned or destroyed the men of military age; they took the marriageable women to their harems.' Turkey, it was alleged, was hell bent on extirpating a Christian presence whose roots could be traced to the Lycus Valley communities St Paul had first fostered at Colossae, Laodicea and Hierapolis almost 2,000 years before.

At Lausanne it was also established, of course, that many Muslims faced expulsion as well; these were the Turkish peoples of Greece who were to make the same journey now being forced upon Anatolia's Christians but in reverse. The numbers were unequal, with some 400,000 Muslims affected by the exchange, though this did not justify the sheer lack of Western interest in their plight. One commentator 'wondered whether it was realised that the Moslems had suffered only a few degrees less than had the Christian subjects of the Porte. In the . . . so-called exchange of human beings, as if they were goods and chattels, the wretched Musulmans . . . were being dumped on the devastated coast of Asia Minor, to take up, as best they could, the holdings of the departed Christians.'

The wider historical truth, which the pro-Greek powers had consistently ignored, was that this influx of Muslims into Turkey was just the latest in a long series of mass arrivals there. For centuries Turkey had been receiving refugees rather than making them. From the 1820s until 1913 Anatolia opened its door to an almost unbroken flood of Muslim refugees from the Balkans, southern Russia and the Caucasus. Those lands, an arc-shaped swathe wrapped around the northern shores of the Black Sea, were progressively lost to the Ottomans in the series of defeats they suffered to Imperial Russia as well as to newly independent Greece and Bulgaria.

With every victory these states set about zealously Christianising lands that had formerly been home to mixed populations under the Ottomans.

The victims, inevitably, were the resident Muslims: the Tartars of Crimea, the Circassians of the Caucasus and the various exotically named populations – the Koniari, the Vallahades, the Pomaks – of Greece and Bulgaria. The intention, to reduce or remove the Muslim presence, was sometimes achieved by administrative pressure, with extortionate taxation proving persuasive, or by sustained campaigns of harassment. In other cases, however, Muslim villages were plundered of their cattle and equipment, and the residents were ordered to leave. As the ceaseless catalogue of wars raged, villages were often destroyed and their residents massacred; there were instances of Muslim women being repeatedly raped before they were herded into barns piled high with harvest straw and immolated. Mosques were turned into latrines. Cavalry units fell upon the columns of refugees and the survivors carried nothing with them out of their lands other than festering sabre wounds. In the course of a process barely acknowledged in the West, where the atrocities perpetrated by the Ottomans alone appeared to be worthy of condemnation, an estimated five million Muslims were driven from their homes; the survivors among the expelled largely found refuge among their co-religionists in Turkey.

The Ottomans, by contrast, had continued to tolerate their own minorities for much of the nineteenth century; they had even permitted, as we have seen, fresh waves of Greeks migrants to settle and prosper in areas like the Meander Valley. The discrepancy between the population sizes involved in the exchange, which the West cited to justify the concentration of its resources in aiding the Christian arrivals in Greece, should instead have been taken as indicative of a telling nineteenth-century truth; Christians evidently found life in Anatolia more tolerable than Muslims did in the Christian lands. The West had it that Turkish barbarism played a leading role in endorsing ethnic cleansing by the nation's participation at Lausanne, and that the Turks' brutal slaughter in 1915 of the Armenians constituted the original genocide of the industrial age. In fact, the 'monstrously wicked' solution that Turkey agreed to in 1923 was nothing more than a formalised version of the one it had for a century or more watched its Orthodox Christian enemies inflict upon the Muslims of those benighted lands beyond the Black Sea.

With the first call to prayer I walked out of Aydın. The city was half-lit. On the empty streets I now noticed the number of businesses and properties – a freight company, an apartment block, a money-changing booth, an electricity supplier and a café – that called themselves *Menderes*. Given the state of the river, however, these seemed like empty acknowledgements, and for once I was not tempted back to the high dry banks. Instead I let the rail tracks I had first followed from the Meander's source, a daily presence since Sarayköy, guide me out of the waking city. I followed the roadside railway past the lorries fuming at the traffic lights, past the sign that forbade horse-drawn carts from joining the nearby motorway to Izmir, past the track-side warehouses of the farming syndicates and out into the fig orchards.

At the town of Erbeyli a man was painting the railway station's waiting room with long pink licks of his wide brush; another had wedged a parasol, spokes protruding from the faded and ripped fabric, into the cracked platform and raised a precarious stack of strawberry punnets beneath it, and when I pointed to a lower tier he laughed and held up two fingers, but in encouragement rather than insult, lowering one the moment I indicated that a single punnet would do; and a third man, watering the flower baskets that hung along the platform, invited me with a companionable grunt to wash my strawberries beneath his hose. The man asked about my vehicle, and upon discovering that I did not have one he turned out his pockets to signify the pennilessness that we had in common. We shared the strawberries. Then, rinsing my hands beneath the hose, I wandered down the platform to investigate a curious obelisk that rose beside the road.

The slender memorial was dated 21 June 1919 – precisely a week before the fighting for Aydın began – when rising tensions had triggered a skirmish between Erbeyli's Turks and the occupying

Greeks. *Lest We Forget the Heroes Who in Firing the First Bullets Against the Enemy Gave Their Lives to the Motherland*, the memorial declared. The grand rhetoric gave way to more homespun sentiments, however, when it came to the roll-call; for this time the heroes were not merely listed as the sons of fathers in the traditional way but rather were named for the attributes, however humble or informal, that best distinguished them. Among Erbeyli's dead were Durmuş from Izmir and Hafiz from Isparta; the barber Sadık and the porter Mehmet; Mustafa the son of Osman the shoemaker, and Ahmet the sheep farmer's son; the carter's son Ahmet and Hasan the son of the lame Abdullah; Bald Ibrahim's son Ahmet, the Cretan carter Hasan and Hasan the son of the islander Ali.

It was a memorial I might easily have missed and with it the moment that I had been anticipating, I now realised, all through my journey: evidence of ordinary Anatolians asserting rights to identities, however modest, of their own. If my journey had taught me anything about the history of these people, it was that they had been accounted an anonymous, uncouth and secondary herd for millennia. Ever since the time of the ancient Greeks they had been dismissed as common barbarians compelled to bow before successive conquerors and their gods, and to fight their distant wars. They had then been left impoverished, uneducated and unrecognised in their flea-ridden hovels. In honouring their sacrifice the memorial

398

at Erbeyli acknowledged them, at last, in something like the fullness of their individual selves – where they were from and what they did, even fleshing them out with the inherited traits they might have developed, like baldness, or the features they might have accidentally acquired, like lameness, if their own lives had only been long enough. Anatolia's peasantry, its porters, carters and the rest, had for centuries been condemned as 'Turks', even as stupid 'Turk-heads', by those who ruled over them. But now the disgraced Ottomans were gone, along with the Rum Christians, and it was as Turks that a newly proud people took belated possession of a land, however shattered, which should have always been their own.

Nowhere did that pride flare more memorably than in the Turks' response to one of the last of the great Westernising reforms; the surnames that they were required to find for themselves, in the manner of the expelled Rums, in 1934. They might have been expected to make conventional selections, based on the likes of their father's first name, or the family's profession or provenance, as the memorial at Erbeyli only appeared to anticipate. But during the eighteen months they were given to decide, many followed rather the lead of Mustafa Kemal, their beloved President, whose own choice – Atatürk, Father of Turks – confirmed the widespread hunch that splendid brio was the form when it came to the Turkish version. For his close acquaintances, especially favourite generals,

Atatürk took pleasure in proposing the names of the battles they had won or the mountain ridges their men had heroically defended during the war; for others he suggested such inflated surnames as Sublime, or Spiritual Companion.

So his people went for Trueturk, Bravelion, Greywolf, Whitestar and Overthrower-of-Mountains, and, in the case of the forebears of those I had encountered along my own journey: Darkeye, Truehero, Fearless, Skirmisher, Blessed, Greatspring, Flag, Trueblueeyed, Bluedanube and Ironhand. The choice proved easier for others, especially those who were already confirmed in their two-part names, like Yörük Ali, who simply transposed them to become Ali Yörük; so that on the occasions that bureaucracy required, no doubt with all due deference, a surname of the revered freedom fighter, Nomad Ali went as Ali Nomad.

And now the offspring of modern Turkey's first generation, their aged children and their grand-children, travelled the road westwards where I walked. All morning they and their own young passed me in speeding lorries and trundling tractors, and in *dolmuşes* hung with football pennants, which drew up with a jolt to pitch them into the dusty verge by the shabby towns of the wide valley; grey-haired men in their worn suits and women with their baskets of aubergines, who stepped over gutters littered with the discarded shells of water-melons and the puddles of sump oil, and walked past the car repair shops and machine works, the grimy glass-fronted kebab houses, and the occasional offices of provincial doctors, dentists and lawyers where every premise bore the proud surname of its Turkish owner.

The road was hard, the sun high and a woman put up dust as she appeared out of the fig orchards. I noticed her earrings and curly hair before it occurred to me that the woman wore no headscarf, which was unusual out in the countryside. As she crossed the tracks towards me I was pushed to remember when a woman had last gone out of her way to make my acquaintance; the one, I reckoned, who had stopped me in the uplands village near Bahadınlar to tell me of her children who were now making prosperous lives for themselves in Switzerland. Rarely did the sexes stray from their appointed spaces in rural Turkey, I had learned, unless they were sufficiently young or old that it did not signify. Or unless it was themselves that they sold, in whatever place provided a degree of privacy, like the depths of the trackside fig orchards where the woman with one word now invited me. I had backed away from her graphic proposition, making for the quiet of the river, when it occurred to me that I was leaving the railway for the last time.

The railway and the valley had run together since Sarayköy. Now they were diverging, the one veering north towards Izmir's quaysides, the other trending south on its final mazy leg to the delta. The odd thing, it now struck me, was that I had not seen a single passing train since the beginning of my journey, and I remembered something Mehmet Trueblueeyed had said; that only the poorest people were prepared to endure the long waits that Turkish train travel entailed. The railway had not stopped paying, it seemed, for its collaborationist past. Certainly, the infidel line had long since lost out to the roads, with their constant flow of *dolmuşes*, and to the new motorway, and all the efforts that had lately gone into the neat station platforms, with their freshly painted waiting rooms and flower baskets, and all the labour of line gangs like the one I had seen that first day near the source could do no more to save the railway, I now feared, than the whips the drivers had uselessly raised that their camel trains might compete with the advance down the track of the newly laid sleepers 150 years before.

I walked through a very long day and was within a few miles of Söke, stumbling in the darkness, when a *dolmuş* stopped for me. The nondescript cotton town (alt. 27 metres) was quiet but for the rumble of closing shop grilles and the clang of gas canisters being unloaded off truck beds. The one hotel, the Ephesus Palace, appeared to date from the agricultural boom the town had enjoyed in the 1950s. The receptionist had since retreated into his little glass office and turned his back towards the television, posting a handwritten sign that forbade guests from entering his sanctuary, as if to barricade himself against a weight of grievances, however reasonable, and the pot plants had gone from the stair-side alcoves where cigarette butts gathered, and a little pink bin, with a black trim where its plastic liner showed, stood guard outside my door.

I was sore and exhausted, and had gone out in search of something to eat when I spied a window whose grille was yet to fall; it was a tackle shop, with a display of rods, nets, hooks – and an orange life jacket. I took encouragement from that jacket; as a reminder that the sea must be near, like a whiff of wind-blown salt, it would have been a welcome sight even if it had not been for the image of a paddling canoeist above the word TURKEY printed large across the chest. At up-country tea houses and regulators the account I had so often given of myself, as a sea-bound canoeist, had been greeted with such silent incomprehension that I had long yearned for the least acknowledgement; so I was happy when it finally came, even if it was from a buoyancy aid.

The town of Söke, which Italian forces had occupied for much of the Independence War, had fared somewhat better than Aydın; the Greek quarter had largely survived, even if its name – Kemalpaşa Evleri, or General Kemal's Houses – was a pointed reminder that the place now belonged to Atatürk's Turkey. An erratic wind was gusting as I wandered among the elegant merchant houses, some still bearing their Greek inscriptions and late nineteenth-century dates, where I spotted the same extensive motifs – the flowers, rosettes, festoons and the hand-shaped door knockers – I had seen at Aydın.

The most common pattern in evidence, however, was the meander. In Söke's old quarter it all but ran amok. There were meanders in the exterior plaster, in the rusted brackets beneath the rotting wooden balconies and in the filigree ironwork above the doors; through windows I saw how they also ran round interior plaster cornices and how they bordered staircases and doorways.

In its Söke setting, in short, the motif seemed insistent; what I had taken to be merely decorative now appeared to endow the houses where they were inscribed with the overt affiliations, even the political aspirations, of their owners. I speculated that the meander, for all the shifting significances that had attached to it over the ages, had by the beginning of the nineteenth century become, at least in the region, a tacit embodiment of nothing less than the Great Idea; the assertion of a territorial claim that would eventually lead to occupation. It had acted, I guessed, as the badge of a prosperous and influential minority whose loyalty lay with the Hellenic invaders. In their turn the Turks might even have regarded the meander with something of the same unease that the swastika – and the two motifs, I had noticed, were commonly entangled – had signified to those in the path of Nazi Germany's blitzkrieg. It was a thought, that said, that I had never heard expressed. On a whim I waylaid a passing Turk, a man carrying a radiator, and asked what the patterning meant to him. With the shrug of one, however, who had a life to be getting on with, the man patted his radiator and continued down the lane.

It was a warm morning and I was content to buy a sesame bread ring, or *simit*, and chew upon it as I rested my sore feet in the Warriors' and Martyrs' Park. Children played about their mothers, and elderly men, comfortably canted on the benches, raised wrinkled eyes to the sunshine and ran prayer beads through their fingers. One, whose name was Yusuf Grape, came to sit beside me. Yusuf, who was seventy-seven, took pleasure in telling how he had once worked precisely where we now sat when the four chimneys of Söke's liquorice factory, since demolished, had dominated the country town's skyline. Liquorice, yet another of the Meander Valley's many crops, was

405

a thickly rooted weed, which prospered in the deep silt soils. It had once grown wild, across the untended lands and in the fields alike, and the factory owners had prospered on exports to America and Europe where liquorice was used in confectionery and medicine, and to flavour tobacco and cigarette papers, and thoughts of the opium trade of the valley's uplands reminded me that the Meander region had always served narcotic pleasures.

Yusuf had spent much of his working life in the liquorice business. 'Every spring, when the ground was wet,' he explained, 'my brothers and I used to go down into the delta, around villages like Atburgazı and Güllübahçe, and dig up the spidery liquorice roots thick as a child's wrist. We had some half-dozen camels we used to load – 100 kilos on each flank. In those days you could see mountains of the root piled by the pathways. We sold the liquorice at the factory gates. Later, when I was in my thirties, I worked in the factory, boiling the dried roots time and again until they formed a thick syrup, which hardened into a black paste. We sent the liquorice to Izmir, and from there it went overseas.'

I wondered why the factory had closed.

'Things got difficult from the 1950s,' explained Yusuf. 'That was when the tractors first came, and with their deep ploughs they tore up the liquorice roots. Then they began to sow the big cotton fields, and we liquorice diggers and the holes we made were no longer welcome. The owners shut down the factory in 1969, and the Western managers left, and all us workers, some thirty men, lost our jobs.'

Yusuf's elegy explained why no liquorice digger commanded the plinth in Söke's square; a shawled young woman, a Soviet-style heroine of the cotton fields, instead stood beside a wicker basket that overflowed with her pickings. I left the town by the main road and soon arrived at a new mall, complete with Starbucks and McDonald's, which might have finally confirmed the end of traditional inland Turkey if it had not been for an adjacent sign offering Sacrificial Lambs for sale. I worked my way back to the river where there were ruined farm buildings, their ceilings lathed with sagging reeds, and in the midst of a big field inch-high with red-stemmed cotton seedlings a farmer stood tiny in his torn waistcoat.

'Filthy water,' he said despairingly – and not enough of it, so the season's cotton harvest was sure to be miserable, the pickings meagre as the previous year when the crop had been barely a fifth of the usual yield. The fields were shadowless except where storks passed high overhead, and by the riverbank old metal ferry rafts had been flipped onto their low gunwales to rust away. Lines of eucalypts, planted in the 1960s to help drain the malarial marshlands, shaded me along the river until the ruins of a Byzantine bastion rose from the far bank, and at last I knew myself to be close;

for here, at ancient Myus, my journey would once have ended.

Once, that is, being back in the fifth century BC when the sight of 200 warships riding at anchor might have greeted me on my arrival at the seaport. Five centuries later I would have yet had a way to go, however, when the same place was only reached by heading 'inland for three miles in rowing boats'; and further still a century later yet when Myus, beset by the gnats that swarmed from the encroaching marsh, stood largely abandoned. The Meander, a sophist wrote, 'had taken the sea from the navigator, and given it to the husband-man to be divided into fields; that furrows were seen in the place of waves, and kids sporting in the room of dolphins; and that instead of hearing the hoarse mariner, you were delighted with the sweet echo of the pastoral pipe'. What stretched ahead, in short, were the delta lands that the river's alluvial deposits had reclaimed since the beginning of recorded time.

At the village of Sarıkemer an old stone bridge spanned the river; its arched underside was riddled with holes where the sloughed skins of snakes hung, creating a hollow rattle in the breeze. The river remained as low as ever, and only in the memories of the old villager I met at the tea house was the water abundant. Hüseyin Crane, whose surname celebrated the great birds that had once visited the delta villages in profuse numbers, recalled the winter days when he had operated the

Meander ferry between the villages of Atburgazı and Balat; when the receding waters stranded vast numbers of fish across the April flats, and the *dalyans*, the fish traps, had harvested prodigious quantities of eels and grey mullet; and when men like the Grape brothers came with the spring to dig for the damp liquorice, and made a mess of the fields and the irrigation canals where they rooted for the deep weed like the filthy pigs the Rum people had once kept in their villages.

I thanked Hüseyin Crane for the tea and passed out of Sarıkemer, and to my left I could soon make out the watery expanse of Bafa Lake. A few fields separated river and lake. Then the two began to close and when I judged they were at their closest, with not a football pitch between them, I left the river and walked down to the lake. All around the mountains flared pink, taking their evening colour, it seemed, from the flamingos that stood shadowed in the shallows until something put them up, and they took off down the wide waterway, a swished gauze, and were gone from view.

I walked beyond the crusted mud where the water lay and bent before raising a dipped finger to my lips; the water was warm like blood and – preserving a memory from the time of those ancient warships, when the lake had been a gulf of the Aegean – there was also salt in it.

CHAPTER 22

In the morning I retrieved my canoe and returned to the lake, dragging the assembled craft down to the water. When I looked back, I saw that the canoe's rubber underside had left a broad smear, wiping my tracks from the soft grey mudflats. After the succession of exhausting valley walks that had brought me here – from Feslek, from Yenipazar, from Aydın, from Söke – I was glad to see my footprints go.

I was back on the water, though not on the river, and so might have been accused of wandering off course; but I was not about to be censured, not on the Meander, for doing so. The river had always mingled, at any rate, with the waters that I now paddled. Once, of course, its sweet outflow had mixed freely with the salt waters of the Latmian Gulf, as the Aegean inlet was then known. What was striking was how the river's physical separation from that gulf, by the actions some 2,000 years ago of its very own silts, had not prevented a continued association; the regular spilling of the river's winter flood waters into the lake, raising the levels there by fully a metre or more, meant that the two had shared seasonal reunions ever since – the last twenty years pointedly excepted.

The waters were clear under the sun and I paddled east up the old inlet, through the shoreside reed stands, until the lake lay wide open within its hem of hazed mountains. The heights that rose from the northern shores, wooded with olives and scrub oak, were strewn with house-high boulders, all suggestively smooth, even spherical, as if countless tides had rolled them there; there were mysteries in the high folds of that mountain – holy Latmus to the ancients – which had been 'a grand resort of fanciful devotees, and secluded hermits, a nursery of saints, another Athos' from the seventh century.

A good wind had gathered at my back. It pitched me across the shimmering lake until there rose out of it an island, wooded but whitened, the olives, bays, figs and tamarisks serving as the shit-splattered roosts of countless waterbirds. The cormorants held their ground at my approach but the egrets and herons put up in their hundreds, and from their raucous wheels overhead they cast me in a strobe-like dapple of wing shadows. Over the weed-rimmed base of a fluted column, which protruded from the shallows, I looped my painter and went ashore.

The old bastion walls had been reduced in many places; above the dusted brambles their unevenly exposed courses were occupied by lines of cormorants, black as the notes of a tumbling musical score. In the wall rubble I could make out column drums, and broken bits of pediment and frieze from an edifice of the Hellenistic era. I thought how these mountain-ringed, moated Byzantines had with the stones of their forebears once raised here their own innermost defences, no doubt hoping that the Turks or Saracens or Persians, or whichever Eastern peoples were then taking their turn to maraud the land, would content themselves with the region's more accessible settlements. The sun was high now and the flow tide of its glare had submerged almost all the island, and the few resident goats jostled for space in the last remaining banks of shade. They were reluctant to concede ground when I claimed their shelter for my picnic site, and soon they were back, stumbling boldly about me, hot and rank, as I broke into my olives, cheese and bread.

Later, when the wind strengthened, the lake increasingly resembled the sea it had once been. I drove on, struggling to keep the canoe from shipping the waves that broke at the bow, and it struck me that I might have done more than admire – like buy – the orange life jacket I had seen at Söke. I did not doubt, however, that I could safely beach the canoe even if the waves did cause it to founder. In the heat the water looked positively inviting. At that moment it occurred to me that I was enjoying myself. I wondered how it was I had only now noticed that the worrying – about handling the canoe, dogs, maps, the sinister significance of watermills, fallen willows, dams and regulators, sleeping arrangements, crossing points, river levels and trowels – had largely ceased. I was doodling along, as I had always meant to, and I felt fine.

The canoe, bucking and flexing, fell down the big waves that the sea wind, the *meltem*, pushed up the lake through the afternoon. I passed another fortified island, broken walls toppling from the rocks, where a terracotta cross showed between the paired narrow window arches of a basilica, and an intact ring of grey crenellations crowned a nearby promontory. I came into the lee of the long bay at the head of the lake where the mountain slopes withdrew, and there were low-lying fields, and a shoreline curious with apparently miniaturised ruins; one-room cottages of whitewashed block, with single chimneys cornering the tiled pitches of the roofs, cracked patios shaded by tumbledown vines, and bleached window shutters hanging askew from their hinges.

The lake's main inhabited settlement lay well beyond the abandoned cottages. Directly opposite the ruins of yet another fortified island, this one flying a Turkish flag, was a bone-white strand where I ran the canoe ashore among blue fishing caiques, the high prows piled with rank-smelling nets, and wandered up the lane, past the turpentine trees and a sign to the Selene Restaurant, into Kapıkırı.

From the profusion of downed columns and shattered platforms, tottering arches and ashlar tiers, it was clear that the villagers of Kapıkırı had themselves followed the Byzantine example in settling among the ruins of earlier civilisations; but whereas the visible evidence was that the Byzantines had forever been in retreat, forced back to the last stands they made behind the walls of their offshore Alamos, finding safety as sparse as the shade today's goats sought on those same islands, the current occupants now squatted secure. They occupied the heart of Hellenistic Heraclea, and while that one-time city's own impressive walls, complete with gates, parapets and towers, suggested that life back then can barely have been safer than the latter-day Byzantines were to find it fifteen centuries later, today's Turks appeared to have no use for them other than to confine their cattle. All through the present-day village the doors of their rough homes stood open. The old dangers had evidently receded; perhaps the greatest threat to the current community was from a national museum service in thrall to the tidying tendency, which might one day seek to remove the modern settlers from the ancient city, as it had done at many of Turkey's other historical sites.

For now, however, Heraclea's uncurated stones had been left to the villagers of Kapıkırı. The column drums served as their garden tables, the agora doubled as their football pitch and an old man at his door stopped to press an arthritic heel against a length of fallen column, having learned over the years that its fluted rim was just the thing to assist him in easing off his rubber boots. The villagers' casual customisation of the old city, alive to the historical continuities that museums thought to arrest, was evocative.

The tourists certainly thought so; they had been visiting the village for some years now. I took a cabin in a *pansiyon*, home to the Blueeyed family, which occupied a bluff above the strand. In the gardens I drank beer as the farmers returned from the fields, their donkeys piled high with fodder or firewood, and the herons made for their island roosts. The light slipped by degrees until all was charcoal – the birds and the smooth ashlar of the temple walls, the stilled water and the rounded boulders and the five peaks of Latmus – except for the wash of moonlight; the moon, of course, for the myth of Endymion, which some had set among the spilled secretions of Pamukkale's travertines, was first and for ever associated with Mount Latmus. I remembered the beautiful shepherd, and the moon goddess who had machinated to make him hers, and the divine stupor into which she had cast him high on this mountain, and I guessed it had probably begun with the nocturnal fantasies of some lonely shepherd who could sleep neither for the brilliance of the moon nor for the longing within; and my main thought was that such shepherds had less to fear than the women reduced to selling sex in the fig orchards along the Aydın road.

The advice, that said, was that I should not wander the mountain on my own; according to the locals, who knew it for its distinct peaks as Beşparmak, or Five Fingers, it was easy to be lost among the viewless boulders and rifts. So Mehmet Blueeyed led me in a chill dawn through gates roughly wickered from bleached brittle sticks and over olive groves and meadows of poppies, crocuses and orchids. The air was sweet with the scent of the pinkish Chaste Tree, a verbena named for its supposed bromide-like qualities, and I wondered whether it was the local celibates, seeking preservation against the abandonment that had befallen Endymion, and doubting their power to resist, who had themselves cultivated the shrub in such profusion. But these were fanciful thoughts, and among the wrecked fortifications and rib arches of the acorn-eating ascetics' sanctuary at Yediler, Monastery of the Seven Brothers, there grew only grasses and pink rock roses. One hermit's cave, a weather-hollowed boulder, was ceilinged with a frescoed Crucifixion; a naked Christ, ribcage raised in torment, racked against a sky cobalt with divine insult.

Then Mehmet led me to a cave of older paintings. They were of a time before Messiahs, angels and expiation, about 8,000 years old, and were rendered wholly in rust reds and mustard yellows. The paintings, of rudimentary stick figures, animals, ideograms and handprints, were thick with the fascination of their makers; with the dawning realisation, perhaps, that their handwork might express meaning. Here was what the painters saw, even what they meant, but perhaps before they had the words to articulate those meanings and most certainly before they had developed the written wherewithal to record them.

The invitation was to comprehend, then, what they had intended by their painted representations; the animals they plainly had rendered for the nourishment their flesh afforded and for the warmth of the skins, and their own hands they honoured as the miraculous tools of human will. Which left

417

the less immediately explicable patterns that they had made. Much of their work consisted of repeated geometrical motifs. In a moment of purest pleasure I recognised the pattern that ran up and down, up and down the walls of the cave; it was the squared-off wave, the meander pattern in its purest form. Only the day before I had glimpsed what the meander may have come to mean – an assertion of cultural, even territorial domination – in its play on the walls of Söke's Greek quarter. Here, on earlier walls, I had the faint but insistent sense that it had once conveyed a more universal meaning; the painters' experience that everything went around, days, seasons, lives, the things that threatened and that gave strength, and everything came back, and so the red-dyed stick beneath their fingers ran not straight but turned and turned again, through the generations, until they left their caves and words came to them and writing too, and the people emerged into the half-lit history with which this narrative began.

We headed back through the scrub oak and the boulders, making for Kapıkırı's landmark minaret, and Mehmet spoke of the village. The villagers counted between them some ten surnames; theirs was a close community, originally of Yörük stock, though I had seen their poorly watered mountains and guessed that the Beşparmak range neither rose nor extended sufficiently to sustain the alpine meadows essential to seasonal nomadism.

'Our forebears never spent their summers in the

mountains like typical Yörüks,' Mehmet conceded. 'These days we go to the mountains in the winter to harvest the olives. A few goatherds do summer up there and some of us go up to hunt wild boar, but that's about it.'

I asked about the boars and Mehmet explained that a good number of the younger villagers regularly ate the meat, though the imam was not to know. Mehmet thought the flesh delicious; an admission I would never have heard in Dinar. I felt the old orthodoxies lose their grip as the coast drew close; in this respect at least I had travelled out of one world and into another.

Mehmet's elder brother, Muammer, was preparing dinner when I got back to the Blueeyeds' *pansiyon*. It was bass, straight off the fishing boats, and so in a final crucial detail – its fish – the windy, wavy, salty lake was confirmed as an inland sea.

'In the winter the fish, the bass and the grey mullet, leave the Aegean for the river and reach the lake by the fishery canal,' Muammer explained. 'Though we do get some freshwater types, like carp, as well.'

I'd seen fish surfacing around my canoe, I told Muammer, as I passed by the little ruined cottages.

'You mean the old summer village,' said Muammer. It had once been the habit of the village, he explained, to abandon Kapıkırı through the summer for the lake shore; in the absence of suitable mountains the water and cooling breeze there had served instead. So the people of Kapıkırı had been nomads, but adapted ones, whose seasonal migration had amounted to a walk of no more than fifteen minutes.

Muammer fondly remembered the summer village and the improvements they had made there over the years: the tiles they laid on the roofs, the reed-lathed ceilings and the cupboards, the mosque they built and the grocery shop, and even the little tea houses where the grandparents liked to sit, watching the children learn to swim. There were games of football and afternoon naps, fishing lines wound around little fingers, and light work tending the aubergines, black-eyed peas and onions, and the lemon groves, and all through the long summer the village camped in contentment; in every regard, in fact, their summers were long holidays by the sea.

From the canoe, however, I had seen the abandonment that had overtaken the settlement; the place had gone to wrack, the rough plaster peeling off the block walls around the hearths, the tiles teetering on the roofs, the broken shutters and the invading reeds, and I remembered all the ruins I had witnessed along the Meander: the ancient cities and temples, the Byzantine monasteries, the abandoned upland villages beneath their tottering minarets, the brick shells of the buildings around the town of Dalama, and now the summer village at Kapıkırı. I had the inescapable sense that the ruination was not simply the result of the wars that had ravaged this land but was somehow endemic to the place. It was difficult to imagine why the villagers should otherwise have abandoned a way of life that struck me as idyllic. Muammer smiled and excused himself, for he had guests to attend to, and I then knew what he would have said if he had not been too gracious to do so: *People like you began to arrive.*

So Western tourists had discovered places like Kapıkırı. The villagers now had *pansiyons* and restaurants to run. The men had hikes to lead and boat trips to organise; the women were busy cooking bass and making beaded scarves, which they touted from plastic bowls on the agora where they also raised pyramids of honey jars. The people of Kapıkırı found that they no longer had time to spend at the summer village. It was the Westerners who lay by the beach and the Turks who served them.

CHAPTER 23

O
n a hot morning I rejoined the river where I had left it some days earlier and walked its wandering banks across the delta grasslands. In the heavy air I heard regular rasping sounds, which appeared to come from a cluster of riverside trees; the Turkish flag flapping among the mulberry crowns might have been planted precisely to mark their source.

The flag actually flew over the old *dalyan* or fishery. Beyond a broad loop the river unbraided into a fray of caged and netted channels, which I crossed by a concrete bridge and found myself in a shaded yard. On every side stood decrepit buildings whose former functions were announced by varnished signs fastened above peeling jambs. The curious noises came from the middle of the yard where a solitary man, Adem Thunderbolt, was scything at the high grass around a gilt bust of Atatürk and its adjacent flagpole.

The fishery controlled the narrow channel between the lake and river where the sea shoals migrated, when water levels allowed, to their winter spawning grounds on the lake. Adem paid for the fishing rights, but the fee was nominal.

'Oh, I get a few grey mullet between September and March,' he said. 'The odd good-sized one, even as much as five kilos. The rest of the year I grow a little cotton and wheat, keep the place tidy. I was born here, after all.'

It had not always been like this; the factory sheds, offices, canteens, machine rooms and living quarters, the channels, the Atatürk bust and the flagpole, the boats and the rotted nets were all evidence of the bustling concession that had once employed an extensive workforce, Adem's father included. By an expressive gesture, miming a sack of coin he repeatedly weighed on an open palm, the forty-two-year-old remembered the prodigious catches he had witnessed at the *dalyan* in his boyhood. I myself knew of the formerly productive fishery from the travellers, Lord Patrick Kinross and Freya Stark among them, who had visited the *dalyan* in the 1950s.

At that time the fishery maintained the usual exceptional standards of Turkish hospitality – Kinross, Atatürk's biographer-to-be, described luncheons of salted eels and grey mullet, 'a profusion of pears and apricots', plentiful rakı, and peasants who sprinkled water on the ground beneath the guests' feet 'to lay the dust' – even as the staff saw to the daily business of the place: the packing of the fish roe, or *tarama*, for the island tavernas of nearby Samos, the freezing or curing of the mullet, and the readying of the eels for export to Holland and Germany. The formidable Freya

Stark, who spent three days at the *dalyan* during the winter floods of 1952, wrote how the daily catch was such that 'twenty camels, each with a box on either side of it', were required to carry it away to market. Now, however, there was only the Thunderbolt family who dared to hope that each winter might throw up a few good-sized mullet.

The reasons for the fishery's fifty-year decline were wearyingly familiar; excessive fishing and irrigation, the polluting of the waters by fertilisers and by industrial run-off, had all been compellingly cited. In recent years large numbers of dead fish had repeatedly washed up on the shores of Bafa Lake. Some blamed the phenol-rich effluent from the oil presses in the olive groves around Bafa Town; others suspected the deaths were due to a lack of oxygen in waters starved of circulation, to the point of stagnation, by the influential representations of the downstream cotton growers who meant to protect the river, their irrigation source, by restricting the inflow of fresh water into the lake and the amount of saline water permitted to leave it.

Kinross and Stark were witness, then, to the historical moment when industrialisation began to degrade the Meander Valley, though at the time a more positive transformation appeared to be under way. Halil Özbaşı, then the fishery's affluent concessionaire, told Freya Stark that the rich summer grasslands of the delta were visibly dotted with the traditional camps of the Yörüks and their grazing herds during 1952. Özbaşı added, however,

424

that he did not expect to see the distinctive black-wool tents there again. 'Next year there will be no Yürüks,' he predicted; 'it will all be under cultivation.' The nomadic herdsmen, like the liquorice diggers, were being driven from the fertile delta. New bridges would soon put the ferrymen and their traditional triangular rafts out of business. Some 40,000 tractors, largely paid for by American aid, were flooding into Turkey; 2,000 of them, according to Özbaşı, in the Meander Delta alone where their powerful ploughs would soon erase the crescent-shaped depressions from the relict channels of the former river braids, the faint dust circles left by the Yörüks' tents, and the liquorice diggers' pits alike. New farms were being built. Dams, power stations, harbours and metalled roads were under construction. Malarial marshes were drained and thirsty eucalypts planted to aid the process. Millionaires were being made in Söke, and even the peasants were enjoying a modest prosperity. The government, according to Kinross, had brought the country people 'new canalization, fertilizers to enrich new fields no longer flooded with silt, tractors to cultivate them, loans to develop them, usually in terms of cotton subsidies for the price of their crops'. A 'Menderes regime for the Menderes Valley', as the term went, had been established; for it was a local man with a local surname, Meander, who had been Turkey's prime minister since gaining power in 1950.

The home farm of the Menderes family stood

near the valley village of Çakırbeyli which I had visited some days earlier while in Aydın. Çakırbeyli was a neat, shaded place arranged around a spring of noted sweetness; the marble fountain was inscribed with the name of Adnan Menderes. It stood in the centre of the Adnan Menderes Park and Family Tea Gardens; a prominent framed portrait of the man – urbane, intelligent, clean-shaven, brilliantined black hair, spruce in his suit and tie – had been hung above the rose-scented gardens to confirm the devotional impression. Numerous institutions, most notably the university at Aydın and the airport at Izmir, commemorated the name of Adnan Menderes; statues had been raised in his memory.

The head of the village, who bought me tea, was also keen to honour the man. 'What they did to him,' declared Mehmet Iron, 'was an outrage against democracy.'

Adnan Menderes was born in 1899 into a prominent landowning family. He came to the political fore during the 1940s when, in the aftermath of Atatürk's death, the national establishment began to allow a tentative transition from dictatorial rule to multi-party democracy. The consequence, unexpected in its immediacy, was that Menderes' Democratic Party crushed Atatürk's ruling Republican Party in Turkey's first free elections.

It was as if, with the century's arrival at its halfway point, Turkish society could wait no longer to make the next step in its development; the one-party elite installed by Atatürk – urban, intellectual, professional, bureaucratic, military – was rudely unseated by the powerful alliance the Democrats had succeeded in arraying against it. Menderes, who championed free enterprise over state control, counted among his constituents the increasingly influential business class of industrialists and managers. His family background meant he was also able to attract the support of the landowners and the wider rural vote they were able to deliver. Menderes, with his acute understanding of the Turkish peasantry, was quick to buttress their support by paying court to that innate rural conservatism, not least in terms of faith – 'the entire frame of everybody's existence'

– which the Westernising state over the previous three decades had so determinedly quashed. Many of the country mosques were reopened. The call to prayer was once more permitted to be made in the traditional Arabic. Religious schools opened. Islamic periodicals were published.

As the popularity of the regime faltered through the 1950s – it was running record trade deficits and manifesting an increasingly authoritarian streak – Menderes was to identify himself ever more closely with Islamic sentiment. His government was duly accused of conniving at the flouting of secular law in the hinterland where turbans had begun to reappear, not least on the heads of imams who performed polygamous marriage ceremonies and commonly reminded their congregations that those who withheld their vote from Menderes thereby declared themselves infidels. An imam forbade people from having their teeth filled, fillings being a sinful innovation unknown in the time of the Prophet. People were threatened for smoking in the streets during Ramadan, and it was said that one father would not permit his dying daughter to take medicine during the Fast.

The state increasingly feared that Atatürk's legacy was in danger of wholesale betrayal. The Democrats might have filled Turkey with modern machinery, but they had largely paid for it on unsustainable lines of credit and at once had exposed the national mind to the forces of reaction, thereby undoing much of the educational progress credited to Atatürk. All of which Menderes might have got away with, not least because his rural support remained solid, if he had not also incensed precisely those people who could act against him: the military.

We have seen how Turks had historically held soldiering to be the noblest of callings. High standards were expected of the Turkish officer; the reward was the regard, even the sanctity, that he commanded. Through the 1950s, however, Turkey's armed forces experienced a dramatic erosion of their traditional prestige. The job had never been a lucrative one, but as the cost of living soared – prices at the end of the 1950s were more than ten times what they had been at the beginning of the decade – the very same military men who had served so heroically in the Independence War were effectively paupered. Politicians and entrepreneurs grew rich while retired generals were forced to take teaching jobs. Landlords with burgeoning property portfolios did not trouble to show military officers around the plusher apartments, assuming the rent to be beyond them. Mothers advised their daughters against military matches which would once have been considered highly prestigious. Militarism, guardian of the constitution, had lost out to materialism. The army duly decided that the national adventure in democracy had gone far enough. In 1960, the government of Adnan Menderes was overthrown by a military coup.

That day at the fishery happened to be the

anniversary of the intervention, 27 May, a coincidence that no doubt crystallised the parallels between 1960 and the political situation at the time of my journey; a disgruntled military class was once again acting against a democratically elected government by accusing it of violating Atatürk's secular constitution through pandering to the Islamic constituency. There appeared to be a broad difference, of course, though it effectively came down to style; where they had once used tanks and soldiers the military were now relying upon a blatantly biddable judiciary to close down the ruling party and ban its leaders from politics. Turks knew that the land's highest court was to rule on the case later that summer and many feared the outcome. Any closure of *Ak* would cause public outrage, but if the case against the governing party was dismissed, then it was possible that a thwarted military might be provoked into more direct intervention. Nobody was about to forget the army's form in this regard, nor the fate that had befallen Turkey's first democratically elected prime minister, Adnan Menderes, whom they had hanged along with two of his leading ministers in 1961.

The last regulator lay a few hundred metres below the fishery. The difference with this one, however, was that the river beyond it was full of water. I assembled my canoe with practised ease beneath the wide road bridge where cattle took the shade.

The river's recovery appeared miraculous; the explanation, in fact, lay not in the supernatural but in nature, as it had always done. A close look revealed no current whatsoever. Physical law dictated that the waters flowed through the low-lying delta, effectively a sump, only when the upstream river brought to bear the brimful force of its falling weight to flush out the lower reaches, something the dams, regulators and irrigation schemes had combined comprehensively to prevent. With only puddles at its back, and all out of incline, the Meander had done its running.

The greater marvel of the water, deep through these final flatlands, was its sudden clarity; the river bubbled and flashed with fish, and at last the inelegant turtles were back. They basked in the sun, the wavelets nudging their black shells where they protruded beyond the compacted platforms of rotted canes at the foot of the reed stands. Out on the open reaches of the river, where a stiff sea wind raised the waves to little hackles, progress was slow. I kept to the shaded shelter of the high reeds, reaching between the curving banks where the fallen seed husks dusted the still water. In one cleared break lay a dinghy piled high with nets, the floss-like filament weighted by a pair of slender-bladed oars, while an old carpet lay draped across the seat at the square stern; it was the first working boat I had seen on the river since my arrival at the fish farm at Gökgöl – on my very first day in the canoe.

A first glimpse of ruins – nothing more than a low ridge of rubble that a few rising courses, once walls, at least did something to substantiate – prompted me to put ashore; from my beginnings at Dinar I had now reached the city, once the greatest in all the Greek world, at the other end of the Meander. Only as I closed on the ridge did more of Miletus come into view; these were prestigious civic additions of the Roman period – a colonnaded agora, the intact platforms of temples, a monumental baths complex – which had initially been beyond my view precisely because of their low-lying position. Where they stood, below the elevated promontory site of the earlier Ionian city, the sea had formerly lapped.

In the centuries immediately prior to the time of Christ, however, those waters had grown increasingly shallow; they had then thickened into alluvial flats, as they had already done to choking effect at other delta cities like Myus and Priene. It was as if the standard concerns of the modern port city had been reversed; as the citizens of Venice now laboured to raise defences against the sea's advance, so the Milesians had once built to keep pace with its retreat. If Miletus was to preserve its port status, the mainstay of its wealth, the city was obliged to retain its waterfront, which it did from the fifth century BC by progressively relocating to the plain. It was hard, however, to keep pace with the silt, which advanced some twenty feet every year, as it would continue to do until the

1950s, and by the second century BC the port's approaches were peppered with hazardous shallows. The waters around Miletus were turning to mud and extensive dredging was required if the city's harbour was not to go the way of Myus, abandoned in its malarial marsh.

It was a natural process, but to a port it was natural as death, and the sophist who had rhapsodised over the landscape's transformation – the harsh calls of the mariner giving way to the melodious notes of the shepherd's pipe – must have had interests in agriculture rather than in trade or shipping. Otherwise he might have taken a less pastoral line in describing how it was that 'the great maritime city of the archaic period, mistress of the Aegean and birthplace of science and philosophy', found herself knee-deep in the Meander's evacuated soils. As Vesuvius had buried Pompeii beneath its ash, so the river had shat the great port unto death.

I made my way through the tamarisks and grazing sheep to the shallow depression that had once been the city's harbour, reflecting as I went that many of those already encountered on my journey, individuals and peoples alike, had also been at Miletus: Freya Stark and Patrick Kinross, of course, and a century before them the treasure hunters who had removed the city's prize antiquities to Berlin, and in their time early antiquaries such as Chandler and Pococke; the Turks who built their mosque from the Romans' stones in the

433

fifteenth century, as the Byzantines had built their castle above the theatre before them; St Paul, who summoned the neighbouring Ephesians to Miletus to hear his goodbyes before he continued towards Jerusalem where he was to face arrest, denunciation and eventual deportation to martyrdom in Rome; Alexander, who subdued Miletus before continuing on a journey that would lead him to Celaenae, Gordium and the conquest of all Asia; Xerxes' Persian forces on their retreat from Salamis in 479 BC; and fifteen years earlier the Persians of King Darius whose more successful battle fleets in 494 BC had defeated the forces of the Ionian Revolt off the island shores of Lade, now a hillock in the delta plain, before razing the rebels' promontory capital.

For Miletus's heyday, however, I was required to spool back to the city that stood here roughly a century before Darius punished its insurrection with that vengeful sack. In the sixth century BC this terminus of the Meander Valley trade route, hub of an extensive network of colonies, and producer of its own highly prized speciality vines and wools, was accounted the first city of the Aegean world. Posterity was to remember Miletus, however, not for its commercial prosperity but for more durable achievements in the artistic and intellectual spheres – and largely for a citizen called Thales.

Thales appears to have lived between about 620 BC and 550 BC. None of his writings survive; what we know of this geometrician, astronomer and philosopher derives from the posthumous acknowledgements his example was to elicit from such illustrious successors as Herodotus and latterly Aristotle. Many of the stories associated with Thales certainly seem constructed from the usual recycled spoil of legend, with no footing in reliable fact, which is not to say that the central achievement widely attributed to this shadowy ancient should simply be dismissed. Thales is commonly celebrated as the source of rational inquiry; he is credited with first positing the revolutionary notion that natural process rather than divine action might be behind the shaping of phenomena. Thales' reflections on the nature and substance of matter challenged an old order which, ignorant as to inquiry's value in bettering the world, had never thought to look for causes beyond the arbitrary waving of the deity's wand.

For a man known only vicariously, such grand claims may appear grossly inflated. It may be that he is more compellingly evidenced, however, not in the subsequent commendations of Herodotus and his like but rather in the very fact of the exceptional crop of geniuses whom Thales' example appears to have inspired in the decades after his death: the historian of Halicarnassus himself, of course, Herodotus, who told it as men told him; Hippocrates of Kos, first to believe that diseases might have natural rather than divine causes; Heraclitus of Ephesus, who surmised that the universe was defined by change and opposition; the original mathematician Pythagoras of Samos; and Hippodamus, himself of Miletus, credited with originating the city grid and urban planning in general. It happens, as the map reveals, that the home cities of these scientists and philosophers, proto-rationalists all, are oriented in a compellingly compact seaward circle around Miletus; they serve to place Thales at the eye – and so make him the very cause – of the singular ripple that spread to revolutionise the intellectual outlook of the region in the immediate aftermath of his death. By his example Thales delivered mankind, in the words of Freya Stark, 'into the world of Athens and Augustine and Dante and Stratford and Rome'; all cities and men, ironically, from those western lands beyond the sea that would one day be known as Europe.

The Thales legends tout a composite portrait in which a broad wisdom is prominent. The distinguished man of Miletus is canny and worldly, if not also prone to the stock distractions and pitfalls common to genius. His main virtue may be said, however, to be an absolute faith in the value of observation; a unarguable starting point in the pursuit of reason. Herodotus wrote roughly a century after Thales' death how the venerated Milesian had been the first to predict a solar eclipse. A century later still Aristotle made less, however, of that celestial *coup de théâtre* and more of Thales' conclusions as to the comparatively stealthy processes at work beneath his feet. For in seeking to know the basic nature of matter Thales came to believe that it all derived from a single substance, which was water.

The ancient Babylonians had long established wetness at the heart of their own cosmogony. Where, however, they imagined the universe had begun when the great divinity, perhaps with a nudge from its magic wand, had stirred some inert primordial sludge into life, Thales sensed that the miracle was inherent in water itself. Moisture self-evidently gave life to seeds. Water was brimful with life.

These were general perceptions, even if they were remarkable for the sixth century BC, but it may be suggested that the transforming catalyst was the particular setting in which they took place. For at Miletus, exceptionally if not uniquely, Thales was privy to an extraordinary phenomenon – one we now recognise as alluviation – whereby water appeared to metamorphose into earth itself. In its season and from inland came the brown swirl that resolved with every passing year into drying earth. This inconvenient alchemy was evident in the grumblings of grounded ships' captains, and in the way old men spoke of lifetimes observing the shores thicken around the gulf and its islands. Thales saw how water turned to mud and thence to earth, and the very land solidified out of the water on which it floated.

The Meander's alluvial spews were eventually to engulf great Miletus, but not before their inexorable workings had set a man of the city on his intellectual course, his thoughts flawed but free, so that men first raised science above their idols. Miletus, we may even speculate, was not so much lost as sacrificed for the lasting benefit of humanity; the very process that did for the city showed one of its citizens where our minds might go and what they might truly do. As gravity began in an apple orchard, so reason itself was born by the Meander's silting mouth.

Halil Özbaşı was wrong about the Yörüks. I found a last family of them by the stones of the old harbour, like those first wild Turcomans who had pitched their tents in the war-racked ruins of Dorylaeum. They were a ragged couple, dark with the sun, who busied themselves with gathering up the shorn fleeces of their flock and piling them on a brown tarpaulin slicked with lanolin. Their son, twelve years old, straddled a prone sheep. He had tripped it by the marble lion, once a proud mark of the harbour entrance but now sunk so low in the silt that only its eroded mane protruded. The boy worked with an old pair of iron shears, deftly squeezing the sprung blades so that the fleece fell away intact, and at the last he ran the shears, lovingly, along the sheep's brow. Then he threw the tool aside and stood, and the sheep rose from its fallen fleece and stumbled free, and the boy wiped his own brow and looked about him. A flock of bee-eaters, yellow and red, passed low overhead.

I made my way to the great baths complex, which the Empress Faustina had commissioned in the first century. Beneath high walls the baths were open to the blue sky. In the frigidarium, where bathers had once plunged into the cold waters of a low square pool, I came at last across the god of the river. For here at the head of the pool a bearded, muscular Meander reclined, naked but for the sheet slung loosely at his navel. I might have acknowledged the deity whose river I had followed from the source if a nearby sign had not declared him an impostor; it was a concrete cast of the statue that had once stood here. So I turned away and walked out to the road.

CHAPTER 24

That evening a *dolmuş* delivered me to Didim. The town, some fifteen kilometres south of Miletus, had grown up around the ancient temple of Didyma. This name replaced Yeronda, a corruption of the Greek word for temple, as the almost exclusively Christian population had known the place. The ruins of elegant Rum houses, classical and compact beneath the sagging loads of their tiled hip roofs, still lined the edges of the temple enclosure.

The Turks had generally kept their distance from the place they called infidel Yoran. From 1922, however, they were free to make the town their own. In recent years they had transformed it into a sprawling tourist resort. The consequence was that it once more attracted a largely infidel population, albeit one condemned to occupy rather less appealing homes than those of their Christian predecessors. Turkish developers, rushing to beat the breaking crest of Europe's holiday property boom, had raised a miserable thicket of concrete apartment blocks across the town. Many of these blocks stood empty in their fresh plots, the windows plastered with discounted prices and telephone numbers, and the first stains already showing up the poverty of the workmanship. On a few balconies bicycles and barbecue sets had appeared, and the replica T-shirts of English football teams flew from the washing lines. The streets brimmed with estate agents, hotels and tourist restaurants.

Around the archaeological site the developers had been kept at bay. By the temple I pushed my way through the gate of a simple *pansiyon* where an old man was dozing on a patio beneath an awning of vine-clad corrugated iron. Ahmet Heart waved me in the direction of his son, Mahmut, who showed me upstairs to my room.

'Basic,' Mahmut conceded gravely. 'But I dare say you'll enjoy the view.' From the window I looked over a vast stepped platform where a walled edifice was set within a peristyle of broad columns; much of this stone thicket, 120 columns in all, had been reduced to truncated stubs though a surviving trio, intact unto their scrolled capitals, a pair even bearing a section of architrave, conjured the structure in all its original splendour.

Didyma was among the greatest temples of the ancient world. From roughly the eighth century BC until the Byzantines officially established Christianity in the fourth century visitors came here in search of answers. They sought divine counsel from the god of prophecy. The familiar old martinet of the upper Meander, he who had flayed Marsyas for his presumption and bent the hapless Lairbenes to his will, had turned up again. Along these shores, however, he controlled rather by the power of oracular utterance. Apollo's coastal business was in analysing risk; with nineteen major oracular outlets along Anatolia's Aegean shores and with another ten in Greece, his was a lucrative and influential franchise.

The Anatolians were the horoscope readers of their day, a weakness Apollo had long since learned to exploit. A consequence of his success was that he no longer deigned to serve the humbler sorts, leaving them to rely instead upon the value-brand utterances of the street-corner opportunists – their divinations based on dice throws or the inspection of the entrails of chickens lately surprised by, and prised from, the wheel rims of passing carts – when it came to deciding, for example, whether the time had come to sell the family cow. Prestigious Apollonian institutions like Didyma targeted weightier pockets and the concerns that came with them.

The oracle at Didyma, whose priesthood claimed descent from an honoured favourite of Apollo's, stood within an extensive precinct where the temple, the various ceremonial buildings and the initiates' quarters were arranged among sacred laurel groves. Didyma's lavish scale served to remind its clients that they must pay top whack to keep the oracles on side; generous retainer payments would not only guarantee clients preferential access to advice but might even advantageously influence the very futures on which the oracles pronounced.

The oracle boasted a varied client list, not least the nearby city of Miletus, which was linked with Didyma by a paved, colonnaded and statue-lined Sacred Way. The Milesians no doubt considered themselves the oracle's preferred sponsors, though that special relationship was not exclusive; it certainly did not prevent Apollo's agents from mining a wider seam of high-grade clients. Prominent among these was Croesus, proverbially wealthy king of neighbouring Lydia, whose exceptional largesse further contributed to Didyma's swollen coffers.

Oracles like Didyma were considered, even so, to have earned every last coin of their considerable wealth, not least because the issues on which they were commonly consulted – on affairs of state or of international geopolitics – were often so complex as to tax even the supposedly omniscient Apollo. The oracular science, as even clients appeared to acknowledge, was not always exact, and Croesus commonly hedged his position by retaining the services of a range of oracles.

The Lydian king certainly needed all the help he could get. It was Croesus's fate that he should have been beset by the political, diplomatic and strategic burdens of kingship at a time of particular foment; not for him the intellectual musings that his close contemporary, Thales of Miletus, was free to entertain. Croesus found himself confronted, in fact, with the defining dilemma of the age: what was he to do about the Persian power rising to threaten him in the east? After an exhaustive selection process the Lydian king went to the oracle that by general consent outranked even Didyma – Greek Delphi – to ask whether he should deploy his Lydian armies against the Persians. Delphi's apparently encouraging advice was that Croesus would thereby destroy a great empire; the empire that the king duly destroyed in a series of engagements during 546 BC famously turned out to be his own.

By that fateful decision Anatolia was first exposed to the foreign subjection it would endure for millennia; it was also, of course, a personal disaster for Croesus, who felt let down, stiffed even, by a deity who was supposed to be on the payroll. Delphic Apollo's flagrant disingenuousness hardly seemed like a fair return for the patronage Croesus had lavished upon the Greek oracle. In the welter of recriminations Delphi was repeatedly obliged to remind its client where ultimate responsibility always lay. For all these attempts to absolve itself of blame, Delphi's reputation did not appear to escape unscathed; certainly, the next embassy of note steered clear of the oracle for its advice and went instead to the one at Didyma. The issue in this case was a particularly knotty one, which had arisen, it happened, out of events leading directly from Croesus's defeat at the hands of the Persians.

With the fall of Lydia, Croesus's Persian conquerors immediately set about establishing their new authority over the conquered lands. Focused as they were on territorial objectives in the distant East, however, the Persians mistakenly apportioned key administrative posts to Lydians who were not yet ready, as they soon proved, to be ruled by Persians. Chief among the promoted natives was one Pactyas who, entrusted with crating up and delivering the brimful Lydian treasury into Persian hands, instead began distributing its contents among the mercenary army that he promptly raised to restore Croesus's Lydian empire.

All might have been well, of course, if only the patriotic Pactyas had been able to win over an effective coalition of what he naïvely supposed to be like-minded neighbours, not least in Ionia, to join his insurrection against the Persians. The problem was that many of the coastal city states, alive to the precariousness of their predicaments, had already sought terms with the new power, and though they had mostly been rebuffed, very few of them could be persuaded to declare against the all-conquering Easterners. In no time Pactyas found himself faced by the advance of a Persian army intent this time on fixing Lydia more firmly into place, and liquidating the ringleaders in the process. The failed rebel fled north to the Aegean port of Cyme where he was promptly followed by Persian envoys demanding his surrender.

It was the people of Cyme who now dispatched their embassy not to Delphi, freshly discredited by the fallout following the loss of their account with Croesus, but to Didyma. How, they asked Apollo, should they respond to this moral dilemma? Should the city violate the fugitive's sanctuary rights by abandoning Pactyas to the Persians? Or should it rather honour them and thereby risk the wrath of precisely the power with whom it had recently sought an accommodation? Apollo's oracle at Didyma replied that the Lydian fugitive should be surrendered.

The answer was refreshingly unequivocal; it came even so as such a surprise, sanctuary being an inviolable right, that some in Cyme thought the oracle's words must be falsely reported. A second embassy, led by a Cymean citizen called Aristodicus, returned to Didyma to confirm for themselves the oracle's answer. On receipt of the same response, and in defiance of protocol, Aristodicus casually wandered off among Didyma's sacred laurel trees to remove the baby chicks he found nesting there. Over much cheeping and the gasps of scandalised priests a booming voice demanded to know how the impious Aristodicus dared to interfere with creatures within the confines of the divine sanctuary. Aristodicus airily replied that since Apollo was so ready to protect those in his care, it might be asked how he could command the citizens of Cyme to give up the man in theirs.

It was a good retort; even the exalted gods, it seemed, could find themselves in predicaments like the Cymeans. In fact, Apollo's position was especially compromised since Didyma's coffers, stuffed with

Croesus's gold, naturally obliged the oracle to declare in support of the Lydian patriot who meant to restore Croesus; the problem was that Didyma had also run up a substantial tab with Miletus, and Miletus had already reached a settlement with the Persians, which it would not suffer the local oracle to jeopardise.

It was left to the Cymeans to figure for themselves that they might just have sufficient steerage to slip between both civic dishonour and Persian offence – by the tried expedient of passing the buck. The citizens shipped Pactyas off to the island of Mytilene until the fugitive's position became as uncomfortable there, when they removed him to nearby Chios. The Chians had been already sweetened, however, by land rights the Persians dangled before them. The Chians took it upon themselves to drag the rebel Lydian from sanctuary in a local temple and to deliver him up. We may only imagine how the Persians dealt with the wretched Pactyas; it is recorded that they certainly showed no mercy to the few cities that had called it wrong by backing his failed revolt. The Persians sacked the towns of Priene and Magnesia, and enslaved their citizens. They then pillaged the plain of the lower Meander.

The incident revealed the seamy web of loyalties and obligations in which even Apollo could be snared. It perhaps even hinted at a secret from the god's deep past. In the Greek tradition Apollo was born in the sanctified light of Delos in the Cyclades. In fact, the god's true origins were not Greek but

Anatolian and in ages past, as Aplu and Apaliunas, Apollo had served such Bronze Age Anatolians as the Arzawans and Hittites. He had form, moreover, when it came to taking the Eastern side; Homer had cast the god in the *Iliad* as the enemy of the Greeks, divine sponsor of the Trojans. Even Apollo could find himself in the classic Anatolian bind; here on the world's cusp the question, as ever, was where one belonged and where one's loyalties lay.

'My people were Muslims from Macedonia,' Ahmet Heart explained. 'They came from a village near the port of Kavala.'

We sat among the potted geraniums and the ancient temple stones on the patio of Ahmet's *pansiyon*. In his old age Ahmet had turned slight. His speech was gummy, his beard grizzled and his blue eyes were rheumy. His trousers hung slack from his braces and he wore a thick shirt against a chill I did not feel. He had been here for a long time.

'They were tobacco farmers from a coastal village called Kuçkar. The first thing they knew of the exchanges was when the Christian refugees from Anatolia started arriving in the area during 1923. These arrivals were poor and ill. They had nothing. My people gave some of them jobs. They wondered why these refugees had been sent to them; they gradually realised that these were the people who would take their houses once they were forced to leave. So it came about the new arrivals in turn told the locals of the lives that they could expect in Turkey.'

The prospects were appalling. Much of western Anatolia had been destroyed in the course of the Greek forces' retreat to Smyrna. Infant mortality rates stood at 80 per cent. Food supplies were pitifully short. Tuberculosis, malaria and dysentery were endemic. The local Turks had already taken possession of any surviving buildings; the Muslim arrivals from Greece were often reduced to settling in wreckage. They made their homes in derelict German-built train carriages abandoned in station sidings. A witness in Smyrna saw them 'at every step lodged in excavations, in the cellars of burned houses, under temporary roofs made of pieces of sheet iron supported on stones'. Nine hundred refugees were in one instance dispatched to new lives in Söke; within a year 250 of them were dead.

The people of Kuçkar were braced for a hellish future when they surrendered their papers at the gangplank of a Turkish ship that steamed out of Kavala one day in 1924. But they were to be lucky. On their arrival at the little port of Mavişehir they found that camels had been supplied to transport them and their possessions to the nearby town where their new lives were to begin. The town happened to lie, moreover, beyond the scorched line of the Greek forces' retreat. The Turks for their part had certainly looted and desecrated this Rum settlement where 'torn account books lay scattered about among fragments of bottles and debris of all sorts' in the shops and taverns, and 'everything was smashed, torn, trampled upon' in the school. The houses were 'littered with wrecked boxes, ripped-up mattresses, broken floors', with 'cupboards, sofas, shelves and broken petroleum lamps; children's toys, sewing machines, gramophone records and household utensils'. In the churchyard trunks lay empty, the lids ripped away and the locks pilfered. The church itself had been reduced to 'heaps of boards, seats, ornaments, ikons, crosses, lamps, lecterns, all in pieces and thrown about anyhow'.

But the refugees, who had feared the worst, saw that much could be put right. The new arrivals were even able to select for themselves houses in which 'a good deal of the furniture was still in position'. One couple, newly married, chose to make their home hard by the huge piles of temple stones and columns in the middle of the town and set about making Turks of themselves. The following year their son was born in the house where he was to live all of his life. They called him Ahmet. The same Ahmet, born in the third year of the Turkish Republic, raised a bony finger and pointed to the wall where a framed photograph showed a view, beyond vineyards and country lanes, of a little town before a blue Macedonian sea.

'I won't get to Kuçkar now,' said Ahmet. 'But it may be that my son will.' He gestured that he wished to sleep. As we parted, I was overcome by a powerful valedictory sense. It was as if the old man had finally led me out of Anatolia's colourful but brutal past to emerge into a peaceful if prosaic present. The trade seemed like a good one. I left Ahmet dozing in the shade and, stepping out into the bright sun of summer, I blended with the hatted tourists as they made their way among the courts and colonnades of the great temple.

In the morning I returned to Miletus. The site was deserted and the eucalypts hung motionless in the still air. Outside the half-built museum stood the arrayed marbles – carved lions, friezes, capitals – which were to be exhibited there. Among them the original Meander reclined in magnificent ease beside a watchman's ancient motorbike. I thought of the distance I had come and thanked the river god for keeping me safe. Laying my hand on the statue's shoulder, warm in the returning sun, I particularly thought of the kindness and courtesy I had experienced among these barbarians. At no point had anybody threatened me or barred my progress; they had only wished that I might drink tea with them or take up their offer of a lift. They had befriended me, bought me meals and put me up, and generally treated me to exceptional hospitality. I now wondered if I was the beneficiary of a historical debt – if it was precisely the same kindness that their arriving forebears had once received that they in turn showed to strangers like me. Whatever the answer, Anatolia had turned out to be my ark, as it had also been theirs.

451

It felt odd, even so, all this kindness in a blood-soaked land. The hope was that the warring was finally done and all the people I had met would live out their lives in a peace the Meander Valley had rarely known. It might be that these Turks would never know where they belonged in the wider world, would never quite choose between Europe and Asia, but would learn instead that they were cursed and blessed to live between them. It certainly seemed that the Turks had freed themselves from the threat of invasion, which left them to work out the considerable contradictions that existed among and even within themselves. There were worse things, certainly, than peace and the politics, however fraught, which preserved it.

I walked past the old stones and came down to the river for the last time. I clambered into the canoe and pushed off. Swallows swooped to pluck the water's stiff surface and my strokes sounded clear in the silence. The land lay low now; across the salt flats flamingos stood on bamboo-thin legs among the clumps of samphire. An early sports fisherman was chewing on sunflower seeds beside his planted rod.

'Where have you come from?' he greeted me. And when I told him the man's eyes flared.

'By God, that's something!' he exclaimed. 'Not far now!'

The widening river now appeared to merge with the vast blue sky. From either bank there rose the reed walls and roofs of motley shacks, and water dripped from the frayed tethers of the fishing boats. In the soft sunshine weathered men mended their nets beneath the vertical plumes of cigarettes, raising lazy hands to me.

I could now see the scored line where the first wave broke at the river mouth. Beyond it rose the low outline of the Aegean islet that Greeks and Turks alike knew as Donkey Island. Out on a final sand spit a washed-up traffic sign, an injunction against overtaking, had been planted in the sand. As I paddled onto the Aegean, at the end of 500 horizontal kilometres and one vertical one, my canoe shied at the unfamiliar notion of the long swell and I gave its battered gunwale a reassuring pat of gratitude. Then I pulled out the little tablet jar, sniffed at its garlic-scented memories, raised it above my head and poured the source water into the salt.

I turned to face the way I had come. All up the long valley of the Meander the morning sun was hazing the mountains. The flamingos lifted in a line. As I paddled past the reed shacks the Turks invited me to join them for tea.

EPILOGUE

A few days later Turkey's constitutional court cancelled the amendment that would have opened the way for women to wear headscarves in public offices. It subsequently ruled that the *Ak* Party had violated the secular principle enshrined within the constitution.

A month later still the same court convened to decide on what was to be done with *Ak*. Of the eleven judges six voted to close down the party; a majority, but where a qualified majority – seven out of eleven – was required. *Ak* received a substantial fine but was permitted to continue in office. Many Turks were relieved by an outcome which averted a judicial coup while fostering the convenient impression that the old secularists continued to retain something of their former authority; many considered the result so fortuitous, in fact, that they suspected it had not been arrived at by chance. In the meantime the investigations into *Ergenekon*, that shadowy cadre of secular activists, continued.

The year had not run its course before the people of the Meander Valley noticed something unusual; the winter rains were heavier than many of them had known. These rains persisted. Rivulets poured off the drenched heights above Pınarbaşı to swell the springs along the foot of Samsun Dağı. They brimmed down the ditches of Dinar. Beneath black skies the lakes at Gökgöl and Işıklı rose to their brims, and spuming torrents clattered through the dam gates where Mehmet, concealing his hair loss beneath a woollen cap, had pushed my canoe out onto the stagnant shallows. By Kavak the river had burst its banks, and the farmstead and orchards of the Fearless family were flooded out. The waters lapped at the fringes of the Skirmishers' farm and thundered past the old watermills below Aşağı Seyit. All along the deep gorge at the base of Çökelez Mountain they boiled, and passed below the temple of Apollo Lairbenos to pour into the lonely lake of the waterskiing blonde. Onwards they swirled into the newly built dam at Çindere.

This empty dam, a welcome sump, was able to absorb vast quantities of water. It could do nothing, however, about the rains that had fallen quite as heavily along the lower valley. In spiralling slicks the water slid through the regulator gates at Feslek. By Kuyucak it had breasted the banks and poured out across all the wide plain. It inundated the old bridge at Sarıkemer and spilled into Bafa Lake, raising the waters there by several metres. At the *dalyan* Adem Thunderbolt, hopeful for mullet, found himself knee-deep in water. At Miletus there was so much water, all stirred with silt, that it was as if the sea had returned and all was back as it had been before this story began.

CHRONOLOGY AND CAST

Aregional timeline, with explanatory notes on historical and mythical participants.

6000 BC: The Neolithic cave paintings found on Beşparmak (Mount Latmus) have been dated roughly to this period.

2700 BC: Rise of the Minoan Civilisation in Crete. Emergence of ancient Anatolian fertility deity, **Cybele**, the forerunner of **Artemis of the Ephesians** and characterised by pendulous and multiple dugs.

2000 BC: Rise of a civilisation, tentatively identified as Arzawa, in western Anatolia.

1800 BC: Emergence of the Hittites in Central Anatolia.

1700 BC: Sack of the Arzawan palace at Beycesultan.

1300 BC: Wars between Trojans and Greeks. Emergence of Olympian/Anatolian deities including **Apollo**, god of music and prophecy; **Marsyas**, satyr and virtuoso pipe player; and

Endymion, a beautiful shepherd of Mount Latmus seduced by the moon goddess.

1000 BC: Gradual colonisation of Anatolia's shores, especially the mid-Aegean – Ionia – by mainland Greeks.

800 BC: Rise of Phrygian Empire in central Anatolia under the legendary **Midas**, who was given asses' ears by Apollo as a punishment for championing the pipe playing of Marsyas, and further chastised for his foolish greed when the gods granted him the golden touch. Midas is supposedly related to the mythical **Lityerses**, a Meander Valley deity notorious for killing his harvesters.

600 BC: Miletus celebrated as commercial and cultural centre of the Aegean world, and home to residents such as the scientist, philosopher and proto-rationalist **Thales**.

580 BC: Apogee of the Lydian Empire under **King Croesus**, byword for inordinate wealth.

546 BC: Defeat of Croesus by the Persians after the Lydian King misinterprets the advice of the Delphic Oracle. The beginning of Persian rule in Anatolia.

(?)545 BC: Attempt by **Pactyas**, a Lydian, to lead a revolt against Persian rule. On his flight to Cyme the citizens of that Aegean port ask the oracle at Didyma whether to honour the Lydian's request for protection.

499 BC: The Ionian Revolt against Persian rule.

494 BC: End of Ionian Revolt and the sack of Miletus.

c.490 BC: Birth in Halicarnassus of **Herodotus**, so-called Father of History.

481 BC: Persian invasion force under **King Xerxes** at Celaenae, and his meeting there with **Pythius**, a Lydian, who thinks to curry favour with the King by offering him his entire fortune.

480 BC: Xerxes crosses the Hellespont into Greece. Heroic Spartan defence at Thermopylae. Defeat of Persian fleet at Salamis.

479 BC: Further Persian defeats at Plataea and Mycale.

460 BC: Persian defeat at the Battle of Eurymedon.

401 BC: The anabasis, or expedition, of a Persian prince, **Cyrus the Younger**, and his 'Ten Thousand' Greek mercenaries passes through Celaenae en route for the East. After the prince's death near Baghdad it is **Xenophon**, an Athenian, who takes the lead – at least according to the *Anabasis*, his own eyewitness account of their heroic retreat to the Black Sea.

334 BC: **Alexander the Great**, King of Macedonia, passes through Celaenae en route for Gordium and an encounter with a legendary knot. He conquers all Asia, bringing to an end Persian rule in Anatolia.

312–188 BC: A Hellenistic dynasty, the Seleucids, rule the region. At the Peace of Apamea (188 BC) all western Anatolia is ceded to Pergamum, a client state of Rome, which progressively extends its administrative influence across the Hellenised region.

47: **St Paul** makes his first missionary journey, visiting Antioch in Pisidia, Iconium, Lystra and Derbe.

60: Earthquake flattens Hierapolis, Laodicea and Colossae.

c.100: Progressive silting of Meander Delta cities including Miletus, Priene and Myus.

c.200: Christian conversion at its height in Phrygia.

312: Legalisation of Christianity across the Roman world.

324: Adoption of the city on the Bosphorus – the newly named Constantinople – as the Eastern Roman Emperor's new capital announces the Byzantine Empire.

542: **Bishop John of Ephesus** persecutes pagan communities in the Meander Valley.

650–750: Raids by Muslim Saracens into Anatolia. Pergamum besieged in 717. At around the same time Turkish tribes begin their long migration west from the lands surrounding the Gobi Desert.

1045: Raids by Selçuk Turks and Turcomans reach the Lycus Valley.

1071: Defeat of the Byzantines by the Turks at Manzikert, eastern Anatolia.

1097: Knights of the First Crusade defeat the Turks at Dorylaeum. Establishment of Selçuk Turkish Sultanate with capital at Konya (Iconium).

1145: Turks raid west as far as the Aegean.

1146: Byzantine Emperor **Manuel Comnenus** skirmishes with Turcomans at the head of the Meander.

1148: Knights of the Second Crusade under **Louis VII** defeat the Turks by the Meander. They then suffer a major reverse in the mountains above Laodicea en route to the Mediterranean port of Adalia.

1176: Defeat of Byzantines by the Turks at Myriocephalon.

c.1200: Increased fear among settled Turks and Byzantines alike of unruly Turcoman raiders.

1282: Sack of Nysa and Tralles by Turkish clan chief **Menteşe**.

c.1300: Eclipse of Selçuk Turks and gradual rise from the competing Turkish clans of the Ottomans.

1453: Fall of Constantinople to the Turks. End of Byzantine Empire.

1529: Siege of Vienna. The pinnacle of Ottoman imperial power.

1683: Second siege of Vienna, marking the beginning of the Ottomans' decline.

1682: **George Wheler**'s *Journey Into Greece*, among the first of many Western accounts of travels in Anatolia, is published.

c.1740: **Richard Pococke**'s exploration of the Meander Valley and the surrounding region's ancient sites coincides with the rise of European neoclassicism. Another antiquary, **Richard Chandler**, follows in 1765.

1821: The Greek War of Independence focuses European prejudices against Turks. Over the next century the loss of further Ottoman territories in the Balkans, the Crimea and the Caucasus triggers a flood of Muslim refugees into Anatolia.

1826: **Reverend Francis Arundell** identifies the site of Celaenae-Apamea. Other scholars and antiquaries, among them **William Hamilton** and **Charles Fellows**, subsequently publish accounts of their travels in and around the Meander Valley.

c.1830: Outlaw zeybeks, popular rebels against Ottoman authority, rife in the Meander Valley. **Bald Mehmet** heads a local insurrection near Kuyucak.

1856: A British company begins to build Turkey's first railway line up the Meander Valley, connecting Smyrna with Aydın.

1911–12: Ottoman–Italian War in Libya.

1912–13: Balkan Wars between Ottomans and a coalition of Greeks, Bulgarians and Serbians.

1915–17: Caucasus Campaign against the Russians. Among the deserters is **Yörük Ali**, a peasant of the Meander Valley.

1915: Defence of the Gallipoli Peninsula against Allied invasion forces where **Colonel Mustafa Kemal** distinguishes himself.

1918: Surrender of the Ottomans to the Allies.

1919: Treaty negotiations at Sèvres, Paris, where the dismemberment of Anatolia among the victorious powers is proposed.

15 May 1919: 13,000 Greek forces land at Smyrna.

19 May 1919: Mustafa Kemal leaves Constantinople to lead the nationalist resistance in Anatolia.

27 May 1919: Greek forces occupy Aydın.

27 June–4 July 1919: Battle for Aydın where the Turkish zeybek bands are under the command of Yörük Ali.

1919–21: Greek forces advance east to threaten the Turkish nationalists' capital at Ankara. In August 1921 their advance is finally halted.

August 1922: The Turkish counter-offensive routs the Greeks, who fall back on Smyrna, which the Turks take in September.

1923: Turkey is reborn as a republic under the leadership of Mustafa Kemal, who will take the surname **Atatürk**. For the next fifteen years the country is radically Westernised.

1923–4: Anatolia's Greek Christians, more than a million, are forcibly exchanged with Greece's Muslims.

1938: Death of Atatürk.

1950: Election of **Adnan Menderes'** Democratic Party.

1960: Overthrow of Menderes, who is executed by command of a military tribunal in 1961. Further military interventions follow every decade or so.

2007: The Islamic party, *Ak*, wins a commanding majority in Turkey's national elections. In 2008 it is fined for attempting to undermine Atatürk's secular constitution but remains in power.

2008–9: Record rains cause floods along the Meander Valley.

For years the earl had led a disorderly, unsatisfactory private life, full of intrigue and mired in gossip. He was the last of his line—and a good thing too, many said, considering his disgraceful ancestry—and he wanted a son. Not a bastard son, but a legitimate heir, born of a recognized marriage to a woman willing to live down the inevitable disapproval of the queen. He had a number of liaisons (his enemies counted dozens), and a long-lasting mistress, Douglas Sheffield, who bore him two children, but his preferred choice as a wife was Lettice Knollys, the queen's beautiful cousin. They were secretly married sometime after Lettice's husband died in 1576, and two years later, when she was heavily pregnant with Leicester's child, her father Francis Knollys demanded that a more formal private ceremony take place. It was a great risk, for the queen was sure to discover the truth in time, yet Knollys did not trust the notorious womanizer Leicester to have carried through a valid wedding ceremony; he had to see with his own eyes that his daughter was properly married.

Simier found out about the marriage, and told Elizabeth, only weeks before Alençon was due to arrive in England. She was already tense and overwrought with fear and expectation; the discovery of Leicester's treachery shocked, then enraged her. It was like Leicester to act behind her back, his pusillanimity was as contemptible as his deceit. As for Lettice, that traitorous "she-wolf," no words were harsh enough to describe her. Leicester, though, would have reason to fear for his life. She ordered him seized and shut up in an isolated tower in Greenwich park, to await stricter imprisonment in the Tower of London.

Angry and wounded though she was, and eager for revenge, Elizabeth must have glimpsed a kind of perverse symmetry in the courses her life and Leicester's were taking. It was said among the people that they had been born in the same hour, so that their lives were attuned from birth; now, having reached their mid-forties, both had decided to marry. And just as in fact the earl was a year older than the queen, so he had married the previous year; she would follow in her turn. There was a melancholy appropriateness about Leicester's marriage, for however she might lament his loss as a potential husband his union with Lettice Knollys left her completely free to choose elsewhere. However tenuous her enduring romantic tie to him had been, it was now formally severed. She could marry Alençon with nothing weighing on her heart.

On August 17 Alençon arrived. There was no public welcome, for though the fact of his visit was an open secret, it was unofficial, and no one was allowed to speak of it. The secrecy, and the private, clandestine meetings between Elizabeth and her boyish admirer added a strong erotic overtone to their encounter. No one recorded what went on at their first meeting, whether the duke played the ardent, aggressive wooer or let Elizabeth set the tone, her warmth and heartiness breaking through the brittle artificiality of her overadorned, overrouged person. They were prepared to find one another at least tolerable; in fact they took pleasure in each other's company, and ended by becoming infatuated.

"The queen is delighted with Alençon, and he with her," the Spanish ambassador Mendoza reported with chagrin. She was "much taken with his good parts," she found him pleasing in manner and, presumably, acceptable in appearance. In short, "she admired him more than any man." Simier was her Monkey, Alençon became her Frog. He presented her with a brooch commemorating his nickname—a golden frog sitting on a golden flower, with the duke's face painted on the frog's back.

To the men of affairs who were accustomed to keeping themselves informed about events at court the near-total privacy of the wooing couple was maddening. Not even the council members were involved. They "shut their eyes and avoided going to court," while letting it be known that they disapproved of the entire proceeding and were disturbed about it. The very fact that the queen was in sole control of her dealings with Alençon and Simier seemed to indicate the uniquely serious character of these marriage negotiations. "Many people who were wont to smile at it now see that appearances are all in favor of its taking place and believe it," Mendoza wrote.

Elizabeth was enjoying every minute of the intrigue, both for its own sake and because it was distinctly unsettling to her councilors. She used Alençon to tease her courtiers, entertaining them at a ball where the duke was hidden, conspicuously, behind a tapestry. As he looked on from his concealment she danced for him—more vigorously and more often than she usually did—and made secret signals to him that called even more attention to his presence.

The wooing, the game of secrecy and the erotic attentions of the personable young duke energized Elizabeth and drew her further and further along the path toward final commitment. She saw in Alençon the "Defender of Belgian Liberty Against the Tyranny of Spain"—the title the Netherlanders had bestowed on him. He was small but mighty; had he not declared, when warned that the French would never accept him as king if he married Elizabeth, that "he would look upon as his enemy any person who advised him to the contrary"?

She must marry, she had declared. Since she must, let it be this man. There were no more wry smiles, no more self-deprecating remarks. ("What a fine idea for an old woman like me to talk of marriage!" she had said only a few months earlier.) Let the closing stages of the negotiations begin.

Alençon's coming had been private, but his parting with Elizabeth was public, and "very tender." She gave him a handsome jewel, and in return he slipped onto her slender finger a sparkling diamond ring whose worth was estimated at ten thousand crowns. The afterglow of their courtship was vivid. For weeks after the duke's departure Elizabeth talked of his virtues, his "good qualities," even the goodness of her future mother-in-law Catherine de' Medici, whose character and policies she had always before despised.

The frog brooch shone from her bodice, the diamond ring gleamed on her finger. For her part, Elizabeth said, choosing her words with care, "she would not prevent his being her husband."

27

The King of France shall not advance his ships in
* English sand,*
Nor shall his brother Francis have the ruling of the land:
We subjects true unto our queen the foreign yoke defy,
Whereto we plight our faithful hearts, our limbs, our lives
* and all,*
Thereby to have our honour rise, or take our fatal fall.
Therefore, good Francis, rule at home, resist not our
* desire;*
For here is nothing else for thee, but only sword and fire.

Alençon was barely off on his homeward journey—pausing at Dover to write his sweetheart Elizabeth four passionate love letters, and at Boulogne to write three more—when a pamphlet was published which denounced him as a scheming, debauched opportunist.

John Stubbs, a lawyer and country gentleman who spoke for the stern, uncompromising reformers known as Puritans, published *The Discovery of a Gaping Gulf Whereunto England is Like to Be Swallowed by Another French Marriage if the Lord Forbid Not the Bans by Letting Her Majesty See the Sin and Punishment Thereof*. The treatise was as infelicitous as its title, yet its plain-spoken arguments were forceful.

What sort of sordid lovemaking was this, that linked a scurvy young lecher to a gaunt old maid of forty-six? (The pamphlet's appearence coincided unflatteringly with the queen's birthday.) Everyone knows the true purpose of "these younger men that seek their elder matches," Stubbs insisted; they are always deceiving rogues, out to steal the woman's money —or in Elizabeth's case, her kingdom. She herself was a pitiable victim; he hated to see "our dear Queen Elizabeth (I shake to speak of it) led blindfold as a poor lamb to the slaughter."

And slaughter it would surely be, for a woman of her years to submit to the agonies and hazards of childbearing. True physicians would certainly confess, if they were candid, "how exceedingly dangerous they find it by their learning for her majesty to have her first child at these years, yea, how fearful the expectation of death is to mother and child: I fear to say what will be their answer." (Cecil, only a few months earlier, had fully satisfied himself from information provided by the queen's physicians and waiting women that she had "no impediment . . . nor lack of natural functions in those things that properly belong to the procreation of children." Her "aptness to have children" was to him beyond doubt; indeed the physicians predicted another six years of fertility, and added that the process would most likely prove rejuvenating.)

The thought of Elizabeth's fleshly union with the disease-ridden Frenchman was repellent to Stubbs. She who exercised a "princely priesthood in Christ Jesus" ought never to touch a man scabrous with venereal disease, "God's punishment on flesh and bones," a man whose immoral pleasures had brought on him the "inevitable plagues" that follow overripe lusts.

Above all the queen must not be deluded about Alençon's true motive: "to seduce our Eve, that she and we may lose this English Paradise." Just as the hated King Philip had once brought to England a swarm of greedy, slovenly Spaniards when he married Mary Tudor, so Alençon hoped to invade English shores with his train of "needy, spent Frenchmen, the scum of the king's court, which is the scum of all France which is the scum of Europe." They would attach themselves like horseleeches to the prosperous English, until they drew off all their wealth and all their strength, then, with Elizabeth under her husband's command, unable to resist, they would complete the conquest in earnest.

The *Gaping Gulf* was monarchical insult of a high order. Stubbs's condescension toward Elizabeth was as maddening as his language was offensive; he assaulted her sovereignty, her judgment, and her statecraft as well as her nubility—and the latter alone was enough to warrant severe punishment. She ordered all copies of the *Gaping Gulf* to be burned, and ordered Stubbs, his printer and his publisher to be hanged.

In reacting as strongly as she did Elizabeth was responding not merely to one outrageously offensive pamphlet, but to an outspoken and influential group of her subjects. By punishing Stubbs she meant to punish all Puritans, and to rebuke their insolence and self-righteous presumption. They were an affront to her rule, for they answered to no authority but the Bible, as they interpreted it, and they did not hesitate to serve as arbiters of morality to anyone and everyone around them, including the queen.

The church Elizabeth had established at the beginning of her reign was a church built on compromise and concessions, politically workable but spiritually insipid. It was inoffensive to the indifferent, but to men and women of fervid religion it was a stale and bland thing, its rituals a hollow if eloquent exercise, its clergy few and mediocre, its doctrine too remote to nourish warm belief.

Many Catholics never accepted it at all, though most of them conformed outwardly to its usages; many Protestants began early in the reign to form a Puritan "counter-church" within it, dedicated to the moral transformation of the entire society. Earnest Puritan ministers met weekly to devote themselves to Bible study and prayer, and strove to purge every vestige of sin from their lives. Inspired lay parishioners joined these weekly "prophesyings," and became consumed by a holy mission to uncover and correct wrongdoing in themselves and others.

The strength of the Puritan movement lay in its radical, uncompromising view of the human condition. Nothing short of absolute commitment to godliness must be tolerated; there must be no accommodation with Satan. Life was a battleground where good struggled with evil, and only those ironclad with righteousness and profoundly serious of purpose could come through the fray unscathed. "Satan is roaring like a lion, the world is going mad," one Puritan wrote to a likeminded friend in 1578. "Antichrist is resorting to every extreme, that he may with wolf-like ferocity devour the sheep of Christ."

Seen from this grim perspective, ordinary events took on the magnified proportions of omens and portents, signs of things to come. Ominous times called for preternatural vigilance. Therefore there must be, in every parish, men who spied out the sins of the erring and wrote them down for correction at the weekly meeting. "Notorious blasphemy, whoredom, drunkenness, railing against religion, scolds, ribalds and such like"—all must be reported, and the perpetrators admonished. But this was only the beginning. Prayers, attendance at endless, hair-raising sermons, long Sundays filled with heart-searching meditations, Bible study and church services: these were the rudiments of the godly life, to be lived in agonized expectation of the end of the world. Puritan children carried their spiritual burden in their names: Reformation, Tribulation, Dust, Deliverance. Flee-Sin kept company in the nursery with Praise-God and Be-Thankful; the baptismal records of the 1570s and 1580s are a theological lexicon of pious names, with Repent and Eschew Evil and Faint-Not frequent among them.[1]

The more frivolous Elizabethan pastimes drew disapproving Puritan frowns. Players were chased out of town, morris dancers forbidden to dance. Seasonal festivals were outlawed when it was found that the pageantry drew greater crowds than the sermons which competed with them. Everywhere the unregenerate complained of Puritan clergy "too sour in preaching away their pastime," everywhere the lighthearted music of pipe and drum was drowned out by the mighty sound of fervent hymns. The Puritans managed to exert far more influence and attract far more attention than their numbers warranted, perhaps because they felt, and looked, alien and out of place among ordinary, worldly men and women. Their faces were compressed into masks of self-denial and censure; they held themselves rigid, and walked with unswerving purpose. Unadorned, plainly dressed, their clothes were a mortification of the flesh and a warning to the gaudy.

Nowhere were they more conspicuous than at Elizabeth's court, where their dull black gowns stood out from among the flashing, gem-encrusted doublets of the other courtiers. The unruly, shoulder-length hair of the redeemed made a strong contrast to the well-tended coiffures of fashionable men, who "frounced their hair with curling irons" and wore long "love locks" tied with ribbons or silk favors. Exaggeration vied with exaggerated plainness, flamboyance with exaggerated sobriety. And the Puritan emerged the more memorable.

Courtly pastimes came in for particular condemnation. Drinking, gambling, dining on dainty foods and indulging illicit lust all brought forth God's wrath and the preachers'. Dancing the violent, exhausting Elizabethan dances, "with disordinate gestures, and with monstrous thumping of the feet, to pleasant sounds, to wanton songs, to dishonest verses," the Puritans decried as contrary to Scriptural law, while swearing was a dishonor to God and an abomination to the Christian community. The queen, who was unusually gifted at both dancing and swearing, was not spared her measure of censure. Her language was especially reproved.

"Your gracious majesty," a Puritan named Fuller told Elizabeth in a book he left for her to read, "in your anger hath used to swear sometime by that abominable idol the mass, and often and grievously by God, and by Christ." She swore, in fact, by Christ's wounds, his death, his head and other venerated organs, and by all the saints, forgetting entirely about the biblical injunctions against such blasphemy. And her subjects imitated her. "By your majesty's evil example and sufferance," Mr. Fuller wrote reproachfully, "the most part of your subjects and people of every degree, do commonly swear and blaspheme, to God's unspeakable dishonor, without any punishment."

This same tone of personal reproach was taken by Puritans in Parliament, where they formed a strong and formidable opposition group. Their strident voices were raised in long-winded and often keenly perceptive diatribes against the clerical hierarchy of bishops and archbishops—"a thing introduced into the church by Satan"—against the Book of Common Prayer—"an unperfect book, culled and picked out of that popish dung-hill the breviary and mass book"—and in particular against Elizabeth's headship of the church. On this issue, and on Elizabeth's general fallibility, the Puritans became increasingly vehement in the later 1570s. At Easter of 1579 a preacher addressing the lord mayor and magistrates of London railed at the queen so violently that he had to be seized and removed from his pulpit. In Parliament, the Puritan leader Peter Wentworth began a tirade against the queen's ineffectual efforts to reform her church. He went on and on, exceeding the bounds of his subject and attacking Elizabeth with unprecedented impropriety. "Certain it is," he shouted, "that none is without fault, no not our noble queen, since her majesty hath committed great faults, yea dangerous faults to herself." He would have said more, but the Commons members themselves, "out of a reverend regard for her majesty's honor, stopped Mr. Wentworth before he had fully finished."[2]

Wentworth was sent to the Tower, yet he and his coreligionists in Parliament were valuable to Elizabeth's government, for along with their fearless criticism went unfeigned admiration for their Judith, their Deborah, their treasured Gloriana. Elizabeth was a sinful, fallible woman whose political judgment failed her when it came to matters of conscience; she was also the Protestant figurehead of her Protestant realm, the ruler evidently chosen by God to lead her people. With their bluff forthrightness the Puritans were among the loudest in pledging to support their queen with their lives and goods, and in articulating that cult of the queen which grew throughout the 1570s. The eternal struggle between good and evil was in the late sixteenth century embodied in the struggle between England and her Catholic enemies, in the Puritan view; it was their clear duty to stand behind their queen in her hour of danger. There was a tenderness in their fervent protectiveness. "It makes my heart leap for joy to think we have such a jewel," one Commons member said of his sovereign, adding that "it makes my joints to tremble for fear, when I consider the loss of such a jewel."[3]

Much as she valued their patriotism and cherished their affection Elizabeth was wary of the Puritans, for their visionary fanaticism often led them astray. At Cambridge, where the movement had its intellectual stronghold, students disobeyed college rules en masse when they went against Puritan beliefs, and smashed windows and pulled down monuments in an upsurge of iconoclasm. Apoplectic Puritan preachers lost control of themselves, until their shrill invective came close to hysteria. Misguided individual believers were driven to acts of madness. One day, while the service was being performed in Elizabeth's chapel in the palace, there was a frightening interruption. A man ran up to the altar, beside himself with rage and shouting "heretical and shameful words." Before anyone could stop him he had thrown down the cross and candlesticks—the ornaments which to

Puritans represented Catholicism—and crushed them by stomping on them with his boots, cursing and swearing at the top of his lungs as he did so. He was crazed, but not with ordinary madness, and instead of being locked away as a simple madman he was brought before the royal council and questioned. Why had he done this thing? they asked him. He held up a Bible, an English translation of the New Testament. "That book had made him," he said. There was no need to say more.[4]

Vehement, irrational, socially disturbing, the Puritans were as much an abomination to Elizabeth as her swearing was to them. Their way was one of ultimatums and absolutes; hers was one of approximations and evasions. They were clearly "dangerous to kingly rule," and she meant to halt the rapid spread of their influence.

The weekly "prophesyings" must stop. She ordered her archbishop of Canterbury, Edmund Grindal, to command the bishops to end them. But Grindal demurred. The clergy needed revitalizing, he said; why should she want to suppress a movement that was so beneficial to spiritual life? He could not bring himself to do it. She could remove him from his see if she liked, but the prophesyings would go on. And while he was on the subject, Grindal went further. Elizabeth's attempts to govern the affairs of her clergy, he said, were dangerously reminiscent of the pope's attempts to control his priests. "Remember Madam that you are a mortal creature," Grindal warned, "and although ye are a mighty prince, yet remember that he which dwelleth in heaven is mightier." There was a strong Puritan flavor in the archbishop's final admonition. Let Elizabeth take heed that she not repeat the error of the biblical king Joash, who "when he was strengthened, his heart was lifted up to his destruction, and he regarded not the Lord."

The queen ignored her archbishop's righteous growlings and, angrily noting his disobedience, sent out her own command to the bishops that the prophesyings must cease. Grindal was suspended from exercising his jurisdiction, but there was no major scandal, for if she had reacted strongly every time one of her servants showed sympathy with the Puritans she would have had leisure for little else. Not only Grindal but Cecil and Leicester aided them and sided with them on occasion; Knollys and Walsingham were Puritans themselves, and in fact it was the inscrutable, sardonic principal secretary whom she suspected of being behind the publication of Stubbs's *Gaping Gulf.*

Francis Walsingham, who had been principal secretary for the last six years, presented Elizabeth with a unique problem. Of all her councilors, he was least likely to allow anything to dissuade him from speaking his mind, and she valued his candor. Yet when he did voice an opinion she had difficulty deciding whether it was the Puritan ideologue speaking or the cultured, sophisticated diplomat and man of the world. For Walsingham was a paradox, a stern, inflexible follower of the purer religion who was at the same time a well-rounded Renaissance courtier. He looked at life through a narrow apocalyptic lens, yet he was capable of delivering his judgment upon it in facile and cultivated French or Italian or German or Spanish. His superb education—he had studied with John Cheke at Cambridge—had been deepened by two years of travel and study on the continent, and he was as adroit and subtle an ambassador as Elizabeth possessed.

But if she relied on Walsingham to draw on his wide knowledge of foreign courts and tongues in advising her she had always to keep in mind that his views were those of a Marian exile, a grim enemy of what he saw as the Satanic forces of popery. He was at his best in seeking out devious plots at home and abroad, while when it came to the feints and tergiversations and half-truths of Elizabethan statecraft he was somewhat ill at ease, especially when to him the way of godliness seemed overwhelmingly clear.

Walsingham's perception of England's situation left no room for ambiguities. The Catholic powers of Europe, he believed, with overmighty Spain in the vanguard, would soon launch a military assault on Protestant England. They would be certain to involve Mary Stuart—who represented a grave danger to Elizabeth and should have been put to death years ago —and would rely heavily on seditious Catholic subjects within England to accomplish their purpose. Since Armageddon must come, Walsingham argued, it would be best to go out armed to meet it. England must fight vigorously and wholeheartedly against Spain and the powers of darkness on every holy frontier—in the New World, in France where the Huguenots fought the Catholics, in the Netherlands where Dutch Calvinists struggled to oppose Spanish arms. An alliance with Alençon, heir to the Catholic throne of France, was from this point of view unthinkable; it was tantamount to an alliance with Satan. Elizabeth must not marry him, no matter what the cost to her personal happiness or to the continuity of the Tudor line.

That Walsingham was the most determined opponent of her proposed marriage Elizabeth felt sure. Yet much as she would have liked to discount his views as those of a blind and bigoted fanatic, she could not; she had too much respect for his intelligence and sophistication. To be sure, he had said, "I wish God's glory and next the queen's safety," putting religion before patriotism and personal loyalty, but in this he was typical rather than idiosyncratic. No, she would continue to rely on his prescience, his indefatigable energy—he worked harder, and for longer hours, than almost anyone else in her government—and on his dark vision of reality. But she would not tolerate his behindhand propaganda. If he had been to any degree responsible for the Stubbs pamphlet, then he must be made to feel her displeasure.

Elizabeth had said that Stubbs, his printer and his publisher would be hanged, but when it came to charging them there was a dispute over the illegality of what they had done. Was it really unlawful to raise arguments against a prospective bridegroom before the queen married him? The lawyers had not had to face this issue for a generation, not since Mary Tudor had been forced to provide protection to her hated husband Philip of Spain. Some found Elizabeth's vengefulness against Stubbs intolerable; one judge resigned rather than join in the verdict.

On the appointed day in early November the author and his publisher were brought to face their punishment—the printer was pardoned—on a scaffold built in the marketplace at Westminster. There was a large crowd, and people waited uneasily for the cruel spectacle they were to witness, stamping their feet and hugging their arms to keep warm. The weather was unseasonably cold; it would be a harsh winter. Already there was talk of the unusual frosts and storms, and of what they might foretell. Throughout September there had been extremely heavy rains and floods, stopping up the "crannies, pores and vents" in the ground and impeding the earth's customary "windy exhalations and vapors." A comet had been sighted in October, and this, combined with the climatic aberrations, was clearly a portent. It was not difficult to infer its meaning: it foretold a dark event —the death of a great personage, war or natural calamity, or perhaps an ill-omened marriage between the English queen and the French duke.

Stubbs and his publisher William Page had been sentenced to lose their right hands. Stubbs came forward, baring his wrist and placing his hand on a wooden block. His wit did not fail him. "Pray for me," he was heard to say, "now my calamity is at hand." The hand was "cut off with a cleaver, driven through the wrist by the force of a mallet," and the victim, reeling from the shock of the blow and from the sight of his own gushing blood, pulled off his hat with his sound hand and cried loudly, "God save the queen!" Then he fainted.

"The multitude standing about was deeply silent," wrote an eyewitness, "either out of an horror at this new and unwonted kind of punishment, or else out of commiseration towards the man, as being of an honest and unblameable repute, or else out of hatred of the marriage, which most men presaged would be the overthrow of religion." Or, he might have added, out of disbelief at Elizabeth's bloody spite.

Her behavior was indeed erratic as she struggled with her recalcitrant councilors, now commanding, now cajoling them, weeping with vexation one minute and the next squabbling angrily with whoever opposed her. What the Spanish ambassador Mendoza called "her little witcheries," which often brought her the outcome she desired, failed her utterly. Instead the men of the council played on her fears and anxieties. "Knowing her pusillanimity and fear of any adversity," they tried to alarm her with threats of invasion and treachery. How could she possibly think of marrying a Catholic, Knollys cried, when she had forbidden her Protestant subjects to do so? She glared at him; she had not forgotten his complicity in Leicester's marriage to his daughter, nor did she forget that he was a Puritan like Stubbs. "He might pay dearly for the zeal he was displaying in the cause of religion," she said. This was "a fine way to show his attachment to her, who might desire, like others, to have children."[5]

She exasperated Cecil, and quarreled so bitterly with Hatton that he had to stay out of her sight for a week. Walsingham, who spoke his mind as usual and told her flatly what his objections to the marriage were, she dismissed peremptorily. He was good for nothing, she said, but to be a protector of heretics, and she sent him away. Her moods grew more and more unstable, and for the three months following Alençon's departure in August she was crotchety, imperious and demanding. And when for all her moodiness and insistence she found her councilors as adamant as ever in their refusal to endorse her marriage, she became "extremely sad" and was "so cross and melancholy that it was noticed by everyone who approached her."

As for the beleaguered councilors themselves, it was all they could do to put up with their sovereign. Their ranks had thinned. By 1579 many of the names familiar from the first decade of the reign—Pembroke, Northampton, Arundel, Norfolk—had been struck off, with death or retirement or, in Norfolk's case, execution accounting for the absence. Others were aging, and growing querulous with age. Sussex, whose advice was still valuable, complained of being slighted by Elizabeth; he was treated like an old broom, he said resentfully, useful enough when needed but then thrown outside the door and left to rot.[6] Knollys was becoming prim, and strident on the subject of court morals. He wished aloud for "that realm where virtue is honored and vice is bridled," and had to be humored on moral issues. Hatton, now coming into his own as a suave and skillful reconciler of factions and mediator between opposing points of view, gave place to the efficient secretary Walsingham and to Cecil, who still anchored the council with his moderate opinions.

Cecil was getting on in years. He had his ailments, and wore his doublets "cut and voided in the back" for fear of the stone. For years his government work had kept him in "a continual agitation both of body and mind," and as he got older he took more and more pleasure in such undemanding pastimes as telling stories to his grandchildren around the supper table and "riding privately in his garden upon his little mule." Yet Elizabeth continued to rely on him. He was thoughtful, sober, wise. What he called his "dullness" she prized as balanced judgment, a quality she needed when her thoughts were, as she told him once, "in a labyrinth" and needed unraveling.

Leicester was in a kind of limbo, superficially reconciled to the queen yet not restored to anything like his former place in her regard. She had thought better of her initial reaction to the discovery of his marriage, when in cold anger she had ordered him imprisoned. He had spent a week in involuntary isolation, but it was given out that he had merely been shut away to take medicine, and after the week was over he left court to stay at one of his own houses.

Clearly he had forfeited a measure of that sentimental concern Elizabeth had always felt for him, and he feared to lose his power and perhaps his wealth besides. He wrote to Cecil, lamenting his loss of favor and predicting morosely that having sacrificed his youth and liberty to the queen he was about to give up "all his fortune" besides.[7] He felt wronged, a victim of his enemies' malice and a martyr to his own selfless devotion to his unappreciative sovereign. For twenty years he had "faithfully, carefully, and chargeably" served Elizabeth, and had been honorable in all his acts and intentions, he told Cecil. Yet now she had "grown into a very strange humor, all things considered," and her bitterness knew no bounds. He felt like a faithful dog being whipped by an ungrateful master; all in all, he had little to show for twenty years of service. Leicester's capacity for self-pity, which had always been great, was now at its height, and his counsel was not likely to be of much use to the queen or anyone else in the near future.

After weeks of frustrating and stormy deliberations Elizabeth broke through to action. On November 20 she ordered the marriage articles put into final form, and a few days later Simier, who had stayed on after his master Alençon's departure in order to conclude the diplomatic formalities, left England, taking the articles with him.

The thing was done. If the council members had meant to call Elizabeth's bluff, they found she had all along been sincere. She did not dare face the Commons. Parliament, scheduled to meet in October, was prorogued, and popular opposition continued unabated. Through the bitter winter months, when an "unlooked for great snow" froze the rivers and piled in high drifts along the roads and in the towns, Puritan preachers as usual exhorted their congregations to eschew evil and reject the French marriage. The queen swore she would have them whipped, but forbore. In tender letters to her sweetheart Francis the Constant she confessed to a growing concern about his religion. He was her very dear Frog, and she would rather spend the rest of her life with him than with any other prince in the entire world, she wrote, yet her subjects would have no king who professed the Catholic faith. Unless a way around this obstacle could be found, their infatuation might never come to fruition.

Was it the first sign of a rift? Observers in England and elsewhere watched the queen's behavior closely. One observer had never been convinced that all the lovemaking, all the negotiations had been anything but a ruse. "I have always looked upon the idea of a marriage between the queen and Alençon as a mere invention," King Philip wrote from Madrid to his ambassador Mendoza in England.[8] "I nevertheless believe they will continue to discuss it, and even may become reconciled for the purpose, but I believe that she herself is the person who will refuse."

28

Some gentler passions slide into my minde,
For I am softe, and made of melting snowe;
Or be more cruell, Love, and soe be kynd,
Let me, or flote, or sinke, be high or lowe;
Or let me live with some more sweete content;
Or dye, and soe forget what love ere meant.

I n April of 1581, King Philip went to his coronation in Lisbon. He was dressed entirely in black, for he was in deep mourning for his wife, but his doublet was cut of rich brocade and his few ornaments were kingly. He stood solemnly before the altar at the coronation mass, decorous and reverent, as he was invested with the crown of Portugal and with Portuguese lands stretching across the known world from Brazil to the East Indies to the Persian Gulf. Spain had brought him the wealth and treasure of the New World; Portugal brought him added riches, riches enough to conquer what lands and kingdoms he did not already possess.

King Philip had reached the summit of his power. No European sovereign had ever ruled over so much land or commanded so much wealth. Yet beneath the carapace of royalty stood a shrunken figure with a gray beard and sad eyes. "They want to dress me in brocade, much against my will," he wrote later to his daughters, describing the coronation. Finery was alien to him; it went against his deep-seated asceticism. But he had resigned himself dutifully to the expectations of his new Portuguese subjects. "They tell me it is the custom here," he explained.

Philip came to his newfound might in a mood of infinite resignation. Adult life had brought him much more sorrow than joy, and he had only recently lost his most cherished companion, his fourth wife Anne of

Austria. Her tight-lipped self-denial had matched his—"she never leaves her rooms, and her court is like a nunnery," a visitor to the palace had noted —and since her death her bereaved husband had aged noticeably. He had now buried four wives in all, and two heirs to his throne as well. Few of Anne of Austria's many children had survived, and those that had the king treasured with a fiercely paternal concern tinged with fatalism. He clung to all the people he loved, yet stood ready to yield them up should God desire it, for he had learned to look on his private griefs as oblations offered by a humble soul to an inscrutable providence. It was the same with his triumphs. They were not his, but God's, and he accepted them reverently but with a devout indifference.

Contemplation of his worldly dominion brought Philip far less satisfaction than his enemies thought. Others were more quick than he to calculate the benefits of his Portuguese conquest: vast lands in Africa, the New World and the Far East, treasure so incomparably rich it made him wealthier than all the European sovereigns combined, twelve great Portuguese fighting galleons, with the dockyards to service them and the skilled mariners to sail and man them. Already the colossus of the known world, in 1580 Spain was becoming even more gigantic, and those who feared her might counted up her men and arms and warships and tried to imagine what was in the abstracted, austere old king's mind to do with them.

To the pope, to Catholic English exiles in Spain and elsewhere on the continent, the answer was clear. Philip should turn his immense fighting forces against "that guilty woman of England," Elizabeth. He who had conquered Portugal, through his great general Alva, in only a few weeks, he whose fleet had crushed the naval forces of Islam at the battle of Lepanto and was indisputable master of the world's oceans—save for an occasional loss to English pirates—should not hesitate to snuff out England. It was not even a question of calculating the military odds. The suppression of Protestant heresy in England was a holy obligation, part of a larger spiritual war between the forces of the church and the forces of the devil. With all the visionary impracticality of homeward-yearning emigrés the English conspirators dreamed of a grandiose "Enterprise," a voyage of conquest in which Spanish arms would unseat Elizabeth and put Mary Stuart on the throne to restore Catholicism.

But it was not the impractical English exiles alone who urged the Enterprise on Philip; it was the pope himself. Gregory XIII, the fiery, impatient leader of Catholic Christendom was inordinately devoted to the annihilation of the "wicked Jezebel" who ruled England, and as the 1580s opened he had begun to attack her on several fronts. He had sent military expeditions to Ireland, the last of which, landing in the summer of 1579, had succeeded in gaining a foothold in the country and defending it against the English for more than a year. He was sending missionaries into England to revive the Roman faith—and with it the determination to change the government. And he had persuaded himself, with a sophistry common in the later sixteenth century, that to condone the assassination of a ruler who was an enemy to the true faith was to act correctly in the sight of God. Through his secretary of state, the cardinal of Como, Gregory XIII had proclaimed that since Elizabeth was the cause of such injury to the church of Rome and was responsible for the loss of so many Catholic souls, anyone who "sent her out of the world" would not be committing any sin.

Philip was certainly in agreement, in principle, with the cause of destroying Protestant England. He had never approved of Elizabeth, either as a sister-in-law or a prospective wife or a fellow sovereign. He had promised the pope that he would rescue Mary Stuart from her captivity and help her to gain her rightful place as queen of England, and he had made, and honored, in part, a pledge of financial support for an invasion. Self-interest too urged action against Elizabeth, and a desire for revenge. For years she had been opposing him in the Netherlands, financing rebellion there and causing him untold trouble and expense. Her captains harassed his treasure fleets and stole his silver—which she then sent to pay the Dutch rebels— and her vigorous wooing of the heir to the French throne played havoc with the precarious peace between Hapsburg and Valois. And if he wanted revenge, it was now in his grasp, for with the combined fleets of Spain and Portugal at his disposal he could at last confront Elizabeth's small but powerful navy in an invasion launched from his own Portuguese coastal ports.

All this Philip knew, yet as he sat at his plain wooden desk, pen in hand, pondering the state of Christendom and praying for guidance, he often became distracted and slipped into a sort of pious reverie. His servants noted the vacant gaze and bemused expression, and worried over their master's health, for he was frequently melancholy and had difficulty taking pleasure in anything but his children and his great womblike palace.

The Escorial was an outward expression of Philip's wayward inner moods, a dark, cavernous edifice whose core was a monastery. The king's own small and sparely furnished rooms faced down onto an ornate, cathedral-like chapel; lying in his simple bed he could watch the mass being performed and hear the choir intone the ethereal anthems of his court composers. He bought masterworks of medieval art for the palace, and commissioned sumptuous new pieces by gifted craftsmen, but all in the service of faith, not beauty.

The Escorial was as much a gigantic reliquary as it was a Renaissance palace; the king applied the same meticulous care to correspondence with relic merchants as he did to government dispatches, reading every word with squinting slowness and writing comments in the margins with a careful and deliberate hand. He was amassing an unusually complete collection of venerable bones and skulls. He found such objects of devotion consoling; like the countryside around the palace, they helped to "elevate his soul and sustain his pious meditations."

The Protestant English, indeed Protestants everywhere, imagined King Philip far differently than this—not as a nearsighted, bemused old man frowning over his relics, but as a dark conqueror brooding in his secret fortress. What they knew of him was ugly rumor: that he had murdered his son Don Carlos, that he was "more papal than the pope," and murderously bigoted, that his cruel soldiers in the New World had killed millions of Indians, chaining them like dogs and starving them to death or torturing them by searing their skin with hot bacon grease.

They heard, through the reports of spies or ambassadors abroad, how Philip presided in grim majesty over the mass burnings of heretics. In an open square at the center of Valladolid or Madrid a high wooden structure was erected where the king sat on his throne, surrounded by the terrifying inquisitors of the Holy Office. He spoke gravely to the crowd, swearing to defend the pure faith against all who would corrupt it, then gave the signal for the awful spectacle to begin.

The bells of the city's churches began to toll as the mounted escort appeared leading the procession of the condemned. They dragged along in their hundreds, wretched figures broken by miserable confinement and wasted from lack of food, wearing the black tunic of prisoners sentenced to execution. On their heads were high conical caps painted with grimacing devils and leaping red flames—images of hell—and on their wrists and ankles they wore chains, or the wounds and welts where chains had been.

As the king and the vast crowd looked on, a preacher delivered a long and chastening sermon. Afterward, with the spectators on their knees and the executioners heaping wood and straw around the heavy stakes to prepare them for the torches, the grand inquisitor intoned the final rites of absolution and condemnation. Then, stern and remote on his high throne, Philip watched as the victims were tied to the stakes and the fires were lit under them.

The horrors of the Inquisition were graphically described in Protestant propaganda, and the English had no difficulty envisioning the moans and screams of the dying, the acrid, smoke-filled air, the snorting and neighing of the guardsmen's horses and the solemn bells. It was said at Elizabeth's court that such open-air burnings were common in Spain. Early in his reign

Philip reportedly ordered two thousand people apprehended for heresy—men, women and children—and though a great many of these escaped death, hundreds had suffered.

The Spanish conquest of Portugal came at a time when Philip's fortunes were rising elsewhere. The American silver mines that financed Spain's war machine suddenly boosted their yield. The war in the Netherlands looked more hopeful than it had for years, and the papal adventuring in Ireland had shown how vulnerable England was in the north, and had tested her military resources. The Irish rebellion had attracted substantial Scots support, forcing the government to reinforce the garrison at Berwick and to muster five thousand fighting men.

If nothing else, the improving leverage of Spain in the European arena caused increased uncertainty in London, where after two years the outrage of the queen's French wooing had not died down. Elizabeth had counted on the chaos in the Netherlands to continue to distract and drain Philip's energies and treasury, but now a breakthrough seemed possible. And another safeguard had been removed, albeit a shaky and impermanent one. Civil war had been resumed in France, making it unlikely that the French would be able to intervene to block Philip's advance, should he decide to launch the Enterprise of England after all.

Like it or not, the English would have to choose between the menace of Spain and the distasteful prospect of a French prince as Elizabeth's husband. As King Philip submitted to his coronation in Lisbon, Elizabeth unfolded the most lavish and extensive entertainment yet offered to visitors from abroad. Her guests were envoys of Francis the Constant, still her long-suffering suitor and devoted slave—or so his letters said—weary of waiting for his elusive bride-to-be but ever hopeful nonetheless.

There were more than five hundred in the French suite, including many nobles of the highest rank, and one of Elizabeth's own houses was emptied to lodge the grandest of them. London and Westminster were crowded with servants and petty knights and liveried retainers, for in addition to the hundreds of French servitors all the English peers had been ordered to come to the capital and to bring their full trains with them. If there was to be a minor invasion of Frenchmen it was just as well to have a countervailing English force close at hand. Leicester, as conspicuous as ever among the principal councilors, was amassing kinsmen and servants with frantic urgency, eager to make the most ostentatious display possible to impress the French.

A fortune had been spent on a newly built banqueting house at Whitehall. Forty tall, thick ship masts held up the canvas roof, which was painted and gilded with clouds and stars and gleaming sunbeams. Three hundred glass lanterns lit the huge open hall, illuminating fantastic ornaments bright with paint and shining with gilt. The entire structure was completed in three weeks, with two of the nearly four hundred workmen breaking their legs in the process, and at a cost not much less than two thousand pounds.

This expense, plus the cost of feeding and lodging the hundreds of guests and distributing some ten thousand pounds' worth of silver plate among the official marriage commissioners, should have severely strained the English treasury. But in fact it was Spanish, not English, silver that was being paid out, Spanish treasure captured by Francis Drake on his way around the world.

Only six months earlier Drake had sailed into Plymouth harbor, his ship leaking badly and riding low in the water, weighed down by her precious cargo. During his three-year voyage he had not only circumnavigated the globe but also shattered the myth of Spanish dominion of the seas. To contemporaries this, and not the unprecedented feat of seamanship and navigation, was Drake's principal achievement. He had sailed freely in waters swept by lofty Spanish galleons and heavy-laden treasure ships. He had cruised the coastal lanes, raiding shipping and stealing from the unprotected colonial ports, walking off with jewels and bars of silver. The treasure ship *Cacafuego* had fallen to him, its hold full of silver in such quantities as to be almost incalculable.

This treasure—the many tons of silver, the pearls and rubies and rare priceless emeralds, the chests of gold and plate—had been stored in the Tower, for though Drake's share in it made him a very wealthy man the profits of the voyage belonged to the shareholders: among others, Hatton, Leicester, Walsingham and the queen.

Elizabeth had backed Drake from the start, and many of her leading courtiers had helped to finance the voyage. John Dee, her astrologer and adviser who by the 1580s had become one of the most eminent mathematicians and scientists in Europe, may have been the moving spirit of the enterprise.[1] Dee's profound knowledge of cosmography and navigation— he was a close friend of the globe-maker Mercator, a teacher of explorers such as Frobisher and later of Humphrey Gilbert—was coupled with a kind of antiquarian imperialism. The fascination he and many other Elizabethans had with King Arthur was closely tied to their exploring venture, for Arthur was looked on as a conqueror whose claims to New World kingdoms Elizabeth inherited. Through Drake, Dee reasoned, England was destined to resurrect the Arthurian empire, and in time to overthrow the empire of Spain.

The Spanish ambassador Mendoza wrote sourly to King Philip that Elizabeth was cheerfully dipping into the stored Spanish treasure to pay for the French entertainments. Everything was being financed "from the bars brought by Drake," he wrote, adding that, as if to emphasize the insult to the Spanish, Elizabeth was going out of her way to show personal favor and approval to the adventurer. He was seen entering her apartments frequently, and envious rivals took note of how she seemed never to go out in public without speaking to him. Drake and the queen walked together often in her private garden, and Mendoza's informants told him that they were plotting to raise a new fleet to harass Spanish shipping.[2]

Of course, the ambassador had officially protested Drake's piracy and demanded the return of the treasure, but nothing came of it. Why should Elizabeth return valuables worth £160,000—which was a sum equal to what Parliament ordinarily granted her, and which represented some nine months' customary crown revenue—when it was so much easier to acquire the income this way than through cajoling Parliament or collecting crown debts? Besides, by keeping King Philip's money, she accomplished two further purposes. She interrupted his expected revenue, inconveniencing and hampering the operations of his government, and what was more important, she did grave harm to his credit. The bankers of Antwerp could no longer be certain that the treasure ships from Peru would reach Seville in safety; the English might seize them. Therefore they would have to raise the interest rates they charged the Spanish crown, to compensate for the added risk, and even then they would be reluctant to make new loans. Damaging Philip's credit meant damaging his ability to wage war, and she was more than willing to face Mendoza's indignation and Philip's frowning anger far away in the Escorial for the sake of forestalling war.

Elizabeth had Mendoza convinced, once the French arrived, that nothing could be less important to her than affairs of state. Leaving the marriage negotiations to her advisers, she concerned herself solely with "whether there were any new devices in the joust, or where a ball was to be held, or what beautiful women were to be at court," and so on. She wanted her ladies and gentlemen to look their handsomest; their finery should compare favorably with that of the tasteful and elegant French. The most practical way to ensure this was to lower the price of luxury cloth, and so she commanded all shopkeepers to sell their velvets and silks and fine metallic weaves at a one-quarter reduction.[3]

The queen's long-smoldering passion for Alençon seemed to leap again into flame with his envoys' coming. She sent her beloved a "wedding ring," and said loudly and fervently that "every hour's delay seemed like a thousand years" until she should have her Frog by her side again. Certainly the little duke was rising in the world's esteem, and no doubt in Elizabeth's. He had been offered, and accepted, sovereignty over the Netherlands by the Protestant rebels, and it looked, for the moment at least, as though he might take on the much larger sovereignty of France. His brother Henry III was said to be "much broken" in health, perhaps near death.

If this was true, the courtship took on a much more serious dimension. If Alençon was soon to become king of France, it was not only essential that his suit to Elizabeth be continued—it was essential that he be kept from looking elsewhere for a bride. As king of France the duke would inherit a Catholic throne, and might think better of taking a Protestant bride. Not long before, his mother Catherine had talked of matching him with a Spanish princess, a nightmare eventuality that must have complicated Elizabeth's attitude toward Alençon and clouded her own emotions.

The French were entertained with fairytale magnificence. There was feasting in the extravagant banqueting house, with Elizabeth presiding in a golden dress ornamented with flashing jewels. There were smaller banquets given by the councilors, more intimate but no less superb in the quality of the food and wines. And there was elaborate jousting in which the young paragons of the court, among them Philip Sidney, rode to their sport in fantastic costumes of glittering engraved armor and metallic lace and stiff feathers of gold and silver. The jousting was an allegory of seduction, in which the chaste Fortress of Beauty, representing the queen herself, was besieged by Desire, or the ardent wooer Alençon. The Fortress was assaulted with mock cannons shooting perfumed water and "sweet powder," and the attackers threw flowers against the walls, but no assault on the queen's purity, however metaphorical, could be allowed to succeed. Desire's siege was turned back, and he was instructed by one of the actors in the pageantry to "content himself with a favorable parley, and wait for grace by loyalty."

There were parleys in plenty, but none completely favorable. By early June a marriage treaty had been drafted, but the English had insisted that it contain a clause making it inoperable until Alençon himself returned to England to sign it.

The French envoys went home, overfed and disgruntled, and Elizabeth sent Walsingham to France to press for a military alliance as an alternative to marriage. She had learned that Henry III was not gravely ill after all; this gave her time to explore a fresh diplomatic initiative. But Walsingham, imposing though he was with his sober talk of the need for France and England to join together to oppose Spain before all opposition became futile, could not move the French king or his mother to commit themselves. They mistrusted Elizabeth, and insisted that she marry Alençon to prove her good faith. She would have to continue her intervention in the

Netherlands no matter what they did, after all; it was in England's interest to go on supporting the rebels' cause, with or without a strong ally.

The recent exchange of envoys had strained relations between the two courts, for King Henry was offended that after sending nearly six hundred of his courtiers to England he got only one, Walsingham, in return. (The secretary sent word to Elizabeth in cipher that the king had been overheard to threaten his life.) What was worse, Alençon had become completely unmanageable and haughty. He had an interview with Walsingham— whom he knew to be a long-standing opponent of Elizabeth's marriage— at La Fère in Picardy, with the dowager queen Catherine present. When Walsingham raised the all-important issue of popular dissatisfaction with the French marriage among the English, the duke nearly exploded. He refused to listen to anyone but Elizabeth herself on the subject of their marriage, and he refused, furthermore, to consider an alliance between Elizabeth and his brother to be in any way a political alternative to it. Had his mother not been there, Walsingham told Elizabeth, the little duke would have become far more vehement. As it was, he said flatly that, if an alliance were to be formed, he would personally break it—unless Elizabeth married him.[4]

Obviously Alençon had to be mollified, and Elizabeth immediately sent off a loving letter in which she expressed her affection "most sweetly" and tried to soothe her admirer's wounded vanity. She also sent him the sum of thirty thousand pounds, "brought out from the Tower, in gold, secretly at night by water," with which to mount a new campaign, and he lost no time in putting the money to use. Levying fresh troops he seized Cambrai from the Spanish, leaving the mighty commander Parma disconcerted and, for the moment, in retreat.

Fresh from this victory Alençon sailed for England, arriving at the end of October, out of money but in buoyant spirits. For three years he had pursued the elusive queen of England, convinced of her passion for him and convinced, too, that in time her passion would overcome her political caution. It could no longer be said that he lacked either maturity or manliness; he had proven himself, he was the conqueror of Cambrai. And he was impatient to put an end to Elizabeth's coyness and to demand that she demonstrate the sincerity of her love by pledging herself to become his wife. After all this time his honor was at stake, and his military future as well, for he relied almost entirely on English gold to finance his warmaking.

Soon after his arrival he wrote confidently to his brother and mother, his letter full of hopes. Elizabeth had come privately to meet him when he disembarked, "in order that he might catch sight of her before he arrived," and this romantic meeting made him more optimistic than ever. They spent the better part of each day together, either alone or out of earshot of the councilors and the queen's women, and in private, Mendoza believed, she "pledged herself to him to his heart's content, and as much as any woman could to a man." To everyone's surprise Leicester was not only affable to the duke but ostentatiously servile, waiting on him as he dined and remarking "that there seemed to be no other way for the queen to secure the tranquillity of England but to marry Alençon."

Walsingham too abandoned his Puritan distaste for the queen's Frog, nodding sagely in agreement with Leicester and complimenting Alençon on his abilities and intelligence. "His only fault," the secretary said archly, in the queen's hearing, "was his ugly face."

"Well, you knave!" she blurted out, "why have you so often spoken ill of him? You veer round like a weathercock!"[5]

After ten days of apparent bliss and high spirits Alençon was unnerved when Elizabeth suggested that he take another thirty thousand pounds and return to Flanders. He balked. He would not leave England—indeed he would not set foot outside his apartments in the palace—until she gave an unequivocal response to his proposal of marriage.

Suddenly on November 22 the response came, and in a far more dramatic form than anyone had expected.

It was midmorning, and Elizabeth and Alençon were walking together down a long gallery in the palace. Leicester and Walsingham were nearby —Cecil was in bed suffering from gout—and were keeping watch, from a distance, on the royal pair. By now they had become a familiar sight, she tall and spare, he short and small, she smiling and joking in her broad French, he returning her witticisms with flowery compliments and gallantry. Their exchanges must have been more pointed than usual that morning, since on the previous day the duke and his followers had seemed quite disenchanted with the vacillating English, and discontented to the point of anger with the queen's failure to make up her mind to the marriage.

The French ambassador came into the gallery and spoke to Elizabeth. He was on the point of writing to King Henry, he said, and needed to hear from Elizabeth herself precisely what her intentions were. Her face brightened. Impulsively she turned to her little companion and cried out, "You may write this to the king: that the duke of Alençon shall be my husband!"

Then, to the astonishment of Leicester and Walsingham, she took off one of her rings and gave it to Alençon, and kissed him on the mouth. The meaning of the ritual was clear to everyone present. It was the ritual of marriage by ring and pledge, the time-honored ceremony of union in medieval Europe going back centuries to a time when men and women married without the presence of a priest, merely by promising themselves to one another.

Delighted and amazed, Alençon took the ring and, pulling off one of his own, handed it to Elizabeth. With this they had fulfilled the prescribed formalities of marriage according to the old custom. They were man and wife.

Quickly the queen summoned all the courtiers in the presence chamber into the gallery and repeated her verbal pledge to the duke "in a loud voice." Their excitement at the announcement must have been very great, not only because of its spontaneity—a rare phenomenon at a soporifically overceremonialized court—but because it was a romantic and even an erotic gesture. Traditionally, couples pledged to one another by promise began to sleep together, even if they planned to repeat their vows later before a priest.

This thought may have been behind Leicester's indignant reaction to the dramatic scene in the gallery. His courtly attentions to the duke, which had been so marked before the exchange of rings took place, ceased abruptly, and when he confronted Elizabeth about what she had done a few days afterward he asked her, rather rudely, "whether she was a maid or a woman." Was she sleeping with the man she had informally made her husband?

No, she was still a maid, she told him, adding that she was likely to remain a maid since the condition under which she had given Alençon her pledge—that King Henry would agree to her new extravagant demands in the marriage bargaining—was not likely to be fulfilled. The question was of course a rhetorical one. Like the queen's impetuous embracing of Alençon, Leicester's outburst was largely for show, though in both cases a strong undertone of heartfelt sentiment went into the display. Nothing that had happened between them in the course of their lifelong infatuation—certainly not Leicester's marriage—had weakened his sharply proprietary affection for Elizabeth, and he was jealous of the strutting young duke.

Hatton, ever the queen's faithful, moonstruck suitor, was inconsolable to think he had lost his love—and to a man who would bring her only ruin. Throughout Alençon's courtship Hatton had continued his own, offering thoughtful advice, eloquently expressed, sending charming letters ("I love yourself. I cannot lack you," he wrote disarmingly), giving gifts of clothes and jewels and purses of coins. He was solicitous of her health, and in plague season sent her a ring which "had the gift of expelling infectious airs." It was to be worn, he explained, "betwixt her sweet breasts, the chaste nest of pure constancy."

It was because he cherished the queen so dearly that he hated to see her take the foolhardy step of making an unpopular marriage. When he saw her pledge herself to Alençon he took the scene so much to heart that he spoke to her "with great boldness and many tears" about it. She could only bring trouble to England, he said, and by going so forcefully against her subjects' wishes she was provoking rebellion—and quite possibly deposition and even death. Perhaps because Hatton was so visibly moved, she listened to what he had to say with uncharacteristic mildness. Or, more likely, she restrained herself from interrupting him because she saw now that the thing he feared would never really happen.

The longer Alençon stayed in England the more obvious it became that marriage to him was neither the political expedient Elizabeth clutched at in moments of fear nor the sentimental epiphany she dreamed of. The end of the year found her no closer to formal alliance with Henry III than before, partly, to be sure, because she had begun to press for such impossible conditions as the return of Calais and a virtual declaration of war against Spain. At the same time she was discovering how ugly and truculent her Frog could become when thwarted—a sobering foretaste of what married life with him might be like.

His veneer of lustful gallantry wore thin, and revealed the money-hungry adventurer beneath. He demanded larger and larger payments, thirty thousand pounds, fifty, a hundred. He demanded war subsidies, guarantees of future sums, finally a huge monthly pension. She owed him this, he said, his tone acid with spite. She had toyed with his affections and given him nothing in return. Everyone was bound to laugh at him, and it was her fault. In public the duke kept up his sugary speeches, as she did her warmth and rapt attention to them, but in private the honeyed words dissolved into bullying and blackmail.

And the hypocrisy of his "burning desire" for her was only too obvious. Even as he swooned, or appeared to swoon, with passion and to yearn inconsolably for "the sweet consummation that he desired more than his life," he was finding abundant consolation in the arms of the London whores, some of whom made off with most of the official papers in his lodgings and sold them to the English diplomats.

And what of the quaint, old-fashioned pledge of marriage? Alençon had taken it as seriously as everyone else—except possibly the bride—and had written to his brother immediately to say that he was wedded to Elizabeth as surely as he, King Henry, was wedded to his wife the queen. How could he have written that? Elizabeth asked Sussex. Surely, knowing her intention as he did, he must have realized that the pledge was conditional on completion of the French alliance.

"No, no, madam, you are mine," Alençon cried out in exasperation as he saw everything the English had led him to expect, including a fortune in English pounds, slipping away. "You are mine, as I can prove by letters and words you have written to me, confirmed by the gift of the ring, of which I have sent intelligence to the king my brother, my mother, and the princes of France."[6] He had witnesses, he had documents, he had everything but the ultimate means to make Elizabeth do what he wanted.

"If I cannot get you for my wife by fair means and affection I must do so by force, for I will not leave this country without you." Whatever he may have meant by that—elopement, kidnapping, or more likely simply blackmail—the threat crushed what remained of the romance.

"I grieve, and dare not show my discontent," Elizabeth wrote, beginning a poem on the occasion of Alençon's departure. "I love, and yet am forced to seem to hate." She was two selves, of two minds, not so much about this surly, insistent little man she had loved but about love itself. Though there was a public pretense that Alençon's stay abroad would be brief, and that he would soon return to England to resume his ever-hopeful vigil at the shrine of his beloved, the truth was evident: he was Elizabeth's last hope for marriage, and he was leaving for good.

With him went her long flirtation with the dream of domesticity, her longing to have what remained of her beauty fully, enduringly appreciated by a lover who was also a husband. Whatever his faults, and she had only begun to uncover them, Alençon had brought out in her the sort of cozy intimacy she had never enjoyed with anyone else except Leicester. She had been able to idle away time with him, shut up happily in a small room hour after hour. She had visited him in bed, carrying little cups of soup to him and possibly feeding him herself. As his wife she might have been able to cheat time, to recover through his youthfulness the lost decades of her spinsterhood.

That Elizabeth was at all times hardheaded about the political dimension of her love affair takes nothing away from the poignancy of her loss as Alençon sailed away out of sight in February of 1582. Not that she really wanted him back, for she had had terrible trouble getting rid of him, but once he was really gone her profound disappointment spent itself in a fury of irritability. She scolded her women rudely, no doubt adding slaps and body blows to the insults she shouted at them. She swore mightily and articulately. She greeted everyone who entered the privy chamber with exceeding ill temper, and had a phenomenal battle with Leicester, accusing him of treason and likening him to his faithless, luckless father and grandfather.

Her wound was very deep, but not fatal. She saw the absurdity as well as the poignancy of her last love, and she saw, too, the way to turn it to her advantage in her subjects' eyes.

Having worried the English for years about her desire for Alençon, she soothed and relieved them with her ultimate decision to send him away. Her rhetoric, as usual, did not fail her.

"O what may they think of me," she had thundered on the eve of Alençon's arrival, "that for any glory of my own would procure the ruin of my land!" Let none think that, like some foolish girl, she had considered even for a moment putting her own personal interests before the well-being of England. No marriage could possibly mean more to her than her people's love. "My mortal foe can no ways wish me a greater loss than England's hate," she announced with solemnity, "neither should death be less welcome unto me than such mishap betide me."[7]

But in her poetry she struck a different tone. "I am and am not; I freeze, and yet am burned," she wrote, "Since from myself, my other self I turned." She was forty-eight, and her life had indeed reached a new turning. At an age when most women were ending their fruitful years, Elizabeth Tudor's greatest challenge was just beginning.

29

With brinish teares, with sobbing sighes,
I, Englande, plunge in paine,
To see and heare such secret sectes
amongst my people raine.

A few months before Alençon left England, three Roman Catholic priests were brought out from their imprisonment in the Tower and taken to Tyburn to be hanged. They were tied to a low wooden sled which sank into the mud under their weight. Horses dragged the sled through the streets to the place of execution, through Cheapside and Holborn and on westward along the Strand. Crowds gathered to watch the holy men pass, their gaunt faces shining and smiling despite the suffering to come. A priest who saw them go by wrote later that, as they neared the scaffold, the condemned men actually broke into laughter. "But they laugh!" the onlookers were heard to say. "They don't care for death!"

The joyous fortitude of the Jesuit Edmund Campion, Father Alexander Bryant and Father Ralph Sherwin came as no surprise to the hundreds who gathered to witness their final agony, for already there was talk of miracles. At Campion's trial, with his condemnation a foregone conclusion, the judge had taken off his glove and found his hand all bloody, though he had felt no wound. Bryant, during his wretched Tower imprisonment, had begun to receive divine revelations. His ecstatic visions had fortified him, it was said, as he lay far below ground in a black and airless pit, his body useless from repeated torture and his spirit tested sorely as he was denied sleep and food. Clearly all three men had withstood pain so intense and so interminable that the life had been all but bled out of their rag-shrouded bodies, yet, miraculously, they lived on.

They lived—so that they might die in this way, their sacrifice a potent instrument of conversion. The Catholics in the huge crowd drew nearer to the scaffold, clutching jars and mugs and other vessels in which to catch a few drops of the blood of these holy martyrs when the dismemberment and disemboweling began. A lucky few would be able to snatch bits of hair or torn flesh or scraps of clothing, but this was dangerous, as rank on rank of armed footmen stood by and mounted guards as well. To show any sympathy for the sufferers, to shout out encouragement to them, or utter prayers, or to try to touch them or their remains was to be tainted with their treason, and so to risk death.

For officially these were traitors, and nothing else. That they were Catholic priests was, if not exactly incidental to their treason, extrinsic to it. Francis Knollys and several other royal servants announced this from the scaffold before the executions began, assuring the crowd in stern language that the spectacle they were about to see had nothing to do with religion; it was to be the just punishment of convicted traitors, enemies to the queen.

Yet to Catholics the radiant faces of the three men, pale and emaciated yet lit with fervor, belied Knollys' words, as did Campion's scaffold speech. "If you esteem my religion treason," he told them, "then am I guilty; as for other treason, I never committed any, God is my judge." His voice was reasonable, his words both cogent and persuasive. Some of those who heard him knew that his interrogation in the Tower had been interrupted several times so that he could take part in public disputations, for he was learned and well-spoken. Then he had been denounced as "an unnatural man to his country, degenerate for an Englishman, an apostate in religion, a fugitive from the realm, unloyal to his prince." Then, as now, he had answered the accusation in the moderate, logical fashion that had made him an outstanding scholar at Oxford and won him the personal patronage of the queen. He had discriminated carefully between his faith and his political conscience, between his priestly work—the conversion of souls—and the darker labors of political subversion, "from which he did gladly restrain and sequester his thoughts." His loyalty to Elizabeth was absolute. He wished her, he told the crowd, "a long quiet reign with all prosperity." It was noted as Campion spoke that he had no fingernails; iron spikes had been driven up under his nails until they were torn off.

Campion, Sherwin and Bryant were not the first priests to be sentenced to death in Elizabeth's reign, but their executions had far-reaching significance. For one thing, they came at a time—early in December of 1581— when it was generally believed that the queen was about to marry the

Catholic Frenchman Alençon, and when in consequence there was heightened ill feeling between the hopeful Catholics and the outraged, outspoken Protestants, especially the Puritans.

More important, they coincided with a sudden resurgence of the Catholic faith in England, as astonishing in its swiftness as in its scope.

In the late 1570s English Catholicism awoke, roused from within in response to the unaccountable rhythms of popular piety and from without by a new generation of fiery young priests schooled for martyrdom in the seminaries of Douai and Rome.

That the immemorial religion of the English should revitalize itself after two generations of dormancy—with brief irruptions of vitality during Mary's reign and in the Northern Rebellion of 1569—was perhaps to be expected. Among the common people Protestantism was still the "new religion," though its newness had in fact worn off in the reign of Henry VIII. A surprisingly large number of elderly priests, some of whom had been quietly, devoutly performing masses without interruption since King Henry's days, kept alive the memory of the old Catholic realm, while the legal profession, the peerage, even to an extent the royal court were all strongholds of the ancient faith. It was impossible for even the most scrupulous Puritans to avoid contacts with Catholics, for they were everywhere—in the law courts, where they occasionally defended the archbishop of Canterbury and the queen, at the social gatherings of the aristocracy, serving as officers in noble and ecclesiastical households, in the House of Lords and, of course, crowding the jails and grinning from the gibbets.[1] Of the sixty peers in 1580, twenty were Catholic. Of the others, Leicester and his brother aided Catholics, Cecil had Catholic relatives (as did Walsingham, who boasted of his peerless Protestant son-in-law Philip Sidney but said little of his Catholic son-in-law the earl of Clanricarde). Given the close-knit Tudor networks of kinship and alliance, confessional enmity was imperfectly sustained. Protestant courtiers gave advance warning of raids and investigations to their Catholic intimates, and the queen herself occasionally lent her protection to her Catholic friends.

There were Catholics everywhere, and in the late 1570s and on into the 1580s their numbers grew rapidly, and their attitude changed from one of tacit complicity in the rituals of established Protestantism to militant refusal to conform. They became recusants—subjects of the queen who would not follow the usages of the queen's church. They stayed away from the service, they did not take communion, they did not listen to the sermons. In secret, they heard mass instead.

They gathered wherever there was a priest to sing mass, in the countryside where several hundred might come together in the open air, in caves or barns or the lofts of houses, in the jails, in the capital where they ran great risks and where many were seized while worshiping and taken to prison. With them were seized the articles of worship that nourished their devotion—"their superstitious stuff," the queen's agents called these objects scornfully, "their abominable relics, their vile books." Shiploads of religious pictures, manuscripts, rosaries and images blessed by the pope were confiscated at English ports, with the bones and garments of the saints among the contraband.

And there were new relics to bolster the faith and confirm the recusancy of believers: the remains of English martyrs whose growth in numbers kept pace with the increasing population of nonconforming Catholics.

A priest was executed in July of 1580, and to the many recusants who came to see him die his suffering was particularly edifying. His conversion, or "reconciliation," to the Catholic church three years earlier had been a triumph for the resurgent faith, for until then he had been a Protestant minister. Following his conversion he had gone to Douai to study, had become a priest, and then had decided to return to England to work among the imprisoned Catholics. In the midst of this spiritual labor he had been seized and interrogated, his captivity made nearly intolerable by filth and hunger and vermin; finally he had been brought to his execution, dying with "invincible constancy and fortitude, greatly to the edification of the Catholics," a coreligionist wrote, "and the surprise of the heretics."

So eager were the devout onlookers to participate in the holy death that they caught up every drop of the dead man's blood, wiping it from the boards on which the body was laid and scooping it out of the earth beneath the scaffold. Every trace of the martyr was spied out and preserved, either by believers impelled by devotion or by opportunists eager for profit. "Two days after his martyrdom," it was noted, "there was not a bit of ground left which had been touched by his blood, it having been taken by the faithful, who also offered large sums of money for his garments."[2]

It was this voracious, all-consuming piety that alarmed the queen and her councilors most, for behind it was an ominous fatalism, a commitment to death as well as to religious truth. Seminarists studying for the priesthood at the Douai college—a vital agency of the Catholic renaissance which by 1580 had sent a hundred priests to England—lived and worked in expectation of martyrdom; the college walls were painted with graphic depictions of torture chambers and grisly torments, beatific faces on rent bodies. Ecstasy through carnage: that, in crude terms, was the watchword of the priestly vanguard, and if to the individual this meant simply self-sacrifice in imitation of the crucified Christ, to the queen and her government it was more reminiscent of the St. Bartholomew's Day Massacre than of the life of Jesus.

To care so little for life, to glory in self-destruction, made the priests and the lay Catholics to whom they ministered natural candidates for extremism, or so royal officials presumed. The pope had exonerated in advance anyone who assassinated Elizabeth, and assassination was already becoming the supreme political weapon of the enemies of Protestantism. Even if this fearsome possibility could be forestalled, an armed rising threatened, more widespread and far more harmful than the Northern Rebellion, with its adherents stiffened by uncompromising leadership and made ruthless by their resolute faith.

Where there was one staunch Catholic in 1559, now there are ten, Cecil confided glumly to a colleague. Their fortitude seemed all but unbreakable —though some did, of course, break, and many died. Pain and delirium drove a few to reveal what they knew of the underground church, and even to offer to serve as spies for the government. But to the treasurer these turncoats were highly exceptional, for his informants told him of fresh conversions in staggeringly large numbers. A single priest could reconcile as many as eighty former Protestants a day to Catholicism, and there were many priests at work. The scale of the religious transformation "almost exceeded belief." It had to be stopped, and immediately.

Urgent and thoroughgoing enforcement of the laws against recusancy reached new heights in the summer of 1580. Royal agents spread out through the countryside, raiding houses and buildings suspected to be centers of recusancy, hunting down priests, arresting any Catholics reported to be staying away from the Protestant services and subjecting them to a variety of punishments. At the very least, they were fined—twenty pounds for every month of absence from church, two hundred pounds for a year's absence—and ordered to resume attendance or risk more severe retaliation. "Constant" recusants were interned in castles or other fortified places, their goods forfeit to the government unless they agreed to conform. During August the council stepped up its campaign, sending new orders to every county demanding heightened activity on the part of local officials and notifying all Catholics who had been released from prison on bail to return at once.

"The persecution is now very grave," a contemporary wrote. "New prisons are appointed in every county, as the old ones are full of recusants." Thousands were taken, many of them gentlemen and others of substance; thousands more waited fearfully for their lives to be disrupted, perhaps destroyed, by the sudden appearance of grim-faced officers at their gates.

There were other tactics, counter-evangelism being the most obvious. Sermons of recantation by former Catholics were a frequent occurrence in London, though it is questionable whether any staunch Catholics heeded them. Aylmer, bishop of London, tried to persuade Cecil to finance a plan to send committed, rigorous Puritans into Catholic regions—Lancashire, Staffordshire, Shropshire "and such other like barbarous countries"—to reconvert them, but the idea came to nothing.[3] By the time Campion and his companions arrived in England in the summer of 1580 the jails were full of recusants, and many of those who had so far escaped capture were living hunted lives.

The odyssey of Campion and his Jesuit partner Robert Persons lasted only a year, but during those few months of eventful sojourning much was accomplished. Guided by cohorts of eager young Catholic gentlemen they traveled throughout the country, staying in the houses of recusants and always moving on before they could be discovered by the authorities. They preached, heard confessions, celebrated masses and reconciled men and women to the church, welcomed wherever they went by great numbers of the devout. They became famous, both because the royal agents searched high and low for them and because Campion's written explanation of his mission—"Campion's Brag," as his enemies called it—reached a wide audience.

The journeys of the two Jesuits put new heart into an already revitalized Catholicism. Absolutely confident of the ultimate success of the Jesuit Order, Campion looked forward to the probability of his own execution with joyous humility: "We have made a league," he wrote, "cheerfully to carry the cross you shall lay upon us, and never to despair your recovery, while we have a man left to enjoy your Tyburn, or to be racked with your torments, or consumed with your prisons." Many were caught up in this spirit of hope and of fearlessness; Persons recorded how the believers he encountered showed a "wonderful fortitude of mind and readiness to suffer any travail on account of religion," and heard mass with such "sighs and frequent sobs" that he was moved to tears.

Fear of imminent discovery intensified the mood. At any moment, the Jesuits and their hosts knew, royal agents might burst in and arrest them, led by an informer or a heavily bribed servant. "Sometimes, when we are sitting merrily at table," Persons wrote, "there comes an insistent rapping at the door we associate with the police. We all start up and listen, hearts beating, like deer who hear the hunters halloo." There was no time for flight, only for prayer. "Not a word is spoken, not a sound is heard, till the servant comes in to say what it is. If it is nothing, we laugh—all the more merrily because of our fright."[4]

For Campion the tension ended in capture in June, 1581. (Persons escaped to the continent; he was to remain a moving spirit behind plots against Elizabeth.) After months of questioning and torture he came, with the other two priests, to his execution in December.

Hard rain had turned the earth to deep mud around the scaffold by the time the condemned men were in position and the queen's councilors had harangued the crowd into uneasy silence. The onlookers stood huddled together in the cold and wet, miserable yet watchful, waiting to be caught up in a transcendent drama. Campion addressed them, and Sherwin, and the young visionary Bryant, who "with his naturally innocent and angelic face" moved his hearers by his expression of profound joy.

The three stood in wheeled carts beneath the gallows, and the ropes were put around their necks. It was their last moment of life; they prayed, and the crowd prayed with them. Then the carts were jerked out from under their feet. The weight of their bodies pulled the nooses tight, breaking their necks instantly. But Bryant's noose had been carelessly placed, so that when his cart was pulled away he was left hanging by his chin, in great pain, but still living.

Almost at once the bodies were cut down so that the methodical butchery of disemboweling and dismembering—routine for the corpses of traitors—could begin. But Bryant, resisting the executioners, "made great efforts to rise," and continued to cling to life "in full consciousness" as his abdomen was cut open and its organs disgorged. The spectators pressed closer, awed, horrified, amazed at the young priest's unnatural fortitude. This was the miracle they had come to see, a dying man, his body carried beyond bodily limits, defying death.

"Ere the limbs were severed," an eyewitness wrote, "evidently in the extremity of agony," Bryant "raised his mangled body and stood upright on his feet to the great astonishment of all beholders."[5]

All the eviscerated corpses were beheaded, then cut in four sections and displayed prominently in places where Londoners gathered. The ghoulish spectacle was meant to be a chilling warning against treason, but it was a clear invitation to relic-collecting as well. Part of Campion's quartered body was placed on one of the City gates. Someone cut off a finger, and the incident set off "great efforts" in the royal council to investigate and locate the thief. For these executions were set apart from all previous executions of priests and lay Catholics. Within days of the event stories of the queen's cruelty and bigotry were circulating, and Catholic propagandists in England and elsewhere were making the names of the martyrs widely known.

Pamphlets, libels, broadsheets denouncing Queen Elizabeth and the merciless persecutors who served her appeared in great numbers. One book told of "Mr. Norton the Rackmaster," who was in charge of the dreaded oak frame on which prisoners, tied down at the wrists and ankles, were stretched to the bursting point. Norton was said to have boasted that he racked Bryant until he was "one foot longer than ever God made him," and to have kept the wretched Campion stretched on the frame for the whole of one endless night. (Norton, himself tortured by various "domestic afflictions," was much distressed by his adverse celebrity and wrote in his own defense that he acted "only in pursuance of orders and in conjunction with others."[6])

The ghosts of the dead priests proved to be more pernicious than all their sermons and masses when they were alive. The report of their martyrdom was spread by word of mouth and in print, and this, combined with the attacks on the queen and government, led to more conversions to Catholicism. To counteract the slander official declarations of policy toward recusants were issued, in which Elizabeth's mercy and clemency were stressed along with her habit of pardoning at least some of those condemned to execution. But such statements failed to lessen the impact of the recent deaths, especially at foreign courts. "There be men in the world which drink blood as easily as beasts do water," wrote one European Jesuit of the English councilors. And at their head, he added, was the wicked, bloodthirsty English queen.

The queen, just then, was troubled by a pain in her hip, and this, plus upsetting news of a military reverse for the rebel forces and the English troops supporting them in Flanders, made her unusually bad tempered when the Spanish ambassador Mendoza arrived for an audience.[7] He was led into the privy chamber at Richmond, and found her sitting under her canopy of estate, with two councilors and three ladies in attendance.

It was Elizabeth's custom, when receiving ambassadors, to step down from the raised dais beneath the canopy and, extending her hand to be kissed, to greet them formally in Italian. *"Sia il ben venuto, signor ambasciatore,"* she would say gravely, then return to her place. Now when Mendoza entered, however, she was pointedly rude, disregarding his entrance entirely and taking no notice as he approached her. When she did speak it was not to greet him but to complain of the pain that was annoying her and to add that it had been bothering her for a long time.

Though irritated and fatigued himself, Mendoza took the queen as he found her, sweeping off his hat with a respectful gesture and replying that, though she had delayed granting him an audience for a very long time— unconscionably long, he was thinking—he would gladly have waited longer rather than vex her with business while she was in pain. His words were remarkably gracious, under the circumstances; having been put off day after day, he was abruptly told at noon this day that the queen would see him in two hours. He was ten miles from the palace at the time, but rode there as fast as possible, only to be icily informed by three of the tall gentlemen pensioners and then by the haughty lord chamberlain, once he arrived, that he was very late.

Mendoza stood, hat in hand, waiting for Elizabeth to acknowledge his sentiment with thanks as she usually did. Instead she remained silent, holding her hip.

"How about the letter which you have from his majesty?" she asked at length.

Mendoza gave her a letter from Philip II, which angered her as she read it with its accusations of English belligerence and provocation. With "much hectoring and vociferation," the queen said roundly that, had she genuinely wanted to stir up trouble, it would have taken King Philip's fleets far off their courses to prevent her.

Boastful talk was one thing, action another, Mendoza replied, adding without emphasis that the fleets of Spain were so well prepared that they could triumph over any enemy, no matter how large and powerful. He went on to list the mounting irritations that were exacerbating England's conflict with Spain: the money Elizabeth was giving Alençon to enable him to fight the Spanish in the Low Countries, the English pirates plundering Spanish ships, the vast treasure seized by Drake and never returned. How could she have done more than this, the ambassador asked plainly, without openly declaring war on King Philip?

Without a moment's hesitation Elizabeth snapped back "that she neither knew nor understood anything" about any of these things.

But he himself had been telling her about them for three and a half years, Mendoza insisted. Perhaps "it would be necessary to see whether cannons would not make her hear them better."

If he thought to frighten her, Elizabeth said, stiffening in her seat, she would "put him into a place where he could not say a word." But her voice was low and lacking in its customary note of fierce challenge, and Mendoza found the change noteworthy.

In all probability, Elizabeth was weary. Her painful hip throbbed mercilessly, and as she disliked taking medicine she was most likely doing nothing to alleviate it. She was under a good deal of strain. The situation in the Netherlands nagged at her, forcing her ever closer to the brink of actual war, draining her treasury, playing havoc with her private life. Foreign policy demands clashed with the strongly felt desires of her subjects. The men around her, men made increasingly shrill in their counsel and brittle in their views by age and the tense political climate, delivered themselves of their vehement opinions and disapproved of what use she made of them. Cecil shook his head in dismay at England's dangerous position, Walsingham insisted that Elizabeth must strike the first blow at the Catholic enemy, and immediately. Leicester bemoaned the growing numbers of recusants and the queen's apparent blindness to the threat they posed. "The Lord of his mercy open her eyes!" he wrote to Walsingham, praying that God might do what the royal councilors could not.

Elizabeth and Mendoza exchanged threats, but before long both saw nothing to be gained from continuing this and Elizabeth signaled an end to the personal discussion by asking Mendoza to call in his secretary, she in turn dismissing her ladies and summoning two of her councilors to join the talks.

Elizabeth repeated the ambassador's reference to "bringing in cannons" for the benefit of her advisers, resuming her boastful tone, and told Mendoza once more that he need not try to frighten her. At once he became condescending and gallant. Smiling at her "fury and perturbation," he conceded that monarchs were never afraid of mere private men—and as for Elizabeth, "a lady and so beautiful that even lions would crouch before her," she need fear nothing at all. ("You know how timid and pusillanimous she is," he wrote to Philip II afterward in cipher.)

Her anger was soothed at this, or so Mendoza believed, and the conversation turned from insults and threats to substantive diplomatic matters. But there was no escaping the rancor that colored the meeting, or the unspoken issue—the queen's persecution of her Catholic subjects—that overshadowed it. Before long Mendoza and Elizabeth were quarreling again, with the Spaniard passing on a threat from his master that, unless Drake's treasure was returned, the goods of English merchants in Spain would be seized as compensation.

She would do nothing about Drake, she answered firmly, until Philip had made amends for his role in the attempted invasion of Ireland, and after repeating this twice she took leave of the ambassador "very drily."

Hoping to have the last word Mendoza called out that in future he would communicate with the royal council, raising his voice so that the councilors, hearing him, would think that he had initiated the breach and not the queen. But her voice could carry as well. As he was making his way out of the privy chamber he and everyone else in the room heard Elizabeth say, with a great sigh, "*Volesse a Iddio che ognuno avesse il suo, e fosse in pace.*" "Would to God that each had his own, and was at peace!"

30

Here lieth the worthy warrior
Who never blooded sword;
Here lieth the noble councilor
Who never held his word
Here lieth his excellency
Who ruled all the state.
Here lieth the earl of Leicester
Whom all the world did hate.

In mid-December of 1585 a fleet of fifty English ships sailed into Flushing harbor, carrying "the flower and chief gallants of England." In command was Leicester, his stout torso and pot belly encased in parade armor and his spirits as high as they had ever been.

Destiny called him—at last. Though he was well into his sixth decade he had been given a command—nay, a sacred mission—that many a younger man might envy. He was to lead the English army in the Netherlands, to make war on the army of Spain.

Many saw an epoch-making confrontation in the offing, a battle, not just between overmighty Spain and truculent little England, not just between Catholic and Protestant, but between the forces of the Roman Antichrist and God's chosen people. Protestant patriotism blazed high. "The freehold of England will be worth but little if this action quail," wrote one of Leicester's valiant captains. "The fire is kindled; whosoever suffers it to go out, it will grow dangerous."[1]

Leicester strode the deck of his flagship self-importantly, now giving orders, now looking out across the water in a pose of farsighted leadership. No one was more aware than he that he had not been near a battlefield for thirty years, and that the summit of his military experience was brief service as ordnance master in Picardy during Mary Tudor's reign. He had no military bearing; his paunchy body, thinning gray beard and tired, lined eyes suggested dissipation and world-weariness rather than stout-hearted combativeness. Yet the queen had chosen him as her commander—not her ambitious new favorite Walter Ralegh, nor Leicester's nephew Sidney, whom she disliked, nor any of the other hotheaded younger men who longed to prove themselves in war and who tried their best to push the reluctant Elizabeth into full-scale conflict with her old enemy King Philip.

She had, in the end, chosen Leicester, but not without grave misgivings and maddening changes of mind. His inexperience, his inability to get along with either subordinates or equals without awakening their violent dislike, his questionable statesmanship were all against him; in his favor were his rank and wealth—though he had to borrow very heavily to finance his expedition—his known intimacy with her and his princely status in the eyes of the Dutch. In his favor too was his somewhat diffuse ambition and mildly befuddled grasp of affairs. Elizabeth feared war in that, as a woman, she would have to yield something of her authority to male commanders; in Leicester she hoped she had a commander who would, partly for want of clear-headed schemes of his own, do as she told him.

With her usual "strange dealings" she had made the preamble to the journey a nightmare for the earl. First he was informed of his appointment, then, having ordered a great deal of armor and supplies and having sent some two hundred letters of summons to his fighting men, he received word that the appointment had been held up. She found she could not spare him after all. She was fearful; an ailment plagued her, and she needed Leicester to comfort her when the attacks came and she lay in her bed fearing that "she should not live." He half expected the change of heart from her. She had always been dependent on him, and had never before been willing to let him go so far away from her for so long. She was not only dependent, she was often malicious, never allowing Leicester to forget that he had wounded her mortally by his deceitful marriage to Lettice Knollys and "ever taking occasion," as he put it, "to withdraw any good from me."[2]

From the time of his original appointment in early September until the very day he sailed, December 8, the queen kept him in uncertainty. She exasperated him to the point of collapse. ("For my part," he wrote to Walsingham when he felt he could take no more of her caprice, "I am weary of life and all.") He felt sure that, whatever force he assembled and however well he equipped it, she would disapprove of it and give the command to someone else. Or her illness might return, or some other minor issue might arise to pique her and cause her to cancel all his carefully made preparations.

On the eve of his departure she gave him one final fright. She withheld the money to pay the six thousand footsoldiers and the thousand mounted men that were to make up his army. In panic, he sent a hurried message to Walsingham. If only she would release the funds, he begged, he would sell her some of his lands at a tremendous loss. The lands were worth sixty thousand pounds; she could have them for thirty, and if she sold the wood on them as well, she could make a profit of forty thousand in all.[3]

The funds were released, and the fleet set sail from Harwich, the queen's proud lieutenant Leicester in the van.

As soon as they caught sight of the English ships the citizens of Flushing signaled a noisy greeting. With every encouragement from Sidney, who had been made military commander of the town, bells were rung and cannons fired in a cacophony of welcome. The earl of Leicester was here at last, the mighty English peer, great Elizabeth's devoted lover—almost a king himself.

Certainly he came with a king's retinue. Over a thousand fighting men made up his personal train, and their huge warhorses and grooms and chests of weaponry weighted down the *Sea Rider*, the *Golden Rose*, the *Swan*, the *Crab-Joint*, the *Golden Hag* and the other English vessels as they anchored in the harbor. Leicester's household was enormous—a hundred yeomen and grooms, six dozen titled lords and gentlemen, scores of menials to wash and clean and serve and carry. His chaplains with their gowns and books and golden candlesticks, his choirboys, his cooks and stable staff and company of actors added another hundred at least to the rolls, and beyond these there were the purely military personnel—paymasters and purveyors, messengers, engineers, armorers and ordnance men, trumpeters, drummers and fife-players to march with the troops. Even so the list was not quite complete. Somehow Leicester had overlooked the office of herald, and had to send home for one—hoping to be supplied with a reliable man who could speak Dutch, Latin and French as well as English.

It was a splendid retinue, and Leicester himself looked splendid walking through the streets of Flushing surrounded by his soldiers and liveried servants, as the townspeople cried out "God save the Queen!" and threw down wreaths of flowers in his path.

Leicester was clearly the savior—more than that, the ruler—they had been waiting for. Elizabeth had refused to accept the sovereignty of the United Provinces—the rebel areas, chiefly Holland and Zeeland, still resisting Spanish domination—when it was offered her five months earlier, but Leicester would accept it, or so Sidney told the Dutch.

The idea of an Anglo-Dutch state had been mooted for a decade, but never before had it seemed so inevitable. The United Netherlands brought into being in 1576 by the Pacification of Ghent had split apart three years

343

later, when the predominantly Catholic southern provinces came to terms with the Spanish governor Parma. The north sought to save itself by appealing to Alençon, then to Henry III, and most recently to Elizabeth, but Parma and his Spanish armies marched virtually without resistance into Brabant and Flanders, seizing Ypres, Bruges and Ghent in 1584 and finally capturing Antwerp in this year of 1585. If Holland and Zeeland were to be spared a similar fate, England would have to rescue them, and this meant virtually annexing them to the English crown.

It would have to be England, not France: France had become little more than a feeble ally of Spain. This more than any other recent shift in continental affairs had pushed England into war. In 1584 Alençon, heir to his brother Henry's throne, had died—plunging Elizabeth, his "widow," as she called herself, into deep mourning and causing her to lay aside business for a time while she wept for him. The Protestant Henry of Navarre was next in line, and to make certain he never made good his claim the Catholic duke of Guise conspired with Philip to exclude him. France, once strong and hostile to Spain, had become weak and submissive to her, and this, plus Parma's series of successful campaigns in the Netherlands, left England directly in the path of Philip's devouring armies.

On the day Leicester reached Flushing news came to the English court that in fact the Spanish were preparing for "some great enterprise against England." Military and naval forces were converging on Lisbon: there were sixty ships in the harbor, twenty of them great warships, or galleons, and over sixty thousand troops were billeted in or near the town.[4] Leicester's modest fleet and minuscule army were toys by comparison. Yet the courage of the English made them admired. Elizabeth, one French courtier remarked, seemed "determined to lose like a man, and not like a woman." Whether Leicester would prove to be as manly remained to be seen.

He came to make war—and found himself compelled to make merry instead. For four months he and his train were escorted from town to town, greeted with fulsome Latin orations and poetry, music and cannonades. They walked under gorgeous triumphal arches, admired pageants in which Leicester was likened to the biblical Joshua, sat down to sumptuous banquets of baked swan and roast pheasant and spitted pork. There were fireworks, water spectacles, plays and a "variety of all sorts of wonderful welcomes." There was wine in great abundance, and the English became abundantly, extravagantly drunk—so drunk that, at a banquet in Amsterdam, they amused themselves by throwing puddings and cakes out the windows and watching them splatter over passers-by in the street below.

In letters to the court in London Leicester tried to put all this frivolity in a serious light. The Dutch towns were valuable to Elizabeth; the lavish hospitality of their devoted citizenry was worth whatever delay it meant in warmaking. "I could be content to lose a limb," he wrote enthusiastically, "could her majesty see these countries and towns as I have done." But there was much that he left out of his letters. He did not tell the queen how flattered he was to be the honored, praised center of attention when for nearly thirty years he had been forced to remain in her shadow. He did not send an accounting of all he had had to spend—out of money designated to pay soldiers and wage war—on expensive gifts to the Dutch towns and feasts for the town officials. Most important, he did not tell Elizabeth that, contrary to her express command, he had accepted the title governor-general, and had taken on, for all practical purposes, the sovereignty she had explicitly ordered him to refuse.

Ignorant as yet of this intolerable disobedience, Elizabeth spent the dark winter days in her privy chamber, within whose richly adorned, perfumed confines she worked and read, interviewed ambassadors and councilors, received visitors and friends and supervised and reprimanded her women.

Smothered in adornment, the chamber was dim and stuffy—there was only one window—and frequently overcrowded. For it was here that the sixteen or so women of the queen's entourage dressed their mistress and served her meals and waited for her orders. They were always present or on call, the four chamberers who slept at the foot of her bed, the half dozen "great ladies," all married, who were her official companions and the six young, unmarried waiting maids or maids of honor whose youth grew more offensive to her with each passing year and whose virtue she guarded as possessively as she did her jewels and treasure.

The great ladies had few formal tasks, which meant that during their long hours of attendance on the queen there was much idle time for gossip and flirtation and malicious spreading of rumors. These were Elizabeth's peers, the women she played cards with and talked with and scolded, the women from whom she expected flattery and pampering. They knew what pleased and what offended her, how she liked looking at handsome young men and hated men with bad breath ("Good God," she burst out after meeting with one malodorous ambassador, "what shall I do if this man stay here, for I smell him an hour after he is gone from me!"). They knew—and dreaded—her dark moods, her infirmities, her womanly secrets.

They saw her, as very few others did, without the elaborate mask of creams and lotions which softened and clarified her pockmarked skin and the oily cosmetics, mixed with egg and spread on in thick swathes of dead white and blazing vermilion, that brightened it. They knew intimately that proud, suspicious, handsome, careworn face, the small, squinting, deepset eyes, the nose growing sharper and more hooked with age, the sagging

345

cheeks and jowls and wrinkled neck. Elizabeth's scent, compounded of her syrupy perfume of musk and rosewater, the sweet oil she used on her hands, and the sharp lemon and vinegar odors of her toiletries, must have hung in the air and clung to her attendants even after they left court or retired to their own beds for the night.

To the young maids of honor the queen was a less familiar and more terrifying figure, a strident, querulous taskmistress who though capable of generosity and even of rough good humor was more treacherous than affable. She expected them all to be well educated and to play the lute and have sweet singing voices. More important, she expected them to be docile and decorous, to form a pleasing backdrop for her own overpainted maidenliness. They dressed to complement her dress, and unless they were very foolish indeed they toned down their youthful good looks so as not to outshine her—at least from a distance.

When walking behind the queen on her way to the royal chapel on Sundays or when waiting on her while she ate her dinner in the privy chamber the maids were at least marginally well behaved, though occasionally they talked back to her in a way that "did breed much choler" in her. But when on their own, especially in the coffer chamber where they all slept, they laughed and shouted and created such uproar that the household officers—who slept in nearby chambers—complained indignantly about the noise.

The maids flirted, were occasionally seduced, occasionally married in secret or became recusants, calling forth the queen's fearsome wrath. They were the object of ribald attention. "The maids of honor desire to have their chamber ceiled, and the partition that is of boards there, to be made higher," reads an instruction to the surveyor of the works at Windsor Castle in 1580, "for that their servants look over."[5] It was bad enough that the maids kept the senior servants awake at night; peeping servants added intolerably to the chaos.

While the great ladies and waiting maids gossiped and fondled their lapdogs and pet squirrels and monkeys, the more humble chamberers took on the laborious tasks that fell to them as practical caretakers of Elizabeth's person, hygiene and wardrobe. With their assistants they attended her while she bathed, cleaned her teeth by rubbing them with tooth soap and then with a linen cloth, and applied her beautifying creams and waters and oils. They dressed her hair, combing and brushing it into mounds of curls, building it outward with swatches of false hair, fastening into its serpentine involutions an array of pearls and rosettes and jewels to match those in her gowns and at her ears. They laced and tied and fastened her into eight layers of clothing—from smock to petticoat to bodice, skirt, kirtle, gowns, and sleeves—and then added to these collars, cuffs, stomachers, a ruff, high-heeled shoes in colored leather or silk, scented gloves, jewelry (a great deal of it, the rings tied to the wrists by a twist of black silk), a ribbon at the waist on which were fastened a pomander, a watch, a fan, perhaps a silken mask.

In middle age Elizabeth abandoned the flattering pastels of her youth for dramatic gowns of black and white. In the mid-1580s, while in mourning for Alençon, she wore only black, though an envoy who saw her at court at Christmastime in 1584 recorded how she brightened her costume for the holiday. She was dressed in black velvet, he wrote, "sumptuously embroidered with silver and pearls. Over her robe she had a silver shawl, that was full of meshes and diaphanous like a piece of gossamer tissue. But this shawl gleamed as though it were bespangled with tinsel." Swathed in this shimmering mantle, sitting under her canopy of cloth of gold, Elizabeth must have resembled a goddess, and her regal air and fragile physique can only have added to the otherworldly effect.

Beyond the chamberers were scores of servants and tradespeople who made their contributions to the vast royal wardrobe: seamstresses, dressmakers, jewelers, wigmakers, milliners who supplied gilded trinkets, ornament-makers who brought glittering spangles and tiny golden or silver aglets to besprinkle a gown, grooms to clean, brush and tend the delicate fabrics between wearings, laundresses for the linen and silk women to provide the stuffs from which new petticoats and kirtles were made. The household rolls recorded one woman whose sole daily work was removing the tiny seed pearls that decorated certain garments and sewing them onto others.

Surrounded by the women who served and attended her—women whose unremitting companionship she could never easily escape—Elizabeth resigned herself, in her fifties, to life as a spinster. With Leicester away in Flanders she was more acutely aware of her unenviable status than ever before. To be sure, she had male companions as well. There were the "handsome old gentlemen" of her council—gouty Cecil, flinty Walsingham, tortured now by kidney stones but still driven to untiring labor by his convictions, silver-haired, lovesick Hatton, who was to become chancellor in 1587. There was young Walter Ralegh, a dark, good-looking intellectual and adventurer whose poetic gifts and brilliantly speculative turn of mind nourished Elizabeth's own ever-hungry intellect even as his infatuation with her soothed her vanity. In Ralegh's eyes she was, if not young, at least womanly and desirable, a mysterious and alluring being to be saluted in delicate rhymes.

But there was no substitute for Leicester, and as the weeks passed and there was no news from Flanders of military activity—only of pageantry and overeating, and requests for money—Elizabeth became more and more uneasy about his campaign, and more and more crotchety and unbearable toward her women.

The mood of the court did nothing to soothe the queen's temper. The palace was a hothouse of frenzy and anxiety. The excitement of war and of mounting danger, the growing conviction among the courtiers that theirs was an age writ large in human destiny, and that they must secure for themselves leading roles in the coming drama, made them desperate. The climate of frenzied desperation fed on itself; every time word came of new belligerence from Spain the tension mounted, with whispers of fear alternating with bullying shouts of defiance.

A new generation of gorgeous, swaggering young men came into their own in these tense years, "sword and buckler men" who burned to engage with England's enemies and to stifle fear in the oblivion of slashing combat. Most of them knew only the glory to be gained in war, not its dust and pain and bloody destruction. As they fitted themselves out with fine horses and gilt swords and richly engraved armor they thought little of the risk they undertook; their arrogance and narcissism eclipsed all else.

With their armor off they paraded in gaudy, grotesquely cut painted doublets, huge, jewel-encrusted sleeves and monstrously wide padded breeches, stuffed with wool or rags or bran until they stood out stiffly from the legs and made walking an art. Friends kissed one another's well-tended hands when they met, enemies squared off and glared at one another through intervening knots of admirers. Detached onlookers, new to court or precariously neutral in its web of internal politics, stood nervously apart, balancing themselves carefully on their high-heeled, diamond-studded silk shoes, sniffing their golden pomanders or elegantly picking their teeth with gilded toothpicks.

All was flash, harsh color, vulgar display, along with the din of intense, insistent voices. The queen, with her blazing gowns and high-colored cheeks, her roaring oaths and free talk of severed heads, seemed at one with the strident young warmongers. She sat in the presence chamber at Whitehall amid "pictures of the wars she had waged," plucking the men by their cloaks and pulling them over to talk with her in private.

A visitor to court watched her one day, and afterward described how she "summoned old and young" to her side, one after another, talking constantly and at the same time watching the acrobatics of a group of dancers. She "chatted and jested most amiably" with all who came before her, and singled out Ralegh to tease. "Pointing with her finger at the face of one Master or Captain Ralegh," the visitor wrote, she "told him that there was smut on it. She also offered to wipe it off with her handkerchief, but he anticipating her removed it himself." The incident evoked whispers. "They say that she now loves him beyond all others," the foreigner recorded, "and this one may easily credit, for but a year ago he could scarcely keep one servant, whereas now owing to her bounty he can afford to keep five hundred."[6]

Neither the queen nor Ralegh seem to have danced that day, but those who did caught the tone of hysteria in their mad leaps and "sprightly fire and motion." Slow dances were gone forever, at least for the young and middle-aged; instead they danced the volta, a violent, whirling two-step punctuated by strenuous high jumps and hectic turnings. The Puritans were outraged at this new example of worldly folly, which called for men to embrace women "lasciviously" while turning and lifting them and which led to the unseemly eroticism of skirts raised as high as the knees. But their protests only fed the mania for dance. New steps, old steps quickened to double time, entirely new and tortuously difficult patterns were invented.

What "new kind of dances, and new devised gestures the people have devised, and daily do devise," only God could say, a contemporary wrote. Dancing schools sprang up, with dancing-masters who "leapt, flung, and took on" wonderfully as their eager students watched. Court gallants tried to keep pace with the professionals, but their fevered efforts—made all the more awkward by their outlandish, restricting costumes—often resulted in injured dignity or worse. Often they leaped high—only to fall down hard on their padded breeches. Some "broke their legs with skipping, leaping, turning and vaulting." A few broke their necks.

It was as if they sought to pour all their restive energies into the galliard and volta, to exorcise the infuriate spirit that possessed them through the mindless exertions of dance.

In everything they courted excess: in flirtation and lust, the "ordinary infection" of the court, in the extravagantly flowery language the queen exchanged with her cultured admirers, a language coruscated with excessive alliteration and topheavy with overwrought metaphors, in the inordinate number of epithets—Lady of the Sea, Phoenix of the World, Peerless Oriana, Astraea, Cynthia, Belphoebe, Gloriana—with which the new generation of poets saluted the aging Elizabeth.

Courtly corruption, never suppressed, now flourished with unprecedented venality. Men came to the royal court, joined its ranks, learned its rules and mastered its unsavory politics for only one reason: to make a fortune. (Women came to marry men with fortunes.) It was understood that money was to be made through sophisticated bureaucratic practices involving bribery and theft. To gain an audience with the queen, the lord chamberlain or any other official the suitor had to present "gifts" of money or valuables; lucrative appointments were acquired through favoritism, and favoritism had to be purchased, usually at a very high price.

But once the courtier found a place, however insignificant, within the governmental hierarchy he could begin to broaden his leverage and sharpen his acquisitive powers. Even the most minor posts offered opportunities for graft and embezzlement and large-scale misappropriation of funds. For if official salaries were small, the perquisites that came with them were profitable. Most profitable of all were monopolies, which put into private hands what under another system would have been state regulation of trade and manufacturing. Armed with the power to regulate, the courtier could also bend the regulations—if paid enough to make it worth his while. Conspicuous examples of profiteering were offered by Leicester, Ralegh and Hatton, all of whom were ostentatiously, lavishly guilty of enriching themselves through bureaucratic theft—with the queen's indulgent help.

No group at court, it might be thought, was in a better position to advance their own and others' fortunes than the queen's waiting women. But in practice their influence was limited. They were "like witches," Ralegh said, "capable of doing great harm, but no good." They could tarnish reputations but not enhance them, and only the latter power could be turned to substantial profit. So unlike other highly placed court officials the great ladies and maids of honor had to be content with such modest profits of office as the queen's cast-off gowns and perfumed shoes, and with what fees they could earn by selling information about Elizabeth's private life and habits to foreign ambassadors and their agents.

Theirs was a frustrating role, made more frustrating by their mistress's unforgiving scrutiny and bad temper. It was no wonder that, when an opportunity for real malice and revenge against the queen presented itself, they took advantage of it, and did great harm indeed.

By early February the news from Flanders—a good deal of which reached Elizabeth through her waiting women—was becoming alarming. Leicester had made himself Absolute Governor of the United States of the Netherlands, a blunder which greatly increased English obligations to the Dutch and which was bound to escalate Spanish belligerence. Worse still, he had failed to send a letter of explanation to Elizabeth, or a personal envoy who could make her understand why he had gone against her orders. (In fact, Leicester had dispatched his servant William Davison to do just that, but foul weather was delaying Davison's crossing.)

But what increased Elizabeth's "extreme choler and dislike" tenfold were the rumors—entirely without foundation—about Lettice Knollys.

Lettice was preparing to join her husband, to cross to Flanders and take her place as wife of the Absolute Governor. Her pride and presumption knew no bounds. She was planning to take with her "such a train of ladies and gentlewomen, and such rich coaches, litters, and side-saddles," that she would seem more a queen than Elizabeth herself, whose own gilded vehicles would seem mean by comparison. Lady Leicester was to be nothing short of a second queen, in effect, with "such a court of ladies as should far pass her majesty's court" in England.[7]

The image of the handsome, auburn-haired Lettice Knollys, ever Elizabeth's despised rival, at the head of a competing court was unbearable. It was no good telling the queen that the rumors were "most false," that Lettice, as surprised as anyone when the story reached her, grew pale and trembled with fear, knowing what Elizabeth's anger could lead to. The malicious rumors had their effect, and they not only caused the queen endless vexation but nearly wrecked Leicester's entire campaign.

All the furies were let loose. Those who thought they had seen the full extent of the terrifying Tudor wrath now saw that they had been mistaken. She shouted her rage, at Leicester's unimaginable arrogance, at his traitorous disobedience, at the unforgivable insolence that had led him, ingrate that he was, to think that he could drag his unmentionable wife across the Channel to play at being queen while he played king. The hand which had created Leicester an earl, which had raised him from dishonor to position and wealth, could "beat him to the dust." Every day she drew up new plans to abort his military mission and order him home; every day Cecil, braving her fury, besought her to "suspend her judgment" until she heard from Leicester directly, or through an envoy.

She drew up a peremptory letter blasting him for his unheard-of effrontery. "We could never have imagined, had we not seen it fall out in experience, that a man raised up by ourself, and extraordinarily favored by us above any other subject of this land, would have in so contemptible a sort broken our commandment, in a cause that so greatly touches us in honor," she wrote imperiously. "So great a wrong," she went on, should not remain "in silence unredressed." Leicester was to obey the bearer of the letter—who would insist on his immediate return—without fail, or he would surely "answer the contrary at his uttermost peril."

But Cecil and his fellow councilors detained the bearer of the letter until after the belated arrival of Leicester's servant Davison, who undertook the unenviable task of placating the deeply injured queen. The incident had stirred up all her old grievances against Leicester, and she recited them one after another in "long and tedious" fashion. Her bitterness overflowed;

clearly it would take more than soothing words from a subordinate to assuage her mood. (Hatton sent word to Leicester that an expensive gift —bought, of course, from the military funds—would help.)

Eventually Davison and the councilors wore her down, and persuaded her, with some difficulty, that the stories about Lady Leicester were nothing more than the inventions of troublemakers. By June all talk of recalling Leicester ended. But by then his campaign was dissolving in enmity and squalor, and the beleaguered earl was wishing he had never left Harwich.

Even before the long honeymoon of feasting and pageantry had ended, he had found himself in conflict with the Dutch, who continued, much to his bewilderment, to oppose and hamper his authority while they looked to him to save them from the armies of Spain. Despite himself he was swept into the vortex of religious and political faction, while constantly called on to make peace between his captains and their fractious counterparts among the local forces. Elizabeth was more angry with him than she had ever been since his rash marriage, yet he was at a loss to know how to satisfy her, for her instructions had warned him "rather to make a defensive than an offensive war," and "not in any sort to hazard a battle without great advantage." Heavily outnumbered as he was by Parma's troops, he could hardly expect to stumble into a situation where "great advantage" would be his; even more discouraging was word from England that the queen was undermining his warlike posture by trying to negotiate peace terms with the enemy. He was condemned to preside over an expensive, ignominious stalemate, and the realization broke his morale.

The one military effort he launched, a daring assault on a fort dominating the town of Zutphen, resulted in a loss that broke his heart. His nephew Sidney died of wounds suffered in the assault, and the elaborate hero's funeral Sidney was later accorded could not disguise the relative insignificance of the English gain.

"Forget not money, money," Leicester wrote to Walsingham, and the plea echoes plaintively throughout his correspondence with the court. Elizabeth promised further funds, but did not keep her promises, especially after she learned that Leicester had flouted her parsimony by increasing his own and his soldiers' rate of pay. But she was far away in London; he was on the scene, and knew that the excess money was needed if the men were to have enough food, not to mention boots and cloaks and arms. He had come to lead stalwart soldiers into battle; instead he was forced to listen while "sick, lame and shrewdly enfeebled" men cried out to him for help. He contributed what he could from his own money, but as he had gone deeply into debt his ready funds were small. He did what he could; meanwhile the summer campaigning season ended, and in the fall the Absolute Governor was quietly summoned back to his sovereign's court.

Leicester made the return journey from Flushing in as disheartened a mood as he had ever known. Glory had been within his grasp, and then had been denied him. He found the courage to face the queen, but his tired eyes were full of self-pity. He had failed her, and whatever her share of that failure, the blame must be his. Unutterably weary, he made a brief appearance at court, then left Elizabeth in a monumental quarrel with her advisers and made his way to Bath to take the waters.

31

But sorrow and plagues for their offences,
Battle and famine, and all pestilences,
As a desolate land, brought it shall be;
What shall be more, none know but He.

E ngland in the 1580s was a land ravaged by profound unease. There
was cause for anxiety everywhere: in the war, and rumors of war, that took
on substance when Leicester sailed for Flanders; in the shouted exigencies
of the Puritan preachers, exhorting men and women to hold firm against
the devil; in the alarming rise in the number of witches, so virulent they
threatened to "overrun the whole land"; in the severe food shortages that
drove people to riot and curse the times, the gouging middlemen, and the
queen.

Certainty had vanished. There were only guesses, conjectures, troubled
whispers. Elizabeth warned her subjects in a proclamation "not to be
moved by murmurers and spreaders of rumors, the dissemination of which
is to be punished as the spreading of sedition."[1] Yet the rumors persisted,
for this was an age with no consensus of received fact, and without such
a consensus to rely on, hearsay was more comforting than fearful ignorance.
Prophecy, however grim, was most comforting of all, for it made the future
the product of past foresight, a preconceived, and therefore tamed, prospect.

The queen would live only a few years—or a few months—more. The
queen would die a violent death. An invasion was imminent. (It would have
taken a very poorly informed prophet indeed not to predict this.) A Dread-

354

ful Dead Man was coming, who would rise from his grave to overturn the present order and install a new one. These pronouncements were made, sometimes with the aid of a large folio book of "painted pictures of prophecy," to villagers hounded by worry over their failed crops and hungry children.[2] Grim as the prognostications were, they were eagerly received, for they offered a glimpse of something transcendent, something visionary and otherworldly, that lifted the burden of everyday want and brought a sense of awe and wonder.

The credulity of Elizabeth's subjects gave their anxieties very broad scope. They were fearful not only for the future, but that in some occult fashion history might reverse itself, forcing them to contend again with the past. Many associated the Dreadful Dead Man of prophecy with the late king Edward VI, and imagined that he would soon return to them. "Up Edward the Sixth, the time is come," began one prophetic saying, and in response to expectations held by "great multitudes of the simpler sort," he did indeed return—in the form of several impostors. The impostors were seized and locked away, but not before many people had seen and heard them, and they had helped to strengthen the widely held conviction that the boy-king lived on. There was nothing in King Edward's tomb but a lump of lead, an Essex blacksmith said. A soldier returning from the Low Countries swore that Edward was alive and well in Spain, or perhaps it was France. Another man, a "very simple person," told the authorities the same story he told his neighbors. King Edward had not died in 1553; instead a substitute boy had been put to death in his place, while the king himself was taken secretly to Denmark, where he became the reigning monarch.[3]

The unsettled past returned in many forms to haunt the Elizabethans. There were stories of a child born to the childless Mary Tudor, smuggled out of England to be raised to adulthood on the continent, where he awaited the propitious moment to claim his throne. Tales had been told since the start of Elizabeth's reign about the children she had with Leicester; currently, in the 1580s, a boy representing himself as their son was making himself known at Catholic courts abroad. Imagination merged with sacrilege in the disordered mind of an Englishman calling himself "Emmanuel Plantagenet," who was brought before Cecil in 1587. He was the son of Queen Elizabeth by God the Father, the madman told the treasurer haughtily. And greater than the Archangel Gabriel's was his authority in heaven.

The ultimate prophecy was that the end of the world was near. History was clearly in its "last days," people told one another, for the signs and wonders predicted in the biblical Book of Revelation were everywhere apparent. There were comets and eclipses in the skies, and downpours and snowstorms and heavy flooding on the earth. There was even groaning and travail under the earth, for during Easter week of 1580 a mighty earthquake shook southern England, tearing huge gashes in the walls of castles and knocking down chimneys and church towers.[4]

A loud noise like roaring thunder broke over Kent, and then the earth jerked and heaved with a "wondrous violent motion, and shaking of all things." In London stones fell from venerable buildings onto the heads of people rushing into the streets, and the playhouses swayed so violently that playgoers leaped down out of their seats into the pit for safety. New prayers were introduced into the litany for protection from earthquakes, but the disaster was feared less for its own sake than as a portent "terrible in signification of things to come."

Three years later, on an April Sunday in 1583, the same crowds that had fled the great earthquake were watching the heavens, waiting in fascinated terror for "some strange apparition or vision in the air" that would signal the end of the world. Saturn and Jupiter were in conjunction, and the astrologers predicted "either a grievous alteration of empires" or "an utter destruction of this world." Many had made an effort to cleanse their lives in expectation of Christ's Second Coming. A contemporary noted how they "talked very religiously, seeming as though they would become sanctified people," and their faces were very pious as they turned them toward the sky.

But as the day went on and the heavens failed to open, the expressions of innocent piety gave way to cynical smirking and by nightfall the crowds were jeering at the astrologers for their "extreme madness and folly." Yet hope, or dread, lived on. For every scornful voice there was a voice of expiation: the calculations were off by a few years, there were other factors to be considered besides the exact positions of the planets. New calculations produced new expectations. The world would end in 1588. It was "most certain."

But for the queen, time might run out sooner than that. In the 1580s, fears were redoubled that she might be assassinated.

The risk had been there since the early years of the reign, when in response to rumors that an Italian poisoner had infiltrated the royal household Elizabeth dismissed all the Italians currently in her service. Another alarm led her to confiscate every key to every door leading to her privy chamber, and to ensure that "great care" was taken by the officers of her guard. She might take consolation from her archbishop of Canterbury, who assured her that no harm would come to her "so long as Virgo," her birth sign and informal regal symbol, "was in the ascendant," but every time word came of new designs on her life there were fresh fears. Wax replicas of the queen and two of her councilors were found in the house of a Catholic priest, who meant to use them to end her life by magical means. One of her chamber ladies was accused of trying "by witchcraft" to discover Elizabeth's life span; from there it was but a small step to shortening it.

In the 1580s the attacks increased in numbers and in gravity, prompted by a macabre fashion for political assassination on the continent and by the violent and uncertain climate of the age. These were the years of the rack and the torture chamber, of the English spy network which set snares for Catholics and conspirators but terrorized the entire population. Londoners became habituated, though hardly immune, to "general searches" undertaken by justices and agents of the queen, who threw the city into panic by going from house to house and routing out wanted or suspected persons. Any "unknown men"—those without certain employment or reliable friends or connections—were seized and locked in churches while the raid went on to its end. The searches themselves were only part of a broader campaign of fear; Walsingham's men "prepared the people's minds" for the raids weeks in advance, by spreading talk of "great stirs" and dangerous foreigners abroad in the capital.

London life was a pattern of alarms and ghoulish horrors: wild shouting in the streets in the middle of the night, torchlit interrogations, the clump of boots on cobblestones. And, in growing numbers, hangings, and their grisly aftermath, the display of heads and chunks of flesh on London Bridge.

In the fall of 1584 there was a particularly ghastly execution. Eighteen people, "among them two women and two young lads," were hanged at one time, and the butchery was rounded out by a barbarous act of mercy. The victims' friends, wrote a visitor to the capital present at the executions, "went up to the gallows, tugged at their legs and struck them over the breasts in order to hasten their death."[5]

The attempts on the queen's life were in keeping with the mode of disordered violence. A Warwickshire man fell into a "frantic humor" and started off, glassy-eyed, for the court where he meant to shoot the queen. Elizabeth was a "serpent and viper," he shouted to anyone who would hear him. He wanted "to see her head set upon a pole." Catholic animus had shaped his thinking—a priest was sheltered in his household—but what pushed him to undertake his desperate mission is less clear. When captured and tried, he strangled himself in his cell.

Another intended murderer was a member of the House of Commons. William Parry looked to be above suspicion. He was not only an MP but an employee of Walsingham's, and in fact his connection with the intelligence network makes his guilt somewhat problematical. Still, he bragged of his plans to kill the queen, and an accomplice denounced him, telling how the two of them had decided to surprise her as she rode in her coach. They would ride alongside her, one on each side, and shoot at her head; she would be an easy target, either out of doors or in the palace, where Parry as a trusted royal servant could assault her during the course of a private audience.

A story was told later that Parry had actually gained his private audience, and had come to it with a knife hidden in his sleeve. He lost his courage, otherwise there would have been regicide and chaos.

True or not, the story added to the general apprehension, and supported the common people's view of their ruler as an endangered, beleaguered treasure whose safety was a matter for grave concern. They imagined her, overwrought and weeping, walking in her garden and lamenting "that she would fain know why so many people sought her life." She tore her breast, the tale went, and said she was "defenseless and unarmed, a miserable woman," yet she "trusted in the Lord God to have compassion on her."[6]

This was the account a traveler heard in London, the romantic, tender fabrication of a worried citizenry. People had told similar stories about Mary Tudor many years earlier, their chivalrous feeling for a woman in peril taking precedence over their respect for their sovereign's courage.

In the fall of 1583 there were revelations of a Catholic plot for an invasion force to land in Sussex and proceed to the liberation of Mary Stuart. The Spanish ambassador Mendoza was heavily implicated, and was expelled. Just as the danger was coming to light and the conspirators, under torture, were revealing what they knew Elizabeth was riding under guard from Hampton Court to London, with the French ambassador Mauvissière beside her. They were deep in conversation, with Elizabeth talking effusively about the Jesuit plots that threatened her.

"Just at this moment," Mauvissière afterward recalled, "many people, in large companies, met her by the way, and kneeling on the ground, with divers sorts of prayers wished her a thousand blessings, and that the evil-disposed who meant to harm her tonight be discovered, and punished as they deserved."

As always Elizabeth stopped her horse to acknowledge the good wishes, and broke off her talk of the Jesuits. It was clear, she remarked to the Frenchman tartly, "that she was not disliked by all."

The prayers of the people were echoed in Parliament. Just before the Christmas recess in 1584 the queen thanked the Commons for their care and concern, and then Hatton spoke. He had with him a prayer, he said, written by "a godly man." It was a prayer "for the queen's preservation," and he asked if he could read it aloud. He began to read, and as he did so the members fell reverently to their knees and repeated the words after him, as if they had been the words of a psalm or a response from the Book of Common Prayer.

In a more militant vein was a movement to circumvent assassination by undercutting its potential benefits. In the summer of 1584 the royal council had prepared a document called the Bond of Association which pledged its signatories to pursue to the death any person on whose behalf an assassin might act. Since any attempt on Elizabeth's life (save the random assaults of madmen) was bound to be undertaken on behalf of Mary Stuart the Bond of Association was in effect a vast counter-conspiracy against her, and as the number of signatures grew—there were many thousands, from every part of the realm—the depth and strength of popular opposition to Mary became more and more clear.

Of all the dark clouds that overshadowed the decade the menace of Mary Stuart was the most abiding, and the least tractable. Would Elizabeth outlive her, or not? The nine-year difference in their ages, and the hazards to which Elizabeth was subjected, suggested that Mary might one day rule England, even if the plotters she so fervently encouraged never managed to bring off the grandiose schemes they concocted to sweep her onto the throne.

The days were long past when the two queens were rivals for admiration. Vanity, wigs and cosmetics aside, they were old women, their bones and temperaments brittle and their façade of mutual gentility worn thin. Mary, in her forties, looked ten years older; captivity had turned her hair white and left her "poor, languishing, sickly body" stiff and aching. Her letters to Elizabeth were querulous, yet not so full of complaints as to risk anger or irritation in her royal relative. It was essential to Mary—indeed to them both—that a semblance of goodwill be preserved. Indeed Mary was full of proposals. Why not make her co-ruler of Scotland with her son James, now entering young manhood? Elizabeth considered the proposal, sent negotiators to Scotland to look into it, and concluded that it was completely impractical. In addition to the risk to England in releasing Mary from captivity, the Scottish lords refused to have their dishonored, deposed queen back—and her son too was most unfilial in his negative response. But the correspondence continued.

With her letters Mary sent Elizabeth wigs and embroidered cuffs and caps ornamented with her own needlework, a reminder of her tedious and empty hours. The damp and drafts in her apartments, she informed the queen, were putting her in "danger of her death," yet she hoped Elizabeth's own health was good. Meanwhile, in secret, she read the letters of English

Catholics in France and Spain, letters full of plans for raising armies of liberation, and wrote them commanding, impassioned, traitorous replies.

Elizabeth, for her part, sent Mary wigs in return and bolts of satin and taffeta and, to improve her health, sent her own physician as well. Elizabeth signed herself "your good sister and cousin," and affixed her royal seal. In her council chamber, however, she wondered aloud what to do with her untrustworthy relative, and saw only too clearly that she would never be able to free her. "Her head should have been cut off years ago," she once remarked to an Italian visitor.[7] As the years went by the queen of Scots' execution seemed imperative, and at last inevitable.

To Elizabeth's advisers and to Parliament, the elimination of Mary Stuart was long, long overdue. She was the "monstrous and huge dragon" that menaced England's security, the lodestar of rebellion and treachery and danger from abroad. Her morals were as low as any woman's could be; she had murdered her husband, she was an adulteress, she had seduced her jailer Shrewsbury (according to Shrewsbury's spiteful wife Bess of Hardwick) and borne his child. She had shown herself to be faithless where Elizabeth and her government were concerned. "It is evident," the fairminded Cecil concluded, "that the Scottish queen has never entered into any treaty but only of purpose to abuse the queen of England with some treacherous attempt or other." In fact there was more to Mary's story than this, but by the mid-1580s only the broad outlines mattered.

Then in 1586 a trap was set for her, leading her to provide the evidence needed to find her guilty of treason. She approved, in writing, a plan for Elizabeth's assassination, and when in October of 1586 she was tried at Fotheringhay Castle by a group of commissioners appointed by the queen her guilt was confirmed.

As sovereign, as guardian of her people's lives and her nation's safety, Elizabeth had no choice but to order the issuing of the proclamation setting forth Mary's death sentence and to sign the warrant authorizing her execution. But something held her back. The fears that gathered around her people clutched at her as well, adding to the deep personal misgivings she fought as the year came to a close.

It had been a hard year, a year of bitter disappointment and failure. War had taken Leicester from her for many months, and had led to conflict and ill feeling between them. War had been waged, and the cost had been great, yet save for the minor triumph at Zutphen there had been no victory. Now a decision had to be made about the Scots queen.

The political hazards in sending Mary to her death were substantial. First, Scotland, and the succession. With Mary dead, her claim would pass to her son James; what was to prevent him from attracting to himself all the powers that had previously supported his mother's claim, then using their forces to conquer England? True, James had only recently signed the Treaty of Berwick, pledging himself to an alliance with England and accepting an annual pension from Elizabeth. He was her presumed successor, and he might be content to wait for the crown to come to him in the course of nature. But what if he chose to betray the treaty? What better excuse could she give him than to put his mother to death?

Then there was France, where Mary was still recognized as queen. French envoys had come to Elizabeth's court to ask that her life be spared, and with war at hand the English could not afford to drive the French, already submissive to Spain, into King Philip's camp. The creation of a Catholic martyr in Mary Stuart might well have that effect.

And what of Spain, and King Philip? Would the death of the woman he looked on as England's rightful queen abate Philip's determination to crush England in battle? Or would it merely shift the explanation of his warmaking, from conquest on Mary's behalf to a war of vengeance, a war to punish Mary's murderers?

For a time Elizabeth took counsel with Cecil on this most difficult of her decisions, but before long she ceased to ask his views and pondered the matter alone. Parliament had shouted for Mary's death, begging the queen to "take away this most wicked and filthy woman" before it was too late. But however unanimous the views and feelings of her advisers Elizabeth could not bring herself to acquiesce. William Davison, recently made a secretary of state because of the increasing burden of office on Secretary Walsingham, believed that it would take more than intellectual and political logic to persuade the queen to sign the death warrant. She would never take Mary's life, Davison said, unless compelled by "extreme fear."

Among the prophecies being spread abroad in 1586 was one concerning the queen of Scots. Once she came to harm, it was said, there would be horrible results. An army of invasion would sail to England and land at Chester. Queen Elizabeth, abandoned by her quarreling Parliament, would become a fugitive seeking safety in Wales. The people would rebel; a rising of "clubs and clouted shoes" would end in victory for the peasants, and meanwhile the Tudor crown would be lost and won by a series of claimants.[8] It was a long, intricate vision of disaster, encompassing most of Elizabeth's worst fears. And it would all come about the moment Mary Stuart's head was severed from her shoulders.

Alone with her thoughts, was Elizabeth haunted by this dire prediction? Did it deepen her already strong reluctance to send a female relative to her death? ("What will they not now say," she asked a parliamentary delegation, "when it shall be spread that, for the safety of her life, a maiden queen could be content to spill the blood even of her own kinswoman?") As a highly educated woman, and one who had more than a slight interest in the occult, Elizabeth believed in the doctrine of correspondence—the teaching that every created thing was linked to every other by a powerful psychic force. To disturb one element in the carefully balanced whole was to send shock waves through the rest of creation. For Elizabeth to authorize the taking of an anointed queen's life was a sacrilege of sorts, a rending of the web which encompassed all; it might well bring death back on her.

There may have been another theme in Elizabeth's tortured musings, made up of antiquarian curiosity and long-buried memories. A queen had been executed in England, fifty years earlier. Anne Boleyn had stood accused of treason, as Mary Stuart was now; like Mary, Anne had been denounced as a wicked, unrepentant woman, faithless to her husband, an adulteress who had plotted the death of her lord and lawful sovereign. Was there in Anne's daughter a superstitious dread of replicating her father's terrible revenge against Anne? Or did Elizabeth merely note the parallels, nod with interest, and then return to her efforts to calculate the reaction Mary's death was likely to produce at foreign courts?

In January of 1587 fresh alarms swept the country. Rumors sprang from one another, creating unprecedented panic and breeding ever more fantastic news of imagined events.

The Spaniards had landed. They were at Milford, thousands strong, their huge cannon rumbling through the Welsh countryside and their grim legions of cutthroat troops marching ever closer to the capital.

The north was in revolt. It was a rising as stubborn and as ill-disposed toward the queen as the rising of 1569, only this time the Spaniards would aid the rebels and nothing could stop them.

London was in flames. The queen—was she still living, or had she been assassinated, as some said?—had had to flee. In all the confusion, the queen of Scots had escaped. She was on her way to the northern rebels. Spaniards were moving toward the burning capital, their crested helmets silhouetted against the red glow of the night sky. Surely, these were the last days of the world.

The whirl of rumor engulfed the court. The image of a realm in chaos shimmered in the air like a horrifying mirage, unreal yet threatening. Elizabeth fought toward her decision, pressed as much by the wildfire of panic as by the urgent necessity for action on a matter of great import.

"For mine own life," she insisted, "I would not touch her." Yet Mary had to die. There was no escape—unless, as a number of people hinted darkly, Mary's jailers took it upon themselves to carry out the pledge of death they had sworn to in the Bond of Association. Elizabeth asked it of them, but the deed was not done. She cursed them, blasting "the niceness of those precise fellows who in words would do great things but in deed perform nothing."[9]

Then came word of yet another plot against her life—on Mary's behalf. The French ambassador and others made plans to kill Elizabeth, though when their conspiracy came to light they had not yet determined whether to poison her stirrup or her shoe, in the Italian manner; or to kill her "by laying a train of gunpowder where she lieth."[10]

There was no longer any reason to stay Mary's execution in order to placate the French. As for James Stuart, she would have to gamble on his coldheartedness toward his mother and his often asserted, carefully protected succession rights.

At the end of January Elizabeth wrote to James. Mary, she said, is "the serpent that poisons me." If she saved Mary, she would herself be destroyed. The agony of decision had passed. Only one simple, fateful course was open to her.

On February 1, Elizabeth summoned Davison, signed the death warrant, and sent Davison off with it to the bedside of the sick Walsingham. It was a solemn moment, but she added a grim joke. "The grief thereof," she said, referring to the document in his hand, "would go near to kill him outright."

32

When after Christs birth there be expired,
Of hundreds fifteene, yeares eighty eight,
Then comes the time of dangers to be feared,
And all mankind with dolors it shall freight,
For if the world in that yeare doe not fall,
If sea and land then perish ne decay,
Yet Empires all, and Kingdomes alter shall,
And man to ease himselfe shall have no way.

T he Most Fortunate Armada rocked at anchor in Lisbon harbor, its white sails with their bright red crosses fluttering in the chill wind. There were well over a hundred ships, half of them towering galleons and galleasses and hulking armed merchantmen that loomed "so high that they resembled great castles." These monstrous vessels were meant to frighten the enemy as much by sheer size as by force of arms or firepower, and as the tiny supply boats darted in and out among them, rising and dipping in the strong chop of the harbor waters, they seemed to stand, stately and majestic, like grandees attended by their scurrying valets.

In command of the vast flotilla on this spring day in 1588 was Don Alonso Perez de Guzman, duke of Medina Sidonia, Lord of San Lucar, and Knight of the Golden Fleece. King Philip had made him Captain General of the Ocean Sea only two months before, and in the interim he had struggled to learn what he could about ships and guns and naval warfare, about which, when appointed, he knew virtually nothing. He watched now as the ships were loaded with chests of muskets and pikes, corselets and morions, cannon balls and powder. Horses and cattle were slung aboard in nets and stowed below decks, along with casks and barrels of salt meat and fish, rice, cheese, and other provisions, wine and water. In accordance with the captain general's orders, more men were being put aboard the ships along with the beasts and provisions, sailors kidnapped from other ships in Lisbon harbor, invalids from the hospitals and criminals from the prisons, even laborers who had never before seen the sea, taken from their fields and put to work for the king aboard the great Armada.

There was a shortage of men. Some months earlier, when word of a vast expedition had first gone out, men had come to Lisbon from all over Spain and Portugal, eager to sail with the fleet. But since then, epidemics had reduced the size of the crews and desertion too had become a problem, and as the time for departure neared it had been necessary to make up the losses by commandeering all the men to be found, no matter how unsuitable.

Medina Sidonia had other worries. The gigantic ships carried too few guns, and there were nothing like enough gunners to man them. Many of the vessels leaked, or responded badly under sail, and there were far too few smaller craft to act as a proper escort for the greatships. Food and water were bound to be a problem, for the purveyors to whom the task of provisioning had been entrusted were notorious for supplying tainted meat and sour wine. In addition, it had not been possible to buy enough seasoned barrel staves to supply the entire fleet; most food, wine and water were stored in casks and water butts made from green wood, which were not watertight and in which perishables spoiled quickly.

For this, Drake was to blame. A year earlier, in the spring of 1587, the daring Englishman had raided the harbor at Cadiz, then supply center for the Armada, and in the course of his raid he had burned tens of thousands of seasoned barrel staves—along with some thirty-seven warships and smaller vessels. To Elizabeth's great satisfaction, he had also seized a merchant ship whose cargo of spices, silks and jewels was worth many fortunes. But in the long run, the lumber was the greater loss to the Spaniards, for though the ships could be replaced, the lumber could not.

A strong, almost wintry wind set the colorful pennants and flags flying. Each ship was "furnished and beautified with trumpets, streamers, banners, warlike ensigns, and other such like ornaments," gilded and painted, and as they fluttered from the masts and spars they lent the vast flotilla an air of joyous celebration. But the duke was far from joyous. He found the tasks of command irksome, and the men under him—haughty, jealous commanders who quarreled with one another and looked askance at any admiral set over them—hard to rule. Moreover, he was more fatalistic than sanguine about the Armada's chances for success. The astrologers and prophets were predicting disaster for this year, and given the unsatisfactory state of his ships and crews, they were likely to be right. Certainly the weather was no help. "Unsettled winds" bedeviled navigation, and unseasonable storms sent huge waves crashing against the coast with heavy rain and blasting gales. It promised to be the stormiest summer in years, and the captain general imagined with dread what perils awaited his ships in the dangerous waters of the North Atlantic.

The king too was fatalistic, but with the granite certainty of one absolutely convinced that God is on his side. To King Philip, the Armada was a crusading navy, its mission a holy war. For years he had been urged to turn the might of his soldiers and his ships against England; now, at last, he had made up his mind to do so. By what saurian involutions of thought he had reached this determination no one could say, for with advancing age his abstractedness and self-absorption had increased to the point of opacity. But sometime in the mid-1580s his predestined path had become clear to him. He came to realize that all the wealth and power he had amassed in his long reign, all the gold and silver from the New World, all the lands he had seized and plundered had been brought together for a single purpose: to destroy the heretical rule of Queen Elizabeth.

With an alacrity that startled his ministers—who were accustomed to infinitely protracted decisions from the king, clouded by infinitely detailed objections—Philip ordered the preparation of an enormous fleet. It would sail for the Netherlands, where Parma would be waiting with his soldiery to commence the conquest of England. The Armada would not be itself a fleet of conquest, it would aid in the military invasion. Together, the towering warships and the fighting men in their tens of thousands would overcome England's formidable navy and much less formidable land defenses.

Just where and how the two halves of the Spanish attack force would join together was unclear. In particular, it was left vague how a fleet requiring a deep-water port was to rendezvous with a land army in a region whose one deep-water port was in enemy hands. But these and other tactical considerations were not allowed to deter the expeditious assembling of ships and men and supplies that culminated in the splendid panorama spread before Medina Sidonia's gaze in Lisbon harbor in the spring of 1588. In record time, the most formidable, the most extensive, the most intimidating naval force that ever put to sea had been assembled. Soon it would set sail, and Philip, as the English told one another excitedly, would attempt to "devour all Christendom with invasion."

The English would have been surprised to learn with what alarm their own defensive preparations were viewed by the Spanish sailors manning the Armada. "The enemy now make but little reckoning of us," said Lord Howard of Effingham—half-brother of the traitor Norfolk, and now appointed admiral of the English fleet—"and know that we are but like bears tied to stakes, and they may come like dogs to offend us."[1] In fact, among the intelligence reports reaching the English court from Lisbon were one or two declaring the "great fear" felt throughout the Spanish fleet that England was more than adequately prepared to encounter their ships and men.[2] Drake was especially terrifying. The Spaniards called him "El Draque," the dragon, and found his powers of navigation and extraordinary luck in combat too remarkable to be explained by human abilities alone. He was a sorcerer, they said, who sailed and waged war by means of magic.

Yet taken overall, the reports were much more disheartening than encouraging. Wildly inflated estimates of the Armada's size and strength reached the council chamber: there were over two hundred ships, carrying thirty-six thousand men; there were three hundred ships, half of them giant ships of war; there were four or five hundred ships, ready to debouch onto English soil the largest land army ever assembled.[3] And it was surely assembling, the spies in Dunkirk wrote. There were thirty-seven warships in the harbor, ready to ferry Parma's men to their rendezvous with the hulking escort fleet. Horses were being brought to Dunkirk in great numbers, and all the abbeys in the region were pressed into service grinding wheat to bake biscuits for the soldiers.

So vain was King Philip of his monster fleet that he publicized its specifications. Detailed lists of the ships, their guns and their crews were available in Rome and Paris and Amsterdam in the spring of 1588, and though the numbers on these lists were inflated they were more reliable—though no more comforting to the English—than the dispatches of spies. Printers in Amsterdam, ever eager to incriminate the Spaniards, augmented the official itemization by listing the scourges and whips and instruments of torture the great ships carried in their holds. By the time these lurid documents reached England they were fleshed out by stories of how, once the invasion force landed, all adult English men and women would be tortured and killed, leaving their orphaned infants to be suckled by an army of seven thousand Spanish wet nurses—to be carried, along with the scourges and whips, in the Armada's capacious holds.[4]

Throughout the stormy spring and early summer the English defense was mounted. The lords lieutenant of the counties were ordered to muster bands of footsoldiers and the nobles and gentry received messages from the queen commanding them "to attend upon her with such a convenient number of lances and light horse as might stand with their ability." In the interest of security, watches were to be set in all towns by night and all suspicious persons detained. The hunt for priests and for the recusants who concealed them was intensified, for no one could predict what English Catholics might do once their Spanish coreligionists came ashore in force. All along the coasts, villagers were told to prepare beacons, to be lit as warning fires when the Armada hove into sight. Nothing of possible use to the invaders was to be left unguarded; even cattle grazing near the sea were driven inland, to prevent them from falling into Spanish hands.

An ingenious if somewhat makeshift barrier was erected to block the passage of any enemy ships up the Thames. Huge, heavy chains and ships' cables were locked together and stretched across the river from Gravesend to Tilbury, held in place by a cordon of small boats anchored in the river and by a hundred and twenty tall ships' masts laid end to end.[5]

But the main line of defense was the navy, and in addition to Admiral Howard's main fleet there were two smaller squadrons, one at Plymouth under Drake, who was named vice admiral, and another light squadron to patrol the Channel, headquartered at Dover. A full complement of sailors was mustered ("There is here the gallantest company of captains, soldiers and mariners that I think ever was seen in England," the ebullient admiral remarked), and even the Thames watermen were called to serve. Carpenters and shipwrights had labored to fit the ships until, in Howard's words, "there was never a one of them that knows what a leak means," though this had often meant working by torchlight at night as well as during the day, and persisting despite the "extreme gales of wind" that lashed at the harbors.

By June the fleet was ready, the ships dancing out the recurrent storms "as lustily as the gallantest dancers at the court." Ashore the trained bands were beginning to converge on Tilbury, designated as the headquarters of the land forces. If any resisted serving the queen in that perilous hour, no record of their resistance remains—though there was some concern on the part of the country people that taxes levied to support the soldiers might become a permanent burden. For many the approaching confrontation with the Spaniards must have come as a great relief. To meet at last the enemy they had dreaded for so many years can only have filled them with a sort of millenarian exhilaration. Whether they prevailed or were defeated, the outcome would at least be clear, the long uncertainty ended. "It was a pleasant sight," a contemporary wrote, "to behold the soldiers as they marched toward Tilbury, their cheerful countenances, courageous words and gestures, dancing and leaping wheresoever they came."

As the English marched toward Tilbury and their expected rendezvous with the enemy, the ships of the Most Fortunate Armada were foundering in a howling storm off Cape Finisterre.

Since leaving Lisbon in early May, the fleet had been overtaken by a series of disasters. First contrary gales had kept them windbound off the Portuguese coast, with some ships unable to hold their own against the headwinds and drifting off far to the south. Then, once the fleet finally began its northward progress—traveling with exasperating slowness because of the leaden pace of the supply ships and the fitful, unpredictable winds—the men began to fall sick from drinking foul water and eating rotten food. The green barrel staves were taking their toll. Cask after cask of provisions was opened and found to be stinking and crawling with worms; only the rice was unspoiled. Then, just as the captain general was about to halt the expedition, a sudden tempest had arisen, scattering the vessels and seriously damaging some of them, and forcing a general run for port.

After so many delays and catastrophes it was hard to see the beneficent hand of God guiding the Armada's destiny. June, so Medina Sidonia had been led to understand, was the best sailing month of the year, when calm seas and fair winds prevailed even in the roughest waters. Yet June had been even more stormy than May. If God could not seem to provide a safe passage even in the most halcyon season of the year, then perhaps it was a sign that he meant the fleet to fail in its mission.

Yet such a suggestion hardly seemed credible. How could God be displeased with an undertaking which in every particular bore the stamp of a holy crusade? The ships had been christened with the names of the saints: *San Francesco, San Lorenzo, San Luis* and *San Martin.* Holy images and crusading crosses had been painted on every waving ensign and pennant. The flagship's principal banner, blessed with elaborate ceremony in Lisbon cathedral just before the fleet's departure, carried on its face the crucified Christ and on its back the Virgin, her eyes upraised in supplication. *"Exsurge, Domine,"* read the scroll beneath, *"et judica causam tuam!"* "Arise, O Lord, and vindicate thy cause!"

None of the usual vulgarities incident to expeditions of sailing men were allowed to defile this sanctified campaign. Before leaving the harbor the ships had been swept clear of prostitutes, and the men had purged themselves of their sins and communicated in the cathedral. Nearly two hundred monks and friars sailed with the fleet to perform daily masses and lead the crews in prayer. At sunrise and sunset the ships' boys gathered at the mainmasts to sing religious hymns, and the sailors were dissuaded from indulging in "profane oaths dishonoring the names of our Lord, our Lady and the saints." The watchwords for each of the days of the week—for Monday, Holy Ghost, for Tuesday, Most Holy Trinity, for Wednesday, Saint James, for Thursday, the Angels, and so on—were a pious reminder of the Armada's transcendent purpose. "From highest to lowest," King Philip's instructions to the men read, "you are to understand that the object of our expedition is to regain countries to the church now oppressed by enemies of the true faith. I therefore beseech you to remember your calling, so that God will be with us in what we do."

"God will be with us"—so Medina Sidonia had believed, especially after a most holy man, a friar, had expressed to him his most profound certainty that Spain would be the victor in the coming contest. His officers too, men of long experience in battle, seemed serenely content to anticipate a victorious outcome, though they were candid in admitting that the English would have the advantage of them in ordnance and maneuverability. "We fight in God's cause," one of them explained. "We are sailing against the English in the confident hope of a miracle."

Yet as he sat in his flagship in the harbor of Corunna, surrounded by his storm-battered ships, the captain general lost heart. The expedition might be in God's hands, but the immediate responsibility was his own, and he could not in conscience proceed with it. Even an inexperienced sailor such as he was could see that the galleys, formidable though they might be in Mediterranean waters, were holding up badly as oceangoing ships. The bulky merchantmen listed badly and lagged far behind the more responsive vessels. The storm had underscored the fleet's vulnerability, but even without it there would have been reason enough to reconsider the entire venture.

"To undertake so great a task with forces equal to those of the enemy would be inadvisable," Medina Sidonia wrote in a sobering letter to King Philip, "but to do so with an inferior force, as ours is now, with our men lacking in experience, would be still more unwise." "I am bound to confess that I see very few, or hardly any, of those on the Armada with any knowledge of or ability to perform the duties entrusted to them." He particularized the difficulties one after another, hoping that his sovereign, with his logical mind and reverence for detail, would find the disadvantages overwhelming. "I have tested and watched this point very carefully, and your majesty may believe me when I assure you that we are very weak," he concluded. "The opportunity might be taken, and the difficulties avoided, by making some honorable terms with the enemy."

Philip found the duke's letter disconcerting, especially as Parma, in the Netherlands, took the same overall view. (Parma's army had fallen from thirty thousand to seventeen, which made him doubt whether an invasion of England could be attempted without leaving too few men behind as garrison troops.) But it did not disconcert him for long. Human limitations, however severe, could not be allowed to impede a divinely appointed mission. At the Escorial, the masses and prayers in the huge, ornate royal chapel went on day and night; in the towns and villages of Spain statues of the Virgin and the saints were carried in procession through the streets to ask God's blessing on his Invincible Armada. The captain general must have faith that all would be well, that the troubles he faced would be surmounted. King Philip ordered him to proceed.

Obediently Medina Sidonia complied, and on July 12, with his fleet re-victualed and repaired, he gave the command to weigh anchor.

A week later, on the afternoon of July 19, an English captain sighted the Spanish fleet while his bark was cruising the mouth of the Channel. He came into Plymouth to report. By evening the beacon fires were burning along all the headlands, their thick columns of smoke and red glow visible far inland and out across the Channel to Dunkirk. Within hours the chain of warning lights had spread far to the north and west, until by morning it had reached the Scots border. The Spanish were upon them. The great battle was at hand.

Three days after word reached the capital that the Armada was within striking distance of the English coast, the queen appointed Leicester to be commander of the Camp Royal at Tilbury. The appointment warmed the heart of the sick old earl, who ever since his return from the Netherlands campaign had suffered nearly as much from Elizabeth's coldness and angry neglect as he did from the illness that was slowly killing him. His old age was proving to be harsher and bleaker than he could have imagined. His marriage had grown cold and was in any case disfigured by bereavement. (His son by Lettice had died in infancy—of epilepsy, so Leicester's enemies said, as a punishment from God for the father's immorality.) A sensational book, *Leicester's Commonwealth*, revived in lurid detail every scandal ever spread about him, accusing him of seducing most of Elizabeth's women (sometimes "keeping a mother and two or three daughters at the same time"), of being "plunged, overwhelmed and defamed in all vice," of murdering those who stood in the way of his advancement and generally of making himself the most hated man in England, which he very probably was. The years of lechery and criminality had left him "broken within and without," the anonymous author said, and in 1588 the phrase was not far wrong.

The hatred he aroused, and his wealth and apparent power at court, made the earl a target for assassination. Several of the plots against the queen included killing Leicester as well, and during 1587 a conspiracy had come to light that envisioned his murder by one of a grisly variety of means. Either he was to be killed when his house at Wanstead was burned, or he was to be poisoned, possibly by a lethal liquid slipped into his perfume.[6]

Early in 1588 Leicester wrote to Elizabeth "beseeching her to behold his wretched and depressed estate, and restore him to some degree of her former grace and favor." Her belated reply had been the appointment as commander of Tilbury, and even though he realized that the command was a restricted and somewhat honorific one, he accepted it gladly. The title was grander than the post itself: Lord Steward Her Majesty's Lieutenant Against Foreign Invasion.

Elizabeth sent Leicester off to Tilbury with words of "great comfort," spurring him to squeeze the maximum of activity out of his aging frame and inflating his self-importance to new heights. "Nothing must be neglected to oppose this mighty enemy now knocking at our gates," he wrote to the council, dashing off the letter in great haste while en route from Gravesend to Chelmsford to supervise the raising of troops. "There is no looking back now to any oversight past." Present oversights offended him, however. There were too few officers appointed to serve under him, an implied insult to his rank. And he was jealous of Hunsdon, appointed to command the special forces raised to protect the queen; he asked the council to word Hunsdon's commission "so as not to interfere with his own authority."[7] He tangled with the arrogant earl of Oxford, who refused the command Leicester offered him and made such a disdainful nuisance of himself that the earl was "glad to be rid of him" after he stalked off in anger.

In his first expansive days as lord steward Leicester encouraged Elizabeth to visit the camp in person to "comfort these thousands" as she had comforted him. Fortunately for him, her coming was delayed for some days; in the interim he was able to turn the chaos of unprovisioned troops, half-erected fortifications and rain-soddened equipment into something like an orderly camp.

The military crisis with Spain pulled Elizabeth out of an ugly contretemps with her advisers. All the hidden strain in her personal life had broken to the surface with the execution of Mary Stuart, and in the aftermath of that infinitely distasteful event she had lost not only her self-control but, for a time, her governmental sense. The chief scapegoat, William Davison, was sent to the Tower while the queen sought to have him hanged without a trial. (Finding this impossible, she had him tried, condemned to an indeterminate imprisonment and heavily fined.) The councilors feared for their lives.

It seemed for a time as if the brash, bullying woman with her loud talk of severed heads was about to order executions in earnest. She inquired of the justices "whether her prerogatives were not absolute" and succeeded in calling up, in the minds of her senior advisers, the specter of her terrifying father Henry VIII. With advancing years both the old king and his father, Henry VII, had now and then lapsed into a twilit sanity in which they stumbled about, red-faced and speechless with anger, or attacked their companions with lunging violence. The older Henry had withdrawn into secretive paranoia, the younger into raging tyranny.

There was more than a hint of this affliction in Elizabeth Tudor, but unlike her father and grandfather she had never until now allowed her personal eccentricities to damage her discrimination as queen. In the three or four months after her royal cousin's death she came very close to losing her judgment, and allowing her feelings of resentment to lead her into direct conflict with the men through whom she ruled. In the end she did not provoke a governmental conflict; instead her revenge took the form of excluding from court those she meant to punish, then, after a period of painful exile, allowing them to return but exposing them to savage and bitter abuse. Cecil, whom she at first wanted to imprison in the Tower along with Davison, was exiled, then vilified in this way; though old and ill he was made to suffer through the queen's tirades, being called "traitor, false dissembler, and wicked wretch" in tones far sharper than the words themselves. Walsingham stood up better to such ill treatment than Cecil, though he too was ailing and the stormy scenes must have worn down his nerves. The queen addressed him with icy disdain to his face and spoke viciously about him behind his back; he confessed to behavior toward her that was "nothing gracious."

The military emergency that began to loom in the spring of 1588 relieved this atmosphere of sordid tensions and turned the queen's enmity in a more appropriate direction. Not that she welcomed the Spanish assault: in fact she shut her eyes to its inevitability until the last possible moment, doling out funds to pay troops and victual her navy with a tightfistedness remarkable even for her ("King Harry, her majesty's father, never made a lesser proportion of supply than six weeks," complained Admiral Howard when he found out he was to be allotted only a month's provisions at a time) and continuing to negotiate with Parma until mid-June, many weeks after the Armada had left Lisbon harbor. But once she accepted its inescapability the danger began to lift her spirits; she rose to meet its challenge, in a flamboyant gesture of self-display that left an indelible mark on English memory.

On August 8 she sailed on the ebb tide to Tilbury in her royal barge, surrounded by a small flotilla of other rivercraft carrying her trumpeters, her tall gentlemen pensioners and the yeomen of her guard. A flourish of trumpets and drum rolls announced her arrival, and as she disembarked a great shout went up from the men.

She rode through their ranks on a huge white warhorse, armed like a queen out of antique mythology in a silver cuirass and silver truncheon. Her gown was white velvet, and there were plumes in her hair like those that waved from the helmets of the mounted soldiers.

Every man the queen passed fell to his knees and called on God to preserve her, until the extravagant reverence became as embarrassing as it was repetitious. She sent a messenger to precede her and to beg the men to forbear. Yet the shouts of blessing could not be restrained, and the soldiers appointed to stand guard outside her lodging that night toasted one another with cries of "Lord preserve the queen!" until the early hours of the morning.

It had been more than two weeks now since the first sighting of the Spanish fleet, and very little news had reached the Camp Royal about the fate of the two navies. Word came that Drake had seized a galleass, and captured the fleet's "admiral or vice admiral" along with it. One of the greatships had sunk. Two Spanish carracks had been taken by the ships of Flushing and Zeeland. So far, it seemed, English losses had been small. The arrival of the queen greatly encouraged the men, but they knew well in what peril they lay. There were perhaps ten thousand in the neighborhood of the camp, all told—a respectable, but hardly an invincible force. They could not stand long against the Spaniards if they landed; they could not even protect London, for the huge boom of ships' masts and chains that had been built across the mouth of the river had collapsed, leaving open to invaders the pathway to the heart of the country, the court and government.

The following day, August 9, Elizabeth again rode through the camp, this time with a retinue of heralds and sergeants, guardsmen and musicians. Leicester and Lord Grey, marshal of the camp, rode before her, richly dressed "in princely garments of great price, bearing their hats and feathers in their hands." Eight footmen escorted her warhorse, her ladies riding behind her and a troop of guardsmen bringing up the rear.

This time the queen did more than acknowledge the shouts of the men by energetic nods and waves and brief words of thanks. She made a speech, at once rousing and moving, her words carefully chosen to appeal to their patriotism and to their lifelong affection for her.[8]

"My loving people," she began, "we have been persuaded by some that are careful for our safety, to take heed how we commit ourselves to armed multitudes, for fear of treachery. But I assure you, I do not desire to live to distrust my faithful and loving people. Let tyrants fear. I have so behaved myself that, under God, I have placed my chiefest strength and safeguard in the loyal hearts and good will of my subjects; and therefore I am come amongst you as you see, at this time, not for my recreation and disport, but being resolved, in the midst and heat of the battle, to live or die amongst

374

you all, and to lay down for my God and for my kingdom and for my people, my honor and my blood, even in the dust."

She spoke simply, her words interrupted often by cheers. Only the men nearest to her could make them out; to most of those at the camp she was a tiny, gesticulating figure in white, her cuirass gleaming dully and her orange wig bobbing enthusiastically up and down with each shout of approval.

"I know I have the body of a weak and feeble woman," she was saying, "but I have the heart and stomach of a king, and of a king of England too, and think foul scorn that Parma or Spain, or any prince of Europe should dare to invade the borders of my realm; to which, rather than any dishonor shall grow by me, I myself will take up arms, I myself will be your general, judge, and rewarder of every one of your virtues in the field."

Thunderous noise greeted this appeal of the thin, aging woman to lead her troops into battle, and with a final promise to pay the unpaid, meanly fed men—a promise she was to break—Elizabeth ended her speech.

Had this been stage drama rather than plain reality battle would immediately have been joined, or word would have come of a decisive clash between the fleets, decisively ended. But in truth the sequel was anticlimactic.

There had been fighting in the Channel, as it turned out, some of it fierce and prolonged. But according to the messages reaching Tilbury, it had been inconclusive, and had ended in confusion in the first days of August.

The Armada had sailed majestically up the coast, a massive crescent of seagoing castles. Forbidden by King Philip's orders to land, the fleet had anchored off Calais to wait for Parma's men, fending off the English ships as best they could but suffering a good deal of damage from the furious pounding of the latter's awesome guns. Admiral Howard had been wrong: it was not the English but the Spanish ships which were like bears tied to stakes, lumbering and clumsy for all their strength, with the smaller but more deadly English mastiffs tearing at them from all sides.

Medina Sidonia sent message after message pleading with Parma to embark with his army, yet there was no sight of them; in fact the Spanish forces were blocked in by the Dutch. Alternately blinded by thick smoke from the English cannonades and by the driving rain and heaving seas that washed over their bows and broke their bowsprits and foremasts, the Armada captains raged against their commander, against Parma, and against their own ill fortune. On the night of July 28, the English sent blazing fireships into the midst of the enemy vessels; they scattered, and several foundered. Pounded on the following day by the English off Gravelines, and then by yet another in the series of gales that made winter of this freak summer, the Invincible Armada sailed northward, pursued by the English until, short of powder and provisions, they had to give up the chase off Scotland.

A wreckage of spars and sails, ropes and bodies floated in the Channel, witness to much destruction, but the English captains felt cheated of victory and speculated anxiously about the Armada's imminent return. Surely the fleet would not sail home to Spain without making another attempt to complete its task; it must have taken shelter somewhere— perhaps Denmark—to refit, and would be back soon. In the meantime Parma must be belatedly preparing his invasion, and would cross in his own ships with the next favorable tides in a matter of days.

And the English seamen, who had served bravely despite widespread illness from rough seas and sour beer, and had gone on uncomplaining when the fresh water ran out and they were forced to drink their own urine, had now begun to die of typhus by the hundreds. Shipboard mortality left some vessels with too few men to weigh their anchors. "They sicken one day and die the next," wrote the admiral. "It is a most pitiful sight to see the men die in the streets of Margate."9

In all the Catholic cities of Europe the bells were rung for a great Spanish victory. The Newfoundland fishing fleet, on its way to Dieppe, had witnessed a monumental naval battle with the English losing many of their ships. Other reports told how Drake had been captured, and gave assurance that Parma must already be in London. From Paris to Venice to Rome the fantastic news traveled, with the few contrary reports dismissed as unreliable. It was to have been a year of disaster, and disaster had indeed fallen on the English, as all good Catholics had known it should. In the Escorial the royal chapel resounded with masses of thanksgiving; in Seville and Madrid rejoicing crowds gathered around bonfires to celebrate the defeat of the wicked heretic Elizabeth and the capture of the devilish dragon Francis Drake.

But the revelry, like the misgivings of the English captains, was premature. The Armada, many of her ships listing badly and others damaged beyond repair, was battling vainly to return home, and losing ground with every mile. Another storm caught them nearing the Orkneys, and by the time the fleet was opposite the Galway coast more and more of the great-ships were wallowing low in the water and sinking out of sight. New tempests drove many of the remnants onto the Irish coasts, where survivors were executed by English soldiers or by the Irish in their pay. Of the overmighty fleet assembled in Lisbon in the spring, only half the ships made it back to their home waters.

Not for many weeks was it known in England that a great victory had been won, the great power of Spain checked for a season. Parma and his army did not come, nor did the Armada reappear. Instead, there were stories of dead horses and mules washing ashore—to save water and excess weight the Spanish had thrown all their animals overboard—and of wrecked galleons driven onto rocky shores or broken up by giant waves. Gradually it became clear that the boasting on the continent was nothing more than wishful thinking. The Armada had been shattered, a victim of the English guns, the treacherous weather, and its own inherent weakness.

"She came, she saw, she fled," read derisive Protestant broadsheets celebrating the miraculous defeat of the unconquerable Armada. In retrospect her proportions seemed impossibly vast, her menace unprecedented. She had come, Ralegh wrote, with "so great and terrible an ostentation" that no other fleet could ever match it; the ships were so huge, Camden recorded with Vergilian pomposity, that the winds were tired of carrying them, and the ocean groaned under their weight. A mistimed, mishandled venture was seen as a providential debacle, an epic chapter in the canon of Protestant history.

But the depositions of the few Spanish survivors who were not at first killed restored the disaster to human scale. They told stories of slow starvation on the crippled ships, of drownings, of wounded men crying for food and water, of scurvy and maddening despair. By the power of the saints a few, a very few, had come through their hour of martyrdom alive.

Late in October, nearly three months after the battle in the Channel and its tragic aftermath, Geoffrey Fenton, secretary for Ireland, went walking on the coast of Sligo. The secretary had been an official of the queen's government for many years, and had seen much slaughter and bloodshed in the Irish wars. Yet nothing in his experience matched the spectacle that awaited him on that raw autumn day. In a walk of less than five miles, he wrote to Cecil afterward, he counted more than eleven hundred Spanish corpses on the beach, washed up, bloated and decaying, by the incoming tide.

PART SIX

"A Lady Whom Time Had Surprised"

33

I weepe for ioy to see the world decay,
Yet see Eliza flourishing like May.

I t was a brisk December afternoon when André Hurault, Sieur De
Maisse, disembarked from the royal barge at the privy stairs of Whitehall
Palace and greeted the gentlemen who waited to receive him there. He
came as ambassador of Henry IV of France—the former Henry of Navarre
—and he had been entrusted with the unenviable task of sounding out
Queen Elizabeth on the subject of the war with Spain.

The year was 1597, nine years after the Spanish had surprised themselves
and all Europe by failing to conquer England with the Invincible Armada.
But far from ending the war the Armada debacle had, paradoxically, tough-
ened Spain so that a decade later her navy was stronger than ever, far
stronger than it had been when Medina Sidonia left Lisbon harbor with
his doomed flotilla. The rejoicing in England in 1588 had soon turned to
apprehension, for Spain not only rebuilt her warships but moved her land
forces into Picardy and Brittany in an aggressive attempt to acquire a
French port from which to invade England.

Recently King Philip had been active in Ireland as well, sending supplies
and gold to support the rebel leader Tyrone and ordering soundings taken
along the coast to locate a deep-water landing site. Even as De Maisse
mounted the river stairs behind his escort and made his way along the
covered walkway leading to the lower rooms of the palace, the court was

alive with talk of the latest news from Ireland. The English governor had just died—some said of poison—and Tyrone and his Spanish allies had begun to burn dozens of villages and slaughter all who opposed them.

The ambassador was led into the presence chamber, where he was requested to seat himself on a cushion. The queen, he was told, would see him presently.

In contrast to the dark, low passage into the palace from the river side, which De Maisse had found "passing melancholy," and "with no appearance for a royal house," the presence chamber was all garish color and coruscation. Tapestries flowed in bright blues and reds and burnished golds on the walls, whose surfaces, where they were not covered by the rich hangings, were painted and gilded. There were thick Persian and Indian carpets draped over every table and cupboard, as well as soft rugs on the floors. Oddities of all sorts—ostrich eggs, coconut cups, earthenware art objects and miniatures in crystal and mother of pearl—were mounted in silver and displayed about the room, while outsize ornaments in the shape of frogs, salamanders, golden flowers and giant walnuts gleamed with semi-precious stones.

But the dozens of courtiers who stood about the chamber, brilliant in their overstuffed, overembroidered finery, outshone by far all other ornaments in the room. With their orange and purple beards and their flashing earrings, their jeweled swords and daggers and bright doublets in fashionable shades of "Lusty Gallant," "Drake's Color" and "Dead Spaniard," their sheer gaudiness inspired awe.

But remarkable as they were, the splendors of the presence chamber were not what the Frenchman had come to see. They were nothing more than a backdrop for the principal treasure of the court, and of England—the rare, peerless and altogether extraordinary sixty-four-year-old queen.

In the forty years since her coronation Elizabeth Tudor had never ceased to be the object of intense speculation and scandal, but in the last decade her fame had transcended itself. She had become the stuff of legend.

She had outlived most of her contemporaries. Few in Europe could remember a time when she was not England's monarch. She had outlived nearly all of those who, at her own court, had shaken their heads over her sickliness and fragile woman's body, and muttered that her reign could not be a long one. Among her councilors and intimates, Hatton was dead, and godly Walsingham, blind Blanche Parry, and her beloved Leicester. His brief lieutenancy at Tilbury had been his last; he had died, virtually alone and certainly unmourned, save by the queen, a few days after that command ended. Only Cecil, a portable invalid carried from room to room in an upholstered chair, was left to carry on.

Elizabeth seemed immemorial—and unique. For forty years she had governed alone, without a husband (though certainly not without lovers, it was said), showing, at least in retrospect, an amazing capacity for stubbornness as well as for rule. Her unmarried state—which in fact she had several times been on the point of cheerfully abandoning—had become in her old age the centerpiece of her legend. By an irony of history, this woman of exceptional passions would be known as the Virgin Queen.

Her gorgeous palaces had become half-museums, half-mausoleums where aristocratic tourists paid to see the great queen's perfumed virginal made all of glass, her bed with its gilded beasts and multi-colored ostrich plumes spangled with gold, her brown velvet throne "studded with very large diamonds, rubies, sapphires and the like that glitter among other precious stones and pearls as the sun among the stars." They were shown her "bathing rooms" at Windsor, their walls and ceilings all mirrors, and the breathtaking throne room at Hampton Court, called the Paradise Chamber for its incomparable richness in gold and silver and gems. A very few of these tourists received brief audiences with the queen herself, but none of them wrote down their impressions of her with anything like the penetrating scrutiny of De Maisse.

As he waited on his cushion in the presence chamber the ambassador must have had in mind all that he had been told about the old queen's habits and personality.[1] For his own part he was already favorably impressed, for she had paid him the honor of giving him apartments "wherein Drake had formerly lodged," pleasing him very much. His informants, however, described her as an aging termagant, "a haughty woman, falling easily into rebuke," inclined to think herself far wiser than her councilors and mocking them contemptuously and holding them up to ridicule. Diplomats found her exceedingly difficult to confront, it was said, because she only listened to them as long as what they said was agreeable; as soon as they raised a disagreeable subject she interrupted them with a harangue of her own, often managing to misinterpret their point of view in the process. Usually she misrepresented the entire conversation to the council afterward, so De Maisse was advised to write out his message and arguments and present the written document to her advisers. Worst of all, he learned, Elizabeth was particularly inclined to show her noisy bad temper whenever she heard the name of France or of Henry IV.

After a while the Frenchman was led along a dark passage into the privy chamber, the inner sanctum of the queen, and there, "seated in a low chair, by herself," he found Elizabeth.

Her appearance was startling. She wore, not the customary English gown and kirtle, but a gauzy dressing gown of cloth of silver, unfastened in front

383

so that "one could see the whole of her bosom." Her high-piled red wig was stuck full of gold and silver spangles, and was made still higher by a crowning garland of silver cloth. Two long, fat curls hung down almost to her shoulders, ending at the high jeweled collar of her gown.

She rose and came forward to embrace him, and De Maisse noted that, although her body was still youthful and her movements graceful, her face was long and thin and "very aged." As she greeted him, and began to apologize for not having received him sooner, he found it hard to understand her. She was missing a great many teeth, especially on the right side of her face; those she retained were "very yellow and unequal," and unbecoming in the extreme.

Straining to catch her words through her lisp, he managed to grasp her meaning. She had been ill, she said, looking at him kindly, with a swelling in her right cheek—indeed she could not remember ever having been so ill before. Then glancing down at her robe, she began to excuse her informal dress. "What will these gentlemen say to see me so attired?" she said, looking over at her councilors who were grouped together at the far end of the room and scolding them. "I am much disturbed that they should see me in this state."

De Maisse was a diplomat seasoned in years and experience, yet he found this bizarre mixture of bawdiness and coquetry disconcerting, especially as the queen punctuated her talk by continually grabbing the open front of her gown and flapping it back and forth as if she were too hot, "so that all her belly could be seen." Though her neck was wrinkled, he noted, the skin below was "exceeding white and delicate" all the way down to her navel; the display, though grotesque, made its intended impression.

The ambassador proceeded to the subject matter of his mission, the issue of peacemaking, and found to his relief that the queen neither interrupted him nor flew into a rage at the mention of France. Yet he found her difficult to talk to all the same, for she was never still. At first she sat in her chair, twisting and untwisting the fringe of her gown, then she got up and began to pace around the room—remarking that this was a habit of hers which often tired out ambassadors—and all the time she fairly trembled with nervous energy, showing marked impatience and agitatedly opening and shutting her gown. The fire was too hot, she complained, it was hurting her eyes. She called for her servants to put it out, and the Frenchman paused in his discourse while buckets of water were poured on the sizzling logs.

Elizabeth's overabundant vitality amazed him. He had prepared himself to confront a very old woman, crotchety perhaps, but frail. Instead he found himself faced with a fidgety, restless being whose animal spirits appeared to be waxing rather than ebbing. There was an air of the macabre about Elizabeth; she was like a lively, clacking skeleton whose energetic jerkiness belied her wrinkled cheeks and bare gums. She had in fact lived through her grand climacteric, the dreaded age of sixty-three which few of her contemporaries reached and fewer passed. In that "fatal" year she had for a time seemed to be near death; prolonged insomnia and fevered swellings of her chest and head had prompted her advisers to prepare for a change of reigns, fortifying the court with arms and ordnance and taking steps to guard the treasury at Westminster. But she had recovered quickly enough, and there had been no repetition of the crisis. Even the leg ulcer that had made her limp as a much younger woman seemed no longer to affect her, nor were her hearing or her vision impaired. She had in recent months been troubled by a "desperate ache" in her right thumb, which was as annoying as it was painful since it prevented her from writing. But she hid it, and vehemently denied that it could be gout ("the gout it *cannot* be nor *dare* not be"), and by denying it, she seemed at least for the moment to have cured it.[2]

Under the circumstances, De Maisse made his audience a brief one. He rose to go, and Elizabeth, walking with him to the door, reiterated her coy chagrin "that all the gentlemen he had brought should see her in that condition," and called for them to say their goodbyes. Then, embracing them all "with great charm and smiling countenance," she let them go.

While talking with the queen De Maisse had recognized individuals among the councilors in the room: Cecil, "very old and white," Admiral Howard, much at the heart of affairs and highly honored since his Armada victory, and Cecil's son Robert, who had become principal secretary the year before and who was generally accounted to be "the greatest councilor in England," with whom Elizabeth spent hours in "private and secret conference."

Young Cecil, in 1597 just entering his mid-thirties, was as startling in his appearance in one way as the queen was startling in hers. Elizabeth called him "Pygmy"—a name she knew he detested—but he was not only short, he was hunchbacked, and according to De Maisse, "had small grace and appearance." In an age that believed a crooked soul went with a crooked spine, Robert Cecil was at a severe disadvantage, and his self-consciousness about his appearance did nothing to improve it. He was an urbane and clever man, at home in the witty world of the theater and loving the excitements of gambling and high society. Precocious as a politician and man of affairs, he had sat in Parliament at the age of eighteen and had risen rapidly in Elizabeth's government. Robert Cecil was a worthy successor to Walsingham, to his own father and, reaching back through the century, to

Cromwell and ultimately to Wolsey among the great Tudor drudges who bore the title of royal secretary. All had shared, beyond intellectual force and keen judgment, a capacity for long hours of exceedingly detailed labor; young Cecil was cast in their mold. A man who saw him at court wrote how he hurried his slight, oddly shaped body through the presence chamber on his way to meet with the queen, walking "like a blind man, his hands full of papers and head full of matter."

One figure had been conspicuously missing from the privy chamber: the most flamboyant, the most popular, and many said the most able man at court, the earl of Essex.

Leicester's stepson clearly had greatness of a kind in him. He was built along heroic lines. Tall, broad-shouldered, with the bluff, slightly awkward movements of an athlete and soldier, Essex had the clear, wide forehead, soulful eyes and sensitive expression of a poet. His long face was ruddy in color and grew more so when he talked heatedly of the subject that obsessed him: warfare, and in particular, his own military exploits. "He is entirely given over to arms and the war," wrote De Maisse when he finally met and talked with Essex, "courageous and ambitious, and a man of great designs, hoping to attain glory by arms, and to win renown more and more."[3] The Frenchman also detected his principal flaw. "He is a man of judgment," he wrote, "but one who believes no counsel save his own; when once he has undertaken a thing it is impossible to get it out of his head."

Yet De Maisse would have agreed that, by the mid-1590s, Essex's judgment (coupled with Leicester's patronage and his own marked physical prowess) had brought him a long way. After the death of his penniless, debt-ridden father, Lettice Knollys' first husband Walter Devereux, nine-year-old Essex had been brought up in Cecil's household, along with the hunchbacked boy Robert. By age seventeen he was being advanced at court by his stepfather Leicester, and brought attention to himself by insulting Ralegh and striking him. "What comfort can I have to give myself over to the service of a mistress that is in awe of such a man?" he declared dramatically, running away and hoping to join the fighting in the Netherlands.

He did fight there, and later in France, with considerable distinction, acquiring a reputation not only for brave and audacious soldiery but for old-fashioned chivalry as well. Duels and challenges to single combat suited his temperament perfectly, while drawing attention to his fighting ability and making him popular. But he did not entirely neglect civil for military affairs, and managed to convince Elizabeth of his statesmanship so that she appointed him a member of the council in 1593.

The queen found Essex as exasperating and delightful as a man as he had been as a boy. She called him her "Wild Horse," and felt toward him not only a strong tie of blood—they were cousins, as Elizabeth and Lettice were —but an even stronger one of sentiment. Essex was, after all, the stepson of her lifelong love, and even before Leicester's death she was installing Essex in his court apartments.[4] She put up with his hotheadedness and disobedience, his dueling and violence, though she did complain loudly "that someone or other should take him down and treat [sic] him better manners." He was an intelligent, exuberant, extremely handsome man, good company and a brilliant escort for her, and he knew how to please and flatter her. He sat up late partnering her at cards; he sat at her side for the first performance of A Comedy of Errors; he wore her favor in the tiltyard and organized athletic entertainments for her pleasure. She was in her sixties, he in his thirties, yet there was nothing grandmotherly in her affection for him. His marriage to Sidney's widow infuriated her—though her fury abated in record time for a secret marriage, two weeks—and she rushed at "the fair Mistress Bridges," one of her waiting maids, with "words and blows of anger" when she learned that the girl was flirting seriously with Essex.

Essex was clearly the rising star at court, yet his absence from the privy chamber on the day of De Maisse's audience was not only conspicuous but eloquent. He felt wronged, and he was showing his feelings, as he customarily did, by staying away from the queen and the council table.

"The court is ordinarily full of discontent and factions," De Maisse commented in his written observations, "and the queen is well pleased to maintain it so." In 1597 the factions were very clearly defined: the Cecils, with Admiral Howard, were on one side, opposing Essex, some of the younger men in government and the young military men who admired Essex's swashbuckling style and who had come to maturity during a decade and more of war. Between the elder Cecil and Essex there was respect and a kind of courtly mutuality ("they render strange charities to one another," De Maisse wrote), but greed corroded their relations; Essex was waiting impatiently for Cecil to die so that he could take over the latter's lucrative post as keeper of the wardrobe.

For their part, the two Cecils and their adherents eagerly pushed the bellicose Essex into hazardous military ventures—he hardly needed their encouragement—and then waited smugly for him to kill himself or, equally to their advantage, to damage himself financially and politically. "If he comes back victorious they take occasion thereby to make him suspected by the queen, and if nothing is accomplished then to ruin him." In time, they sensed, Essex would overreach himself and bring about his own destruction.

If he did, it would very likely be because he was blind to the immense personal capacities of the queen. Their relations fell into the time-honored mold of disdainful lady and flattering, admiring courtier. "Most fair, most dear, and most excellent Sovereign," he addressed her in his letters. "While your Majesty gives me leave to say I love you, my fortune is as my affection, unmatchable. If ever you deny me that liberty, you may end my life, but never shake my constancy." But Essex thought little of the abilities of women, and saw no reason to exempt the queen from his belittling censure. The English court, he told De Maisse confidentially, "labored under two things, delay and inconstancy, which proceeded chiefly from the sex of the queen."[5]

These ungallant sentiments were shared by a great many of the men at Elizabeth's court in her last years. "Ah, silly woman! now she shall not curb me, she shall not rule me!" blurted out one of the blunt soldiers who resented a woman's authority. "God's wounds! This is to serve a base, bastard, pissing kitchen woman; if I had served any prince in Christendom, I had not been so dealt withal." The offender was tried for his slanderous remarks—among them, that Elizabeth had "pissed herself with fear" at the time of the Armada—yet it was not possible to bring charges against every man who looked forward to the day when the kingdom would again pass into male hands. However the common people might cheer for the old queen whenever they caught a glimpse of her, the aristocracy and political elite were more than ready for her presumed successor James VI of Scotland to assume power. Her government, the French ambassador noted, "was little pleasing to the great men and the nobles, and if by chance she should die, it is certain that the English would never again submit to the rule of a woman."[6]

Over the next several weeks De Maisse saw Elizabeth a number of times, and with each audience he came to appreciate her more. Her eccentricities of dress and manner continued to disconcert him. Constantly in motion, she talked constantly as well, digressing into long, musing anecdotes or memories so that the ambassador had often to bring her back to the business at hand. She repeated herself, she indulged her musing memory, yet De Maisse was astute enough not to confuse this deliberate, self-flattering self-indulgence with senility.

He had often to humor her vanity. She was forever calling herself foolish and old, "saying she was sorry to see him there, and that, after having seen so many wise men and great princes, he should at length come to see a poor woman and a foolish." This called forth, as it was meant to, overstated reassurances about her "blessings, virtues and perfections," her prudent sovereignty and wise judgment.

Her concern for her appearance was clearly obsessive. "When anyone speaks of her beauty she says that she was never beautiful," De Maisse wrote, "although she had that reputation thirty years ago. Nevertheless she speaks of her beauty as often as she can." Concern for her looks caused Elizabeth to cancel an appointment with the ambassador one day. She had made herself ready, and had already sent her coaches to fetch him and his entourage to the palace, when she thought better of it and called it off. "Taking a look into her mirror," she said that she looked too ill to be presentable, and "was unwilling for anyone to see her in that state."

When presentable she was breathtakingly garbed, either in robes of her favorite silvery white or in elegant black and white. At one meeting she "wore innumerable jewels on her person, not only on her head, but also within her collar, about her arms and on her hands, with a very great quantity of pearls, round her neck and on her bracelets. She had two bands, one on each arm, which were worth a great price."[7]

Yet striking as her appearance was, it was nearly eclipsed by the force of her personality, and by her remarkable sway of mind. Her arrogance about her talent for rulership was absolute. Having been "intended for affairs of state, even from her cradle," she governed with a degree of astuteness none of her present councilors could match. ("They were young," she said, "and had no experience in affairs of state.") She impressed De Maisse as a "very great princess who knows everything," yet her manner was endearingly candid and on occasion playful. De Maisse introduced to her a secretary who was a member of his legation. She "made good cheer to him" as he knelt before her, saying that she remembered having seen several of his letters. "She began to take him by the hair," De Maisse wrote, "and made him rise and pretended to give him a box on the ears."

The more he saw of her the more the Frenchman was astonished by Elizabeth's liveliness. One afternoon she remarked "that she was on the edge of the grave and ought to bethink herself of death," but then abruptly contradicted herself. "I think not to die so soon, Master Ambassador," she said, "and am not so old as they think." And indeed as De Maisse watched her leave the room at the conclusion of his audience, "retiring half dancing to her chamber," he could well believe it.

The true test of the old queen's acuity, of course, was her ability to come to terms with affairs of state. Here he found her to be not only shrewd, calculating and utterly statesmanlike, but minutely informed about recent events and conditions in many parts of Europe. She had spies everywhere, she confided, and especially in the port cities of Spain. She paid them well, but expected complete loyalty and diligence from them. "If they failed to send true advertisement of all that was being done," she remarked simply, "she caused them to be hanged." De Maisse had occasion to see for himself how the queen insisted on being the first to be informed. A courier arrived at Whitehall bringing letters from France. When he made the mistake of giving the ambassador his letters before delivering Elizabeth's, she made her extreme displeasure known and "caused him to be reprimanded for it."

The business on which he had come to England was urgent, yet De Maisse found himself staying on, week after week, without being able to conclude it. Elizabeth beguiled him by her digressions—which he knew full well were meant to delay the negotiations as well as being "her natural way." They talked of the classics ("she knows all the ancient histories, and one can say nothing to her on which she will not make some apt comment"), of her pleasure in dancing and music (she had some sixty musicians, she said, watching her maids dance and "following the cadence with her head, hand and foot"), of how she still liked to play the virginals and how, in her youth, she had "known six languages better than her own."

"A great virtue in a princess," the Frenchman commented at this.

"It is no marvel to teach a woman to talk," the queen shot back wryly. "It were far harder to teach her to hold her tongue."

They talked of religion, with Elizabeth firmly denying as "malice and lying" all the stories then current about her in Rome. It was not true, she insisted with vehemence, that she had ordered a house burned to the ground knowing that over a hundred Catholic women were taking refuge there; in fact there had been only "one or two" women. It was also an absolute falsehood that she had ordered Catholics to be wrapped in bearskins and baited by dogs; the Roman spies sent to London to touch the bears and see for themselves could confirm this. No matter what scandalmongers said, she had never allowed any Catholic to be harmed who was not a traitor, and no one could condemn her for ordering traitors to be punished. Her conscience was "clear and transparent as crystal," she said, sounding very much like her father when pressed on a sensitive topic. And echoing a famous saying of her sister's, she added "that she wished they could see the inside of her heart in a picture and that it was at Rome, so that all could see it as it was."

Christmas came and went, with its elaborate feasting and music and merriment. No doubt the queen danced with Essex—after displays of pique on both sides, they made up their quarrel—and there was entertainment by companies of actors, among them the lord chamberlain's company with its actor and playwright Will Shakespeare.

In the third week of the new year De Maisse pressed for definitive word to take back to King Henry. What did Elizabeth mean to do about the war with Spain, and, more specifically, about the English troops she had in France?

The subject galled her. "They were but thieves and ought to hang," she said, becoming so angry that the ambassador was alarmed. Seeming to forget his presence she ranted on about the worthless soldiers, lisping through her bad teeth and muttering so that he could not make out her words. She had already sent for them to return home, she told him when she became calmer. But they both knew that the larger issue of peacemaking hung over them, unaddressed and unsettling. King Henry was desperate to make peace with Philip II, yet Elizabeth, peace-loving though she was, had to urge him to continue the war—even if it had to be, as in the past, at her expense. She had no choice. Only months before a vast fleet of Spanish ships had sailed against England, and though bad weather had forced it back to its home port there were reports of a fresh fleet being prepared.

She called De Maisse to come closer, and talked to him in a low voice so that none of her advisers could hear. She gave him a private message to take to King Henry. She said to tell him that she was an old woman, and capable of nothing on her own; her nobles were unstable, and changeable in their moods and opinions, and her ordinary subjects, no matter how loudly they might swear their love for her, were nonetheless fickle and inconstant.

She had to fear everything, Elizabeth went on—hostile Parliaments, a depleted treasury, a bitter and war-weary populace that had already sent twenty thousand men to die in the wars abroad. At this she quoted an appropriate Latin tag, and looked "greatly sorrowful."

No one knew King Philip better than she did. In fact she had talked of him often to De Maisse, telling the ambassador again and again how over the years he had sent fifteen assassins to England to kill her. Yet her spies now told her that Philip was little more than a walking corpse, being kept alive "by force" by his physicians and by his daughter who nursed and fed him.

If only King Henry would wait. Only a few months more, at the most, and the old enemy would be dead.

The message would not please his master, De Maisse knew, nor would it stop him from making peace with Spain. King Henry would desert Queen Elizabeth, and there would be a diplomatic rupture. He cannot have enjoyed taking his leave of the great queen with this knowledge weighing on his mind, but her graciousness lightened the parting. She talked briefly of personal things, saying how pleased she was to have befriended De Maisse and complimenting him on his diplomatic finesse.

She embraced him twice, and then embraced the gentlemen who attended him, charming them all as she had on the first audience.

Then she turned to Admiral Howard, who had come up to join the group, and commanded him to give De Maisse a good swift ship for his homeward voyage. Her last words were a dark jest. Watch out, she warned with a laugh, that the Spaniards don't take you prisoner.

34

Fly from her, Age; sleep, Time,
before her throne;
Our strongest wall falls down,
when she is gone.

T he government had run perilously short of money by 1600, and Elizabeth, calculating the value of the heirlooms in her Jewel House, was forced to lay sentiment aside and pawn her family treasures.

Many of them had been her father's. There was his gold admiral's whistle, which he had once worn when he strode the deck of his flagship the *Great Harry*, wearing a sailor's uniform of cloth of gold. There were his thick gold bracelets—far too large for his daughter's reed-thin wrists— enameled with his motto, *Dieu et mon droit*. There was his great seal, and the gold chains he had worn for the annual feasts of the Garter Knights, and even two pairs of spectacles, "garnished with gold," which he had worn when he read his books and perused his documents. These and other precious things—jeweled crucifixes, objects in Venice gold, an enormous sapphire (had it belonged to Anne Boleyn?) "in the shape of a heart, with a hole in it"—brought nearly ten thousand pounds from the merchants who bid on them, while the "coarse rubbish" that remained was sent to the mint to be melted down into gold and silver coins.

There was simply not enough income to cover the painfully high expenses of war. "The receipts are so short of the issue," wrote Robert Cecil, "that my hair stands upright to think of it." It was not only that the costs of government were greatly swollen by bills for weaponry and military provisions, and by the unending demands for soldiers' pay, it was also that severe inflation had caused the actual value of crown revenues to shrink. Parliamentary subsidies were large but inadequate, and when Elizabeth tried to collect on the promissory notes she held from the French and Dutch she had little success. There was nothing for it but to sell crown lands, raise loans and, finally, auction off the heirlooms in the Jewel House.

If the queen was in want the men of the court who looked to her for their livings were fighting to the death for the crumbs from her table. The great fortunes of the 1570s and 1580s were long gone, and the richest courtiers of that era had died greatly in debt to the crown. Hatton left unpaid an immense sum he had borrowed from Elizabeth, and Leicester, however sincerely grieved by his bereaved sovereign, was hardly in his grave before she forced his widow to sell off the contents of his magnificent houses and turn over the proceeds to the royal treasury. Walsingham found at the end that the godly did not invariably prosper; he died so overwhelmed by debt that his coffin had to be hidden away from his creditors, and buried at night.

The "grasping days" of the 1590s clutched at the elegantly ruffed throats of the courtiers and turned their customary greed and acquisitiveness to clawing theft. With trade withered by the war, monopolies were the only route to solvency, and the men in power battled one another for the right to control the sale of soap and leather and wine and starch. That the sale of monopolies led to disastrous inflation for the people at large and to court corruption on a massive scale did not make the system any less appealing to those caught up in it, for if they blamed anything or anyone for the twilight madness of the late Elizabethan economy, they blamed the queen.

It was the old queen's "nearness" with her money, people whispered to one another, that was at the bottom of all the trouble. That, and her damnable spite, which led her to keep men waiting months, even years longer than necessary for appointments or licenses and made her set faction against vicious faction merely for her own amusement. What in a younger ruler they might have admired as political skill they condemned in Elizabeth as an old woman's malice—and to an extent they were right. To the young men at her court she was thrice alien: as sovereign, as female, and as a relic of an earlier, irrecoverably different age and generation. By 1600 they had become "very generally weary of an old woman's government," and were overheard to make "turbulent speeches" calling for a change of reigns.

And in truth, however admirably regal she might seem when appearing in public on Accession Day or the Queen's Birthday, with the fresh young waiting maids around her and the sumptuously attired gentlemen of her guard in her train, Elizabeth was rapidly aging and lapsed at times into slatternly disarray or senile fury.

Usually garish with jeweled coiffure and layers of finery, she sometimes forgot adornment and went "quite disfavored, and unattired." She lost interest in food entirely, even in the sugared sweets she was normally greedy for, and ate only plain bread and soup. No doubt her swollen gums and black teeth gave her much pain, and made chewing a torment.

But it was her black moods that frightened her servants and made the councilors shake their heads and remark that she could not live long. "She walks much in her privy chamber," wrote John Harington, one of the elderly queen's favorites, "and stamps with her feet at ill news, and thrusts her rusty sword at times into the arras in great rage."[1] She always kept a sword beside her now, Harington wrote, for the "evil plots and designs" against her life had become so commonplace that she never felt safe.

The Spanish assassins she had kept such close count of, sent by King Philip, came no more after 1598 when the old king died. But there were others, prompted by revenge or political impatience or lunacy. A desperate military captain with a few sworn companions burst into her private apartments as she sat dining with her ladies; at the last instant, when he was at the threshold of the room where she was sitting, he was captured. In the presence chamber a burly madman, a sailor by profession, drew his dagger and would have plunged it into Elizabeth's heart had the guards not rushed to stop him.

It was no wonder that the frowning queen stamped her feet in rage and lay about her with her rusty sword, for she was closing out her reign as she had begun it, in imminent peril from enemies at home and abroad. France had, as she feared, made peace with Spain in 1598, leaving England completely isolated. Under Essex's supervision, the country was being organized for semi-permanent war, with the county levies brought under the coordinated direction of military superintendents and with new military districts designated. There was talk of compulsory military training for all men aged eighteen to fifty, and there was talk, too, of how much better off the country would be with a bold, vigorous young man to rule it.

He was at hand, that bold young man, and his ill-timed, ill considered bid for power brought to a head all the war weariness and growing popular grievances that blighted the last years of the reign.

Essex, the queen's brilliant, exasperating "Wild Horse," had by the late 1590s outgrown his court offices and was impatient for a new challenge. His breakneck ambition had reached the bursting point, and he felt that his aristocratic, chivalrous spirit was being enervated by the besmirching vulgarities of court politics. His respected enemy, old Cecil, died in 1598 and Essex had no taste for direct combat with Robert Cecil or his allies.

Essex had the rudiments of true nobility: high-heartedness, eloquence, purity of aim and raw courage. Honor, especially his own personal honor, meant a great deal to him and it was an instinct beyond simple arrogance that made him want to keep himself pure from the corrupting influence of ignoble men.

"All the world shall witness," he wrote of his ambitions, "that it is not the breath of me, which is but wind, or the love of the multitude, which burns as tinder, that I hunt after, but either to be valued by her above them that are of no value, or to forget the world and to be forgotten by it."

To be valued by Elizabeth was one thing, to be ruled by her was, for Essex, quite another. The eccentric old queen and the blazing young swordsman confronted one another again and again in a one-sided battle of wills. She invariably won, but he saw each loss as only a temporary setback, and steeled himself for the next encounter. When she struck him at the council table and "bade him get him gone and be hanged," his pride was cut to the quick, and forgetting where he was and whom he threatened, he put his hand to his sword to avenge the insult. He did not strike—others checked him—but with the full force of his outraged manhood he swore that he would never take such treatment from anyone, not even Henry VIII, and left the chamber in a rage.

It was undoubtedly best for all concerned that Essex was allowed early in 1599 to leave court to take on the most galling of England's immediate troubles: the rebellion in Ireland. In the latest and most grave of a series of rebellions Hugh O'Neill, earl of Tyrone, had with Spanish aid so weakened England's hold on Ireland that the situation called for an urgent and heavy counterstroke.

Ireland was a purgatory for common soldiers and commanders alike, a militantly uncivilized region where for many generations the English had tracked the long-haired, treacherous Irish through a quagmire of malarial bogs. Essex set out in the spring of 1599 with an army of reconquest seventeen thousand strong, yet his chance for glory was blighted by the impossible conditions he found once he arrived, as well as by his own mercurial moods and wayward judgment. Six months after he left England he was on his way back, his army reduced to a quarter of its strength and his own fighting fervor quenched by dysentery.

Elizabeth took one look at Essex's muddy face and exhausted body— with typical brashness he had not stopped to think or to wash before rushing into her privy chamber at Nonsuch—and saw that he had become too weak and too unstable to be of further use to her. "An ungovernable beast," she remarked cryptically, "must be stopped of his provender." Essex was tried for misconduct, denied his court offices, and, worst of all, denied the income from his monopolies. More than this the queen dared not do, however, for the hero had grown dangerously popular, and his admirers dangerously numerous and angry.

It was not only that London was full of swaggering swordsmen who toasted Essex and sang ballads about his exploits in the taverns; he had become the cherished idol of the impoverished, embattled populace at large. For the 1590s were a "famine decade," when four successive years of disastrously poor harvests brought the anxious, overtaxed people to the edge of starvation. The number of "poor folks who died for want in the streets" was rising rapidly, and throughout the north and west the years of scarcity led to bread riots and to impassioned outbursts of violence against the royal government. Elizabeth's reign was coming to a close, not with the prosperity and contentment she might have hoped for two decades earlier, but amid groans of hunger and the rancorous shouts of protesters forced, as they said, to feed their children on "dogs, cats and nettle roots." Such people cried for a savior, and with very little provocation they might have been persuaded to follow Essex into rebellion.

When put to the test, however, in February of 1601, their loyalty remained with the queen. Essex, consumed by ambition and maddened by frustration, plotted to seize the court and the Tower, and then to raise the Londoners in rebellion. Elizabeth, forearmed, saw to it that her court was well defended, forcing the earl either to submit or to appeal directly to the people.

He made a hotheaded dash through the London streets, shouting "For the queen! For the queen! A plot is laid for my life!" But though he caused great excitement with his mad alarm, and with the several hundred swordsmen who thundered at his heels, his dash for glory was deadborn. The royal officials were in the streets too, proclaiming Essex a traitor and ordering barricades raised to prevent his passage. Lacking allies on the council, deprived of the income he might have used to finance a civil war, Essex had only his soldierly rabble and the common folk to rely on. These might have been enough, had the rising been carefully timed, but without planning or preparation it could not succeed, and Essex was soon captured and executed.

It was to prove the last crisis of the reign. Disaffection continued, and "turbulent spirits" went on vilifying the queen and wishing her dead, but no new Essex arose to rally them and besides, the next ruler was already hovering over the court like a disembodied spirit waiting to take form.

In Edinburgh, King James VI was "giving it out very constantly but in secret and indirectly that her majesty was sick and in peril." He was Elizabeth's undoubted successor, though no official statement proclaimed him so; his son Prince Henry was referred to as "Prince of Wales" in anticipation of his father's succession. James now played the role that had been Elizabeth's when her sister was queen. There was discreet correspondence between one of his servants and one of Cecil's about the procedure to be followed when the queen died, how the news would be carried north and the new reign proclaimed, with armed men and ordnance brought in to secure the court against any possible disturbance. Courtiers began to send letters and gifts to the Scots king, flattering him and asking to be remembered "when he came into his kingdom." That they should desert the setting for the rising sun was only natural, yet Elizabeth found her subjects' behavior disconcerting and often muttered, *"Mortua sed non sepulta"*—dead but not yet buried—under her breath.

If she showed no remorse over Essex's death it did leave her heavyhearted with regret. She wept for him, and for old Cecil, whose death "often drew tears from her goodly cheeks," as no doubt she wept for the several generations of intimate servants and friends she had outlived. Suddenly, unaccountably, she would burst into tears at the realization of her own mortality, weeping less, perhaps, for the inevitability of death than for the certainty that when it came she would have to face it alone. Essex had been the last of her close companions. Now that he was gone she had no one to confide in, and the thought saddened her.

"A queen's declining," wrote Essex's secretary Sir Henry Wotton, "is commonly even of itself the more umbratious and apprehensive," than that of a king, and in truth all sunsets are misty. Much as Elizabeth fought to keep melancholy at bay there was much to depress her. She had achieved a reputation for greatness, if not for goodness, yet for all her capacity she would bequeath to her successor a distempered and overburdened realm, cankered by an unsound economic system, huge debts, acrimonious religious differences, brutal persecution of Catholics and widespread poverty and misery.

The affection her presence invariably called forth from her excitable subjects still heartened her, yet she knew it to be an insubstantial thing. She was under no illusions about their volatile passions, and she knew that when the time came they would cheer as lustily for King James as they now cheered for her.

The months following Essex's failed rising in 1601 were among Elizabeth's worst. She appeared weakened, physically and emotionally, and contrary to her usual habits she "walked out but little" and "meditated much alone."[2]

She still enjoyed the occasional hospitality of her nobles, however, and Robert Sidney, younger brother of Philip Sidney, described a visit she made to his house in the fall of the year.

It was a progress-time spectacle in miniature. Six drummers and six trumpeters sounded a greeting at her arrival, and the lord and lady of the house stood waiting in their finest garb, he in "goodly stuff of the bravest cut and fashion," she in a purple kirtle fringed with gold. The son of the house made a welcoming speech, to which the queen replied graciously, and then the musicians in the gallery began to play and the women danced for her, making her smile with pleasure. There were refreshments—the queen ate two helpings of sugary cake and drank a cordial from a gold cup—and then the company went outdoors to watch an athletic youth perform "gallant feats" on horseback, mounting and dismounting with agile leaps and charging with a lance.

It was a happy afternoon for Elizabeth, who had herself dressed in a rich velvet gown for the occasion and sat contentedly on an improvised throne while the festivities went on around her. It pleased her that the women dancers stepped out of their order and came up one by one to curtsy to her before resuming their places again, and if she did not join them in the dancing she did feel energetic enough to tour the house. She was "much wearied in walking about" from room to room, and though the effort tired her and she had to call for a staff to lean on when going up stairs, she announced that she wanted to come back another day.

She shone in full glory a few weeks later when in the crowded council chamber at Whitehall she made her last and most heartwarming speech to the Commons, closing out an embittered parliamentary session in which she had lost ground politically. She thanked the members for their loyalty and love, and spoke a little of her troubles ("To be a king and wear a crown is a thing more glorious to them that see it, than it is pleasant to them that bear it"). She assured them of her continued commitment to their welfare. "There will never queen sit in my seat," she told them, "with more zeal to my country, care for my subjects, and that will sooner with willingness venture her life for your good and safety, than myself. For it is my desire to live nor reign no longer than my life and reign shall be for your good."

As always, she moved them by her straightforward eloquence—though she spoke indistinctly now, and her voice was the high, shrill voice of old age—and even more by her presence. There she was, a withered spinster nearing seventy, boasting that God had given her "a heart that yet never feared any foreign or home enemy"; it was enough to make the most recalcitrant of her political opponents want to lay down his life for her. The boast she made had immediacy to it, for there was a Spanish occupation force in Ireland five thousand strong. It was not inconceivable that the queen might yet have to heft her rusty sword and brandish it against the enemy.

But if her heart was still stout the old queen's legs were weak, and growing weaker. At the opening of Parliament, walking in procession in all her heavy robes, she suddenly became unsteady on her feet and would have fallen "if some gentlemen had not suddenly cast themselves under that side that tottered, and supported her."[3] After she had ridden on horseback for a mile or two her legs would become numb, forcing her to dismount and to call her footmen over to massage them; their "earnest rubbing" eventually restored her circulation so that she could go on.[4]

"Lord bless her, lord keep her, lord lengthen her days," the balladmongers sang, and to this Elizabeth added a fervent amen. She was in no hurry to die, and the days as they passed were all too short. The unending work of government went far to fill them. Cecil was always at hand with his stacks of papers, and there was much to read if she was to maintain her reputation as "a great princess who knows everything." Her active intellect strove on, always returning to the classics she had first studied with Ascham so many years before.

She read and reread, translated and retranslated, finding in the Greek and Latin writers much that was enduring, if not eternal. Seneca suited her forthright, fatalistic philosophical stance. "It is best to suffer that thou canst not mend," read her translation of one of his letters. "In this rotten bower our life we must lead." "It is no delighting thing to live, for so thou enterest into a long journey, where sometimes thou must needs slip and then up again, and so sometimes thou fallest, often times art wearied, and driven to cry out."

Such heavyhanded sentiments suited Elizabeth's mind and temperament. She distrusted subtlety—though no one of her generation was more capable of appreciating it—and turned to Seneca's morose truisms with a sense of relief. For the exquisite complexities of contemporary theology she had no patience whatever, though she read the works of Augustine and Jerome with "great pleasure." Religious disputes seemed to her as fruitless as they were murderous. "If there were two princes in Christendom who had goodwill and courage it would be easy to reconcile the differences in religion," she told De Maisse, "for there was only one Jesus Christ and one faith, and all the rest that they disputed about but trifles."[5]

Though as an old woman Elizabeth presided over a cultural flowering as brilliant as any in European history it would be a distortion to imagine that she had more than a minor role in it. As queen she patronized poets and playwrights both actively and passively; she protected them when they were threatened by repressive forces and she was proud to read and attend their plays. But they belonged to the coming generation, not to hers; their effulgent virility was at odds with the reassuring verities she sought in the texts of her youth. Shakespeare besought her to rail against fortune; Seneca taught her to accept it, and to soldier cheerfully on. "An evil soldier is he who with sighs follows his captain. Wherefore let us take our charge not like the grudging sluggard, but as the joyful man, nor let us leave this course of fair workmanship, in which all our sufferance is well engraven."[6]

In her long last years Elizabeth slogged on with the determination of a footsore man-at-arms, rousing herself time and again from dark thoughts and casting off physical frailties with a revitalizing burst of vigor. A visitor to Hampton Court caught a revealing glimpse of her in a small chamber, alone save for one attendant, "dancing the Spanish Panic to whistle and tabor." Not realizing that she was being observed, the old queen was tossing her head and stamping her feet with crazy abandon, beating out a measure in defiance of time and death.

35

Weepe, little isle, and for thy Mistris death
Swim in a double sea of brackish waters:
Weepe little world, weepe for great Elizabeth;
Daughter of warre, for Mars himself begate her,
Mother of peace, for she bore the latter.
She was and is, what can there more be said,
In earth the first, in heaven the second Maid.

It seemed as if the old queen would go on forever. Day after day she roused herself and set off on long, vigorous walks in her gardens and hunting parks, tiring out with her brisk pace the attendants who marched unwillingly at her heels. She took "great walks out of the park, and round the park," striding as energetically "as though she were eighteen years old," and if it happened to be raining or windy, or if there were frost on the ground, so much the better. Her advisers watched her in wry disbelief, her tall, wiry figure bent against the wind, her voluminous skirts whipping around her, knowing they could not dissuade her from her resolute exercise no matter what they said.

Her physicians said, simply, that if old age did not soon kill her, all this exertion would. Yet the physicians came and went—Elizabeth buried five or six of them in her last years—while she went strenuously on, taking a perverse pleasure in the way her arduous regimen disconcerted everyone around her.

With the weather "passing foul," the court was moving from Hampton Court to London. A September storm was blowing, with drenching rain bouncing off the canvas-covered wagons and the roadways a mire of potholes. The queen insisted on making the journey to London on horseback, as she usually did.

"It is not meet for one of your majesty's years to ride in such a storm," young Hunsdon told her gravely. (His father, Elizabeth's cousin and lord chamberlain, had died in 1596.) He did not add, though another courtier did in a private letter, that she was "scarce able to sit upright" at the time.

Elizabeth glared angrily at her relative. "My years!" she called out. "Maids, to your horses quickly!" Before anyone could stop her the queen mounted and rode off, and did not stop until she had reached the capital. Hunsdon was in disgrace for two days.

It was part stunt, part pure contrariness. Elizabeth had always enjoyed doing what people told her she could not do, and now that she was elderly it pleased her to surpass in physical vigor men and women half her age. But it was partly the result, too, of a strong instinct for self-preservation. She had always had her own ideas about medicine (she avoided it) and doctors (she distrusted them). The physicians advised rest and conservation of strength, yet she knew she had always thrived on combativeness and churning activity, and if her feats of endurance sometimes left her panting and prostrate, they seemed to energize her as well.

There was, in addition, a grim political purpose behind her relentless exertions. She knew well that King James—along with all the other monarchs of Europe, and all her enemies abroad—received word of her every faltering step, her every bout of pain or indisposition. Every hint of weakness made the vultures swoop lower. (In Scotland, it was said there was "no talk but England, England, of which they think to make havoc, and every man to be a gentleman with the spoil of the English."[1]) There had to be news of another sort to contradict the accounts of feebleness, so Elizabeth set about making herself look conspicuously strong.

So she walked, and rode, and hunted as often as she could, and danced with foreign envoys "to show that she is not so old as some would have her."[2] She drove out in her jewel-encrusted coach, the manes and tails of the horses dyed as orange as her own false hair, and waved and called out to the people she passed with vigorous graciousness. To impress visitors from abroad she paraded in her privy gardens, elegantly dressed and with a fashionable mask covering her face, then lowered her mask and her neckline to reveal her much-faded handsomeness and snow-white skin. ("Even in old age," wrote a German nobleman who saw her in 1602, "she did not look ugly, when seen from a distance.") She never failed to appear when her public expected her to, at the weddings of her courtiers, at the tilts and other celebrations marking her Accession Day, on feast days and other formal occasions. For her to miss the "preaching, singing, shooting, ringing and running" of the Accession Day celebrations would have been seen as a sad foreshadowing of imminent death, and even though her last

Accession Day in 1602 was marred by suspicion of an assassination attempt, she changed her route to avoid the danger and made her appearance as scheduled.

That November 17 was, in fact, the brightest in recent years. The harvest had been bountiful, Lord Mountjoy, Essex's successor as commander in Ireland, had beaten the invading Spaniards and checked Tyrone, and the plague, which had been virulent in the summer months, had receded. Londoners ran to see the queen, endured a dull sermon at Paul's Cross, and applauded the host of young men who ran recklessly against one another in the tiltyard. The queen was "very merry" when a fool appeared riding a horse no bigger than a dog, and as always she took keen pleasure in the bear-baiting. A swindler caused a commotion by selling a great many tickets for a play to be staged that day, then disappearing with the money. When the theatergoers arrived to find no play in progress, they took their revenge by tearing the tapestries from the walls and breaking the chairs and generally "making great spoil." But somehow the vandalism was absorbed in the mayhem of merrymaking, and the day ended joyously.

To an extent the queen's effort to appear forceful and vigorous succeeded. "Her majesty is very well," reported one court-watcher, "and exceedingly disposed to hunting, for every second or third day she is on horseback, and continues the sport long." Another praised her "health and disposition of body," and said he "had not seen her every way better disposed these many years." Yet among those close to her there were always informers ready to tell how, in truth, an hour's riding so enervated Elizabeth that she had to stay in bed for two days afterward, or how often pain in her arm or weakness in her legs made it impossible for her to try to ride at all. She had to take naps during the day to keep up her strength, and even so she was often exhausted, for the sheer effort of appearing to be vigorous was taking as high a toll as the exercise itself.

In the midst of the Christmas celebrations at the end of the year, Harington found the queen in a "pitiable state." She was sadly in decline, yet she was dying by inches, in an attenuated misery that was as much mental as physical. She continued to govern, he noted, despite failing eyesight and increasing absentmindedness; she shouted hoarsely at her servants for forgetting things, when in fact it was she who had forgotten, and she sometimes sent for her officers, then reacted with fury to see that they had arrived, as she thought, unbidden.[3]

Cecil and the others managed her as best they could. In their letters they cautioned one another against letting her read dispatches containing bad news at night, when it might worsen her insomnia and so make her impossible the next day, and on occasion they misrepresented the true state of affairs in small ways in order to quieten her anxieties. Cecil kept up the gallant tradition in his dealings with her, complimenting her, flattering her vanity. The parchment she wrote on, he declared, was the sweeter for the touch of her hand; he praised "the life of her eyes and color of her lips," the one ruby, the other crystalline topaz.[4] Yet his admiration for her statesmanship was sincere, and as her reign drew to its close he gave some thought to the "memory to be left to all ages" of her papers. Among the records of her rule, he wrote, were to be found the remains of "more piety, learning and dolceness [sweetness] than ever prince did leave behind him." It must have saddened him, as it did Harington, to see her bent over her letters and warrants, squinting vainly in the firelight to make out their words, and then to watch her scribble her name at the bottom, her once fine handwriting now crabbed and spidery.

Early in 1603 Elizabeth caught cold, and on January 21 the court moved to Richmond, as rain poured down, for the duration of the unusually severe winter. The dark skies and harsh storms worsened the queen's cold to bronchitis and, along with the death of her kinswoman the countess of Nottingham, lowered her spirits alarmingly.

"The queen loved the countess well," wrote a foreign envoy who had come to join the deathwatch, "and hath much lamented her death, remaining ever since in a deep melancholy that she must die herself."[5]

She had entered her seventieth year, and her body was protesting its burden in a dozen ways. Her head ached, her bones ached, the rheum in her arm made it painfully tender, she had a cough and suffered from a "continual cold in her legs." Food and drink had lost their savor for her completely, and she could no longer escape from her miseries in sleep, for she was wakeful and fretful at all hours of the day and night. She had always enjoyed coming to Richmond, calling it "a warm winter box for her old age," but now, as she fretted out the long night watches in sleepless anxiety, she took no comfort from her surroundings.

Worst of all her ailments was the heavyheartedness that had become nearly inescapable. She sat on the floor, embroidered cushions under her, staring at one spot for hours at a time, her motionlessness relieved only by noisy sighs and bouts of crying.

Her usefulness had ended, and she no longer had the will to rouse herself from the listless sadness that immobilized her. From time to time she "raged exceedingly" at ministers who demanded money and at her nemesis Tyrone, who had managed to turn defeat to his advantage and to force the angry, humiliated queen to pardon him. But for the most part her "notable decay of judgment and memory" prevented her from attending to the tasks of rule.

"She cannot abide discourses of government and state," it was said, "but delighteth to hear old Canterbury tales, to which she is very attentive."[6] She would see Cecil, but was unpredictable about receiving anyone else; "impatient and testy," she often sent others away.

It injured her greatly that, now that her death was close at hand, her servants and officials grew lax in obeying her and paid as little attention to her as if she were dead already. She was "very much neglected," wrote the bishop of Carlisle, "which was an occasion of her melancholy." To many, especially her "long-worn, threadbare, poor old servants," she was of interest chiefly for the possessions she would leave behind when the end finally came. What would become of her jewels, the rich furnishings of her apartments, her hundreds of gowns and perfumed gloves and swansdown fans? Would the new king bestow these treasures on Elizabeth's long-suffering, long underpaid servants, or would he take them for his wife? (Surely not, the gossip went; James and his queen were on distant terms at best, and it was rumored that he would have had her imprisoned if his councilors had not dissuaded him.)

"All are in a dump at court," an observer wrote. "Some fear present danger, others doubt she will not continue past the month of May, but generally all are of opinion that she cannot overpass another winter." The courtiers were nearly as fretful as the elderly queen, kept indoors by bad weather and forced into anxious inactivity by the deadlock in political affairs. Business and careers came to a standstill at Richmond, while as the long weeks passed the palace began to reek more and more strongly of unwashed bodies and unwashed floors.

In the first days of March the queen's symptoms became more severe, and made her so "full of chagrin and weary of life" that she refused to swallow the hated medicines her physicians urged on her and sank into a coma-like lassitude. She would not struggle to live, but she would not go to bed and die either. She sat on her cushions, aware yet fatally indifferent to her surroundings, not speaking, not eating, not changing her clothes. A swelling in her throat broke open, choking her with fluid and leaving her prostrate "like a dead person," but the doctors "found means to dry it up well," and the crisis passed.

It was a long, slow, wearying death, without drama or color—a death out of keeping with Elizabeth's flamboyant life. Glassy-eyed and emaciated, she lingered on amid her cushions, her body malodorous from disease, her finger in her mouth like an idiot or a dazed child. Finally, on the twenty-first of March, she did not resist the suggestion that she take off her soiled clothes and get into bed.

It may have been word of this significant event that caused fears of a "commotion" among the nervous men and women of the court. With the queen in her deathbed it was time to take refuge against whatever trouble was coming. The council had fortified the palace and, in London, had begun to amass wheat in the storehouses to ensure against bread riots. The military danger, if it should come, would be from the north, where King James was said to have fourteen thousand mounted men ready to put into the field. London's defenses were strengthened by a wide ditch dug around its northern perimeter and on eastward to Westminster, though the city's best defense, it seemed, might be its worst affliction. Plague had broken out in both the city and suburbs, and was spreading so rapidly, and so early in the year, that the contagion promised to be far worse than any in memory.

They put the queen to bed in her high wooden bed with its ornate beasts and gilded plumes, covering her with embroidered sheets and laying her bony head on a silken pillow. She was greatly wasted from lack of food, but apart from a little broth, ate nothing, and continued her dulled vigil by turning on her side and ceasing to speak or to look at anyone. Alone despite the others in the room, her last thoughts shrouded in enigmatic silence, the great queen sank toward death.

There was a murmur of voices in the room as meditations and prayers were read; outside it, and in the realm at large, preachers had been instructed to pray for Elizabeth, "that she might be strengthened in weakness, her grief assuaged, her mind purified, and her health restored."[7] At the name of Jesus and when Archbishop Whitgift, who was with her, spoke of heaven she seemed to brighten fleetingly with hope, and hugged his hand. Within hours of going to bed she found she could not speak, and had to indicate by lifting her hand and eyes to heaven that she had full faith in her salvation "by Christ's merits and mercy only."

It was her last gesture. Late in the evening of March 23 she went to sleep, and her favorite chaplain, Dr. Parry, watched over her. In the corridor outside the bedchamber the chief servants and dignitaries paced back and forth, waiting for word to reach them. A horse stood in the outer courtyard, saddled and ready for its rider, who would set off northward as soon as the announcement was made to carry the news of the queen's death to King James. There was "great weeping and lamentation among the lords and ladies" when several hours later Dr. Parry, perceiving that the end had come and beginning earnestly to pray for the queen's soul, indicated that she was dead.

The word was passed, the rider mounted, and then the sound of galloping hoofbeats echoed through the rainy night.

Notes

ABBREVIATIONS

Burghley Papers

A Collection of State Papers Relating to Affairs in the Reigns of King Henry VIII, King Edward VI, Queen Mary, and Queen Elizabeth . . . left by William Cecil Lord Burghley, and now remaining at Hatfield House, ed. Samuel Haynes and William Murdin. 2 vols. London: William Bowyer, 1740–59.

EHR

English Historical Review

L.P.

Letters and Papers, Foreign and Domestic, of the Reign of Henry VIII, ed. J.S. Brewer, R.H. Brodie and James Gairdner. 21 vols. London: Her Majesty's Stationery Office, 1862–1910.

Relations politiques

Kervyn de Lettenhove, Joseph M.B.C. and L. Gilliodts van Severen, eds., *Relations politiques des Pays-Bas et de l'Angleterre, sous le règne de Philippe II.* 11 vols. Brussels: P. Hayez, 1882–1900.

Salisbury MSS.

Calendar of the Manuscripts of the Most Hon. the Marquis of Salisbury . . . preserved at Hatfield House, Hertfordshire. 23 vols. in 19. London: Her Majesty's Stationery Office, 1883–1973.

Sp. Cal.

Calendar of Letters, Despatches, and State Papers, relating to the Negotiations between England and Spain, preserved in the Archives at Vienna, Simancas, Besançon and Brussels, ed. Pascual de Gayangos, G.A. Bergenroth, Martin A.S. Hume, Royall Tyler, and Garrett Mattingly. 13 vols. London: His and Her Majesty's Stationery Office, 1862–1954.

Sp. Cal. Elizabethan

Calendar of Letters and State Papers relating to English Affairs, preserved principally in the Archives of Simancas, ed. Martin A.S. Hume. 4 vols. London: Her Majesty's Stationery Office, 1892–1899.

State Papers, Domestic   *Calendar of State Papers, Domestic Series, of the Reigns of Edward VI, Mary, Elizabeth and James I, preserved in the State Paper Department of Her Majesty's Public Record Office*, ed. Robert Lemon and Mary A. E. Green. 12 vols. London: Longman, etc., 1856–1872.

State Papers, Foreign, Elizabeth   *Calendar of State Papers, Foreign Series, of the Reign of Elizabeth, preserved in the State Paper Department of Her Majesty's Public Record Office*, ed. Joseph Stevenson et al., 23 vols. in 26. London: Longman, etc., 1863–1950.

Ven. Cal.   *Calendar of State Papers and Manuscripts, relating to English Affairs, existing in the Archives and Collections of Venice, and in Other Libraries of Northern Italy*, ed. Rawdon Brown et al., 38 vols. in 40. London: Longman, etc., 1864–1947.

References to *L.P.*, *Sp. Cal.* and similar collections are to page numbers, not document numbers.

PART ONE

The Improbable Child

CHAPTER 1

1. *L.P.* V, 592.
2. *L.P.* VI, 412, 420.
3. *Ibid.*, 450.
4. *Sp. Cal.* IV:ii:ii, 923.
5. *Ibid.*, 788.

CHAPTER 2

1. *L.P.* VI, 684.
2. *Ibid.* VII, 360.
3. *Ibid.* VI, 658.
4. *Ibid.*, 604, 618.
5. *Ibid.*, 610.
6. *Ibid.*, 629.
7. *L.P.* VII, 424–5.
8. *Ibid.* VIII, 172–3.
9. *Ibid.* IX, 189.
10. *Ibid.* VII, 191.
11. *Ibid.* VIII, 297.
12. *Ibid.*, 204.
13. *Sp. Cal.* V:ii, 39.
14. *L.P.* X, 361–2, 359–60.

CHAPTER 3

1. *L.P.* VIII, 157.
2. *Ibid.* X, 356.
3. *Ibid.*, 380.
4. *Ibid.*, 381.
5. *Ibid.*, 433.
6. *Ibid.*, 380.
7. *Ibid.*, 466.
8. *Ven. Cal.* VI:iii, 1538.
9. *L.P.* X, 104, 339.
10. *Ibid.*, 135.

11. *Ibid.* XI, 346.
12. *Ibid.* X, 377.
13. *Ibid.* XI, 17.
14. *Ibid.* X, 357.
15. *Ibid.*, 333.
16. *Ibid.*, 380, 378. Modern historians concur in finding Anne's guilt an imponderable issue, though one not lightly to be dismissed.
17. *Ibid.* X, 401.
18. *Ibid.*, 371, 382.
19. *Ibid.* XI, 90; Agnes Strickland, *Lives of the Queens of England*, 6 vols. (London, 1873), III, 5–7.
20. *L.P.* XI, 130, 104.
21. *Ibid.*, 202.

CHAPTER 4

1. *L.P.* XIV:i, 507, 515.
2. Strickland, III, 32, citing MSS. Lansd. 1236 f. 35.
3. *L.P.* XIV:ii, 257.
4. Lu Emily Pearson, *Elizabethans at Home* (Palo Alto, 1957), pp. 187–8.
5. *L.P.* VI, 629.
6. *Ibid.* VIII, 101.
7. Cited in Pearson, pp. 183, 186, 190.
8. Roger Ascham, *The Scholemaster*, in *English Works*, ed. William Aldis Wright (Cambridge, 1904), p. 210.
9. Cited in Pearson, pp. 208–9, 191.
10. *Ibid.*, 191, 189.
11. *L.P.* XIV:i, 5; *L.P.* XV, 1.
12. John Nichols, *The Progresses and Public Processions of Queen Elizabeth*, new ed., 3 vols. (London, 1823; reprint New York, 1969), I, x note.
13. M. St. Clare Byrne, *Elizabethan Life in Town and Country* (London, 1954), pp. 208–9; Pearson, p. 182.
14. Ascham, *Scholemaster*, p. 200.
15. *L.P.* XV, 391.
16. *Ibid.*, 636.
17. *Ibid.* XVII, 66.
18. *Ibid.* XVII, 66; *L.P.* XV, 519.

CHAPTER 5

1. *L.P.* XIV:i, 53.
2. *Ibid.* XVIII:ii, 283.
3. *Ibid.*, 115.
4. Frank A. Mumby, *The Girlhood of Queen Elizabeth: A Narrative in Contemporary Letters* (London, 1909), pp. 22–3. There seems to be no evidence to support the often repeated presumption that this period of separation was the result of some misbehavior on Elizabeth's part.
5. *The Whole Works of Roger Ascham*, ed. J. A. Giles, 3 vols. (London, 1864–5; reprint New York, 1965), I:i, 108. For Ascham's life see Lawrence V. Ryan, *Roger Ascham* (Palo Alto and London, 1963).
6. J. E. Neale, *Queen Elizabeth I* (London, 1934; reprint 1952), pp. 23–4; Strickland, III, 225–6.
7. Nichols, *Progresses*, I, x note.
8. Nicholas Udall, preface to *Paraphrases of St. John's Gospel*, cited in G. Ballard, *Memoirs of Several Ladies of Great Britain* (London, 1752), p. 127.
9. Anthony Martienssen, *Queen Katherine Parr* (New York and London, 1973), p. 227.

PART TWO
God's Virgin

CHAPTER 6

1. *Burghley Papers*, I, 100.
2. *Ibid.*, 98.
3. *Ibid.*, 70.
4. W. K. Jordan, *Edward VI* (London, 1968–70), II, 18.
5. *Sp. Cal.* IX, 46–7.
6. Jordan, II, 422.
7. The Good Duke is reassessed in M. L. Bush, *The Government Policy of Protector Somerset* (London, 1975).
8. Ascham, *Whole Works*, I:i, lvi–lvii.
9. For what follows see *Burghley Papers*, I, 99–100.
10. *Burghley Papers*, I, 99.
11. *Ibid.*, 99–100.
12. Martienssen, p. 24, citing Vives, *De Institutione Foeminae Christianae*.
13. *Ibid.*, 24–5.
14. *Burghley Papers*, I, 96.

CHAPTER 7

1. *Burghley Papers*, I, 96. "As I remember," Thomas Parry deposed later, "this was the cause why she was sent from the queen; or else that her grace parted from the queen. I do not perfectly remember whether of both she [Ashley] said, she went of herself, or was sent away."
2. *Ibid.*, 101.
3. Ascham, *Scholemaster*, p. 261.
4. *Apologia . . . pro caena Dominica*, cited in Ryan, p. 96.
5. Ascham, *Whole Works*, I:i, lii–liii.
6. Mumby, pp. 69–72.
7. *Ibid.*, 35–6.
8. *Ibid.*, 37.
9. *Burghley Papers*, I, 103–4.
10. Cited in Martienssen, p. 239.
11. *Burghley Papers*, I, 82.
12. *Ibid.*
13. *Ibid.*, 105.
14. *Sp. Cal.* IX, 346–7. Their vehement disavowal of such backing after Seymour's apprehension suggests their involvement, as does the fact that the French king was closely informed of the admiral's activities. The messenger who brought him news of Seymour's arrest "broke one of his ribs in haste."
15. *Burghley Papers*, I, 80.
16. *L.P.* XXI:ii, 320–2.
17. *Burghley Papers*, I, 96.
18. *Ibid.*
19. *Ibid.*, 100.
20. *Ibid.*, 102.
21. *Ibid.*, 101.
22. *Sp. Cal.* IX, 340. Paget's remark may be the source of the apocryphal comment attributed by the fanciful historian Leti to Elizabeth on Seymour's death: "This day died a man of much wit and very little judgment."

CHAPTER 8

1. *Burghley Papers*, I, 70.
2. *Ibid.*, 70–71.
3. *Ibid.*, 72.
4. This story had a very long life. A version of it was still being told on the continent in 1601.
5. Henry Clifford, *The Life of Jane Dormer, Duchess of Feria* (London, 1887), p. 86.

6. *Burghley Papers,* I, 89–90.
7. *Ibid.,* 94–5.
8. *Ibid.,* 89, 102.
9. *Ibid.,* 106–7.
10. *Ibid.,* 108.
11. Mumby, pp. 55–9.
12. John Aylmer, *A Harbor for True and Faithful Subjects,* cited in Strickland, III, 38–9.
13. *Sp. Cal.* IX, 489.
14. *Ibid.,* X, 6–7.
15. *Salisbury MSS,* I, 60.
16. Jordan, II, 20.

CHAPTER 9

1. *Sp. Cal.* X, 186.
2. *Ibid.,* 209.
3. *The Chronicle and Political Papers [of Edward VI],* ed. W.K. Jordan (London, 1966), p. 71.
4. Viscount Strangford, ed., *Household Expenses of the Princess Elizabeth during her Residence at Hatfield October 1, 1551 to September 30, 1552.* In *The Camden Miscellany,* Vol. II. Camden Society, Old series, LV (London, 1853).
5. Ascham, *Whole Works,* I:i, 175–6; Ryan, p. 112.
6. *Sp. Cal.* X, xxvii, and 114–15.
7. *Ibid.,* 215–16.
8. Jordan, II, 87, 102.
9. Frederick Chamberlin, *The Private Character of Henry VIII* (New York, 1931), pp. 243–4; Jordan, II, 133–4.
10. Jordan, II, 494, 497.
11. *Sp. Cal.* XI, 54–5.

CHAPTER 10

1. *Sp. Cal.* XI, 228.
2. John G. Nichols, ed., *Literary Remains of Edward VI* (London, 1857; reprint New York, 1963), I, cxl.
3. Years later Cecil told his clerk John Clapham that Elizabeth had been in love with Courtenay, and that he was in fact the only man she had ever wanted to marry. John Clapham, *Elizabeth of England; certain observations concerning the life and reign of Queen Elizabeth,* ed. Evelyn and Conyers Read (Philadelphia, 1951), p. 68.
4. *Sp. Cal.* XI, 252–3.
5. John G. Nichols, ed., *The Chronicle of Queen Jane, and of Two Years of Queen Mary* . . . Camden Society, Old series, XLVIII (London, 1850), 69.
6. *Sp. Cal.* XII, 55ff.
7. *The Acts and Monuments of John Foxe,* ed. George Townsend and A.R. Cattley, 8 vols. (London, 1837–41), VI, 414.
8. Patrick Fraser Tytler, *England Under the Reigns of Edward VI and Mary,* 2 vols. (London, 1838), II, 310–11; Mumby, 107–8; Chamberlin, *Private Character of Henry VIII,* 45–8.

CHAPTER 11

1. Neale, *Elizabeth I and Her Parliaments* (London, 1953–1957), I, 148.
2. Tytler, II, 320, 337–8.
3. *Ibid.,* 340–1; *Holinshed's Chronicles of England, Scotland and Ireland,* 6 vols. (London, 1807–8), IV, 56.
4. Tytler, II, 342.
5. Foxe, *Acts and Monuments,* VIII, 607ff.
6. *Ibid.,* VIII, 609.

CHAPTER 12

1. "State Papers Relating to the Custody of the Princess Elizabeth at Woodstock in 1554," ed. Rev. C. R. Manning, in *Norfolk Archaeology,* IV (Norwich, 1855), 176.

2. Tytler, II, 371–2.
3. *Ibid.*, II, 343–4; *Ambassades de messieurs de Noailles en Angleterre*, 5 vols. (Leyden, 1763), III, 95–103.
4. Tytler, II, 366–7.
5. *Ibid.*, II, 415, 396, 367, 405.
6. *Ibid.*, II, 398–9.
7. "State Papers . . . Woodstock," p. 206.
8. Ian Dunlop, *Palaces and Progresses of Elizabeth I* (London, 1962), pp. 16–17.
9. *Ibid.*, 13ff.
10. Nichols, *Progresses*, I, 9–10 note.
11. *Ibid.*, I, 9–10.
12. *Ibid.*, I, 10–11.
13. "State Papers . . . Woodstock," p. 142.
14. *Ibid.*, 176–7.
15. *Ibid.*, 169, 172–3.
16. *Ibid.*, 170, 166, 169.
17. *Ibid.*, 175–6, 179, 182–3.
18. *Ibid.*, 192–3.
19. *Ibid.*, 224–5.

CHAPTER 13

1. *Sp. Cal.* XIII, 135.
2. *Ibid.*, 169; *Ven. Cal.* VI:i, 60–61.
3. *Sp. Cal.* XIII, 145.
4. *Ven. Cal.* VI:ii, 1059.
5. *Ibid.*, 1058–9.
6. *Ibid.*, 1059.
7. *Ibid.*
8. *Ibid.*
9. Carolly Erickson, *Bloody Mary* (New York, 1978), p. 420.
10. *Ven. Cal.* VI:i, 57.
11. Erickson, *Bloody Mary*, p. 413, and sources cited there.

CHAPTER 14

1. *Ven. Cal.* VI:ii, 1059.
2. Peter J. French, *John Dee: The World of an Elizabethan Magus* (London, 1972), pp. 34–5. It is unclear just how Dee came to make the astrological calculations that endangered him.
3. Ascham, *Whole Works*, I:ii, 443–8.
4. *Ibid.*
5. Frederick Chamberlin, *The Private Character of Queen Elizabeth* (New York, 1922), p. 22.
6. Ascham, *Whole Works*, I:ii, 447.
7. *Ven. Cal.* VI:i, 417–18.
8. *Ibid.*
9. Erickson, *Bloody Mary*, pp. 436–7.
10. *Ven. Cal.* VI:i, 479–80.
11. *Ibid.* VI:ii, 484; on the Pope forgeries see Herbert E. D. Blakiston, "Thomas Warton and Machyn's Diary," *EHR* (April 1896), 282–300.
12. *Ven. Cal.* VI:i, 559.
13. *Sp. Cal.* XIII, 238.
14. *Ibid.*, 90.
15. *Ven. Cal.* VI:ii, 1079 and note, 1081 note.
16. *Ibid.*, 1080.
17. *Ibid.* French agents in England were reporting that her jaundice and shortness of breath were likely to be fatal.
18. *Ven. Cal.* VI:iii, 1538.
19. *Sp. Cal.* XIII, 293.
20. Cited in J. E. Neale, "The Accession of Queen Elizabeth I," *History Today*, III, No. 5 (May 1953), 295.

21. *Ven. Cal.* VI:ii, 1058.
22. *Sp. Cal.* XIII, xvi.
23. *Ibid.*, 379.
24. Neale, "Accession," pp. 295–6.
25. *Ven. Cal.* VI:iii, 1563.
26. *Relations politiques*, I, 280–1. On this document see Conyers Read, *Mr. Secretary Cecil and Queen Elizabeth* (New York, 1961), p. 479 notes 2–3.
27. *Ven. Cal.* VI:iii, 1549.

PART THREE

"La Plus Fine Femme du Monde"

CHAPTER 15

1. John Hayward, *Annals of the First Four Years of the Reign of Queen Elizabeth*, ed. John Bruce. Camden Society, Old series, VII (London, 1840), 6.
2. *State Papers, Foreign, Elizabeth*, I, 21, 28, 101.
3. Neville Williams, "The Coronation of Queen Elizabeth I," *Quarterly Review*, CCXCI, No. 597 (July 1953), 398–401.
4. *State Papers, Foreign, Elizabeth*, I, 7. In 1585 or so the number of Elizabeth's personal guard was reported to be about two hundred.
5. *Ibid.*, I, 6.
6. Read, *Mr. Secretary Cecil*, p. 124.
7. *Sp. Cal. Elizabethan*, I, 12, 10.
8. *Ibid.*, I, 12, 10, 8, 7.
9. *Ibid.*, I, 7, 17–18.
10. *Ibid.*, I, 13.
11. *Salisbury MSS*, I, 158.
12. R. B. Wernham, *Before the Armada: The Emergence of the English Nation, 1485–1588* (New York, 1966), p. 237.
13. *State Papers, Foreign, Elizabeth*, I, 209. In his letter Knox ruefully admitted that his "First Blast had blown from him all his friends in England."
14. Nichols, *Progresses*, I, 38. This account of Elizabeth's coronation is drawn primarily from the most reliable contemporary English account, printed in Nichols, I, 38ff and from *Ven. Cal.* VII, 12ff.

CHAPTER 16

1. *Sp. Cal. Elizabethan*, I, 57–8.
2. *Ven. Cal.* VII, 105; *Sp. Cal. Elizabethan*, I, 112.
3. Victor von Klarwill, ed., *Queen Elizabeth and Some Foreigners* (New York, 1928), p. 157.
4. *Ibid.*
5. *Ibid.*, 113–15.
6. *Sp. Cal. Elizabethan*, I, 68, 57–8.
7. *Ibid.*, I, 57, 75.
8. *Ven. Cal.* VII, 27, 80–1, 84; Philip Hughes, *The Reformation in England*, 3 vols. (New York, 1951–4), III, 28–9 and notes.
9. *State Papers, Foreign, Elizabeth*, I, 152–3.
10. *Sp. Cal. Elizabethan*, I, 51.
11. *Ven. Cal.* VII, 91.
12. Nichols, *Progresses*, I, 69–73.
13. Klarwill, pp. 120–1.
14. *Sp. Cal. Elizabethan*, I, 67.
15. *Ibid.*, I, 74.
16. *Ibid.*, I, 95ff, 107.
17. *Ibid.*, I, 119, 110, 101–2. *Burghley Papers*, I, 212.
18. Klarwill, pp. 98, 99, 157.
19. *Sp. Cal. Elizabethan*, I, 141.

CHAPTER 17

1. Read, *Mr. Secretary Cecil*, p. 199.
2. *Sp. Cal. Elizabethan*, I, 175.
3. *Ibid.*, I, 175, 113.
4. *Ibid.*, I, 175.
5. *Burghley Papers*, I, 364.
6. *Ibid.*, 362. One wonders whether any significance ought to be attached to the fact that, within days of writing his letter, Francis Knollys received a large gift of lands from the queen. *State Papers, Domestic*, I, 159.
7. *Burghley Papers*, I, 361–2.
8. *Ibid.*, I, 368. Cecil's minute is undated, but is placed among the documents from fall 1560.
9. Read, *Mr. Secretary Cecil*, p. 202.
10. *Sp. Cal. Elizabethan*, I, 181–2. Frances Brandon, daughter of Henry VIII's sister Mary Tudor and Charles Brandon, had married her steward. Brandon's fourth wife, Catherine, had in her widowhood married a gentleman of her household. Both women were duchesses, and Frances Brandon was in line for the throne.
11. *Ibid.*, 188–9.

CHAPTER 18

1. *Sp. Cal. Elizabethan*, I, 45; Thomas Wright, ed., *Queen Elizabeth and Her Times*, 2 vols. (London, 1838), I, 7–8. The envoys representing the archduke Charles at Elizabeth's court, while pressing for the queen's own consent to marry their candidate, kept Catherine Grey in the background as an alternative should the royal marriage project fail.
2. *Sp. Cal. Elizabethan*, I, 214; Chamberlin, *Private Character of Queen Elizabeth*, pp. 50–51.
3. *Sp. Cal. Elizabethan*, I, 213. On Amy Robsart's death see Ian Aird, "The Death of Amy Robsart," *EHR*, LXXI, No. 278 (January 1956), 69–79 and Elizabeth D'Oyley, "The Death of Amye Robsart," *History Today*, VI, No. 4 (April 1956), 252–60.
4. F. E. Halliday, "Queen Elizabeth I and Doctor Burcot," *History Today*, V, No. 8 (August 1955), 542–4 draws from the seventeenth-century memoirs of Richard Carew an account of Queen Elizabeth's encounter with one Dr. Burcot, a German mining engineer and medical wonder-worker. According to this account, it was Dr. Burcot who cured the queen of smallpox in 1562. But Halliday's inexact chronology mars the plausibility of his argument somewhat, and there are major discrepancies between the course of the queen's illness as described in the later account and the dispatches written by Ambassador De Quadra at the time. Burcot may indeed have treated Elizabeth, but Carew's story cannot be taken as an accurate narrative of that treatment.
   In this reconstruction of the events—whose chronology is somewhat muddled in De Quadra's dispatches—I have relied on *Sp. Cal. Elizabethan*, I, 262ff and in particular the more complete transcriptions in *Relations politiques*, III, 162ff.
5. Chamberlin, *Private Character of Queen Elizabeth*, p. 51.
6. On all the candidates for the throne see Mortimer Levine, *The Early Elizabethan Succession Question, 1558–1568* (Palo Alto, 1966).
7. *Sp. Cal. Elizabethan*, I, 263.

CHAPTER 19

1. *Sp. Cal. Elizabethan*, I, 126.
2. Klarwill, pp. 194, 59.
3. *Ibid.*, 194; *Sp. Cal. Elizabethan*, I, 49.
4. *Memoirs of Sir James Melville*, ed. A. Francis Stewart (New York, 1930), p. 91. Melville's stay at Elizabeth's court in 1564 is well documented in these memoirs, pp. 88ff.
5. Melville, *Memoirs*, p. 92. A formal description of Dudley's elevation is in Nichols, *Progresses*, I, 190–1.
6. *Ibid.*, 82.
7. Cited in Strickland, III, 154.

CHAPTER 20

1. Cited in A. L. Rowse, *The Elizabethan Renaissance, Part 1: The Life of the Society* (London, 1971), p. 134.
2. Allegra Woodworth, "Purveyance for the Royal Household in the Reign of Queen Elizabeth," *Transactions of the American Philosophical Society*, New series, XXXV, Pt. 1 (1945), 3–89.
3. *Ibid.*, 12.
4. *Ibid.*, 13.
5. Dunlop, p. 100.
6. E. K. Chambers, *The Elizabethan Stage*, 4 vols. (Oxford, 1923), I, 15–16 and note.
7. Klarwill, pp. 160, 58.
8. Ascham, *Scholemaster*, p. 207.
9. Klarwill, p. 195.
10. *Ibid.*, 145, 337.

PART FOUR

"A Very Strange Sort of Woman"

CHAPTER 21

1. Wright, I, 331–8. This account of the rebellion comes from Wright, I, 331ff and notes, and Hughes, III, 269–70 and *passim*.
2. *State Papers, Foreign, Elizabeth*, IX, 159, 147; Hughes, III, 269–70.
3. Hughes, III, 247.
4. Wright, I, 331.
5. On Elizabeth's government in the 1560s see Wallace MacCaffrey, *The Shaping of the Elizabethan Regime* (Princeton, 1968).
6. *State Papers, Domestic*, VII, 100.
7. *Ibid.*, VII, 139, 104.
8. *Ibid.*, VII, 114.

CHAPTER 22

1. Hunsdon, Da Silva wrote in 1567, was "not thought much of as a soldier." *Sp. Cal. Elizabethan*, I, 676.
2. *Salisbury MSS*, I, 50.
3. Historians aver that, despite the gossip over Elizabeth's inability to bear children, she was perfectly healthy and able to reproduce. Conyers Read, *Lord Burghley and Queen Elizabeth* (New York, 1960), pp. 210–11; Neale, *Elizabeth I*, pp. 220, 239–40, 244–5; Wernham, p. 259. However, contemporary opinion varied, and rumors were predictably inconsistent. "If my spies do not lie," Feria wrote in 1559, "which I believe they do not, for a certain reason which they have recently given me I understand she will not bear children." In 1561, De Quadra recorded that "the common opinion, confirmed by certain physicians, is that this woman is unhealthy, and it is believed certain that she will not have children, although there is no lack of people who say she has already had some." *Sp. Cal. Elizabethan*, I, 63, 180.
4. Chamberlin, *Private Character of Queen Elizabeth*, pp. 56–7. In February of 1567 the Spanish ambassador Da Silva wrote with tantalizing inexactness that Elizabeth was "apparently well, only she treats her stomach badly." *Sp. Cal. Elizabethan*, I, 615.
5. *Sp. Cal. Elizabethan*, I, 679.
6. Wright, I, 140–1.
7. *Sp. Cal. Elizabethan*, I, 591–2.
8. *Burghley Papers*, I, 444.
9. *Sp. Cal. Elizabethan*, I, 599.

CHAPTER 23

1. The dark side of life in the queen's privy chamber is abundantly illustrated in a letter attributed to Mary Stuart, in *Lettres, Instructions et Mémoires de Marie Stuart, Reine d'Ecosse*, ed. Alexandre Labanoff, 7 vols. (London, 1844), VI, 50–57.

2. *Lettres . . . de Marie Stuart*, VI, 51. It is worth noting a later reference in the same letter to Elizabeth's "having recently ceased menstruating"—a fragment of evidence about her reproductive health. The letter is variously dated 1584 or 1586, though much of its contents are retrospective.
3. *Ibid.*, 54.
4. *The Letters of Queen Elizabeth*, ed. G.B. Harrison (London, 1935, reprinted New York, 1968), p. 52.
5. Nicholas Harris Nicolas, *Memoirs of the Life and Times of Sir Christopher Hatton* (London, 1847), pp. 13–14.
6. Cited in Hughes, III, 261 note.
7. Strickland, III, 207; Nichols, *Progresses*, II, 619 note 1.
8. Conyers Read, "A Letter from Robert, Earl of Leicester, to a Lady," *Huntington Library Bulletin*, No. 9 (April 1936), 17.
9. *Lettres . . . de Marie Stuart*, VI, 52–3.
10. *Ibid.*, 52.
11. Nicolas, *Hatton*, pp. 13–14.
12. Wright, I, 440–1.

CHAPTER 24

1. Roy Strong, "The Popular Celebration of the Accession Day of Queen Elizabeth I," *Journal of the Warburg and Courtauld Institutes*, XXI, Nos. 1–2 (January–June 1958), 91 and *passim*; J. E. Neale, "November 17," in *Essays in Elizabethan History* (London, 1958), 9–20.
2. Nichols, *Progresses*, I, 533–52.
3. *Ibid.*, 485–523. Robert Laneham's account of Elizabeth's sojourn at Kenilworth is in Nichols, I, 426–84.
4. *Ibid.*, I, 601.

CHAPTER 25

1. Much material on the progresses of the Elizabethan court is in Nichols, *Progresses*, Vols. I–III, Chambers, *Elizabethan Stage*, Vol. I, Allegra Woodworth, "Purveyance," Dunlop, *Palaces and Progresses*, and John Buxton, *Elizabethan Taste* (London, 1963).
2. Nichols, *Progresses*, I, 526.
3. Woodworth, "Purveyance," p. 25.

CHAPTER 26

1. *Sp. Cal. Elizabethan*, II, 631.
2. *Ibid.*, II, 627.
3. *Ibid.*, II, 636.
4. On the Anglo–French negotiations, and the issue of Elizabeth's marriageability, see Wallace T. MacCaffrey, "The Anjou Match and the Making of Elizabethan Foreign Policy," in *The English Commonwealth, 1547–1640*, ed. Peter Clark *et al.* (Leicester, 1979).
5. MacCaffrey, "Anjou Match," p. 60.
6. *Sp. Cal. Elizabethan*, II, 675.
7. *Ibid.*, II, 638, 641, 581.
8. *Ibid.*, II, 498.
9. *Ibid.*, II, 641.

CHAPTER 27

1. Nicholas Tyacke, "Popular Puritan Mentality in Late Elizabethan England," in *The English Commonwealth*, ed. Peter Clark *et al.*, p. 78.
2. Hughes, III, 178–9.
3. J. E. Neale, "The Elizabethan Age," in *Essays in Elizabethan History* (London, 1958), p. 26.
4. *Sp. Cal. Elizabethan*, I, 682.
5. *Ibid.*, II, 704.
6. Michael Barraclough Pulman, *The Elizabethan Privy Council in the Fifteen-Seventies* (Berkeley, 1971), p. 48.

7. Wright, II, 103–5.
8. *Sp. Cal. Elizabethan*, II, 664 and note.

PART FIVE
"That Guilty Woman of England"

CHAPTER 28

1. French, *John Dee*, p. 189.
2. *Sp. Cal. Elizabethan*, III, 91, 80.
3. *Ibid.*, III, 93.
4. *Ibid.*, III, 158–9.
5. *Ibid.*, III, 206.
6. *Ibid.*, III, 243.
7. Wright, II, 151.

CHAPTER 29

1. Adrian Morey, *The Catholic Subjects of Elizabeth I* (London, 1978), pp. 133–5 and *passim.*
2. *Sp. Cal. Elizabethan*, III, 153.
3. Carol Z. Wiener, "The Beleaguered Isle: A Study of Elizabethan and Early Jacobean Anti-Catholicism," *Past and Present*, LI (May 1971), 48.
4. Hughes, III, 311.
5. St. George Kieran Hyland, *A Century of Persecution under Tudor and Stuart Sovereigns from Contemporary Records* (London, 1920), p. 292. This account of the executions of December, 1581 is taken from Hyland, pp. 288ff, and *Sp. Cal. Elizabethan*, III, 231–2.
6. *State Papers, Domestic*, II, 48.
7. *Sp. Cal. Elizabethan*, III, 186–90.

CHAPTER 30

1. On Leicester's expedition see Roy Strong and J. A. Van Dorsten, *Leicester's Triumph* (Leiden and London, 1964) and Charles Henry Wilson, *Queen Elizabeth and the Revolt of the Netherlands* (Berkeley and Los Angeles, 1970).
2. *State Papers, Domestic*, II, 265.
3. *Correspondence of Robert Dudley*, Camden Society, Old series, XXVII (London, 1844), 21.
4. *State Papers, Domestic*, II, 291.
5. *Ibid.*, I, 648.
6. Klarwill, pp. 338–9.
7. *Correspondence of Robert Dudley*, p. 112.

CHAPTER 31

1. John Hungerford Pollen, *The English Catholics in the Reign of Queen Elizabeth* (London, 1920), p. 340.
2. Keith Thomas, *Religion and the Decline of Magic: Studies in Popular Belief in Sixteenth and Seventeenth Century England* (London, 1971), p. 422; *State Papers, Domestic*, II, 38.
3. Thomas, pp. 419–21.
4. Alan Haynes, "The English Earthquake of 1580," *History Today*, XXIX (August 1979), 542–4.
5. Klarwill, p. 340.
6. *Ibid.*
7. *Sp. Cal. Elizabethan*, II, 581.
8. Thomas, p. 407.
9. Read, *Burghley*, pp. 367–8.
10. *State Papers, Domestic*, II, 380.

CHAPTER 32

1. *State Papers, Domestic*, II, 461.
2. *Ibid.*, II, 480, 497.
3. *Ibid.*, II, 468, 470, 483.
4. Martin A. S. Hume, *Philip II of Spain* (London, 1897, reprinted New York, 1969), p. 267.
5. *State Papers, Domestic*, II, 507; Miller Christy, "Queen Elizabeth's Visit to Tilbury in 1588," *EHR*, XXXIV (January 1919), 46.
6. *State Papers, Domestic*, II, 391.
7. *Ibid.*, II, 515.
8. On the authenticity of Elizabeth's Tilbury speech, see Neale, *Essays in Elizabethan History*, pp. 104–6.
9. *State Papers, Domestic*, II, 534, 536, 527, 529.

PART SIX
"A Lady Whom Time Had Surprised"

CHAPTER 33

1. *A Journal of All That Was Accomplished by Monsieur de Maisse . . .* , trans. and ed. G. B. Harrison and R. A. Jones (Bloomsbury, 1931).
2. Chamberlin, *Private Character of Elizabeth*, p. 70.
3. De Maisse, *Journal*, p. 7.
4. Alan Kendall, *Robert Dudley, Earl of Leicester* (London, 1980), p. 231.
5. De Maisse, *Journal*, p. 115.
6. *Ibid.*, pp. 11–12.
7. *Ibid.*, p. 83.

CHAPTER 34

1. John Harington, *Nugae Antiquae*, ed. Rev. Henry Harington (London, 1804, reprinted New York, 1966), I, 318.
2. *Ibid.*, I, 312–16.
3. Chamberlin, *Private Character of Queen Elizabeth*, p. 73.
4. *State Papers, Domestic*, V, 252.
5. De Maisse, *Journal*, p. 58.
6. Elizabeth's translation of Seneca is in *Nugae Antiquae*, I, 109–14.

CHAPTER 35

1. *State Papers, Domestic*, VI, 42.
2. *Ibid.*, V, 543.
3. *Nugae Antiquae*, I, 320ff.
4. *State Papers, Domestic*, VI, 260.
5. *Ibid.*, VI, 298–301.
6. *Ibid.*
7. *Ibid.*, VI, 303. Neale sorts legend from authentic incident concerning Elizabeth's last days in "The Sayings of Queen Elizabeth," *History*, New series, X, No. 39 (October 1925), 212–33.

Select Bibliography

ORIGINAL SOURCES

Ascham, Roger. *The Scholemaster.* In *English Works,* ed. William Aldis Wright. Cambridge, England: Cambridge University Press, 1904.
———. *Toxophilus.* In *English Works,* ed. William Aldis Wright. Cambridge, England: Cambridge University Press, 1904.
———. *The Whole Works of Roger Ascham,* ed. J. A. Giles. 3 vols. in 4. London: John Russell Smith, 1864–65, reprinted New York: AMS Press, 1965.
Bullen, A. H., ed. *Lyrics from the Song-books of the Elizabethan Age.* London: Lawrence and Bullen, 1897.
Bülow, Gottfried von and Walter Powell, eds. "Diary of the Journey of Philip Julius, duke of Stettin-Pomerania, through England in the Year 1602." *Transactions of the Royal Historical Society,* Second series, VI (1892), 1–67.
Calendar of Letters and State Papers, relating to English Affairs, preserved principally in the Archives of Simancas, ed. Martin A. S. Hume. 4 vols. London: H. M. Stationery Office, 1892–99.
Calendar of Letters, Despatches, and State Papers, relating to the Negotiations between England and Spain, preserved in the Archives at Vienna, Simancas, Besançon and Brussels, ed. G. A. Bergenroth *et alii.* 13 vols. in 17. London: Longman, etc., 1862–1954.
Calendar of State Papers and Manuscripts, relating to English Affairs, existing in the Archives and Collections of Venice, and in Other Libraries of Northern Italy, ed. Rawdon Brown *et alii.* 38 vols. in 40. London: Longman, etc., 1864–1947.
Calendar of State Papers, Domestic Series, of the Reigns of Edward VI, Mary, Elizabeth and James I, preserved in the State Paper Department of Her Majesty's Public Record Office, ed. Robert Lemon and Mary A. E. Green. 12 vols. London: Longman, etc., 1856–72.
Calendar of State Papers, Foreign Series, of the Reign of Edward VI, 1547–1553, preserved in the State Paper Department of Her Majesty's Public Record Office, ed. William B. Turnbull. London: Longman, Green, Longman and Roberts, 1861.

Calendar of State Papers, Foreign Series, of the Reign of Elizabeth, preserved in the State Paper Department of Her Majesty's Public Record Office, ed. Joseph Stevenson et alii. 23 vols. in 26. London: Longman, etc., 1863–1950.

Calendar of State Papers, Foreign Series, of the Reign of Mary, 1553–1558, preserved in the State Paper Department of Her Majesty's Public Record Office, ed. William B: Turnbull. London: Longman, Green, Longman, and Roberts, 1861.

Calendar of the Manuscripts of the Most Hon. the Marquis of Salisbury . . . preserved at Hatfield House, Hertfordshire. 23 vols. in 19. London: Her Majesty's Stationery Office, 1883–1973.

Camden, William. The History of the Most Renowned and Victorious Princess Elizabeth, Late Queen of England. 4th ed. London: R. Bentley, 1688, reprinted New York: AMS Press, 1970.

———. Remains Concerning Britain. London: John Russell Smith, 1870, reprinted Yorkshire, England: EP Publishing, 1974.

Clifford, Henry. The Life of Jane Dormer, Duchess of Feria, transcribed by E. E. Estcourt and ed. Joseph Stevenson. London: Burns and Oates, 1887.

A Collection of State Papers Relating to Affairs in the Reigns of King Henry. VIII, King Edward VI, Queen Mary, and Queen Elizabeth . . . left by William Cecil Lord Burghley, and now remaining at Hatfield House, ed. Samuel Haynes and William Murdin. 2 vols. London: William Bowyer, 1740–59.

Dee, John. The Private Diary of Dr. John Dee, ed. James Orchard Halliwell. Camden Society, Old series, XIX. London: J. B. Nichols and Son, 1842.

Doughtie, Edward, ed. Lyrics from English Airs, 1596–1622. Cambridge, Mass.: Harvard University Press, 1970.

Edward VI. The Chronicle and Political Papers, ed. W. K. Jordan. London: Allen and Unwin, 1966.

———. Literary Remains of King Edward the Sixth, ed. J. G. Nichols. 2 vols. London: J. B. Nichols and Son, 1857.

Elizabeth I. The Letters of Queen Elizabeth I, ed. G. B. Harrison. London: Cassell, 1935, reprinted New York: Funk and Wagnalls, 1968.

Fénélon, Bertrand de Salignac, seigneur de La Mothe. Correspondance Diplomatique de Bertrand de Salignac de La Mothe Fénélon, ed. Alexandre Teulet. 7 vols. Paris and London: no publisher, 1838–40.

Forbes, Thomas Rogers. Chronicle from Aldgate: Life and Death in Shakespeare's London. New Haven and London: Yale University Press, 1971.

Foxe, John. The Acts and Monuments of John Foxe, ed. George Townsend and S. R. Cattley. 8 vols. London: R. B. Seeley and W. Burnside, 1837–41.

Frescoln, Katharine P. "A Letter from Thomas Randolph to the Earl of Leicester." Huntington Library Quarterly, XXXVII, No. 1 (November 1973), 83–88.

Hayward, John. Annals of the First Four Years of the Reign of Queen Elizabeth, ed. John Bruce. Camden Society, Old series, VII. London: J. B. Nichols and Son, 1840.

Hinton, Edward M. Ireland through Tudor Eyes. Philadelphia: University of Pennsylvania Press and London: Oxford University Press, 1935, reprinted Philadelphia: R. West, 1977.

Holinshed, Raphael. Holinshed's Chronicles of England, Scotland and Ireland. 6 vols. London: J. Johnson, 1807–08.

Kervyn de Lettenhove, Joseph M. B. C. and L. Gilliodts van Severen, eds. Relations politiques des Pays-Bas et de l'Angleterre, sous le règne de Philippe II. 11 vols. Brussels: F. Hayez, 1882–1900.

Klarwill, Victor von, ed. Queen Elizabeth and Some Foreigners. New York: Brentano's, 1928.

Leicester, Robert Dudley, earl of. Correspondence of Robert Dudley, earl of Leycester, during his Government of the Low Countries, in the Years 1585 and 1586. Camden Society, Old series, XXVII. London: J. B. Nichols and Son, 1844.

[Leicester's Commonwealth]. The Copy of a Letter Written by a Master of Arts of Cambridge to his Friend in London, concerning some talk passed of late between two worshipful and grave men about the present state, and some proceedings of the Earl of Leicester and his friends in England. Printed in Bacon, Francis. Collotype Facsimile and Type Transcript of an Elizabethan Manuscript. London, New York and Bombay: Longmans, Green and Co., 1904.

Maisse, André Hurault, sieur de. *A Journal of All That Was Accomplished by Monsieur de Maisse Ambassador in England from King Henri IV to Queen Elizabeth Anno Domini 1597,* trans. and ed. G. B. Harrison and R. A. Jones. Bloomsbury, England: Nonesuch Press, 1931.

Manning, C. R., ed. "State Papers Relating to the Custody of the Princess Elizabeth at Woodstock, in 1554: Being Letters between Queen Mary and her Privy Council, and Sir Henry Bedingfield." *Norfolk Archaeology: or Miscellaneous Tracts relating to the Antiquities of the County of Norfolk,* IV (1855), 133–231.

Mary Stuart. *Lettres, Instructions et Mémoires de Marie Stuart, Reine d'Ecosse,* ed. Alexandre Labanoff. 7 vols. London: C. Dolman, 1844.

Melville, James. *Memoirs of Sir James Melville,* ed. A. Francis Stewart. New York: E. P. Dutton, 1930.

Moryson, Fynes. *Shakespeare's Europe: A Survey of the Condition of Europe at the end of the 16th Century, being unpublished chapters of Fynes Moryson's Itinerary (1617).* 2nd ed. London: Sherratt and Hughes, 1903, reissued New York: Benjamin Blom, 1967.

Mumby, Frank A. *The Girlhood of Queen Elizabeth: A Narrative in Contemporary Letters.* London: Constable and Co., 1909.

Nichols, John. *The Progresses and Public Processions of Queen Elizabeth.* new ed. 3 vols. London: John Nichols and Son, 1823, reprinted New York: AMS Press, 1969.

Nichols, John Gough, ed. *The Chronicle of Queen Jane, and of Two Years of Queen Mary, and especially of the Rebellion of Sir Thomas Wyat.* Camden Society, Old series, XLVIII. London: Printed for the Camden Society, 1850.

Nicolas, Nicholas Harris. *Memoirs of the Life and Times of Sir Christopher Hatton.* London: R. Bentley, 1847.

Nugae Antiquae: Being a Miscellaneous Collection of Original Papers in Prose and Verse, written in the Reigns of Henry VIII, Queen Mary, Elizabeth, King James, etc., ed. Rev. Henry Harington. 3 vols. London: J. Dodsley, 1779.

Osburn, James M., ed. *The Quenes Maiesties Passage through the Citie of London to Westminster the Day before her Coronacion.* Elizabethan Club Series, Vol. I. New Haven, Conn.: Yale University Press, 1960.

Read, Conyers. "A Letter from Robert, Earl of Leicester, to a Lady." *Huntington Library Bulletin,* IX (April 1936), 15–26.

Rye, William Brenchley. *England as Seen by Foreigners in the Days of Elizabeth and James the First.* London: John Russell Smith, 1865.

Strangford, Viscount, ed. "Household Expenses of the Princess Elizabeth during her Residence at Hatfield October 1, 1551, to September 30, 1552." In *The Camden Miscellany,* Vol. II. Camden Society, Old series, LV. London: J. B. Nichols and Son, 1853.

Tytler, Patrick Fraser. *England under the Reigns of Edward VI and Mary.* 2 vols. London: Richard Bentley, 1839.

Wedel, Lupold von. "Journey through England and Scotland made by Lupold von Wedel in the Years 1584 and 1585," trans. Gottfried von Bülow. *Transactions of the Royal Historical Society,* Second series, IX (1895), 223–270.

Wright, Thomas, ed. *Queen Elizabeth and Her Times.* 2 vols. London: Henry Colburn, 1838.

SECONDARY AUTHORITIES

Aird, Ian. "The Death of Amy Robsart." *English Historical Review,* LXXI, No. 278 (January 1956), 69–79.

Appleby, Andrew B. *Famine in Tudor and Stuart England.* Palo Alto, Calif.: Stanford University Press, 1978.

Ball, Bryan W. *A Great Expectation: Eschatological Thought in English Protestantism to 1660.* Leiden: E. J. Brill, 1975.

Beckingsale, B. W. *Elizabeth I.* London: B. T. Batsford, 1963.

Beier, A. L. "Social Problems in Elizabethan London." *Journal of Interdisciplinary History,* IX, No. 2 (Autumn 1978), 203–21.

———. "Vagrants and the Social Order in Elizabethan London." *Past and Present,* LXIV (August 1974), 3–29.

Bergeron, David M. "Elizabeth's Coronation Entry (1559): New Manuscript Evidence." *English Literary Renaissance,* VIII, No. 1 (Winter 1978), 3–8.

Bindoff, Stanley T. "A Kingdom at Stake, 1553." *History Today*, III, No. 9 (September 1953), 642–48.
———. *Tudor England*. The Pelican History of England, Vol. V. Baltimore: Penguin Books, 1950.
Black, John B. *The Reign of Elizabeth, 1558–1603*. 2nd ed. Oxford History of England, Vol. VIII. Oxford: Clarendon Press, 1959.
Bradley, Ian. "The English Sunday." *History Today*, XXII, No. 5 (May 1972), 355–63.
Braudel, Fernand. *Capitalism and Material Life, 1400–1800*, trans. Miriam Kochan. New York, Evanston, San Francisco and London: Harper and Row, 1973.
———. *The Mediterranean and the Mediterranean World in the Age of Philip II*, trans. Siân Reynolds. 2 vols. New York, Hagerstown, San Francisco and London: Harper and Row, 1972.
Bush, M. L. *The Government Policy of Protector Somerset*. London: Edward Arnold, 1975.
Byrne, M. St. Clare. *Elizabethan Life in Town and Country*. 7th ed. London: Methuen, 1954.
Chamberlin, Frederick. *The Private Character of Queen Elizabeth*. New York: Dodd Mead and Co., 1922.
Chambers, E. K. *The Elizabethan Stage*. 4 vols. Oxford: Clarendon Press, 1923.
Christy, Miller. "Queen Elizabeth's Visit to Tilbury in 1588." *English Historical Review*, XXXIV (January 1919), 43–61.
Clark, Peter, Alan G. R. Smith and Nicholas Tyacke, eds. *The English Commonwealth, 1547–1640: Essays in Politics and Society presented to Joel Hurstfield*. Leicester: Leicester University Press, 1979.
Cook, Olive. *The English Country House: An Art and a Way of Life*. London: Thames and Hudson, 1974.
Council, Norman. "O Dea Certe: The Allegory of the Fortress of Perfect Beauty." *Huntington Library Quarterly*, XXXIX, No. 4 (August 1976), 329–42.
Craig, Hardin. *The Enchanted Glass: The Elizabethan Mind in Literature*. Oxford: Blackwell, 1960.
Creighton, Mandell. *Queen Elizabeth*. new ed. London, New York, etc.: Longmans, Green and Co., 1899, reprinted New York: Thomas Y. Crowell, 1966.
Croft, Pauline. "Englishmen and the Spanish Inquisition, 1588–1625." *English Historical Review*, LXXXVII, No. 343 (April 1972), 249–68.
Davies, R. Trevor. *The Golden Century of Spain, 1501–1621*. London and Basingstoke: Macmillan, 1937.
Davis, Eliza Jeffries. "The Transformation of London." In *Tudor Studies presented by the Board of Students in History in the University of London to Albert Frederick Pollard*, ed. R. W. Seton-Watson. London: Longmans, Green and Co., 1924.
Dent, Anthony. "Shakespeare's Horse-borne England." *History Today*, XXIII, No. 7 (July 1973), 455–61.
D'Oyley, Elizabeth. "The Death of Amye Robsart." *History Today*, VI, No. 4 (April 1956), 252–60.
Dunlop, Ian. *Palaces and Progresses of Elizabeth I*. London: Jonathan Cape, 1962.
Durant, David N. *Arabella Stuart: A Rival to the Queen*. London: Weidenfeld and Nicolson, 1978.
———. "A London Visit, 1591." *History Today*, XXIV, No. 7 (July 1974), 497–503.
Elliot, J. H. *The Old World and the New, 1492–1650*. Cambridge, England: Cambridge University Press, 1970.
Elton, G. R. *England under the Tudors*. 2nd ed. A History of England, Vol. IV. London: Methuen, 1974.
———. *Modern Historians on British History 1485–1945: A Critical Bibliography, 1945–1969*. London: Methuen, 1970.
———. *Studies in Tudor and Stuart Politics and Government: Papers and Reviews, 1946–1972*. Vol. I: *Tudor Politics/Tudor Government*. Vol. II: *Parliament/Political Thought*. 2 vols. Cambridge, England: Cambridge University Press, 1974.
Emmison, F. G. *Elizabethan Life: Disorder*. Chelmsford, England: Essex County Council, 1970.
Erickson, Carolly. *Bloody Mary*. Garden City, N. Y.: Doubleday, 1978.

———. *Great Harry.* New York: Summit Books, 1980.

Ewen, C. L'Estrange, ed. *Witch Hunting and Witch Trials.* London: Kegan Paul, Trench, Trubner and Co., 1929, reprinted New York: Barnes and Noble, 1971.

Firth, Katharine R. *The Apocalyptic Tradition in Reformation Britain, 1530–1645.* Oxford and New York: Oxford University Press, 1979.

Fraser, Antonia. *Mary Queen of Scots.* New York: Dell, 1971.

French, Peter J. *John Dee: The World of an Elizabethan Magus.* London: Routledge and Kegan Paul, 1972.

Froude, James Anthony. *History of England, from the Fall of Wolsey to the Death of Elizabeth.* 4 vols. New York: Charles Scribner's Sons, 1881.

Fuzier, Jean. "London and Country Cries: Elizabethan Life in Song and Music." *Cahiers Elisabéthains,* VIII (October 1975), 31–63.

Gilbert, Creighton. "When Did a Man in the Renaissance Grow Old?" *Studies in the Renaissance,* XIV (1967), 7–32.

Gilkes, R. K. *The Tudor Parliament.* The London History Series, Vol. V. London: University of London Press, 1969.

Glanville, Philippa. "Nonsuch: A Lost Tudor Palace." *London Archaeologist,* I, No. 5 (Winter 1969), 111–13.

Granville-Barker, Harley and G. B. Harrison, eds. *A Companion to Shakespeare Studies.* Cambridge, England: Cambridge University Press, 1934.

Haller, William. *Foxe's Book of Martyrs and the Elect Nation.* London: Jonathan Cape, 1963.

Halliday, F. E. "Queen Elizabeth I and Dr. Burcot." *History Today,* V, No. 8 (August 1955), 542–44.

Harbage, Alfred. *Shakespeare's Audience.* New York: Columbia University Press, 1941.

Hardin, Richard F. *Michael Drayton and the Passing of Elizabethan England.* Lawrence, Manhattan and Wichita: University Press of Kansas, 1973.

Hartley, Dorothy. *Lost Country Life.* New York: Pantheon Books, 1979.

Haugaard, William P. *Elizabeth and the English Reformation: The Struggle for a Stable Settlement of Religion.* Cambridge, England: Cambridge University Press, 1968.

Haynes, Alan. "The Cadiz Expedition, 1596." *History Today,* XXIII, No. 3 (March 1973), 161–69.

———. "The English Earthquake of 1580." *History Today,* XXIX (August 1979), 542–44.

———. "Supplying the Elizabethan Court." *History Today,* XXVIII (November 1978), 729–37.

Hitchcock, J. "A Confession of the Family of Love, 1580." *Bulletin of the Institute of Historical Research,* XLIII, No. 107 (May 1970), 85–86.

Hogrefe, Pearl. *Women of Action in Tudor England: Nine Biographical Sketches.* Ames, Iowa: Iowa State University Press, 1977.

Hughes, Philip. *The Reformation in England.* 3 vols. New York: Macmillan, 1951–54.

Hume, Martin A. S. *Philip II of Spain.* London and New York: Macmillan, 1897, reprinted New York: Haskell House, 1969.

Hurstfield, Joel. *Elizabeth I and the Unity of England.* New York: Macmillan, 1960.

———. *The Elizabethan Nation.* New York and London: Harper and Row, 1967.

———. and Alan G. R. Smith, eds. *Elizabethan People: State and Society.* New York: St. Martin's Press, 1972.

———. *Freedom, Corruption, and Government in Elizabethan England.* London: Jonathan Cape, 1973.

———. *The Illusion of Power in Tudor Politics.* London: Athlone Press, 1979.

———. "Queen and State: The Emergence of an Elizabethan Myth." In *Britain and the Netherlands,* ed. J. S. Bromley and E. H. Kossmann. The Hague: Martinus Nijhoff, 1975.

Hyland, St. George Kieran. *A Century of Persecution under Tudor and Stuart Sovereigns from Contemporary Records.* London: Kegan Paul, Trench, Trubner and Co. and New York: E. P. Dutton, 1920.

Ingram, William. "The Closing of the Theaters in 1597: A Dissenting View." *Modern Philology,* LXIX, No. 2 (November 1971), 105–15.

Jenkins, Elizabeth. *Elizabeth the Great.* New York: G. P. Putnam's Sons, 1967.

Johnson, Paul. *Elizabeth I: A Biography*. New York, Chicago and San Francisco: Holt, Rinehart and Winston, 1974.

Jordan, W. K. *Edward VI*. Vol. I: *The Young King: The Protectorship of the Duke of Somerset*. Vol. II: *The Threshold of Power: The Dominance of the Duke of Northumberland*. 2 vols. London: Allen and Unwin, 1968–70.

Kendall, Alan. *Robert Dudley, Earl of Leicester*. London: Cassell, 1980.

Knowles, David. "The Eltonian Revolution in Early Tudor History." *Historical Journal*, XVII, No. 4 (December 1974), 867–72.

Lacey, Robert. *Robert, Earl of Essex: An Elizabethan Icarus*. London: Weidenfeld and Nicolson, 1971.

Levine, Mortimer. *The Early Elizabethan Succession Question, 1558–1568*. Palo Alto, Calif.: Stanford University Press, 1966.

Loomie, Albert J. "The Armadas and the Catholics of England." *Catholic Historical Review*, LIX, No. 3 (October 1973), 385–403.

MacCaffrey, Wallace T. "The Anjou Match and the Making of Elizabethan Foreign Policy." In *The English Commonwealth, 1547–1640: Essays in Politics and Society presented to Joel Hurstfield*, ed. Peter Clark, Alan G. R. Smith and Nicholas Tyacke. Leicester: Leicester University Press, 1979.

——. *The Shaping of the Elizabethan Regime*. Princeton: Princeton University Press, 1968.

Machin, R. "The Great Rebuilding: A Reassessment." *Past and Present*, LXXVII (November 1977), 33–56.

Mackie, J. D. *The Earlier Tudors, 1485–1558*. The Oxford History of England, Vol. VII. Oxford: Clarendon Press, 1952.

Maltby, William S. *The Black Legend in England: The Development of Anti-Spanish Sentiment, 1558–1660*. Durham, N. C.: Duke University Press, 1971.

Martienssen, Anthony. *Queen Katherine Parr*. New York: McGraw-Hill and London: Secker and Warburg, 1973.

Mattingly, Garrett. *The Armada*. Boston: Houghton Mifflin, 1962.

Morey, Adrian. *The Catholic Subjects of Elizabeth I*. London, Boston and Sydney: George Allen and Unwin, 1978.

Morris, Christopher. *The Tudors*. New York: John Wiley and Sons, 1967.

Moss, D. E. "Roger Ascham." *History Today*, XXVII, No. 10 (October 1977), 651–57.

Moss, Jean D. "Additional Light on the Family of Love." *Bulletin of the Institute of Historical Research*, XLVII, No. 115 (May 1974), 103–05.

Neale, J. E. "The Accession of Queen Elizabeth I." *History Today*, III, No. 5 (May 1953), 293–300.

——. *The Age of Catherine de' Medici*. London: Jonathan Cape, 1943.

——. "The Elizabethan Political Scene." *Proceedings of the British Academy*, XXXIV (1948), 97–117.

——. *Essays in Elizabethan History*. London: Jonathan Cape, 1958.

——. *Queen Elizabeth I*. London: Jonathan Cape, 1934, reprinted 1952.

——. "The Sayings of Queen Elizabeth." *History*, New series, X, No. 39 (October 1925), 212–33.

——. "Sir Nicholas Throckmorton's Advice to Queen Elizabeth on her Accession to the Throne." *English Historical Review*, LXV, No. 254 (January 1950), 91–98.

Nuttall, Geoffrey F. "The English Martyrs, 1535–1680: A Statistical Review." *Journal of Ecclesiastical History*, XXII, No. 3 (July 1971), 191–97.

O'Malley, C. D. "Tudor Medicine and Biology." *Huntington Library Quarterly*, XXXII, No. 1 (November 1968), 1–27.

Outhwaite, R. B. "Royal Borrowing in the Reign of Elizabeth I: The Aftermath of Antwerp." *English Historical Review*, LXXXVI, No. 339 (April 1971), 251–63.

Owen, A. E. B. "Sir John Wolley's Letter-book as Latin Secretary to Elizabeth I." *Archives*, XI, No. 49 (Spring 1973), 16–18.

Parker, Geoffrey. "Mutiny and Discontent in the Spanish Army of Flanders 1572–1607." *Past and Present*, LVIII (February 1973), 38–52.

Pearson, Lu Emily. *Elizabethans at Home*. Palo Alto, Calif.: Stanford University Press, 1957.

Pike, Luke Owen. *A History of Crime in England*. 2 vols. London: Smith, Elder and Co., 1873–76.

The Plague Reconsidered: A New Look at its Origins and Effects in 16th and 17th Century England. Matlock, England: Local Population Studies, 1977.

Pollen, John Hungerford. *The English Catholics in the Reign of Queen Elizabeth.* London: Longmans, Green and Co., 1920.

Pollitt, Ronald. "John Hawkins' Troublesome Voyages: Merchants, Bureaucrats, and the Origins of the Slave Trade." *Journal of British Studies,* XII, No. 2 (May 1973), 26–40.

Prescott, H. F. M. *Mary Tudor.* New York: Macmillan, 1954.

Pulman, Michael Barraclough. *The Elizabethan Privy Council in the Fifteen-Seventies.* Berkeley: University of California Press, 1971.

Read, Conyers. *Lord Burghley and Queen Elizabeth.* New York: Alfred A. Knopf, 1960.

———. *Mr. Secretary Cecil and Queen Elizabeth.* New York: Alfred A. Knopf, 1961.

———. *The Tudors: Personalities and Practical Politics in Sixteenth Century England.* New York: Holt, Rinehart and Winston, 1936.

Reid, R. R. "The Rebellion of the Earls, 1569." *Transactions of the Royal Historical Society,* Second series, XX (1906), 171–203.

Ross, Josephine. *Suitors of the Queen: The Men in the Life of Elizabeth I of England.* New York: Coward, McCann and Geoghegan, 1975.

Rowse, A. L. "The Coronation of Queen Elizabeth I." *History Today,* III, No. 4 (May 1953), 301–10.

———. *The Elizabethan Renaissance.* Part I: *The Life of the Society.* Part II: *The Cultural Achievement.* 2 vols. London: Macmillan, 1971–72.

———. *The England of Elizabeth: The Structure of Society.* London: Macmillan, 1950.

———. *Portraits and Views: Literary and Historical.* London: Macmillan, 1979.

———. *Simon Forman: Sex and Society in Shakespeare's Age.* London: Weidenfeld and Nicolson, 1974.

Ruff, Lillian M. and D. Arnold Wilson. "The Madrigal, the Lute Song and Elizabethan Politics." *Past and Present,* XLIV (August 1969), 3–51.

Ryan, Lawrence V. *Roger Ascham.* Palo Alto, Calif.: Stanford University Press and London: Oxford University Press, 1963.

Salgādo, Gāmini. *The Elizabethan Underworld.* London: Dent and Totowa, N. J.: Rowman and Littlefield, 1977.

Schnucker, Robert V. "Elizabethan Birth Control and Puritan Attitudes." *Journal of Interdisciplinary History,* V, No. 4 (Spring 1975), 655–67.

Shakespeare's England: An Account of the Life and Manners of his Age. 2 vols. London: Oxford University Press, 1916.

Smith, Alan G. R. *The Government of Elizabethan England.* London: Edward Arnold, 1967.

Smith, Lacey Baldwin. *Elizabeth Tudor: Portrait of a Queen.* Boston and Toronto: Little, Brown, 1975.

Stopes, C. C. *Shakespeare's Environment.* London: G. Bell and Sons, 1914.

Strickland, Agnes. *Lives of the Queens of England.* 8 vols. London: Henry Colburn, 1851.

Strong, Roy and Julia Trevelyan Oman. *Elizabeth R.* London: Secker and Warburg, 1971.

Strong, Roy and J. A. Van Dorsten. *Leicester's Triumph.* Leiden: University Press and London: Oxford University Press, 1964.

Strong, Roy. "The Popular Celebration of the Accession Day of Queen Elizabeth I." *Journal of the Warburg and Courtauld Institutes,* XXI, Nos. 1–2 (January–June 1958), 86–103.

Thomas, Keith. *Religion and the Decline of Magic: Studies in Popular Beliefs in Sixteenth and Seventeenth Century England.* London: Weidenfeld and Nicolson, 1971.

Tillyard, E. M. W. *The Elizabethan World Picture.* London: Chatto and Windus, 1943.

Trimble, William Raleigh. *The Catholic Laity in Elizabethan England 1558–1603.* Cambridge, Mass.: Harvard University Press, 1964.

Tyacke, Nicholas. "Popular Puritan Mentality in Late Elizabethan England." In *The English Commonwealth, 1547–1640: Essays in Politics and Society presented to Joel Hurstfield,* ed. Peter Clark, Alan G. R. Smith and Nicholas Tyacke. Leicester: Leicester University Press, 1979.

Vines, Alice G. *Neither Fire Nor Steel: Sir Christopher Hatton.* Chicago: Nelson-Hall, 1978.

Walcott, Robert. *The Tudor-Stuart Period of English History (1485–1714): A Review of Changing Interpretations.* Service Center for Teachers of History, Vol. LVIII. New York: Macmillan, 1964.

Wallace, Willard M. *Sir Walter Raleigh.* Princeton, N. J.: Princeton University Press, 1959.

Wernham, R. B. *Before the Armada: The Emergence of the English Nation, 1485–1588.* New York: Harcourt, Brace and World, 1966.

———. *The Making of Elizabethan Foreign Policy, 1558–1603.* Berkeley: University of California Press, 1980.

Wiener, Carol Z. "The Beleaguered Isle: A Study of Elizabethan and Early Jacobean Anti-Catholicism." *Past and Present,* LI (May 1971), 27–62.

Wiesener, Louis. *La Jeunesse d'Elisabeth d'Angleterre 1533–1558.* Paris: Librairie Hachette, 1878.

Williams, Glanmor. *The General and Common Sort of People, 1540–1640.* Exeter, England: University of Exeter, 1977.

Williams, Neville. *All the Queen's Men: Elizabeth I and her Courtiers.* New York: Macmillan, 1972.

———. "The Coronation of Queen Elizabeth I." *Quarterly Review,* CCXCI, No. 597 (July 1953), 397–410.

———. *Elizabeth the First: Queen of England.* New York: E. P. Dutton and Co., 1968.

———. *The Life and Times of Elizabeth I.* Garden City, N. Y.: Doubleday, 1972.

Williams, Penry. *The Tudor Regime.* Oxford: Clarendon Press, 1979.

Wilson, Charles Henry. *Queen Elizabeth and the Revolt of the Netherlands.* Berkeley and Los Angeles: University of California Press, 1970.

Wilson, E. K. *England's Eliza.* Cambridge, Mass.: Harvard University Press, 1939.

Wilson, F. P. *The Plague in Shakespeare's London.* Oxford: Clarendon Press, 1927.

Woodworth, Allegra. "Purveyance for the Royal Household in the Reign of Queen Elizabeth." *Transactions of the American Philosophical Society,* New series, XXXV, Pt. 1 (1945), 3–89.

Yates, Frances A. *Astraea: The Imperial Theme in the Sixteenth Century.* London and Boston: Routledge and Kegan Paul, 1975.

———. "Elizabethan Chivalry: The Romance of the Accession Day Tilts." *Journal of the Warburg and Courtauld Institutes,* XX (1957), 4–25.

Zagorin, Perez. "English History, 1558–1640: A Bibliographical Survey." In *Changing Views on British History: Essays on Historical Writing since 1939,* ed. Elizabeth C. Furber. Cambridge, Mass.: Harvard University Press, 1966.

Index

Clinton, Admiral, 213
Clinton, Lady, 161
clocks, at Elvetham, 293
"close stools," 223–24
clothing, 45, 93, 226, 290
  of Anne Boleyn, 12, 13
  of children, 42
  for coronation ceremony, 162–63,
    169, 177
  for courtiers, 228–30, 257, 285,
    309, 323, 348, 382
  of Elizabeth, 92–93, 100, 177, 186,
    218, 231, 324, 346–47, 374,
    383–84, 389, 399
  French, 12
  French vs. English, 186, 229
  of Mary I, 109
  men's vs. women's, 228–29
  poisoned, 196
  "progress," 285
  of Puritans, 309
cloth manufacturing, 23, 278
Cobham, Lady, 264
coins, double rose on, 275
Comedy of Errors, A (Shakespeare),
  387
comets, superstitious reactions to, 160,
  276, 313, 355
Congregation (Scotland), 201
contortionists, at Kenilworth, 281
Cooke, Anthony, 58, 168
Cooke, Mildred, 77
Cornwall, riots in, 95
Cornwallis (gentleman usher), 133,
  136
coronations:
  of Anne Boleyn, 11–13
  clothing for, 162–63, 169, 177
  of Elizabeth, 163, 168–69, 177–79
  of Mary I, 110–11, 178
  pageantry at, 178–79
  of Philip II, 317
correspondence, doctrine of, 362
cosmetics, 345–46
  men's use of, 228–29, 263, 382
council, royal, 171–73, 212–13, 241,
  339–40, 347
  Alençon opposed by, 299–300, 304,
    313–14
  Bond of Association drafted by,
    359
  Parliament vs., 253
counter-evangelism, 336

country folk, plays and pageants of,
  277–79, 281
court, court life, 223–30, 345–50
  banqueting houses at, 227, 321–22
  corruption in, 349–50, 394
  of Edward VI, 66, 67, 92–93
  entertainment at, 67, 186, 219–20,
    227, 274, 281, 296, 321–22, 387,
    390, 399
  factions in, 257, 387
  favoritism at, 350
  flirtation in, 349
  food division at, 224, 281–82
  hazards of, 227–28
  intrigue in, 66
  masking at, 227, 282
  pastimes of, 226–27, 280–82, 309
  Puritans at, 309, 311
  rituals of, 225–26
  see also household, royal; progresses
Courtenay, Edward, 112–14, 121–22,
  155–56
courtiers:
  clothing of, 228–30, 257, 285, 309,
    323, 348, 382
  debts of, 394
  mansions of, 289–93
  men as, 347–48
  on progresses, 285, 288, 291
  wit of, 265
  women as, 345–47, 350
Coventry, Mary Stuart in, 247
Coverdale, Miles, 79
Cox, Richard, 55
Crab-Joint, 343
Cranmer, Thomas, archbishop of
  Canterbury, 14, 32, 35
crime:
  attendance at mass as, 186, 332
  increases in, 98, 168
  in London, 168
  as travel hazard, 285
Crofts, James, 114, 120, 128
Cromwell, Thomas, 25–26, 28–29, 34,
  37–38, 386
  church reform and, 27
Cyprian, Saint, 76

dancing, 226–27, 399
  Elizabeth's skill in, 219–20, 226,
    267, 268, 304, 309, 390, 401
  morris, 281, 308
  novelty in, 349

rebellions, *continued*
  Five Wounds of Christ as symbol
    of, 236, 237, 245
  in Holland, 343–44
  in Ireland, 318–19, 321, 340,
    381–82, 396, 404
  against Reformation, 95, 235, 237,
    244–50
  in Scotland, 176
  in Zeeland, 343–44
recusants, 333–38, 340, 346, 367
Reformation, English, 26–27, 59, 75,
    79, 103–4, 108–9
  Act of Supremacy in, 186
  Acts of Uniformity in, 103, 186
  counter-evangelism in, 336
  excesses of, 94–95, 184
  international politics and, 26,
    184–86, 239, 274–75, 318–19,
    366, 369–71
  Mary I's suppression of, 143–44,
    148, 161, 168, 178, 184
  Parliamentary regulation of, 253
  Puritans vs., 307–8
  rebellion against, 95, 235, 237,
    244–50
  recusants in, 333–38, 340
Reformation, European, 156
  in France, 206, 298
  in Netherlands, 298
religious issues:
  divorce of Henry VIII as, 15, 21,
    22
  Elizabeth's excommunication as,
    274
  in France, 206, 269, 274–75, 298,
    321
  heretics executed for, 54, 143–44,
    148, 168, 320–21
  humanism as, 56
  in Netherlands, 298–99
  priests executed for, 331–35,
    337–38
  Spain's war against England as,
    366, 369–71
  succession and, 100–104, 110, 161,
    170, 203, 208–9, 217, 235–38,
    259
  see also Reformation, English;
    Reformation, European; *specific
    sects*
Renard, Simon, 109, 110, 117,
    120–22, 130

Revelation, Book of, 355
Riccio, David, 239
Richard II, king of England, 131
Richmond Palace, 405
Ridolfi, Roberto di, 239, 274
Robsart, Amy, *see* Dudley, Amy
    Robsart
Rochford, George Boleyn, Lord, 28,
    33, 50
Rochford, Lady, 50
Rosamond's Bower, 133
ruffs, use of, 229
Russell, Anne, 263
Russell, Francis, 2nd earl of Bedford,
    183–84, 215, 263, 291
Russell, John, 1st earl of Bedford, 95

Sackville, Thomas, Baron Buckhurst,
    293
Sadler, Sir Ralph, 246, 256
St. Bartholomew's Day Massacre, 269,
    274–75
Saintlow, Sir William, 115
St. Paul's Cathedral, 226
Sands, Elizabeth, 133, 136
sanitary conditions, at Hampton
    Court, 223–24
Savoy, Emmanuel Philibert, duke of,
    156, 158, 162
scandals and gossip, 266–70
  about Anne Boleyn, 28, 32–33
  about death of Catherine Parr, 79
  about death of Don Carlos, 320
  about death of Dudley's wife,
    191–98, 205, 212, 257
  about death of Edward VI, 105
  about death of John Sheffield,
    266–67
  about death of Katherine of
    Aragon, 27, 34
  about Dudley, 180–84, 190–98,
    205, 212, 257–59, 266–67, 355,
    371
  about Elizabeth and de Vere, 267
  about Elizabeth and Dudley,
    180–84, 190, 258–59, 266, 355
  about Elizabeth and Hatton,
    267–68
  about Elizabeth and Ralegh, 349
  about Elizabeth and Simier, 296
  about Elizabeth and Thomas
    Seymour, 70–71, 88–89
  in France, 296

Spain, *continued*
  power of, 318
  scandals and gossip in, 320
Spanish Armada, 364–77, 381
  astrological forecast of, 365
  battles fought by, 374–76
  as religious crusade, 366, 369–71
  supply problems of, 365, 369
  weather difficulties of, 365–69,
    375–76
starch, introduced to England, 229
Stuart, Henry, Lord Darnley, 221,
  254
  death of, 239
  description of, 217
  Riccio murdered by, 239, 251
  succession claims of, 217
Stuart, Mary, queen of Scotland, 262,
  264
  abdication of, 240
  Anne Boleyn compared to, 362
  beauty of, 200, 212, 218, 240
  betrothed to Edward VI, 68
  bravado of, 203, 240
  captivity of, 239, 247, 359–60
  Catholicism of, 202–3
  character of, 240–41, 360
  descriptions of, 200, 218, 359
  Elizabeth's attempted subjugation
    of, 202–3, 240, 251
  Elizabeth's decision to execute,
    360–63
  as Elizabeth's rival, 218–20, 359
  escape to England of, 235
  execution of, 372
  as focus of rebellion, 235–38, 241,
    274, 312, 318, 319, 359, 363
  Francis II and, 170
  health of, 359
  height of, 200–201, 218
  marriages of, 170, 239–40, 254
  match with Dudley offered to,
    211–17, 220–21
  Norfolk's engagement to, 235,
    243
  opposition to, 176, 235, 359, 361
  pregnancy of, 239
  return to Scotland of, 200–201
  scandals and gossip about, 239–40,
    251, 360
  succession claims of, 200, 202–3,
    208

Stuart, Mary, queen of Scotland,
  continued
  trial of, 360
  at Tutbury Castle, 239, 247
Stuart, Matthew, earl of Lennox, 217
Stuart line of succession, 208
Stubbs, John, 306–7, 311, 313
succession:
  attempts to change, 80–84, 101,
    104–6, 114–16, 120, 128, 150,
    153–55, 204, 209, 211–12,
    235–37, 239
  candidates in, 17, 34, 59, 97, 103–4,
    157–58, 160, 161, 168, 170, 200,
    202–3, 207–9, 217, 360–61
  Catherine Grey's claim to, 203–4,
    208
  Elizabeth urged to marry for, 183,
    212–13, 242, 253–56
  Henry Stuart's claim to, 217
  James's claim to, 360–61, 363
  Mary Stuart's claim to, 200, 202–3,
    208
  Parliament's regulation of, 34, 103,
    168
  religious issues in, 100–104, 110,
    161, 170, 203, 208–9, 217,
    235–38, 259
  Stuart line of, 208
  Suffolk line of, 208
  York line of, 208
Suffolk, Catherine Bertie, duchess of,
  168
Suffolk, Charles Brandon, duke of, 16,
  18, 208
Suffolk, Mary, duchess of, 208
Suffolk line of succession, 208
Sussex, earl of, 123–26, 314
  conspiracy of, 243–44
  Dudley opposed by, 257, 259, 299
  as military commander, 236, 238,
    246–49
Swan, 343
sweating sickness, epidemics of, 15, 98
Sweden, English opinions of, 189

Tadcaster, rebellion in, 246
Talbot, Elizabeth, countess of
  Shrewsbury (Bess of Hardwick),
  262, 360
  Elizabeth criticized by, 262, 264,
    267